The Jack Benny Times

2000 - 2005

By

Laura Leff

President, International Jack Benny Fan Club

© Copyright 2005, Laura Leff

No portion of this document may be reproduced without written permission of the copyright owner.

ISBN 0-9651893-4-1

© Copyright 2005, Laura Leff

Distributed by:
International Jack Benny Fan Club
P.O. Box 11288
Piedmont, CA 94611
www.jackbenny.org

All rights reserved. No part of this book may be reproduced or transmitted in any form by any means, electronic or mechanical, including photocopying, recording, or any information storage and retrieval system, without permission in writing from the Copyright owner. Address all inquiries to the distributor.

ISBN 0-9651893-4-1

Cover illustration restored by Amanda Osborne
Alo@zhakora.com   http://zhakora.com/odd-designs/portfolio.htm

Contents

Foreword 5

October 2000 – January 2001 7

February – May 2001 29

June – September 2001 55

January – April 2002 77

May – August 2002 99

September – December 2002 127

January – April 2003 151

May – August 2003 175

September – December 2003 203

January – April 2004 227

May – August 2004 255

September – December 2004 283

January – April 2005 305

May – August 2005 327

September – December 2005 351

Index 373

Foreword

I am often asked about the process of putting together a newsletter. This is also often accompanied by the question of, "Where do you find all this material?" These are valid questions, although I am sometimes torn about saying too much lest it detract from the perceived magic of having 20 pages of solid information about Jack Benny show up three times per year.

There is ALWAYS something going on with Jack Benny research—much more than one would think, considering Jack has not been corporeally with us for over 30 years. I have sometimes said that I'm following an 80-year breadcrumb trail from 1894 to 1974 (and even beyond with newer material like the Benny television tributes and Eddie Carroll's shows). So whatever I'm doing with the fan club, whether writing a book, putting together a convention, doing interviews, planting a tree in Waukegan, or even just answering E-mail, there's always new and interesting information coming at me about Jack. Friends have often heard me say "You just NEVER know what is going to turn up in the IJBFC E-mail inbox," as various people who worked with Jack or folks with some kind of story or information will suddenly drop me a line to tell their tales. I am truly blessed that the club has gained sufficient exposure that these people can come to US, as in many cases I would never have known to search them out.

So as this information comes in, I make notes and set it aside. Then at the end of four months (i.e., in December, April, and August), I sit down and open all my information holding places to see what I have accumulated. I also do interviews with folks whenever I can, so I have built up a queue of interviews with a variety of people who worked with Jack. I organize, I prioritize, I decide what's in and what's out, and how much room I have left over for an interview. Then I put it all together, do the layout, mess with the graphics for a while until it's all working the way I want it to, and send it off to the printer. After a big case of newsletters comes back, I sit down with some good television for the mass mailing of stapling, labelling, and stamping. Then off to the post office (or AOL for E-mail subcribers) and it's on its way to you. And that's the mechanics of the magic.

Some people have diaries. I have <u>The Jack Benny Times</u>. In assembling these issues, I have been reminded of many people and events that have touched my life over the past five years....and some events that took over my life (e.g., Waukegan statue unveiling and the 39 Forever convention). Putting together back issues into a single volume is always an occasion that makes you look over your shoulder and say, "We did ALL THAT?" Usually I am looking to the next issue, event, book, etc. So it is an interesting experience to stop and take stock of what has been accomplished.

Everything that was in the original Times issues is contained in this volume, although I've slightly moved some items to better fit within the 8" x 10" dimensions of this book vs. the 8.5" x 11" dimensions of the newsletter. I have modified the cover format for consistency and size considerations, but the cover photos remain intact. Plus, you've got an index for easy finding rather than flipping through a stack of newsletters. I'm going to put that to good use myself.

Don't believe everything you read. There are errors here and there (e.g., that Bill Morrow played Mr. Billingsley…no, Ed Beloin played the role), and I was torn about whether to correct them. But they are true to the original issues, and represent the body of knowledge at that time. Many times you'll find updates or corrections in subsequent issues.

A discussion of the newsletters is not complete without mentioning the semi-cryptic comment at the end of each newsletter: "Please friends, send no bombs." I have occasionally dropped this coda from the newsletters in this volume due to space considerations. But I have been closing newsletters with that for years prior to these issues…what does it mean? It is connected to member Jack Bloom (of the Jack Bloom Pasadena Chapter fame), or as I always called him, "Uncle Jack". Uncle Jack and I shared a love for both Jack Benny and George Gershwin. At some point in our correspondence, I coined a statement based on the first song lyric by Ira Gershwin: "You May Throw All the Rice You Desire, but Please Friends, Throw No Shoes". (Immortal, I know.) I believe I said, "You may send all the letters you desire, but please friends, send no bombs." Just the last part occurred to me as I wrote the next newsletter, and I added it as a tag line as a private joke between Uncle Jack and me. By the time of Uncle Jack's untimely demise, it had become a mainstay and continues to this day. After 9/11, I did think about it a little bit (and the tasteless elaboration of "Please friends, send no anthrax"). But it's now a tradition, and I decided to keep it.

I am also often asked "How do you find the time?" In all honesty, I don't know. I just keep moving. When you have a labor of love in helping people access material that makes them laugh and feel good, it's time well-spent.

I hope you will consider reading these collected issues of The Jack Benny Times time well-spent.

Sincerely,

Laura Leff

President, IJBFC

The Jack Benny Times

October 2000 – January 2001   Volume XVI, Numbers 1-2

President's Message

Hello again, folks! The International Jack Benny Fan Club has traveled an amazing road since the last time I said that in a newsletter. It has been wonderful to get reacquainted with old friends who have been members of the club for years, and to start corresponding with new ones. There is a lot of enthusiasm all the way around, and folks have provided me with many excellent ideas for fan club activities. Please do keep those cards, letters, and E-mails coming!

A few words on my own personal plans for the club. As most of you know, I turned over the operation of the club in 1987 because I had a variety of personal responsibilities that prevented my being able to devote the proper time to it. I want to insure that the club does receive appropriate attention, that members can get information and material on a timely basis, and that everyone knows the overall status. Therefore, I am making the following personal commitment to you: during the rest of 2000 and 2001, I will be spending a great deal of time on the club. We offer the following:

- Three issues of The Jack Benny Times will be published (approximately one every four months), each including a previously unpublished interview with one of Jack's cast, crew, or personal friends. Articles and information contributions are welcomed and encouraged!
- Our new Web page (www.JackBenny.org) is updated frequently, and offers a wealth of information on Jack Benny and his work. This includes the latest club information, an extensive FAQ (Frequently Asked Questions), photo gallery, online tape library listings, and forum where people can post questions and exchange information. A chat room is in the works.
- The tape library is open, with over 450 hours of Jack Benny shows, appearances, tributes, and interviews. I am working on a variety of trades to be able to expand our offerings.
- We are working on being able to offer Jack Benny shows in MP3 format. I am currently researching the restrictions on the copyrights.
- Stay tuned for information on how you can help to update and expand 39 Forever, our log of Jack Benny radio and television shows, appearances, and specials; movies, books, magazine articles, and discography.

Anyone subscribing to the Times at any point before the end of 2001 will receive all three 2000-2001 issues; thus everyone's subscription will expire at the end of 2001. Toward the end of 2001, I will take a critical look at the club and my ability to continue to devote a similar level of time and effort to it. Either the club will continue with a similar level of service and output, or we will determine the best next step and any modifications to our offerings. The result will be communicated to the entire membership base.

With all of our new activities and membership nearing 600 worldwide, this is probably the most exciting time to be a member of the IJBFC! I invite everyone to bring their thoughts and ideas on how we can help provide optimal service to our members, plus enhance and broaden the recognition and appreciation of Jack's work.

My sincerest thanks to all of you for your continued support, help, and enthusiasm.

Tape/MP3 Trading List

A long-standing fixture of the IJBFC has been our Tape Trading List. The updated list will be published in our next issue, and the most up-to-date listing is available on our Web site under the "Programs" section. There has been a lot of interest in finding Jack Benny on MP3, so we are expanding the list to that as well. If you are interested in being included on the list, please send to the address at the end of this newsletter:
- Your name
- Address
- E-mail (if any)
- Formats in which you will trade (audio tape, video tape, CD, MP3), and
- What information you would like listed on the Web site (i.e., some may want to list only their E-mail address on the Web, but full address in the Times).

Tape Library Reopened!

The IJBFC tape library officially reopened in mid-September. We offer over 450 hours of Jack Benny programs, appearances, tributes, and interviews in audio cassette format. Here are the procedures:
- Select up to 10 hours of Jack Benny material from the library, plus 1 hour of alternate selections per every 5 desired hours (some shows may be typos or incorrectly dated, and the listing is corrected as errors are found)
- Send a sufficient amount of C-60 (60 minute) tapes to: IJBFC, P.O. Box 11288, Piedmont, CA 94611; along with a check payable to the IJBFC in the amount of $1 per requested hour of material.
- I will dub the requested material onto the tapes you send and return them to you.

So for example, you could select 20 Jack Benny programs (10 hours) and 4 alternates (2 hours). You would then send 10 C-60 tapes plus $10 to the above address. I would then copy your selected shows (or substitute your alternates, should your desired shows be unavailable) onto the tapes, and return the tapes to you in the same box.

The easiest way of viewing our holdings is by checking our Web site at www.JackBenny.org in the "Programs" section. Printouts of our holdings can be obtained by sending a large manila SASE (77 cents postage) to the address at the end of this newsletter.

Waukegan's Jack Benny Statue

The citizens of Waukegan had established a fund to erect a 9' bronze statue of Jack Benny in downtown Waukegan. The statue will be placed in a plaza near the Genesee Theatre, where Jack broadcast his 6-25-39 radio program, and debuted his movie Man About Town on 7-7-39. I had the privilege of having a private tour of the theatre in 1987, and it is a very striking place. By 1994, it had closed and fallen into disrepair. However, the Friends of the Genesee Theatre are working to raise money for its restoration as well.

You can do your part through a donation to the Jack Benny Statue Fund. Levels of participation are as follows:

- **$.01 to $38 - Pennies for Benny**: Waukegan students are trying to raise 500,000 or more pennies for the statue.
- **$39 to $74 - 39ers:** (Note: this is the name of the Jack Benny Middle School athletic teams) Donors receive a set of 39 Genesee Theatre postcards.
- **$75 to $99 - "I'm THINKING!":** Donor listing at Benefit Concerts through the year 2002.
- **$100 to $499 - Century Club:** Name on a Benny plaza brick, and donor listing at Benefits Concerts through 2003.
- **$500 to $999 - Friend's 500 Club:** Name on five Benny plaza bricks, donor listing at Benefit Concerts through 2004, and Friends of Genesee Theatre membership through 2002.
- **$1000 to $1999 - Millenium Club:** Name on statue plaque, donor listing at Benefit Concerts through 2005, and Friends of Genesee Theatre membership through 2003.
- **$2000+ - Y not Y2K?:** Name on Genesee Theatre sidewalk diamond, donor listing at Benefit Concerts through 2005, life membership in Friends of the Genesee Theatre.

Please send your donation (and please let them know you're an IJBFC member!) to:
>Jack Benny Statue Fund
>Bank of Waukegan, Downtown Branch
>P.O. Box 39
>Attention: Jan, Branch Manager
>Waukegan, IL 60079

Do You Know?

Alan Grossman discovered something called a "VoicOgraph" paste-up, and interested in finding more information on it. The sleeve says "Jell-O presents Jack Benny via VoicOgraph", and the pasteup looks like a prototype for a 10" picture record. Pictures on one side show Jack, Don Wilson, Phil Harris, Andy Devine, and an NBC microphone. The flip side shows Jack (autographed on the shoulder), Mary Livingstone, and Kenny Baker. We estimate that it dates from 1937-38.

Joe Berg of the Sinatra Mailing List asks about a song lyric. Frank Sinatra recorded Sammy Cahn's song "Come Blow Your Horn"—the theme from the movie. There is a line saying, "There'll be no love in bloom come doomsday morn." Is this just a straight Benny reference because of "Love In Bloom", or is it an extended reference to <u>The Horn Blows at Midnight</u>?

On a Babylon 5 episode entitled "Ship of Tears", the villain Bester radios to Captain Sheridan that he can either let him dock at the ship or have the momentary satisfaction of blasting him out of space. This is followed by a pregnant pause, and Bester asks if Sheridan is still out there. Sheridan replies, "I'm thinking it over." Does anyone know if J. Michael Strazinsky was intentionally giving Jack Benny a nod, or if there is any more to the story of this exchange?

The Tale Piece

Reprinted from Mr. Showbizman:

"When Bob Vincent accepted the job as entertainment director, the first thing Bill Harrah wanted was for Bob to get Jack Benny to play Harrah's. Bill had tried to entice him without success.

"The next day Bob Vincent called Bill. 'Bill, I thought of a way that we might be able to get Benny to work for us. What do you think of my buying George Burns, and then inviting Mr. And Mrs. Benny to come up for George's opening? I think he'll come. He and George are best of friends.' I continued, 'Let's try it anyway. Even if he doesn't come, George Burns will draw big for us, and he's also a favorite with the gambling crowd.' Bill said, 'OK, let's give it a try.'

"I called the agency which handled George Burns and we made a deal. Four weeks before George's engagement I wrote a letter to Mr. Benny's manager and invited him and Mr. and Mrs. Benny up for the opening. A week later I received a letter of acceptance.

"Harrah's didn't have a hotel at that time. We did have two great looking lodges with deluxe furnishings, which we were using for whatever headliner we played in the South Shore Room.

"The day comes for Mr. and Mrs. Burns' and Mr. and Mrs. Benny's arrival for the opening. We decorated the lodges with flowers, fruit and both [had] been cleaned from top to bottom. We sent one of our longest, most expensive Rolls Royce stretch limousines to the Reno airport to pick them up.

"When they arrived and saw how beautiful the lodges looked, they were impressed. While we were visiting, prior to going to rehearsal in the main theatre, Mary asked to use the bathroom. As she came out she said in a rather disgusted voice, 'Jack, you could never play this place. They don't have a bathtub here! You don't take showers.'

"I thought we had lost Jack Benny right there, all for the sake of a bath tub. I excused myself and went to the office and called Bill Harrah. 'Bill, I think we have lost Mr. Benny,' 'Why?' questioned Bill. 'Mary just used the bathroom, and told us that Jack wouldn't play here because he only takes a bath, and won't take a shower! You know all we've got are showers.' Bill thought for a moment and then said, 'Bob, what are you going to do right now?' I replied, 'I'm going to take all of them over to the South Shore theatre and give them lunch, and then Mr. Burns is going to rehearse.' 'How long will that take?' replied Bill. 'About three hours,' I answered. Without hesitation, Bill said, 'I promise you there will be a bathtub in that room in three hours!' 'Are you serious?' I asked. He said, 'You can bet on it. Just get them out of the lodge as soon as you can, so we can go to work.'

"With that I asked everyone to follow me to the main theatre so we could have lunch before Mr. Burns' rehearsal. We all left the lodge for the theatre.

"I dragged out rehearsal for a little over three hours and then we all walked back to the lodge. As we walked into Jack and Mary's suite, Mary smelled paint. She sniffed a little and realized it was coming from the bathroom. She walked into the bathroom and I felt my heart sink into my shoes. Mary came out in a second and practically screamed, 'Jack, do you know what these people did? They tore out the shower and put in a bathtub, just for you. You've got to play here!!'

"Bill Harrah, using his determination and his money realized how desperate we were and performed a miracle. His people tore our the complete shower and installed a bathtub, cemented it in and repainted the entire room in three hours.

"Jack decided right there to play for us and we made the deal that afternoon."

♪♫♪♫♪♫♪♫♪♫♪♫♪♫♪♫♪♫♪♫♪♫♪♫♪♫♪♫♪♫♪♫♪♫♪♫

Jack's comment on accepting an award (which one?) was: "I don't deserve this award, but I have arthritis and I don't deserve that, either."

♪♫♪♫♪♫♪♫♪♫♪♫♪♫♪♫♪♫♪♫♪♫♪♫♪♫♪♫♪♫♪♫♪♫♪♫

Jack Benny's lineage:

Father:	Meyer Kubelsky (1868 – 10/14/1946) from Lithuania; at least one sister
Mother:	Emma Sachs (1870 – 11/1917); granddaughter of Rabbi Iser Charriff of Kalvaria, Lithuania, no known siblings
Sister:	Florence Kubelsky Fenschel (9/12/1900 – 8/9/1977)

♪♫♪♫♪♫♪♫♪♫♪♫♪♫♪♫♪♫♪♫♪♫♪♫♪♫♪♫♪♫♪♫♪♫♪♫♪♫♪

In 1937-38, there was a running gag where someone would knock at the door, deliver a line, and then leave. This was Harry Baldwin, Jack's personal secretary, who also oversaw script distribution. He had worked as a minor Paramount executive before going to work for Jack in 1932. His flat voice had become a joke with writers Bill Morrow and Ed Beloin, and they created the running gag for him.

Bill Morrow himself may have played the character of Mr. Billingsley, who was a boarder in Jack's home. After Ed Beloin's retirement, he moved to New England a built a small motel that he ran until his death. (Thanks to Elizabeth McLeod for these tidbits!)

♪♫♪♫♪♫♪♫♪♫♪♫♪♫♪♫♪♫♪♫♪♫♪♫♪♫♪♫♪♫♪♫♪♫♪♫♪♫♪

Speaking of Jack's early writers, many know that his first regular radio writer was Harry Conn. However, there was a period during 1932 when Al Boasberg did Jack's writing, including the first Canada Dry show. Other writers were also used on the early shows, but eventually Conn was used exclusively. However in trade ads, Harry Conn took credit for all of Jack's radio programs until he either quit or was fired.

Boasberg still contributed to the shows occasionally, coming to readings and "punching up" jokes. He was working on the script of Rochester's debut (aired 1-28-37) on the day he died; the scene with Roch was based on an actual incident from his life. (Thanks to Ben Schwartz for these tidbits!)

Search-a-Word

George Lillie provided this Jack Benny puzzle that he created. Solve it just like a regular word search; words can be forwards, backwards, up, or down. Enjoy!

Word list

Jack	Harris	Blanc	Violin	Monroe
Benny (1)	Dennis	Bea	Maxwell	Johnny
Mary	Day	Benadaret	Vault	Ray
Livingstone	Don	Joan	Charleys	Radio
Rochester	Wilson	Benny (2)	Aunt	TV
Eddie	Frank	Carmichael	Fred	Movies
Anderson	Nelson	Cheap	Allen	
Phil	Mel	Well	Marilyn	

```
R  A  D  I  O  O  F  G  H  S  I  N  N  E  D
Y  A  O  N  I  L  O  I  V  Z  N  P  E  X  Z
N  B  C  K  C  A  J  C  H  A  R  L  E  Y  S
N  E  T  V  X  Y  J  O  A  N  P  Q  N  R  C
H  C  H  E  A  P  P  H  I  L  X  N  D  E  D
O  M  A  R  I  L  Y  N  E  B  E  N  N  Y  Q
J  Z  H  A  R  R  I  S  A  B  P  P  Q  B  N
Q  O  S  W  I  L  S  O  N  F  R  E  D  E  O
R  S  T  X  R  Y  A  D  Z  X  R  A  Y  N  S
L  E  A  H  C  I  M  R  A  C  Y  O  A  E  R
X  D  R  E  T  S  E  H  C  O  R  R  U  D  E
Z  D  M  M  O  N  R  O  E  O  Z  Y  N  A  D
Q  I  N  O  D  M  O  V  I  E  S  V  T  R  N
M  E  F  R  A  N  K  M  E  L  Z  A  Y  E  A
O  B  L  A  N  C  Q  U  X  Z  R  U  N  T  Q
L  O  M  A  R  Y  B  O  Z  Y  A  L  L  E  N
L  A  Q  S  L  I  V  I  N  G  S  T  O  N  E
E  B  Y  B  E  A  Z  N  E  L  S  O  N  A  Z
W  Z  R  X  L  L  E  W  X  A  M  S  Y  Z  Q
```

Etcetera

Arthur "Artie" Auerbach (can anyone confirm if the correct spelling is Auerbach or Auerback?) played Mr. Kitzel on Jack's program from 1-6-46 until his death on 10-3-57 at age 54. He played the character on other programs prior to this date. A specific example is the Abbott and Costello show of 6-1-44, with the following exchange:

Bud: It's our old friend Kitzel, the salesman. What do you have for us today?
Kitzel: Today, I'm in the mansion business.
Lou: The mansion business?
Kitzel: Yes, anything you mansion, I got it.

His Variety obituary stated, "For many years a reporter-photographer on the N.Y. Daily News, Auerback switched to comedy more than two decades ago and came to Hollywood with the Al Pearce radio show. He also worked with Phil Baker before joining Benny for the 'Kitzel' character." Spike Jones asked Sir Frederick Gas (alias Earl Bennett) to imitate Kitzel on his recording of "Ghost Riders in the Sky" and "Tennessee Waltz." Jones was actually criticized as being anti-Semitic for the "Tennessee Waltz" recording. Does anyone have thoughts on why Jack never received similar criticism for either the Kitzel or Shlepperman characters?

You probably know about the running gag between Jack and Phil about "That's What I Like About the South". However, you don't see the full lyrics of the song printed very often. Feel free to sing along:

Won't you come with me to Alabammy
Let's go see my dear ol' Mammy
She's fryin' eggs and broilin' hammy
That's what I like about the South

Now, there you can make no mistakee
Where those nerves are never shakey
Ought to taste her layer cakee
That's what I like about the South

She's got baked ribs and candied yams
Those sugar cured Virginia hams
Basement full of those varied yams
And that's what I like about the South

Hot cornbread and black-eyed peas
You can eat as much as you please
Cause it's never out of seas…
And that's what I like about the South

Don't take one, have two
They're dark brown and chocolate too
Suits me, they must suit you
Cause that's what I like about the South

It's a-way, way down where the cane grows tall
Down where they say you all
Walk on in with that Southern drawl
Cause that's what I like about the South

It's down where they have those pretty queens
Keep a-dreamin' those dreamy dreams
Let's sip that absyinthe in New Orleans
That's what I like about the South

Here come ol' Bob with all the news
Got the boxback coat and the button shoes
But he's all caught up with his union dues
And that's what I like about the South

Here come ol' Roy, down the street
Oh can't you hear those scufflin' feet
He would rather sleep than eat
And that's what I like about the South

Now every time I pass your door
You act like you don't want me no more
Why don't you shake your head and sigh
And I'll go walkin' right on by

Gone on, on and on and on
Honey, when you tell me
That you love me
Then how come you close your eyes?

Did I tell you about the place called Doo Wah Ditty
It ain't no town and it ain't no city
It's just awful small but awful pretty
Well, Doo Wah Ditty

I didn't come here to criticize
I'm not here to sympathize
But don't call me those no-good lies
Cause a lyin' gal I do despise

You love me like I love you
Send me fifty PDQ
Roses are red and violets are pink
I'm goin' get all fifty I don't think

She's got back bones and buttered beans
Hamhocks and turnip greens
You n'me in New Orleans
And that's what I like about the South

Jack broadcast on both the NBC Red and Blue networks at different times. The color designations of the three NBC radio networks are said to have derived from the different colors AT&T engineers used on maps showing the routes followed by the permanent long lines set up for NBC beginning in 1926. Prior to Christmas Eve, 1928, the Orange (Pacific coast) network functioned autonomously, with most network shows coming from KGO Oakland/San Francisco (KGO is still in operation today). After the above date, a permanent, high-quality line was established coast-to-coast. A large map designating NBC affiliates with, as appropriate, red, blue, or orange colored lights used to hang on the wall of the old NBC master control room in the NBC Chicago studios in the Merchandise Mart. This map has been preserved, and is anticipated to be displayed at Chicago's Museum of Broadcast Communications.

♪♪

For those in the Los Angeles area who are interested, George Burns and Gracie Allen are at rest together in Forest Lawn Cemetery. They are in the Freedom Mausoleum, in the Sanctuary of Trust (top level).

♪♪

Don Wilson also had his own separate career in movies. He appeared in Danny Kaye's "The Kid from Brooklyn" and "Niagara" starring Marilyn Monroe.

Eddie Carroll as Benny

In 1991, I interviewed Eddie Carroll who had done a one-man show as Jack Benny. I've probably heard more Jack Benny impersonations than the vast majority people, but when Eddie impersonated Jack on my answering machine, it certainly gave me pause! The first part of this interview was published in our September-October 1991 Times; he talked about his career and auditioning for the part of Jack Benny for a one-man New York show. At this point, Eddie and his family had gone to Hawaii on vacation after his audition.

E: We got home, and the day we got home…I went to get the mail, and I got the letter, it was a letter from the New York production office that he was working out of….it looked like a form letter, you know the kind, even thought it's personally typed it looks like it's something that a lot of copies were made…It said, "Dear Eddie, we thank you so much for auditioning for the Jack Benny show," so on and so forth, "You're very talented, we enjoyed meeting you," and so forth, "However at this time, we have decided to go in a different direction…We thank you, and maybe in the future we can get together on another project." Now as I'm reading this, even thought I'm reading what they're saying to me is "you didn't get it," I just know that I don't believe it. I mean, something is terribly wrong here. And as I'm reading this rejection letter, outside the house watching through the front door, my daughter comes to the front door and says, "Dad, Ted Snowden's [the show's producer] on the line from New York."

So I get on the phone, and Ted says, "Hi Eddie, how you doing? How was Hawaii?" I said, "Terrific." And he said, "Listen, I'm glad you're at home because I need to talk to you." And I interrupted him and I said, "Well, Ted, I appreciate you calling me, but what's interesting is that I just got a letter in my hand that says 'Thank you very much, but you didn't get it.'" Well, he started to scream a profanity, "I don't believe it!...I *told* that woman in the office, these people ba-ba-ba, but tell Eddie Carroll that I have to call him...Forget it, throw it away, you weren't supposed to get that letter." And I said, "I knew it!"

L: Talk about timing!

E: Oh, I'm telling you! So anyway, he said, "Look, I'm coming out in another week...It's down to one person and you. That's where it's at...Because it's been a while since I've seen you...I'm not sure whether you were really that good or because the impression that you gave was so startling, I've got to be sure before I make my mind up." So he said..."I'm going to give the guy another reading here in town, and I'm coming out to L.A. and we'll sit down and go through it and then I'll know for sure one way or the other." Well, I already knew that it was already etched in rock, but he didn't want to make a commitment yet. So anyway, Carol [his wife] and I had a good laugh over the rejection letter that shouldn't have happened. So he came out to L.A., we had a meeting, we started talking, and he said, "Why don't you get up and read some of this for me?" I did about three pages, and he said, "Oh hell, let's roll up our sleeves and go to work." So from that point on, we worked very, very hard.

L: And this was 1986?

E: No, this was 1983. So anyway, we spent months rehearsing it, working on nuances, timing, and so forth...In the two weeks of previews we had before we had our official opening to test the material to make sure it was working, I found there were passages that were very historical and very entertaining from a standpoint of information about Jack's life and growing up and going through stages and so forth, but there were moments throughout that...needed bigger laughs in there. Because if someone recreates Harry Truman, for example, or does some historical character that comes from a serious bent, they can take time to get very dramatic. But somebody coming from a comedy background, even if they tell you about something that's sad, to get off it you go to a joke...It just needed punching. The writer kept insisting that I punch the lines that are there harder, and I tried to explain to him having done comedy for so many years that if there's a joke that gets a chuckle, no matter what you do with it, that's all it's ever going to get is a chuckle because of the construction of the joke...You can't time it or stomp on it or force it or push it or anything else, if it's going to get three on a laugh meter, that's all it's ever going to get is a three. And he kept insisting only because he was resisting having to do any more writing to it. He had literally written himself out. So he was giving me notes, the director was giving me notes, and I finally said, "Look guys…I will try everything you ask me to do, but if it doesn't work then you have to start listening to me more." So after four nights of this, I finally said to him, "I've done everything you wanted to…and if you listen to the audience, the audience will tell you where it needs work." So finally I said, "Please do me a favor now, don't go back to the theatre with the writer until you find these areas—pages 9 to 12, pages 14…" and so forth.

Three days he was gone, and I thought oh man, he's going to come back with lots of extra stuff. He came back three days later, Laura, and I said, "Well?" I thought maybe twelve good jokes or something. He said, "I'm working on a line."

L: *A* line?

E: *A* line. Not that he even had a line, he was just working on *the* line for over three days! I thought if this is going to take three days just to come up with one line…we're in very deep trouble. In the interim during the preview days, most every writer that worked with Benny came to see the show…Sam [Perrin], George [Balzer], and Al Gordon came, and Milt Josefsberg and so forth, and came back stage and they were very, very encouraging…Irving Fein came to see the show…So I finally said to the producer, "Look, we need help here…Even the best playwrights in the world, even Neil Simon after a zillion smash hits on Broadway and films when he opens a new show, takes it out of town and goes through massive rewrites because again, comedy needs an audience to tell you where the comedy plays…Since we have the guys who wrote, who better to write for Benny than the guys who wrote for Benny? So between Sam and George, the way the writers worked, Sam and George were a team and Milt Josefsberg and John Tackaberry were a team, and if they worked on the show, one team would take the first half and the other would take the second half. Then of the two, they had it broken down that Sam was the construction guy of the joke and George was the joke master, he was the one line or the "puncher." So I said, "That's the guy we need."

So we talked to George and said, "How would you like to write for Benny again?" He said, "I'd love it. Who gets a second chance in life? That's wonderful."…So we would get together early in the morning in an office in Santa Monica, and we would work for three, four, five hours and find sections of the show that needed work and started adding material, and that night I would plug it in. It was a bear, because then we were taking stuff out of the second act and putting in the first act, pulling stuff out of there and putting it in the second act. Now when you've got about an hour and forty-five minutes of material in your head, and you don't have another actor on stage cueing you, and you're so far forward that even if someone has a book backstage you can't hear them throw you a line if you get lost, you've got all this information in your head and you've rehearsed it for months. Now when you're out there in front of the audience as you're approaching a section you're reminding yourself in advance, "Don't do that now, that comes later in the second act," and you have to put the new piece in, and it's like this little guy running around inside your head directing you like a traffic cop.

L: It's a shell game with the script.

E: Oh, yeah! I mean I had seasoned, well-known performers and actors you would not believe from movies and things come backstage. Edward Mulhare, a brilliant, very tall, austere British actor who's done Shakespeare come backstage and say, "How the hell do you have the balls to go out there every night by yourself and face down an audience with no one else on stage in front of you? I wouldn't have that kind of courage in a million years." But I loved it. I so felt privileged to be able to be the one to carry on the tradition, and recreate and bring this man's wonderment and special talent back again, and so to me it was a joy.

Anyway, the playwright, just had a great deal of trouble adding more material, but with George's stuff it did help a lot. So the bind we came into, the show did very well, but then when we came down to the point where Dick Clark wanted to produce it as a special and then talked about bringing in writers so we could now adapt a different approach to it…and do it as maybe an hour, hour and a half…and maybe bring in some extra writers to punch it up in areas and segmentize it, the writer went nuts. He became totally self-sabotaging. He got so involved in it that he was frothing at the mouth. In fact, he was furious that George Balzer had even come on board because they were *his* lines, it was *his* baby, and he didn't want anybody else touching it. Even though the jokes that were added and the way the show was rearranged, it's like arranging a song with a full symphony orchestra with the tympani coming in just at the right time and then you bring in the strings and then the French horns and then the suddenly music begins to stir and move you emotionally, it started to pay off. Well, he was so furious…he got angry because we had "bastardized" his material. I said, "Your material is in there. We've added elements and rearranged things." He said, "Well, they're just cheap laughs."…He said, "My deal is that if it goes to television, no other writers are involved." I said, "You can't do that…You'll get single plate credit—teleplay or play by, and then there'll be an additional card after that saying 'With additional material by' so on and so forth. It's no big deal." He wouldn't have it. So finally it got so complex and so complicated that Dick Clark threw up his hands and said, "I can't deal with this," and walked away. Then finally at the end of the year when the play had to be reoptioned again, the playwright brought in his attorneys and they got into a whole "I need to have this"…The demands were so enormous that the producer almost had an epileptic fit over this whole thing. So as a result of it, I just then put together my own version of Benny without plagiarizing his material, and then I performed for the next number of years I performed it all over the country with a show called <u>Legends in Concert</u>, and played Las Vegas and the Nugget in Reno, Caesar's Palace in Atlantic City, in Miami, in Boston, in Toronto, and did a very special version of Legends on Broadway with the man that does Al Jolson and a gal that does Judy Garland, and then intermittently between that also did another version of Benny's presentation—about a forty-minute presentation—for various companies for their conventions all over the country. And then did a series of commercials for Zenith, and those were great fun, Laura, because we got Frank Nelson, and we…made the commercials sound like they were lifted right out of an authentic radio show. So when you hear the door open and close, like a ding-dong in a department store, then you hear people mumbling about, Benny's, "Oh excuse me, Mister!" "Yessssss?" "Listen, I'm looking for a television set, I'm thinking of buying a new one." "Oh, is the one you bought during the Civil War broken?" "Now cut that out!" And we had a laugh track and all the rest of that in it, so it was great, great fun. And then I did a series of television commercials and radio commercials for the…cable company in Miami, Florida to promote their new fall season on television.

More with Eddie Carroll in an upcoming issue!

Produced and Directed by Frederick deCordova

Recorded 5/12/95 at NBC Studios, Burbank, California. I turned my recorder on in the middle of our conversation, and Fred was talking about the NBC tribute hosted by Kelsey Grammar, then in development.

F: Well, I understand there is a, according to Irving Fein, that there is a project currently in development or looks like it will be in development of a tribute to Jack Benny on television. One of the problems involved is actually who owns the rights. I think, and this is just off the top of my head and somebody came to see me about it, would I be interested, and I said "Anything about Jack would fascinate me." And then I heard, not necessarily in this order, that the assumptions was Irving owned the rights. I later heard that MCA owns the rights, and that could hold things up, because I think MCA was saying, "Why would they give that project to somebody else when they could do it themselves?" So I don't know the status of it now…There would be, and I think that's where I came into it, a number of people who would give their memories and feelings and regards about Jack.

Over a period of time, and God knows I've been over a period of time, somebody asked me—lots of people asked me—about all the people I've worked with, and that goes back forever and ever, people like Bea Lilly and Fanny Brice and Bert Lahr and Durante and Bolger in the New York days and all the people in pictures and 22 years with Johnny Carson, who was my favorite person? And it is a good but absolutely honest answer that both on and off stage, the one person I miss most is Jack. I continue time and time again to, something will remind me of something about Jack that again will bring back that feeling that there was nobody like him. And Mrs. Benny and Mrs. deCordova became close friends, so we had a great deal of on stage and social evenings. I don't mean necessarily big social evenings, although Mary was a wonderful hostess. He was the kind of a man that if he went out to buy a tie, he bought a tie for other people who were close to him, with a note that would say on it "Kiss my a**." [E.N.: See below.] So anyway, any memory of the time I spent with Jack comes under the heading of just about the nicest times I ever spent.

L: Now you first met him in 1936?

F: I believe I was doing a show with George Jessell and Sophie Tucker on Broadway, and Jessell was an old friend of Jack's, and Jack came backstage after the show to see George and I was introduced then. Then if I remember correctly, Jack left town and Mary was still there, and I invited her out for dinner with some other people, Betty Furness, Johnny Green, people like that, and that led to my being a social friend of the Bennys. When I came out to California, which was not long after that, I came out to direct at Warner Brothers, and the Bennys really opened the social door to me in California. And every memory that I have about all of it is what a good time and how nice it was…

L: I have to ask, do you still have the barrel?

F: The barrel is tucked away near my swimming pool with the brass plate on it: "Love and kisses and kiss my a**, Jack."

[E.N.: Quote of FdC from Jack Benny (Livingstone, Marks, and Borie): "Jack had a quaint, darling wit. His favorite saying was 'Kiss my a**' which represented the naughty-boy quality in him. He never really talked dirty, either at home or out with the boys. I have a big barrel that came from Jurgenson's Gift Shop in Beverly Hills which has a very special place in my home. Originally, it had been filled with liquor, plus all sorts of imported canned goods, fruit and cheeses. On the outside, there is a gold plaque which reads: 'Kiss my a**.' It was a Christmas present Jack sent me."]

L: How was it decided that you would replace Seymour Berns as director of Jack's TV show?

F: I think I replaced Ralph Levy. It was rather interesting that I replaced Ralph Levy with Burns and Allen and with Jack.

L: How was your name brought up for that position?

F: I think my name didn't really come up. We had been seeing each other, and of course if you were close friends of George Burns' you were close friends of Jack's. So when Seymour left…to do something else, either George said or Jack may have said, "What about

Fred deCordova?"…There was not a long period of negotiation. The minute he said it, I said, "You bet." And I'm glad I did.

L: I've talked with almost all the living writers about the process for creating the radio shows. What was the process for creating the television show?

F: Well it was nothing particularly different than happened with other shows. The writers would, as they would on a show today, the writers would suggest a premise to Jack and he would either say , "I don't know whether that will work or not," or say, "That sounds good to me", and disappear for about two or three days. The writers would write it, then there would be a reading in his office in Santa Monica, and what I don't think he gets credit for, parenthetically, is what a contributor he was to what the writers wrote. It isn't as if, as in some cases, writers write something and the star says, "OK, let's go." Jack would make, not necessarily offensive suggestions, but suggestions that were very welcome and almost without exception added to the value of the script. That would lead to going on stage and blocking the show, and of course before that, it would be whether so-n-so was available in addition to the regular cast, whatever guest star was available. We'd have a pretty good idea that most anybody you asked would say, "Mr. Benny? Yes indeed!" And then you block it and make suggestions, and he would make suggestions, and it always surprised me that he technically knew what would work as well as what scriptwise would work. So I was dealing with someone that I had an enormous regard for personally, but also professionally. We did an awful lot of the shows in front of an audience, and as is the case with a vital few, the doing of the show in front of an audience brought him even more to life and the making of the show worked, as opposed to saying, "That didn't play." He knew what to do to take a script and make it better by performance.

L: Doing things like the stare makes so much more sense when playing to an audience.

F: And the little looks that he would do which were not on paper were in his mind, and he just knew what made it better.

L: How did it work with blocking? [E.N.: Blocking is the choreography in the context of the script, such as who enters from where, when a character sits, where characters stand on the set, etc.] How did you start off with the script—some of it's going to be obvious, if the phone rings you're going to cross and answer it.

F: I think if you've been directing for a while and you read a script, you have a pretty good mental picture of what you're hoping to look like. Then you meet with your art director and say, "I need (whatever you need) an elevator door, a door for a waiter to come in," because everything didn't happen always in the Benny living room. So you discussed from what you as the director think would be the proper way for the doors to be or the windows to be, and as you're talking that over with the art director, you have a pretty good idea of where you want to put the camera, and that's kind of not intricate. You have to know what you're doing, but if you do know what you're doing, that works very well. The blocking is part of the pattern when you lay it out with the art director, the walk would be from here to there, and then you get there and then the doorbell rings and you go back. That's pretty much in your mind. Remember, except in a few episodes, it was not particularly intricate. You were still going to focus on Jack in conversation with one, two, three, or four people. Except in some you're trying to duplicate things like the vault. That was enormously difficult to do. Build a vault, put in false crocodiles…But also you often had, when you did a television adaptation of what had been a success on radio, you were frightened about whether or not you would do it as well visually as had been when people could visualize it only in their minds. That was and still is one of my thoughts that certainly television picture is an improvement on radio, but if by any chance you listen to radio scripts, not only of Jack but of other shows too, you are aware how much your imagination gave you as an improvement over what just you see. So I realized in those places where we did a department store scene or something like the vault, that the people who had listened to the radio were probably going to be comparing what we were doing now to what they had heard. That gave me a few moments of trepidation.

L: And things like the Maxwell, you're not going to have Mel Blanc standing to the side doing the sound effects.

F: You had railroad stations with Si-Sy and things like that which were easy to shoot, and since the people doing them were so talented, you didn't have too much worry. Mostly the worry was when you had something rather bizarre on a radio show that could be duplicated on a television show and still have the same impact.

L: What was the difference in creating shows that were situational, like at the railroad station, versus shows done in one [E.N.: "in one" is a stage term referring to an act done in front of a closed curtain, as Jack's monologues were done, often on shows with guest stars.]? What was the rationale of using one format over the other?

F: Well, I think that many of them were a combination of that. The show would start with a monologue, and lead into…he'd say, "I'll never forget…" as part of the monologue. He would do his jokes, his monologue jokes, and then say, "And certainly, walking home that night reminded me of when…" and that would lead into what that reminded him of.

L: I'm thinking of some shows like with Carol Burnett doing the Tarzan episode. The first half is all done in front of the curtain, then leading into a skit.

F: I'd be lying if I told you the exact sequence, but obviously…she was part of the in front of the curtain thing, and then somehow…he asked her to do…the great Tarzan yell. And she did it. That led to the discussion about Tarzan's life, and that led to the dissolve and so forth, of the scene in the jungle in which he was the timid Tarzan.

L: I remember hearing Carol Burnett saying that with that sequence, there was a point where they were supposed to play ball. So she threw a boulder at Jack, and he stumbled back and hit his hand on one of the prop plants. [E.N.: Burnett said that he had hurt his hand quite a bit in the fall, but kept the scene going without making a fuss over it.]

F: True. However, that again is another attribute of Jack's. Whereas somebody else might well have said, "All right, hold it, I've just hurt my hand," if I remember correctly, he played that as something like, "Tarzan hurt arm," and went on with the sketch. He was a consummate performer, and an absolutely darling man.

L: How do you compare the attitudes of Jack and other performers of his time towards their craft to the attitudes of celebrities today?

F: I think I've learned in all my years that it is a great mistake to live only, and admire only, the past. Whether or not there will ever be another Cary Grant, another Clark Gable, another Gary Cooper, is a total waste of time because the older one gets, the less people care about Cary Grant, Gary Cooper…I did several pictures with Errol Flynn, for instance. I thought there would never be anybody as exciting. But whether I agree with it or not, Bruce Willis sells billions of dollars of tickets, and today is a different day. You mustn't say, "There's nobody like so-n-so." But let's be honest. Jerry Seinfeld is a very, very capable and successful television performer. I'm not saying Jerry Seinfeld is as good as Jack Benny, I am saying there ain't no Jack Benny so Jerry Seinfeld is pretty good. And I think that goes with singers. If I had to say that the best singer who ever lived was Al Jolson, nobody knows who the hell I'm talking about. That might go for Judy Garland. I think the only one who has bridged that whole gap at the moment is Tony Bennett, who is now such a success all over again. In other words, what I think I'm saying is one must not be an old fogey who only says, "Well, there's nothing today like there used to be." They may not be identical, but there are an awful lot of major performers today. Nobody was as pretty as Ava Gardner? OK. Melanie Griffith, or somebody else, is attractive too. I bite my tongue every once in a while when I find myself on the verge of saying, "It's not like it used to be." But I find that people look at me and think that I should be put away for talking like that.

L: How about your thoughts on some of the different people you worked with on Jack's show, like Mary and Phil?

F: Well, you lead into certain shows like when the Colmans did an episode, and X number of years later, the Jimmy Stewarts played that part. I believe I have few cogent memories particularly about the other people who worked with Jack because they were primarily outstandingly successful because Jack made them look very, very good. It's an old story, you've heard it often that he said, "Wouldn't it be funnier if Dennis said that?" and I reacted. That's all true. I know once he came back to our show after having an episode with Lucy, and saying, "I think that will be my last episode with Lucy. She's too tough to work with." Having done Lucy as opposed to Jack being casual about doing every show, Lucy was very specific, and that probably wasn't exactly what Jack had in mind at that period in his career to be told, "No, you walk two steps to the right." But I don't remember, and I think this is one of the things that makes Jack a little bit different, I don't remember ever anybody any time under any circumstances, who ever denigrated Jack. Nobody ever said, "He's a pain in the a**" or "I'm not going to work with him again." Everybody left the show, and everybody at his house always, and I mean always, said what a pleasure it was to be involved with him.

I think he was less fond of Phil Harris than the legend of how close they were. Frankie Remley, a member of the band, was personally closer to Jack than many of the others. I think…I've heard so many remarks about "Jack and Phil" and yet I don't personally remember an awful lot of time of Jack and Phil being together. The Remley-Benny situation was remarkable. It is literally true that they used to take automobile trips together, and it is literally true that they packed their bags…and were about to leave the house to get into the car, and Frankie said, "Where are we going?" and Jack said, "Which way is your car facing?" And that's the way they went. And I played a lot of bad golf with Jack. He's the only person I know, even up to including now, where he would call me and say, "What are you doing?" I'd say, "Nothing much." He'd say, "Do you want to play three holes of golf?" And I'd say, "Yes." Nobody ever says, "Do you want to play three holes of golf?" You play eighteen holes, or maybe you only have time for nine. But Jack would say, "Let's play three holes of golf." We'd go to Hillcrest, play three holes of golf.

L: It almost sounds like a cheap joke.

F: Yes. "Well, I'm kind of tired, but I thought we could play three holes of golf."…Jack had a wonderful gimmick with Ripley [Believe it or Not]. He would send me things from all over saying, "I'm enclosing a Ripley which you've probably seen," it would be a piece of the Ripley cartoon which would include four or five different things, "and it's an absolute lie. The Titanic did not sink because it hit an iceberg." Then he'd make up a reason why the Titanic sank. I kept a lot of them, and still have some socked away in my voluminous files. In a strange and certainly not apropos twist, Alfred Bloomingdale who was a dear, darling friend of mine, I used to show them to him. After Jack died…I began getting letters from Alfred Bloomingdale, he said, "I believe since Jack isn't here, I believe that someone should point out that Howard Hughes' was not the largest airplane ever built." Then he would make his joke about something like that. So Alfred died, and I got quite a group of Ripleys with various jokes involved! The joke which followed, "That's not true what Ripley said, he's done it again, he's lying to the public" and then whatever the subject was, his joke was always a very funny joke about what the real truth was.

Once again, the assumption that he himself was not a funny man is not true. He himself was a funny man. He was not a jokester. He didn't tell, "So have you hear the one about…" That would be Jessell. Or Bob Hope. Jack was the best laugher, and George was the most famous member of that combination. And it's actually true. Jack would say something and George would not answer, and Jack would break up because George hadn't said anything in answer to him.

L: I should know this, but in some of the letters Jack mentioned Bert Scott.

F: His secretary.

L: Not Jeanette Eyemann?

F: Bert was the secretary too. Jeanette was more involved with the show. Bert was more involved with his office work. Yes, he would make a note that, "Everything has gone very well here at the office. Bert has been sick." There wasn't much to know about Bert Scott. He was a routine employee and a very nice one. I think he had a daughter, but nothing that I would have anything to say. I remember Jeanette got married over here in the valley. Nothing particularly funny happened with that, but you brought her name up.

L: …I've never asked anybody about working with Hilliard Marks, Mary's brother.

F: Well, he was a big, husky, fairly attractive guy, who was something less than considered an integral part of the organization. There would be, and I don't mean every time his name came up, there would be jokes about him rather than about something wonderful he'd done. I don't mean he was a screw-up, but he was an addendum. He wasn't part and parcel.

L: Also you worked on the special <u>Carnival Nights</u>, and you worked on some of the other specials.

F: I worked on the last one that Mary did. Mary lovingly insisted that if I couldn't do the whole show, and I couldn't, that I direct her section of it. I did the specials, I did the show, I did other specials that Jack was in like the Crosby one, and never left the stage without saying what a good time I'd had.

You have to remember, well you don't have to remember, that all of this was a long time ago. 25 years of <u>The Tonight Show</u>, 4 years with <u>My Three Sons</u>, the years with the Smothers Brothers, chunks of my life. The Benny era is a long time ago. Even without Alzheimer's, there are lots of spaces in my mind about things that happened. But the overall picture is, "My God, what a wonderful man he was."

There is a famous story as you probably know, when Jack was dying, Mary had kind of a soiree every day which Benny fans and friends would come to her house, and you were really waiting for the eventual demise. And whatever it was, we were there at…cocktail time, and finally I said to [my wife] Janet, "I've got to go on working tonight," and we left. Lenny Gersh, who is a writer, and as I remember Joanie came out on the balcony of the living room and Joanie said, "Jack has left us," and Lenny said, "And so have Fred and Janet."

I had one of those things that you speak at the funeral of Jack and speak at the funeral of Mary [E.N.: Fred delivered the eulogy for both of them.], and obviously as time goes by, I quit going to funerals because there's one almost every day of somebody I know. There's not a lot more I can tell you, it would be repetitious because it's essentially based on a period of time that can never return, and I can not and will not and have not made a friend, and I have many friends I'm happy to say, I've not made a friend who could replace Jack…That's as good as it gets.

Jack Benny with Laurel and Hardy in 1929

The Jack Benny Times

February - May 2001　　　　　　　　　　　　　　　　　　Volume XVI, Numbers 3-4

President's Message

Hello again, folks! The interest and activity level of the IJBFC has been at a fever pitch for over five months. Our membership has grown to over 750 (a nearly 50% increase!), and we are getting close to having all available Jack Benny Programs in our audio library. I have had the pleasure of getting to know many new members of all ages, and the enthusiasm is overwhelming.

If you haven't seen it yet, I recommend that you check out our Web site at www.jackbenny.org. I am updating it continually with the latest Jack Benny information, and our Forum allows you to post your questions and areas of interest. We have a monthly chat room, where members from all over have been congregating to discuss a variety of Benny topics, ask questions, and joke around—it's been tremendous fun.

You'll notice that we have an article on Kenny Baker from one of the members. My thanks to Sue for her contribution. I encourage and welcome anyone who is interested in contributing in any way to do so; this club is here to serve everyone's interests, so please help with some of your knowledge or time!

My sincerest thanks to all of you for your continued support.

New Members

**** Russ Butler **** Tanya Shaw **** Joe Caramella **** Lawrence Lewis **** Jay Meade **** Jim Wong **** W. Gary Wetstein **** George Grube **** Edwin J. Kindred **** Keith Lilek **** Jim Holcombe **** Don Belden **** Fred A. Emmerling **** H.K. Hinkley **** Susan Olson **** James A. Darnell **** Melyssa Ching **** Danica Stein **** Wayne Boenig **** Lowell M. Rowley **** Willard Briggs **** John Baker **** Mike Hamm **** Roby McHone **** Anne Botterbusch **** Glenn E. Mueller **** Scott Randel **** Pete & Kerri Lund **** Mitch Weisberg **** Ron Jorgenson, Jr. **** Joe Novello **** Mark Harris **** Robert Purdy **** Bob Graham **** Jeff Bruce **** Robert Kringe **** Scott Critchfield **** Stephan Herschung **** Ron Aicher **** Bill Anderson **** Kermyt Anderson **** Melanie Aultman **** George Coppen **** Rodney Haydon **** Rizwan Kassim **** Jim Kilmartin **** Chuck Matthews **** Ross Nickel **** Jerry Salley **** Chris Stevens **** David Taylor **** Joseph S. Thornbury **** Richard M. Yeast **** Lois Dicker **** Robert E. Rayder, M.D. **** Alexandra N. Hoover **** Elliott Ferber **** Brian Anderson **** Kevin Trotman **** Gary Dear **** Walt Pattinson **** Hinda Lee Sheffer **** James Corner **** Jon Egger **** James H. Fleming **** Kenneth Flowers **** Mike Galbreath **** Keith Houdeshell **** Dr. Michael A. Langer **** Scott Lebensburger **** Antionio Mazzaro **** Phyllis R. McDonald **** Betty O'Brien **** Jerry Shnay **** Kelly Stanley **** Gerald Straight **** John Tisinger

**** Allan Turner **** Al Ward **** Michael Waters **** Harlan Zinck **** Dorian Bowen **** Dan Fisher **** Sean Hirsch **** Lawrence Kraemer **** Michelle Malik **** Bob McNulty ***** Dr. Michael Rudolph ***** Maria Rudolph ***** Bobby Blumofe ***** Joanna Meiseles **** Sol Fox **** Erik Anderson **** Thomas L. Barnett **** Ernest Carbajal **** Alan Cohen **** Peter Heimsoth **** Brian Lacy **** George Mariner **** Owens Pomeroy **** Baughan Roemer **** Barney Sheehan **** Steve Winkler **** Philip G. Harwood **** Edward (Ted) Jones **** Matthew Ernest Mengersen **** Ira Chineson **** Cliff Kahn **** Adrienne Statti **** Elizabeth Stump **** Thomas Trethewey **** Jenna Rebekah Trethewey **** Bernard Tzorfas **** David Siegel **** Mike Ray **** Christine Bagnasco **** Robert Howe **** Sharon Fisher **** Matt Bohn **** Tony BrakeField **** Kevin T. Doherty **** Curtis Gandy **** Edwin Kugler **** Allen Ragonnet, Jr. **** Howard L. Steinberg **** Dr. George Pollard **** Bruce McKinney **** Sandy Singer **** Ronald Paul II **** Butch Huff **** Stephen E. Jaczko **** Tom Kelley **** William B. Moran **** Ethan J. Muse **** Jeffrey Lee Rose **** Chip Shaw **** Deva Taffel **** Stan Taffel **** Katie Armentrout **** Marney Collins **** Tom Fichtner **** Anthony J. Golden **** Rik Hunter **** Charles Kirksey **** Roy D. Maultbetsch **** Chris Mezzolesta **** James Montgomery **** Ellen Pinholt, M.D. **** John Weyand **** Adam Proios **** Rodney Bowcock, Jr. **** Eric Brolund **** Ron Cerreta **** Stephen S. Enzminger **** Peg Fikes **** Tim Mark **** Jean Rencontre **** Gary Robertson **** Daniel Robinson **** Daniel Sulman **** Bill Wilson **** Tom Wyatt **** Joe Pearson **** Clayton Brown **** Lon McCartt **** Russ Counce **** Craig Crumpton **** Scott Ferguson Greene **** Bruce A. Hutton **** Howard R. Katz **** Bryce Lastine **** Patrick Laughrin **** Ross Learn **** Matt A. Lentz **** Dr. Kenneth Miller **** Larry Moore **** Maria Scarvelis **** Carlyn Vinas **** Walt Appel **** Kate Behrens **** Jim Bessman **** Patricia Brown **** D.W. Burhans **** John Conklin **** Scott Crowder-Vaughn **** Scott Erickson **** Ed Howell **** Andrew Lenahan **** Mark LoPresti **** Templeton Moss **** Philip Pearson **** Hans Summers **** Don Todd **** Sally Todd **** Curt Vance

Tape and MP3 Library

In response to the requests from many members, the IJBFC MP3 library opened on February 14. Here are the procedures:

- Select all the shows you want from the library.
- Send the list of your wants plus a blank CD-R to: IJBFC, P.O. Box 11288, Piedmont, CA 94611. A donation to the IJBFC of $10 per CD-R is recommended; please include return postage at a minimum.
- I will copy as many requested MP3s as possible onto the CD-R and return it to you.

The listing of shows available on MP3 can be found on our Web site in the "Programs" section. If you are interested in this listing and do not have access to the site, please send a SASE to the address at the end of this newsletter.

Printouts of our audiotape holdings can also be obtained by sending a SASE to the address at the end of this newsletter. For individuals who requested a listing previously (apologies that I wasn't keeping a listing), please drop a note and ask for an updated list that reflects the latest additions.

Tape/MP3 Trading List

Rob Cohen, 1603 Harrison Pond Dr., New Albany, OH 43054; robcohen@ameritech.net - Rob is also interested in trading MP3s of other comedy shows (e.g., Fibber McGee, etc.)

George Grube, 6402 Rolling Greens Dr., Ocala, FL 34472; Ontime6402@aol.com

Laura Leff, P.O. Box 11288, Piedmont, California 94611, USA; JackBenny@aol.com

Jay Meade, 681 Straits Rd., Gloucester, NC 28528; jmeade@starfishnet.com

Jack Palmer, 145 N. 21st St., Battle Creek, MI 49015; vdalhart@prodigy.net

Jeff Tanner, P.O. Box 65787, Vancouver, WA 98686, USA; TannerJeff@aol.com

John Tisinger, 1998 Clem-Lowell Rd., Carrollton, GA 30116-9253 jdtisinger@peachnet.campuscwix.net

Drew Wiest, 6109 NE 197th St, Kenmore, WA 98028, USA; dwiest12@hotmail.com

Ken Yesson, 4316 – 83 St., Edmonton, Alberta T6K-0Z5 Canada; yesandno@connect.ab.ca

Waukegan's Jack Benny Statue

The work on the Jack Benny statue in Waukegan is continuing, and the dedication is scheduled for September 8, 2001. Per a recent letter from Waukegan Mayor William F. Durkin, "Scheduled to appear at the unveiling will be members of the Benny family [LL: Jack's grandchildren], celebrities from the Hollywood Friar's Club, and plenty of Jack Benny impersonators. Emcees for the affair include Bill Devore, Director of the College of Lake County Foundation, and Joan Hammel, National Vice President of the Grammy Awards. The Jack Benny family will also be on hand to accept an award from Tony Belmont, Director of the National Comedy Hall of Fame, located in St. Petersburg, Florida. A large crowd of Jack Benny fans and enthusiasts from around the world are expected to attend this gala event."

Artist Erik Blome is creating the statue, which features Jack in the famous hand-on-cheek pose, a violin tucked in his right hand. "Renowned artist Erik Blome has created works for the Chicago Bulls, United States Department of Labor, and YWCA of Greater Milwaukee…Those he has profiled include George Washington Carver, Dr. Martin Luther King Jr., former Supreme Court Justice Thurgood Marshall (commissioned by the Mayor's Office of the City of Chicago), and the late James Jordan, father of former Chicago Bull Michael Jordan (for the James Jordan Boys & Girls Club)."

I have been in contact with Tony Belmont, Director of the National Comedy Hall of Fame about their part in the ceremony. As Tony himself said it, "The statue idea was the brain child of the citizens of Waukegan for their favorite son, Jack Benny. They then began a campaign to have Jack inducted into the National Comedy Hall Of Fame. But when they contacted me, I told them he was already inducted, but we haven't had a proper ceremony yet. We were going to have it at the New York Friars Club. After hearing about the statue, we all decided it would be wonderful to have the ceremony in front of the statue. This would give the city national coverage and let everyone know we will never forget Jack Benny."

I will also be attending the ceremony, and hope that I will meet many of the IJBFC members in the Chicago area. Hopefully, I'll finally be able to see the Jack Benny Vault exhibit at the Museum of Broadcast and Communications in Chicago!

The fund is a little under halfway to their goal of raising $50,000, and needs your help! You can do your part through a donation to the Jack Benny Statue Fund, which is tax deductible (501C3 #36-600-6137). Levels of participation are:

- **$.01 to $38 - Pennies for Benny**: Waukegan students are trying to raise 500,000 or more pennies for the statue.
- **$39 to $74 - 39ers:** (Note: this is the name of the Jack Benny Middle School athletic teams) Donors receive a set of 39 Genesee Theatre postcards.
- **$75 to $99 - "I'm THINKING!":** Donor listing at Benefit Concerts through the year 2002.
- **$100 to $499 - Century Club:** Name on a Benny plaza brick, and donor listing at Benefits Concerts through 2003.
- **$500 to $999 - Friend's 500 Club:** Name on five Benny plaza bricks, donor listing at Benefit Concerts through 2004, and Friends of Genesee Theatre membership through 2002.
- **$1000 to $1999 - Millenium Club:** Name on statue plaque, donor listing at Benefit Concerts through 2005, and Friends of Genesee Theatre membership through 2003.
- **$2000+ - Lifetime 39er:** Name on Genesee Theatre sidewalk diamond, donor listing at Benefit Concerts through 2005, life membership in Friends of the Genesee Theatre.

Please make checks payable to "Jack Benny Statue Fund" (and please let them know you're an IJBFC member!). Send all donations to:

Jack Benny Statue Fund
Bank of Waukegan, Downtown Branch
P.O. Box 39
Waukegan, IL 60079

Kenny Baker… "*Gee, It's a Thrill*"

Who was Ann Miller's first kiss, originally cast to play a character called the "Grand Duke" in the classic film "The Wizard of Oz," and sang for Walt Disney's cartoons? That same handsome, young California lad who "wowed" audiences coast to coast on a weekly basis with his silky-smooth, captivating tenor voice on "The Jack Benny Show" from Nov. 1935 to June 1939 – **Kenny Baker**.

Kenny Baker, born Kenneth Lawrence Baker in Monrovia, CA, on Sept. 30, 1912, truly took his career to new heights when he became "Jack's tenor" on "The Jack Benny Show" on Nov. 3, 1935. Although most of you know of Dennis Day and may have thought that Dennis played the original "naive kid" role on Jack's show, this "honor" was originally bestowed upon, and played quite well by, none other than Kenny Baker.

Baker auditioned for Jack's show in 1935 when Michael Bartlett, Jack's tenor at that time, was returning to the movie studios. Mr. Bartlett was a celebrated star of opera, the concert stage and movies. Says Baker in an interview with "Radio Guide" during that time period, "Michael Bartlett had to go back to the movie studios and I knew they wanted someone to fill his place. But I had no idea they would really consider me. I thought they wanted 'a name' in the spot."

An interview with "Screenland" tells about his trial broadcast on Jack's show. Kenny had no sooner stepped away from the microphone, so to speak, than Kenny was given a contract for seven more weeks, followed with a contract for thirteen more.

"WOW!" Kenny exclaimed. "By that time I was so scared and thrilled I could hardly keep inside my own skin!"

Jack Benny straightaway christened Kenny the "Timid Tenor." Jack said that Kenny approached the microphone like it was a coiled cobra waiting to attack! Such was Kenny's nature – he always said a silent prayer before every song.

Baker began professional radio work in 1931 while still a teenager, giving a performance on "Madame Jennie's Hour" free of charge. In 1932 he talked Ted Bliss of KFOX in Long Beach, CA, into giving him 15 minutes twice a week "just for the experience."

This led to radio work in Los Angeles with the Cardinal Quartet, then soloist at the newly opened Biltmore Bowl. Kenny's big break came in 1935 when he won Eddy Duchin's Texaco Radio Contest singing "To Call You My Own." Part of the prize was an engagement at the famous Cocoanut Grove, where Baker's singing impressed movie producer Mervyn LeRoy, placing Baker under contract. When the soloist position became available on Jack Benny's show, Baker auditioned, and the rest, as they say, is history!

Baker worked on various radio shows after Jack's, including Fred Allen's, and Kenny's own show, "The Kenny Baker Show." He appeared in 18 motion pictures, most notably 1939's "The Mikado." His success in radio, film, and stage led to his prestigious Broadway debut with Mary Martin in the 1943 musical, "One Touch of Venus." Kenny was a deeply religious man who ended his radio career with a 15-minute show dealing with man's spirituality. Kenny Baker died Aug. 10, 1985.

Feel free to contact me! Susan Olson -- kennybakerfan@yahoo.com

Jack and Groucho

I've always been interested that there is such a high degree of crossover interest between fans of Jack Benny and of the Marx Brothers. Jack's humor was known for its more relaxed pace, whereas the Marxes were known for their rapid-fire dialogue. Many fans regard Jack's radio work as being his best, whereas the Marxes excelled in films, and a Groucho hosted the legendary You Bet Your Life (which was not nearly as successful on radio). Jack's pantomime was mainly his hand gestures or simply staring, while Harpo chased women across the stage and a stateroom filled to the rafters with people in A Night At the Opera. I love them both, too. Is it simply because they were contemporaries? I would be interested to know what others think about this.
Jack had Groucho on his program a few times, and even did a skit on his television show with himself as a guest on You Bet Your Life. Jack also appeared with Groucho in radio's Pabst Blue Ribbon Town. It is always interesting to hear these two very different comic geniuses working together. Here are a few notes on Jack and Groucho that I have recently received:
"Marx had maintained a strong avowed preference for ad-libbing. In an interesting anecdote, Leonard Maltin shares a perceptive tale in which Marx's predilection appears compromised on at least one occasion. It concerns an encounter Marx had with Jack Benny's gag writers, when Marx was about to make a guest appearance on Benny's show. Sent in advance by Benny to Marx's home to let him see the script, the scribes returned to report that Marx was characteristically caustic and unreceptive to their overtures. "Well, we won't use him, then," was Benny's response, defending his staff's work to the max.
"Some years later the two comedians met at a local country club. Marx asked Benny why he never had him on his show. Benny replied: 'I'd be happy to have you on my

show, but only if you use the script my writers write for you.' Marx agreed and appeared the following week, presumably reading his lines exactly as written, in obvious contrast to his passionate fondness for ad-libs. It would appear that, while that was Marx's preference, when he had to produce throwbacks in rapid-fire succession every week, he -- and his whole show ("You Bet Your Life") -- depended on all the help he could get. He wasn't just gazing at the ceiling like we thought he was!" - Jim Cox

Jack and Groucho were scheduled to have lunch in late 1974, but Jack never showed. Initially Groucho was very angry, but soon found out that Jack was dying of pancreatic cancer. "Groucho felt badly for two reasons: one, he had misjudged his old friend's reason for having apparently 'stood him up' and, more importantly, he was about to lose a longtime colleague and 'a nice man' -- which was Groucho's ultimate praise. I think it was Milton Berle whom Groucho had run into during one of his daily walks that broke the sad news to him. I had lunch with Groucho and Burns shortly before we learned the news. Of course little did anyone realize that Burns' career was about to be rekindled as a poignant side effect of the death of his best friend (i.e. Sunshine Boys, which Benny had been rehearsing when he fell ill)." – Steve Stoliar, author of Raised Eyebrows: My Years Inside Groucho's House, and former secretary to Groucho Marx

"By the way, are you familiar with the Kansas City dinner theater production of the Odd Couple a few years ago? It was adapted slightly, with Jack and Groucho as the roommates. Unfortunately I didn't see the production myself, and it never went anywhere else, but it's an interesting premise. Occasionally a souvenir glass will show up on Ebay." – Paul Wesoloski, The Freedonia Gazette
(LL: Does anyone have more information on this production?)

Do You Know?

Ross Learn asks, "I just finished listening to the radio show that announced that contest. It got me to thinking....whatever happened to those letters? Don Wilson announced that all the letters became the property of Jack Benny and would not be returned. Does that mean that they did, in
fact, end up...somewhere? In light of the episodes that spotlighted the contest, it would be certainly interesting to see what the content of some of those entries were. They would also have some historical significance (as far as the program), it would reflect how audience members (or the hundred million others) handled the challenge put forth by the contest. Does anyone know what ended up happening to the entries?"

Tanya Shaw asks, "Does anyone know when Mr. Billingsly made his first appearance on Jack Benny? I think his character is great! Also, what really happened to the gas man and what episode was it that Carmichael did him in?" (LL: Carmichael first appeared 2-12-39.)

Also from Tanya, "This morning I listened to a show of Jack's dated April 13, 1947 (Jack fixes his phonograph). Throughout the episode, anytime someone mentioned the word 'million', Jack let out a little 'whoop!'. How and when did this joke get started? I think he was saying 'whoop!' the week before, too."

Scott Randel asks, "Does anyone know the name of the double-talker that occasionally appeared on the radio show? He would say things like 'Last Friday I was frazzinbillidaling...'" (LL: Specifically, he appeared on the second broadcast of "Snow White and the Seven Gangsters" on 1-8-39, among others.)

Mike Martini asks, "I know a little bit about most of the Jack Benny writers, but John Tackaberry eludes me. Whatever became of him? Did he have a writing career above and beyond TJBP? Does anyone know where and when he was born? I think he was from Texas."

Nik Kierniesky asks, "I am having some difficulty in tracking down interviews, biographies, and articles about Eddie Anderson. Did he shy away from such activities or am I looking in all the wrong places?"

Ben Wilkie asks, "Once upon a time during WW2 I heard an episode of the Jack Benny Program where Jack contributes his Maxwell to the 'Junk Salvage Drive.' Sad, I admit, but somehow Jack gets the car back later. Is any explanation for this given?"

Joel S. Rothman asks, "It is well known that Jack did a screen test for the role in the Sunshine Boys film which was ultimately played by George Burns as a result of Jack's final illness. The books about Jack also indicate that he was superb in the part. Are there any 'bootleg' copies of his
screen test in circulation? If so, how do you recommend trying to obtain a copy?"

You Do Know!

John Dolezal corrected an error in the last issue about the graves of George Burns and Gracie Allen. George and Gracie are entombed in the Sanctuary of Heritage, eye level (middle), in the Freedom Mausoleum of Forest Lawn Cemetery in Los Angeles. Enter the mausoleum, make an immediate right, they are two doors down on your left. They are surrounded by several other notables, including Jeanette McDonald, Gene Raymond, Alan Ladd, Nat "King" Cole, and Clara Bow. John has visited and placed flowers there many times. Thanks for the correction!

The Tale Piece

I was recently contacted by the husband of Jan Winters, who performed as an extra on the <u>Shower of Stars</u> program of 2-13-58, entitled "Jack Benny's Fortieth Birthday." Others on the show included Dean Martin, Van Johnson, and Jo Stafford, as well as most of the classic Benny gang. It was during this program that Eddie Anderson had a mild heart attack and was hospitalized. A fine article featuring photographs from the rehearsal can be found in the <u>Life</u> magazine of 2-24-58 ("The Many Happy Returns of Benny").

Jan herself can be seen in the photo of the upper-right corner of page 108, just behind Jack. She had this memory of working with him, "Jack Benny was one of the nicest, kind-hearted and most giving persons that I have ever met. He treated us all to dinner after the show, and the next day I met him on the street. He turned around and said, 'Hi' and started talking to me about the show. He was very friendly. I have very happy memories. He loved to laugh. He always had a smile on his face; quite a departure from his stage act and stage personality. I was just an extra on the show but he treated everyone like a star. He was that kind of person."

Etcetera

The American Radio Archives (owned by Pacific Pioneer Broadcasters) is being combined with the collection of the Thousand Oaks Library. The former includes more than 20,000 transcriptions, 6,000 tapes, and countless scripts and other ephemera, and the latter has over 5,000 hours of recordings and 23,000 scripts. This collection also includes many transcriptions of the Benny radio program. The library is in the process of securing funding for a new building to display the full collection.

♪♫

Jack's best-known house (and the only known detached unit still standing) is at 1002 North Roxbury in Beverly Hills, which he had built and lived in from 1938 to 1964. It was last sold in May, 1997 for over $7 million. Per the City of Beverly Hills, it consists of 8 bedrooms (not sure how they calculated this, as Joan's book notes that there were 4 bedrooms) and 7 bathrooms, totaling 9,928 square feet. The lot size totals 35,305 square feet. Other property features include a guesthouse and tennis court.

♪♫

Speaking of Jack's property, I recently rediscovered some notes about the distribution of Jack's estate. (I also have a copy of Jack's will, if anyone wants more specific information.) The source is unknown, but may be the <u>New York Times</u>. I am often asked about Jack's violins, philanthropic efforts, and the like, so here's the accounting:

1/2/75: "Jack Benny, who died last Thursday at the age of 80, left the bulk of his multi-million dollar estate to his widow, his adopted daughter, and his sister, according to probate records. The comedian also left two valuable violins, a Stradivarius worth … and a Presenda to the Los Angeles Philharmonic Orchestra. He had previously donated the violins, but had retained them for his own use. Other bequests went to the Motion Picture Country Home and Hospital and the Los Angeles County Museum of Art.

2/6/75: "Jack Benny converted his jokes about penny pinching into … real estate and personal property, according to documents filed in a Los Angeles court Tuesday by Mary Livingstone Benny, widow of the comedian who died in December."

7/12/75: "The exact amount of Mr. Benny's estate was disclosed in an appraisal submitted to Superior Court Judge Pearce Young…Among the most valuable items left by Mr. Benny was a 1729 Stradivarius … which he left to the Los Angeles Symphony Orchestra."

12/3/77: "A petition has been approved for the final accounting and distribution of the estate of Jack Benny…The matter was approved without contest yesterday by Judge Edward Rafeedie of Superior Court…In accordance with the late comedian's will, trust funds will be set up for Mr. Benny's wife, Mary, his daughter, Joan Blumofe, and his grandchildren."

♪♫

Also from those old notes…
1/4/75: "George Burns and George Jessell, friends of the late Jack Benny, announced today plans to found a Jack Benny memorial forest on the outskirts of Jerusalem. They said friends of the comedian from all walks of life would donate trees."

10/20/77: "…[Frank] Sinatra has instituted a $2 million libel suit against Jody Jacobs of the <u>Los Angeles Times</u>, charging she falsely wrote that he failed to show up at a banquet in time to present George Burns the Jack Benny Memorial Award. He did get there in time, Mr. Sinatra's suit said, he did present the award, and what's more he resents the implication that he had little regard for Mr. Burns."

10/25/77: "[Jacobs] said in her column by relying on second hand information that the singer went to a baseball game rather than show up on time."

Does anyone know whatever became of this lawsuit, who "manages" the Jack Benny Memorial Award, and for what honor it is given?

♪♫♪♫♪♫♪♫♪♫♪♫♪♫♪♫♪♫♪♫♪♫♪♫♪♫♪♫♪♫♪♫♪♫♪♫

From Chuck Caramella: "Found the following in the <u>Time Capsule</u> 1939…Crime and Corruption, April 17: Waukegan Wisecracker: Born to a Waukegan, Illinois clothing merchant on St. Valentine's Day 45 years ago, Benjamin Kubelsky was thrown out of his school orchestra, where he played the violin, for making a wisecrack about the conductor. At 16, he was expelled from Waukegan High School for making one wisecrack too many about the principal. In vaudeville and on the radio wisecracking Benjamin Kubelsky, renamed Jack Benny, fared better. This year Jack Benny's radio program, outranked in popularity only by that of wooden Charlie McCarthy, will gross him some $390,000. Last week Waukegan's gift to the U.S. stood in a Federal courtroom in Manhattan, guilty by admission of cheating the Government of $700 in duty on trinkets for his wife which had been smuggled into the U.S. by notorious Albert N. Chapereau. Before pronouncing sentence, Federal Judge Vincent Leibell remarked: 'You must feel very much ashamed of yourself, Mr. Benny, standing here as you do today.' 'I do,' murmured Benjamin Kubelsky, flushing. Then Judge Leibell fined Benjamin Kubelsky $10,000, imposed a suspended sentence of a year and a day, let him slink from the courtroom."

I am not sure of the veracity of Jack's early wisecracking, and there were other reasons he was expelled from high school (such as his failing every course). I've heard multiple renderings and theories on how much Jack (and George Burns) knew about Chapereau's activities; this article obviously takes the view toward one end of the spectrum. Check out George's <u>Gracie: A Love Story</u> for a somewhat different interpretation.

♪♫♪♫♪♫♪♫♪♫♪♫♪♫♪♫♪♫♪♫♪♫♪♫♪♫♪♫♪♫♪♫♪♫♪♫

Also from Chuck: "'Larry King appointed to the all-powerful, all-classy, all-honorary committee which nominates VIPs to grace our stamps. The first one he'll plump for is Jack Benny. And it'll be announced next month.' I will keep my eyes open, carefully peruse my stamp newspaper, and let you know when and if anything occurs. Maybe he'll be part of the Legends of Hollywood series as Lucille Ball will become on August 6, 2001."

Jack Benny Classifieds

§§§ Patrick Laughrin is offering his rare Jack Benny statue for sale. Photo at right is representative of the statue, but is not of the actual statue offered. Statue is approximately 50 years old. (Note: This is

not the ESCO statue, but an older one.) Serious inquiries only, please; the seller reserves the right to accept or reject any offer. W3752 Harrison Rd., Hilbert, WI 54129; Pglaughrin@aol.com

§§§ Rob Cohen is interested in selling his reel-to-reel copies of a variety of OTR programs. Each reel contains approximately 16 shows. Programs include many drama (e.g., The Shadow) and comedy (e.g., JB, Fibber McGee, Amos n Andy). $5.00 per reel plus shipping. Rob is also interested in trading MP3s of other comedy shows. 1603 Harrison Pond Dr., New Albany, OH 43054; robcohen@ameritech.net

§§§ James Darnell is seeking an 8x10" glossy copy of the picture at left with Jack Benny and Lucille Ball. 4923 Glen Elm Dr., Peoria Heights, IL 61614; agenttura39@hotmail.com

§§§ Adam Proios is interested in getting in touch with other New York area IJBFC members for trading, etc. 351 West 24th Street, #2J, New York, NY 10011

Diamonds in Clubs

Here are some other clubs that may be of interest to IJBFC members:
- **International Al Jolson Society** In operation since 1950. Two newsletters (Jolson Journal) annually, plus a host of other services. $20 for one year, multi-year discounts. Send payment to Tom Nestor, Treasurer, 1709 Billinghurst Court, Orlando, Florida 32825. www.jolson.org
- **The Eddie Cantor Appreciation Society** Bimonthly newsletter, recordings, books, and personal get-togethers. $15 per year for US members, $25 for international members. 14611 Valley Vista Boulevard, Sherman Oaks, California 91403. www.eddiecantor.com
- **National Lum and Abner Society** In operation since 1984. Monthly newsletter, audio library, movies, and annual convention. $15 per year. Tim Hollis, Executive Secretary, #81 Sharon Boulevard, Dora, Alabama 35062. www.synaps.com/stemple
- **The Official W.C. Fields Fan Club** Quarterly newsletters, film list, conventions. $15 per year for U.S. members, $18 per year for Canadian members, $26 per year for international members. Send a SASE to Ted Wioncek, President, P.O. Box 506, Dept Web, Stratford, New Jersey 08084-0506 to receive a membership application. www.webtrec.com/wcfields
- **First Generation Radio Archives** Dedicated to the preservation and restoration of shows from electronic transcription. Free monthly E-mail newsletter. P.O. Box 2193, Sumner, WA 98390-2193, www.radioarchives.org

Harmonizing with Larry Adler

I had the pleasure of talking with Larry Adler at his home during a trip to England in 1998. We had been in contact for over ten years, and finally were in the same place at the same time. Larry has had such an amazing history in show business and known so many people, that our conversation ran to a variety of topics besides Jack. Enjoy.

L: With someone who's been interviewed as many times as you have, there's always the usual questions that you always have to answer.

A: Sometimes I say to the interviewer, "I'll give you a thousand dollars if you ask me a question I've never been asked before." They can't do it. Except a great professional here in England, a guy named Michael Parkington, he is one of them. Does his homework, doesn't try to put down his subjects, he does a good job. And there's a lady named Mavis Nicholson, also very good. But there was one man…that I haven't mentioned at all. He died, but he put Rita Hayworth on television and she obviously had Alzheimer's. She should not have been exposed to the public, and I thought it was cruel to have that lady…and he was interviewing her, and she didn't know who she was. In public.

L: So many things that I'd like to ask you…well, let's start off with Jack.

A: See, what happened is that I was playing at the Palmer House, and my agent Abe Lastfogel, a William Morris agent, he called me and says, "Larry, you said you wanted to go overseas to the troops. I've got a great show for you, I can't tell you over the phone what it is, but you'll have to get out of your job at the Palmer House." So I went to the manager after one show and said, "The Army has ordered me to go overseas."…They let me out, I went to New York and was introduced to Jack Benny, Martha Tilton, and Marie Shaw…no, it was Anna Lee. And Jack and I got on right away. It didn't take any time to know him, we fit as if we had been brothers for a long time, and we did these shows. Working with Jack, for me, was like going to a university of show business, because that man knew, but not only knew, but was generous in imparting what he knew. There was no jealousy in him, there was no envy. I would never have gotten that kind of feeling from Bob Hope. Jack was at ease.

(At this point, Larry received a phone call from a long-time friend, Tatiana)

[Tatiana] is so funny, you know, to find anybody who could make me laugh the way she makes me laugh…one time we were having a terrific argument, and she said…"I quite forgot I was speaking to a genius!" How can you get mad at that?

L: That's one way to end an argument…I'll have to remember that with my husband!

A: Another time she said, "Why do you always have to be so obstropulous [sic]?" These are wonderful words!…She was asked to run once as the President of Peru, and she said she knew it was like being sent before a firing squad, so she didn't run…

L: If I may be so personal, I remembered our discussions about Tatiana at the time of her divorce…has there been anyone in your life since then?

A: Oh yes, the lady who's putting on the concert Monday, I'm mad about her. *But* she's only 38 years old, for God's sake.

L: (teasing) Well, you told me I was too old for you when I was 21.

A: Well you were, but that was different! I'm always falling in love with somebody. My daughter phoned me from Barbados two days ago. Apparently there's a very popular quiz program called Jeopardy. I've never heard of it. But the question was, "Who had affairs with Roberto Rosselini and Larry Adler?"

L: Ingrid Bergman.

A: Ingrid Bergman, yes. I never thought they would make that a quiz program! So there was the most honest woman I've ever met in my life. She was so direct, there was no artifice about her whatsoever. She once said to me, "Why do they say I'm beautiful and sweet when everybody looks like me?" I said, "Ingrid, I've played Stockholm. I know they don't." She was incredibly beautiful, and had the most wonderful character…We met because she was with Jack Benny and Martha Tilton and me in Germany, and I was playing the piano. I knew that an actress was going to join us, but I didn't know who. But this woman walked in, she sat down, she said, "That's very nice, what are you playing?" I said, "I'm just improvising, making it up." She said, "Well you'll write it down, won't you?" I said, "I can't write music." She said, "You're very smug, aren't you?" I said, "What does that mean?" She said, "You're not only ignorant, you're *proud* of your ignorance!" By then I'd caught the Swedish accent, and I realized it was Ingrid. And she made me, when we got back to the States, find a teacher and study composition. Had she not done so, I never would have written the music for the film Genevieve and about twelve other films. So I owe her quite a lot.

L: How long were the two of you together?

A: Oh, I would say our relationship lasted about four years. And it was a great influence on me because you don't meet people like that every day. They don't exist.

L: I remember your comment in the book that you just didn't feel comfortable being "Mr. Ingrid Bergman."

A: Had we married, that's what I would have been. And my ego ain't capable of handling that. It's an awful thing to say, but it's true.

L: Back to Jack Benny…take us through one of the camp shows, what you would do.

A: Jack Benny did something I've never known any other entertainer to do. When the show was over, Jack would mingle with the soldiers, get their names and addresses, and call their parents when he got back to the states. Now I learned to do that from him. But I don't know any other performer who did that. But he really felt for other people…He was a human being. And the only time I ever saw Jack embarrassed, he told me one day, and he said that his business manager, who I think was Mary Benny's brother…There was political trouble [LL: Larry was on the blacklist in the 50s due to alleged Communist sympathizing], and they were afraid I might drag Jack's name into my own trouble. I said, "Jack, you have nothing to worry about. I'm not going to mention you at all." I could see that Jack was very embarrassed to ask me this.

L: I've seen one film of you and Jack, where he's playing one note on the violin and you're playing a whole series on the harmonica.

A: That was our number that we did all the time. He would play "dah" and I'd play "deedle-lah dah dah dah", then he'd play "dah"…that was the whole number.

L: What were some of the jokes back and forth?

A: I tell you, Ingrid, when she was still in our show, wanted to read excerpts from <u>Joan of Lorraine</u> by Sherwood Anderson. I said, "Ingrid, you're dealing with people who read comic books. They are not going to understand Sherwood Anderson." So I wrote a sketch…

(interrupted by another phone call)

…that was the secretary of the 38-year-old lady. Marina is really the head of the whole Greek community here, and this concert is for a museum of Jewish music in Selonica. Now Marina's father is not Jewish, but he was interested in all Jewish affairs. He should know about *my* Jewish affairs!…He founded a museum for Jewish music in Selonica, because they're Greek. So in my program on Monday which is being done for this museum, I'm going to play some Jewish Greek music…I do <u>Rhapsody in Blue</u> with the digital piano, Gershwin's piano roll. I always like to do that if I can, and Yamaha is giving me the piano. Incidentally, they used to have a game at the [Algonquin] Round Table, "I can give you a sentence with" and you say the word, and my word is Yamaha, and I said, "Your daddy's rich and Yamaha's good looking!" [LL: Reference to a line from "Summertime" from <u>Porgy and Bess</u>]

L: I'm sure Ira Gershwin would be proud of that.

A: Dorothy Parker won it one time by being asked to give a sentence with the word horticulture. She said, "You can lead a horticulture, but you can't make him drink."…Very sad lady. Terribly sad. She took me once, she was making a speech to raise money for Israel, she broke down and cried in the middle of her own speech. She was also very self-conscious about being Jewish, she was a Rothschild.

L: Back to the previous topic, you would go to a camp and do how many performances?

A: We would do usually about two a day. See now Bob Hope would be about six or seven, but he would do only a 15 or 20 minute show. We did a 2 hour show, and we'd dress always in civilian clothes because we thought they saw enough uniforms, and that was a good thing to do, and we did. And I only saw Jack cut off his usual good humor once. We did a show in Bengali (sp?), and there was a sandstorm that blew in our faces and we were deathly ill, and they took us to a Red Cross spot afterwards and gave us some coffee which didn't help all that much. An attendant with a very southern accent came over and said, "Hiya Ja-yack," and he sat down without being asked and said, "Jack, why don't you bring Rochester with you?" That could have been a little trouble, and Jack said, "Well, he had things to do in the States, so he couldn't come with us." "Well, Jack, we listen to you every Sunday, but the highlight of your show, your main asset is Rochester. We love Rochester. I sure do, Mr. Benny." Jack said, "Well, if he was here at our show, he'd be sitting here at this table and you wouldn't be sitting with him. What about that?" "Now just a minute, Mr. Benny, I'm from the South." Jack said, "That's why I didn't bring Rochester."

L: Something that people so often point out about Jack is that if they were on the road, they wouldn't stay at a hotel that wouldn't let Rochester stay there as well.

A: I once said to him, "Why does he have to call you Mr. Benny?" He said, "Larry, once he calls me Jack, we lose all the Southern sponsors." Isn't that awful?

L: Did you ever have any of the other cast—Mary, Rochester, Phil—work with you on the camp shows?

A: No, Mary didn't. When I came back to the States, Jack asked me several times to be a guest on his show, and I met Mary at that time. I didn't like Mary. I didn't get on with her, I thought that she patronized other people. Now, I never saw Jack patronize anybody. And as I say, I learned so much from him and that was one of the things I learned. You see in doing camp shows, someone who's as big a star as Jack had more authority than the Generals. But he never threw it around, he never let you know that he was a star. He never acted the star, and again that was a great lesson learned.

L: I know Joan has told stories about going to queue for a movie, and they'd just be standing around, and finally someone would notice and pull them out and take them to the front.

A: Jack would never ask for a favor for himself. I started to tell you that I wrote this sketch for Ingrid and Jack, I based it on Casablanca, and at one point Ingrid is trying to get Jack to leave his wife and run away with her, and she's shaking him, "Don't you realize this thing is bigger than we are?" And he's supposed to say, "You're bigger than I am!" He couldn't say it because she *was* bigger than he was, and the ridiculousness of it made him laugh, so when he got to that line he couldn't say it. The only time it got said was when Jack had a cold and I did the sketch with Ingrid.

L: Jack was so famous for falling down laughing.

A: Well, there was one joke that Jack would ask me to tell at parties. Now if he asked me to tell it, he knows the joke, he knows what's coming, and he'd burst out laughing every time. The joke is a man says to the doctor, "I'm having terrific difficulty, doctor, I can't pee." He said, "How old are you?" "I'm 92." The doctor says, "Ah, you've peed enough." It's illogical!

L: I remember George Burns told about how Jack called you the world's greatest comedian.

A: Imagine Jack Benny telling George Burns that I was the funniest man in the world. And George says, "Give me an example of what makes Larry Adler the funniest man in the world." And with Jack trying to tell him, it fell flat. From then on, George used it on his radio shows, and one time George came to see my nightclub show, he came with Henny Youngman, and I got him up on the floor to tell that story…[What I said] really wasn't that funny. It was funny at the time, but it really wasn't funny to anybody else.

L: It's one of those "you had to be there" type of things. So you do the camp show, and you'd stay in the barracks?

A: Overnight, yes. I remember one time we were in New Guinea, and we were told we should put everything under the bed and fasten everything, because there was going to be a hurricane during the night. We woke up in the morning, there had been no hurricane….

L: How often would you move between camps?

A: Well, we would do a base and move right to the next base. We were very seldom at any base more than one day. Then we got to Munich, and I wanted to see Dachau. I couldn't get either Jack or Ingrid to go with me. When I came back and told them what I'd seen, they didn't believe me…Then there was another time, we got to Prague in Czechoslovakia…and Prague was occupied by the Russians. Now I knew that Prague was a beautiful city, I went to see it; again, neither Jack nor Ingrid would go with me. What they'd heard was that the Russians would cut your hand off to get your wristwatch. So I went alone, and the Russians were so hospitable, so friendly to me. And Ingrid and Jack didn't believe me.

L: You had done some concerts at the military hospitals—did you do it during the war or after?

A: When we did the shows, very often we had to do shows in hospitals, and they always sent me, not anyone else in our troop, only me into the psychoneurotic ward. I was afraid to find out why. But I was the one who was sent into them. I remember once I was doing a show, and one of the soldiers in the beds said, "Hey Mac." I stopped and said, "Yes?" He said, "Do you have to tap your foot like that when you play?" I said, "I'm sorry." I stopped tapping my foot and went on playing. Then he said, "Hey Mac. Do you have to sway from side to side like that? A guy could get drunk just looking at you." So the nurse said, "Don't interrupt Mr. Adler while he's playing." He said, "Look lady, I'm nuts, ain't I? I'll tell him what I think!"…He said [to me], "Do you think I'm nuts?" I said, "I think you're the first intelligent man I've met on the island." He said, "Shake, Mac. We understand each other. What's your rank?" I said, "I have no rank." He said, "Don't bulls*** me, there's an officer's patch on your shirt. What's your rank?" I said, "We have to wear officers' uniforms. In case we're captured, we're treated as officers by the enemy." He said, "Nobody made you come here?" I said, "No." He said, "I have very bad news for you, Mac. You belong in this ward!"

L: How close to the front lines were you?

A: Only when I went to Korea on my own was when I got near the front lines. With Jack, they never sent us anywhere but into safe territory. Although when we played Guadalcanal, I was told that the majority of the island was held by the Japanese. Then we were sent down to Brisbane to meet MacArthur, who was the biggest ham I ever met in my life! He was impossible! When we left him, Jack leaned against the wall shaking with laughter, and they called *us* hams!…He used to talk like John Barrymore reading Hamlet. He couldn't talk to you as a human being. He was always MacArthur orating to the public at large. He couldn't relax for a minute. He asked us to come and have a drink with his wife and son, and his son had emblems of his father all over his bedroom. I thought, "This is not a way for children to be brought up." Then he also asked us to have a drink with his officers, and Jack and I tossed as to who had to have a drink with the officers because neither of us wanted to, and I lost, so I had to have the drink. There were four Generals and a Colonel and we were waiting for another General. The fifth General came in, and he had a limerick. Here's the limerick:

"Roses are red, violets are blue," said Eleanor to Franklin,

"How long must I stay in the White House with you?"

Said Franklin to Eleanor,

"You kiss the niggers, I'll kiss the Jews,

And we'll stay in the White House as long as we choose."

Everybody *burst* out laughing, and I was all set to explode. Then the Colonel said, "Larry, I know how you feel. I feel the same way, but I've got to live with these guys. And Larry, you must remember, any one of them could put you in handcuffs and send you back to America under military arrest." So I put up, and I still regret that I did.

L: Was it in your book that I read that Jack carried a message to MacArthur or Eisenhower?

A: Well, we wanted to get into Berlin when we were in Germany, and civilians were not yet allowed in Berlin. So we were having a drink with a lady, who turned out to be Eisenhower's mistress. She said, "You want to get to Berlin, you've got to meet Eisenhower." I said, "How the hell am I going to get to meet Eisenhower?" She said, "Leave it to me," and she made a call, and Jack Benny and I went to meet Eisenhower. Ingrid wouldn't go. She said, "Larry, I have nothing to say to him." That's the person she was. But anyway when we got to Eisenhower's office, he looked over our shoulders obviously expecting to see Ingrid, and was disappointed that she wasn't there. But afterwards, he picked up the phone and got us a special plane to take us to Berlin.

L: What was your experience there?

A: Very, very vivid. First of all on July the fourth, we had gone down to Nuremberg and played at the Nuremberg station. I was the first Jew to play a work written by a Jew in a camp in Germany since the war…Then we flew back to Berlin, and Ingrid and I stood on Hitler's balcony, and Ingrid read the Gettysburg Address and I played the Battle Hymn of the Republic, and I now use it in my one-man show. We didn't have a microphone there at the time, but Ingrid was great with her moving Gettysburg Address, and I use it in my show now.

L: Was there ever any concern about traveling in that area as a Jew during that time?

A: Only when…I remember in Berlin, I got between two kids on each side of the street, and they pretended to be throwing stones to each other, but they were actually throwing them at me. And I felt it was only because they knew or felt that I was a Jew. But otherwise, we were not made aware of it. Except in the house that we requisitioned for, a woman came in, I didn't know who she was, and said, "Ist mein zimmer"—her room—and she was obviously very anti-Jewish, and she didn't like the fact that we were requisitioned to live in her house.

L: I guess Jack would have had the same problems.

A: I don't think he was aware of it, I don't think he was made to be aware of it. Jack wasn't really a political thinker. In fact, he would caution me about taking a political attitude. He said, "Larry…you shouldn't be involved in things like that." In my own way…I was concerned about those things. I knew I could get in trouble. I didn't know how much trouble. I didn't know how far I had to go, but I knew I was taking a risk….Whenever I came back to America, Jack had me as a guest on his show. That's how I came to know Mary.

L: I know there were a couple of not-so-great experiences about Mary asking you questions.

A: Oh, you won't believe this. Jack and Mary and my wife and me, we went to a Jerome Kern memorial concert, and we were going to my house for a drink. Well, Jack didn't know how to get to my house, so he drove with my wife and Mary rode with me. As we were driving, Mary said, "Larry tell me, when you were overseas, did Jack cheat?" I said, "Mary, that's the most offensive question I've ever been asked." She said, "Larry, it's just between you and me. I'd never say anything." I said, "Mary, if you weren't Jack's wife, I'd ask you to get out of the car." I don't think we ever spoke again. It was a revolting question! As if Jack really thought I'd tell. The answer was yes, and if I were married to her, so would I!

L: I remember talking with someone about the issues between Jack and Mary, and about [Mary Kelley] whom Jack loved but couldn't marry because of his Orthodox Jewish father. Which reminds me…you kept Kosher at one time.

A: Only when I was a kid, and only between my parents. I never believed it for a minute. In fact…over the past 65 years or so, I've had no religious feeling, no paranormal feeling, no metaphysical feeling of any kind. I'm happier that way.

L: You mentioned Jerome Kern, and I have to admit that next to Jack, my number two idol is George Gershwin.

A: Well, George was a genius. I've worked with Cole Porter, with Jerome Kern, with Harold Arlen, Frank Loesser. Nobody could write in the larger forms the way George did. He could write a piano concerto, he could write "An American in Paris", he could write "Cuban Overture", *and* a magnificent opera, <u>Porgy and Bess</u>. None of the others could come near that…I first met him, I was in Gus Edwards' kiddie revue as one of the kiddies. Paul Whiteman was playing at the Roxy Theatre, and between my shows I would go up and stand at the Roxy Theatre, hoping that somebody would bring me in to play for Whiteman, because I would have loved to be part of Whiteman's band. One day his saxophone player, Frankie Trumbauer, did hear me, did take me in, and I played "The Poet and the Peasant" for Whiteman, and Whiteman said, "Let me hear you play 'Rhapsody in Blue.'" I was 14 years old. I couldn't handle "Rhapsody in Blue". I was one very nasty little kid, and I said, "I don't like 'Rhapsody in Blue.'" [Gershwin] had heard me and I didn't know it….That's how I met him. Then in 1934, there was a farewell party given for me, I was going to London for the first time. Our host suddenly said, "Larry and George are going to play the 'Rhapsody in Blue'." He didn't ask, he didn't even know if I knew it, but by then I'd heard it so many times on the radio and on records—if I hear it and it's in my mind, I can play without rehearsing it. So George sat at the piano, I played, we finished the whole thing, George stood up and put his hand on my shoulder and said, "The g**d**n thing sounds as if I wrote it for you." And he also said something very interesting, "You've got a great ear, kid. Don't study or they'll ruin it for you." But I knew Ira better than George. Ira lived into his 80s, George Gershwin died at 38. That's a tragedy. Remember the line that John O'Hara wrote? "George Gershwin died July 11, 1937, but I don't have to believe it if I don't want to."…

L: I have heard mixed things about George Gershwin as a person…

A: This is all true. He didn't have the warmth of Ira Gershwin, he wasn't the mensch, the human being that Ira was, but you were in the presence of a genius and he wanted you to know it. Then later, many years after George died, Ira gave me a string quartet that George had written but had never had played, called "Lullabies." I had Morton Gould score it for mouth organ rather than strings, and I recorded it. So for several years, I was the owner of the Gershwin string quartet…I was talking about Frank Loesser; Frank's wife, Lynn, was known as the evil of two Loessers.

L: Sounds like the opposite of the wife of Oscar Levant.

A: Oscar Levant *hated* me! He's one of the few people who really hated me, and he hated me because the Gershwin family liked me. He felt they were his personal monopoly…[he and George were] very close. He'd take down what George would say, he played second to George all his life.

L: Are all the things they say about Levant true as well?

A: Yes. He's the only man I ever knew who was on Laudanum, among other drugs. I thought Laudanum had gone out of fashion years ago, and he was on it…It's a drug, like cocaine [LL: an opiate mixed with alcohol].…I was reminded of a joke today, I haven't thought of this in years. A man goes into a psychiatrist and says, "I don't know what my problem is doctor, but nobody pays attention to me. Nobody likes me." The doctor says, "NEXT!"…

L: You mentioned Ira Gershwin…

A: I met Ira when I moved to Beverly Hills, because Ira had a tennis court behind his house, and George and I used to play tennis there. For a while, George and I liked the same girl—Simone Simon. Beautiful.

L: Did you ever do any concerts with George?

A: No, never did any concerts with him. And curiously, although I knew them both so well, there are no photographs of Ira or George and me together…It is unfortunate. I would have loved to have had that. I visited Ira about two months before he died, and he had written a verse that morning which he insisted on reading to me, and the verse was, "Penecillin, strichtomycin (sp?), make a highball, put some ice in." He was a dear man, an absolutely lovable, saint of a man…I never saw evidence of any jealousy of George at all, but Ira as a human being was grand. You don't see people around like that. And his wife, Leonore…she was one tough lady. Once when George collapsed…Leonore said, "Leave him alone, he's just trying to get attention."

L: Going back to some of the other performers, did you ever meet Al Jolson?

A: I met Jolson, yes. In his last year, my agent was planning a tour of Al Jolson and me. But Jolson had contracted malaria in Korea, and he died fairly shortly after that took place. But Jolson was the single greatest entertainer that there's ever to be…I remember once that…Ruby Keeler was giving lectures, and she told me that in one of her shows on opening night, Jolson got up and sang. Everyone thought that was wonderful. Ruby said to me, "I didn't think it was wonderful. It was *my* first night, not Al's."

L: What about some of the others, like Eddie Cantor…

A: I worked with Cantor…he was a marvelous man. He made me write home to my parents, made sure I ate three meals a day. He was terribly nice to me.

L: I think Al Capone did the same thing for you.

A: Yes. Capone, he was so charming to me that I couldn't believe what he did for a living when he told me. He was so nice to me. Bugsy Siegel once told me, we were having coffee together, and he says, "Larry, are you a gambling man?" I said, "No, not particularly." He said, "Well, you don't have to be, but never make a bet unless you know in advance you're going to win." I said, "Seigel, how can you know in advance you're going to win unless the event is fixed?" He said, "You're learning, kid."

L: How about George Jessell?

A: Well, Jessell, I think he went a bit nuts in his later years. I knew him, I liked him, I thought he was a very nice man, and a really funny man. I know Ernest Hemingway invited Jessell to go shark fishing, and Jessell said, "Is that good or bad for the Jews?" But in his last years, he wore a military uniform and there was no need to. I think he went a little nuts…He was a terrific writer of humor…He used to have these imaginary telephone conversations with his mother, call his mother on the telephone and say, "Are there any messages for me?…Can you read them to me?…You can't? Why not?…You haven't got your glasses? Where are they?…They're up on your forehead? So how long will it take to bring them down?"…Red Skelton, very professional comedian. I didn't know him well, he was really a great pro. And Woody Allen, the first time I saw him doing a standup comedy act in a nightclub, I thought "This man is one of the smartest, most creative minds I've ever come across."…I just met him, I came to congratulate him, I never saw him socially ever. Very few people like that, and with such an imaginative mind. Milton Berle I knew. Highly professional comedian…Nothing could put them off. They could handle any situation that would come up…You know, [Henny] Youngman took me up to a show that Lainie Kazan was doing. He said, "I want you to come with me because it's her first night, there are going to be people there who could do you some good." That's how I got an engagement to the Rainbow Room…Again, I found him to be a very generous man. When he was 90, he was still doing one-night stands…A great gentleman was Cary Grant. It was unbelievable what a nice man he was. He decided that I wasn't getting enough work in America, and he got me his own agent to represent me, and he went to great lengths to do this. He was a very considerate man…Again, he was a man completely unaware of his own celebrity.

L: Do you find that as prevalent today…people who just aren't aware of their own celebrity?

A: We haven't got stars like that today. Find people today that are like Cary Grant. Find people today who are like Ingrid Bergman. They don't exist. Mind you, there isn't a training ground any more. See when I was 14 years old, I toured the United States for Paramount. By the end of that tour, I was successful. I knew my job. Where would I learn if I started today? I'm known now, so I have no trouble working. But I'd hate to be starting today.

L: How much do you think that has to do with the studio system?

A: Well, the studio system was a great system, run by bastards, but they loved films. And they built up a stock company of stars with whom they were very careful to get good scripts and make good pictures, and today there's no such thing. There isn't any studio system any more. You just get a bankable star, like Robert Redford or whatever, but there isn't the kind of thing to make a film like <u>The Front Page</u> or <u>Twelve Angry Men</u>. That atmosphere isn't there any more.

L: You also don't have the support system for protecting somebody's image.

A: Tatiana told me about when Bruce Willis came into her restaurant. I wouldn't recognize Bruce Willis. I don't recognize what today's stars look like…Getting away from the studio system was a disaster for show business. I mean, today there'd never be a David O. Selznick to make <u>Gone With the Wind</u>. Nobody would take that trouble. I mean, Steven Spielberg is the nearest thing to that. I read an interview with Spielberg, in which he said his favorite film of all time is <u>Genevieve</u>, which I wrote the music for. I've never met Spielberg, but I'd like to ask him more about it.

L: Changing topics…I've recently become acquainted with Ralph Vaughan Williams' music.

A: Well, I was doing a concert…at the Victoria and Albert Museum, and…a friend of Vaughan Williams brought him to hear me play. And then he brought Vaughan Williams to the house in Brompton Square, and Vaughan Williams said that he'd let me choose any one of his works, and he'd revise it for the mouth organ, then changed his mind and wrote an original work. When we played it…for the first time in history at Albert Hall, it had to be repeated. The applause just went on and on. On the second performance, Vaughan Williams came up and sat in the viola section, and the audience went mad. It was like Elvis Presley meeting his fan club…I went down to…play the work when I got the manuscript of it, and I said, "Mister Vaughan Williams, please forgive my saying this. What you've written cannot be played on the mouth organ. It's impossible." So he paused just like Jack, "So you don't like my music, eh?…If you don't like the way I wrote it, I'll rewrite it. If you don't like it the second time, I'll do it again. IF YOU DON'T LIKE IT THE THIRD TIME, I'LL RESCORE THE WHOLE BLOODY THING FOR BASS TUBA!"…He was a wonderful man. He was a huge man. I said to him,

"Your head should be on Mount Rushmore with the Presidents." He had this magnificent head....I played a concert with the Philadelphia Symphony, and they wanted me to prepare an encore, and I suggested "Bolero". They said, "Well, 'Bolero' is too expensive, you have to pay $450." I said, "Well, the publisher's here in Philadelphia. Maybe if I wrote and told them I met Ravel [LL: composer of Bolero], they might give me a concession." And one of them came out and said he knew all about me, and Ravel had added a codicil to his will, giving me the right…to play "Bolero" any way I liked, at performances at any time, and I was the only one who could have that right.

♪♫

Larry and I continued to talk, although not specifically about Jack Benny. If you are interested in reading more of it, please let me know.

♪♫

The Jack Benny Times

June - September 2001   Volume XVI, Numbers 5-6

Jack Benny and Abbe Lane – Promotional photo for 11-6-64 program

President's Message

Hello again, folks! The activity level of the fan club has continued to increase over the past months. Between Waukegan preparations, new members, keeping up with the Web site, our monthly chats, the new bound back issue, the tape and MP3 libraries, and the general daily correspondence, it definitely keeps me out of trouble.

As many of your know, 2001 was a "trial balloon" for the club, and this is the third of three issues for 2001. Based on the interest level and work required, we would determine its future path at the end of this year. All I can say is that I am overwhelmed and humbled at the enthusiasm expressed by members old and new. This year has brought so much "new" information, from a detailed account of the "Great Lakes Revue" in which Jack played his first comedic role, to an interview with Isaac Stern. With your continued help, there will be enough information to keep the Times going for many years to come. I, personally, am enjoying the privilege of associating with many wonderful members.

I can assure you that the International Jack Benny Fan Club will continue, because you have expressed how much it means to you.

The next issue of the Times (the first of the 2002 issues) will be published in November, and will focus on the Waukegan celebration. $10.39 (or $5.39 for E-mail subscribers) will be due then, but payment for 2002 can be made at any time (makes a great gift, too!). As with this year, anyone joining during the 11/01-10/02 timeframe will receive all 2002 issues. Checks should be made payable to IJBFC, and sent to: P.O. Box 11288, Piedmont, CA 94611.

Now on with the show!

New Members

**** Jeff Gross **** Donna Alvis **** Kerri L. Berney **** Joe Castles **** Denise Dilibero **** John Fitzpatrick **** Bryan R. Guinn **** John Hardekopf **** Danny Howard **** Kenneth Kalitowski **** Charles D. Compton **** Jeffrey Long **** John Migliore **** James Miller **** Dexter Musgrove **** Will Oliver **** John Ordover **** Brendan Roberts **** Thomas A. Ruffino **** Tony Semczuk **** Mark Soennichsen **** Chris Vaughn **** Lynn Wagar **** Gerald N. Eskin **** Rick Botti **** Chris Coen **** Charles J. Denmon **** Scott Doudera **** Hillel M. Ginton **** Ruth C. Hamlin **** Thomas A. Heerter **** Walden Hughes **** Mike Karp **** Tim Kelly **** Christine Kleemeier **** Carl Larsen **** John Laughhunn **** Tim Lones **** Paul Patterson **** Stephen Douglas Smith **** Jessica H. Stewart **** Veronica A. Stulock **** Steve Weseloh **** Dr. David L. Williams **** Laura Case **** Karl Caya **** Joseph J. Eckrich **** George J. Fogel **** Eric Anderson **** Lakota Folster **** Jack Hamilton **** Michael J. Hayde **** Jim Hungler **** Marjorie A. Manners ****

Douglas Mustian **** George D. Paddock **** William H. Powers, Jr. **** Edward Rudman **** Eric and Ross Schmidt **** Guy Sirianni **** Lee Spillenaar **** Wayne Bulthuis **** Robert and Judith Chinello **** Gene DeCapua **** Sunday Decker **** Larry Epstein **** Bob Finn **** Luis Flores **** Nathan Gordon **** Buckey Grimm **** William Hardie **** Chubb Harding **** Susan Havey **** Aaron T. Heverin **** Dave Jaundrell **** Anita Keller **** Michael Levine **** John Murray **** Patrick Ricciardi **** Ernest Richardson, Jr. **** Shawn Rogers **** Howard Rosenberg **** Debby Swanson **** Steve Szilagyi **** Mordechai I. Twersky **** Michelle Susan Varteresian **** Peter H. Vollmann **** Mark Wilson **** Brad Zinn **** Gary Bendo **** Bill Carter **** Brian Dunham **** Mamie Erickson **** Sarah Jimenez **** Laura Jones **** Philip Lockey **** Michelle McLaughlin **** Michael Nella **** John Passadino **** Jeremiah P. Riordon **** Elizabeth Simar **** Christopher Werner ***** Larry Wilde (comedian and author) ***** Marvin Gordon (Jack Benny's cousin) ***** Jack Benny Center for the Arts (Waukegan, IL) ***** Stace Tackaberry (John Tackaberry's son)

Waukegan's Jack Benny Statue

Less than two months until the celebration in Waukegan!

GUESTS OF HONOR
- Joan Benny
- Jack's four grandchildren
- Gisele MacKenzie
- Ray Erlinborn (original sound effects man for Jack's radio show)
- Phil Ford and Mimi Hines
- Tommy Bond ("Butch" from The Little Rascals)
- Illinois Lieutenant Governor Corrine Wood

THE SCHEDULE

Friday, September 7
    6:00 to 10:00 PM - Benny Benefit Dinner
    Bonnie Brook Clubhouse at the Bonnie Brook Golf Course
    $39 per plate and the proceeds will benefit the Friends of Jack Benny Center's Scholarship Fund. Cash bar with hors d'oeuvres, and a buffet dinner of beef or chicken, salad, potato, side vegetable, roll and butter, dessert, milk/tea/coffee.

    AUGUST 22 IS THE DEADLINE FOR DINNER RESERVATIONS. There are a limited number of seats available so please reserve early. Call the Benny Center at 847-360-4740 and ask for Claudia. VISA and MasterCard accepted.

Saturday, September 8

Time TBD - Benny tours
Luxury vans will take people around to a variety of places, including the site of Jack's boyhood home, the Great Lakes Naval Center (where Jack was stationed in WWI), Jack Benny Middle School, and many other locations.

Noon to 5:00PM - Downtown stage
Various musical acts will perform, and **the IJBFC will stage a recreation of the 9/23/51 Jack Benny radio program.**

5:00 to 5:30PM - Induction and unveiling
Jack Benny will be inducted into the National Comedy Hall of Fame, and the statue will be unveiled.

Sunday, September 9

11:00AM - Am Echod synagogue and Kubelsky family graves
Tour the Am Echod synagogue (co founded by Meyer Kubelsky) and visit the graves of Meyer and Emma Kubelsky (Jack's parents) and Florence Fenchal (Jack's sister). Bring a rock to put on the graves (a Jewish tradition).

1:00PM - Museum of Broadcast Communications, Chicago
A trip to Chicago's Museum of Broadcast Communications to see the Jack Benny vault exhibit, and other radio show recreations.

WHERE CAN I STAY?

I have negotiated a group rate of $75 a night plus tax at the Waukegan Ramada. This is one of the newer hotels in Waukegan, and recommended by the city. Call them at 1-847-244-2400 and ask for the "Jack Benny rate". **ROOMS MUST BE CONFIRMED WITH A CREDIT CARD BY August 7th.** For more information on the hotel, please see their Web page at http://www.the.ramada.com/waukegan01082.

THE IJBFC COMMEMORATIVE T-SHIRT

In response to popular demand, special IJBFC limited edition commemorative T-shirts will be offered for advance sale to members only. Wear your T-shirt to the festivities to identify yourself as a proud IJBFC member, and locate other members! More information to come. **Please leave a message at +1-510-914-3257 by August 3rd if you would be interested in purchasing a shirt**. Price is forthcoming, depending on the quantity.

HOW DO I DONATE?

The fund can still use your help in reaching their goal of raising $50,000! You can do your part through a donation to the Jack Benny Statue Fund, which is tax deductible (501C3 #36-600-6137).

$.01 to $38 - Pennies for Benny: Waukegan students are trying to raise 500,000 or more pennies for the statue.
$39 to $74 - 39ers: (Note: this is the name of the Jack Benny Middle School athletic teams) Donors receive a set of 39 Genesee Theatre postcards.
$75 to $99 - "I'm THINKING!": Donor listing at Benefit Concerts through the year 2002.
$100 to $499 - Century Club: Name on a Benny plaza brick, and donor listing at Benefits Concerts through 2003.
$500 to $999 - Friend's 500 Club: Name on five Benny plaza bricks, donor listing at Benefit Concerts through 2004, and Friends of Genesee Theatre membership through 2002.
$1000 to $1999 - Millennium Club: Name on statue plaque, donor listing at Benefit Concerts through 2005, and Friends of Genesee Theatre membership through 2003.
$2000+ - Y not Y2K?: Name on Genesee Theatre sidewalk diamond, donor listing at Benefit Concerts through 2005, life membership in Friends of the Genesee Theatre.

Please send your donation (and please let them know you heard about it from the IJBFC!) to:

Jack Benny Statue Fund
Bank of Waukegan, Downtown Branch
P.O. Box 39
Attention: Jan, Branch Manager
Waukegan, IL 60079

In Memoriam: Hal Goldman and Russell Saunders

Hal Goldman passed away on June 27, 2001 from cancer at his home in Bel-Air. He was 81.

Born Harold Goldman in St. Paul, Minnesota, he began writing comedy in the Army for Armed Forces Radio Service during World War II. Per the Los Angeles Times, "Soon partnered with Al Gordon, Goldman was the urbane and well-read half of the team who typed and polished while Gordon paced and shouted out one-liners."

Jack hired Hal and Al in 1950 as he divided the writing work of the radio and television shows. Again per the LA Times, "Through friends, they learned that Benny needed new material for Rochester, the black valet on his radio show, portrayed by Eddie Anderson. With lightning speed, Goldman and Gordon handed Benny a written sketch." They joined the team known to insiders as "George, Sam, Milt, and Tack" who had collectively worked for Jack since 1943: George Balzer, Sam Perrin, Milt Josefsberg, and John Tackaberry. Jack referred to them as "The Kids" or "The New Writers" until his death 24 years later.

Milt Josefsberg recalled in his book, "Jack was a guest star on a Here's Lucy show that I wrote in 1971, and we were having lunch together. At that time all of his ex-writers were gainfully employed [EN: except Tack, having passed away], and Jack said to me, 'I'm glad everybody is doing well—especially The Kids.' I laughed at this and said, 'Jack, their hair is almost white now. Why do you still call them The Kids?' And Jack said, 'Because they're too young to be called The Old Farts.'"

After the weekly television program was cancelled, Hal and Al went on to write for many other comedians, including: Dick and Tommy Smothers, Carol Burnett, Jim Nabors, Flip Wilson, Dean Martin, Tony Orlando and Billy Crystal. Hal signed on with George Burns in 1979, and wrote for him until George's death in 1996. I had the great pleasure of meeting him at the Television Academy Hall of Fame induction of Jack Benny, Burns and Allen, and others. He was seated at Burns' table with his wife, Betty, Irving and Marion Fein, Carol Channing, and other notables. One of my great regrets is that I did not have more time to talk with him.

His wife, Betty; two daughters, Barbara Garry and Louise Ackerman; a brother, Hilton Goldman; and two grandchildren survive Goldman. The family has asked that any memorial donations be made to the Cedars-Sinai Hospice Fund.

(Excerpted from unknown source) "Russell Maurice Saunders, stuntman: born Winnipeg, Manitoba 21 May 1919; died Los Angeles 29 May 2001.

"One of Hollywood's most famous stuntmen, Russell Saunders was a world-class acrobat who could somersault over 14 people. On screen he performed amazing feats in more than a hundred films for such stars as Charles Boyer, Jack Benny, Gene Kelly and Steve McQueen. It was Saunders who doubled for Alan Ladd in the famous gunfight scene in Shane and who did the series of stunts which win Don Lockwood (Gene Kelly) a film contract in Singin' in the Rain.

"Saunders first performed on screen as part of a troupe of acrobats in The Great Profile (1940) starring John Barrymore, and had one of his first important jobs as a stuntman in Hitchcock's great thriller Saboteur (1942), in which he doubled for Robert Cummings jumping off a 60ft bridge and swimming 100 yards while handcuffed…One of his most famous stunts occurred in The Three Musketeers, in which he leaped from roof-top to roof-top, caught a waving flag that ripped, then swung on its shreds to land in a window. The trapeze artist Fay Alexander (who himself doubled for Tony Curtis in Trapeze and Doris Day in Jumbo) helped Saunders rig the legendary stunt, and commented, 'It took the most co-ordination, timing and ability of anything I've ever seen. He is without a doubt the best all-round acrobat I have ever known one of a kind.'"

[EN: Does anyone know what in movie he doubled for Jack?]

Jack Bloom Pasadena Chapter

The Jack Bloom Pasadena Chapter was started in 1990 as an honorary society for IJBFC members who have been active for four or more consecutive years. Jack Bloom was a dedicated member of the IJBFC, doing extensive research on him for the Times and the original edition of 39 Forever, plus donating hundreds of shows to kick off the IJBFC tape library. Additionally, Jack and I kept a running correspondence for years, discussing Jack Benny and other shared passions, ranging from George Gershwin to bird watching to bad puns. His passing in June of 1990 was a tremendous loss for all the IJBFC members. I still miss him, and am grateful for the warmth and humor that he shared with me.

This feature is returning by popular request. Due to some discontinuities in previous years, anyone who was a member in 1997 and is presently active is eligible for the JBPC. Below is the full JPBC membership, with members added this year indicated by an asterisk. Members of the original JBPC (i.e., members for 15+ years) are indicated by a plus sign.

Jack Abizaid +
Jefry N. Abraham *
David A. Adler *
Michael Avedissian *
Bruce Baker +
Neil J. Baskin
Bernard Beckert
Dennis Benedict *
Jack Bloom +
Hal Bogart
Steve Brent *
James G. Burke *
Charles Burton *
C.A. Caramella *
Rob Cohen
Francis W. Daly
Warren Debenham *
Steve Dillie
Matthew M. Drew *
Robert Duncan *
Wayne Ennis
Phil Evans +
Charles Fair
LeRoy Fillenwarth
Marilyn Fillenwarth
Don Friedrich *

J. Ed Galloway *
Robert L. Garland
Joe Goff *
Joseph F. Gross *
Alan Grossman +
Bryan Haigood *
The Hardings *
Tom Heathwood *
Jon Heinz *
Franklin Heynemann*
Jay Hickerson +
Jimmie Hicks
Richard Hill
Tim Hollis +
Bill Housos *
David Howell *
The Jonases *
Margie Jones
Will Jordan *
Saree Kaminsky +
Larry Kampwirth *
Nik Kierniesky *
Kenneth Klein *
Kenneth Koftan *
The Lakes *
Sam Levene *

Kenneth Levites *
George Lillie +
James A. Link
Patricia Link
Mark R. Linke *
Stephen H. Loeb *
Bobb Lynes *
Tom Mastel +
Russell Myers *
George W. Nichols *
Robert Nystrom *
Bill Oliver +
Robert Olsen +
Jack Palmer
Lewis Pearson *
Paul Pinch
Donnie Pitchford
Alvin Post *
Frank Pozzuoli
Richard Rieve *
Clive Roberts *
The Robertses *
A. Joseph Ross *
Joel S. Rothman *
Rhiman A. Rotz *
Richard Rubenstein *

Rick Scheckman *
John Schlamp +
Scott Severson
Joyce Shooks +
Mel Simons *
W. Robert Smith
Steve Smith *
Helen Songer *
Benjamin Spangler
Bonnie Spangler
David Spangler +
Gus Storm *
Steve Szejna +
Gary Tallman *
Barbara Thunell *
Eva Tintorri
Marion Tintorri
Bill Twillie *
Larry Valley *
Barbara Watkins *
Ken Weigel +
Doug Wood +
Ken L. Yesson *

Back Issue Bound Edition: 1984-1995

The Jack Benny Times issues from 1984 to 1995 are now available in a single, bound edition. It contains over 500 pages of Jack Benny information, favorite scenes, articles from sources throughout Jack's career, and exclusive interviews with Dennis Day, Phil Harris, George Balzer, Sam Perrin, Irving Fein, and many more. **This edition is available for $45.**

Due to the high up-front costs, I need to ask that you prepay for your copy. I will collect the orders I have as of **August 18** and then place the order with my printer. Very few extra copies will be kept in inventory, so order yours now! Checks should be made payable to IJBFC, and sent to: P.O. Box 11288, Piedmont, CA 94611.

Individual back issues are also available. Please send a large SASE (manila envelope) for a listing and prices.

Who Wants to Visit Jack Benny's Vault?
By: Nik Kierniesky, Gettysburg, PA

    1. Below is a quiz for Jack Benny radio fans. It's for fun. No prizes. And no lifelines! Do Benny fans really need them?

    2. There are 15 questions based on content of and knowledge about the Jack Benny radio shows available on tape and CD. They are arranged in order of difficulty from $100 to $1,000,000. The major task that I had in constructing this test was to estimate "increasing" difficulty for already knowledgeable fans of Jack Benny. Since I really didn't know how difficult, or easy, this test would be, I would appreciate feedback on how you did with comments (kiernies@msmary.edu). I will use this information to construct future quizzes, if response merits a sequel. Also send me any inaccuracies.

    3. Remember, these are based on the content of <u>and</u> general knowledge about the available radio shows <u>only</u>. No lifelines! In constructing the quiz, I tried to restrict use of "one episode" questions to important, or classic, shows. Such questions are more likely to be the higher value ones.

ARE YOU READY TO PLAY........WHO WANTS TO VISIT JACK BENNY'S VAULT!?

1. (**$100**) What color were Jack's eyes?
    A) Green. Greener than the eyeball on a one-dollar bill!
    B) Blue. Bluer than the thumb of a cross-eyed carpenter!
    C) Red. As red as the lips of Marilyn Monroe!
    D) Hazel. As hazel as the nuts in autumn!

2. (**$200**) Jack's very first show premiered in
   A) 1926
   B) 1932
   C) 1929
   D) 1936

3. (**$300**) Where did Mary Livingston work before Jack "discovered" her?
   A) The May Company
   B) Macy's Department Store
   C) Schwab's Drug Store
   D) Gump's

4. (**$500**) Place these four sponsors of the show in proper chronological order, starting with the earliest
   A) Grape Nuts, Canada Dry, Jell-O, Lucky Strike
   B) Canada Dry, Grape Nuts, Jell-O, Lucky Strike
   C) Canada Dry, Grape Nuts, Lucky Strike, Jell-O
   D) Canada Dry, Jell-O, Grape Nuts, Lucky Strike

5. (**$1000**) Jack switched from NBC to CBS in
   A) 1944
   B) 1946
   C) 1949
   D) 1952

IF you made no errors to the $1000 level, you have demonstrated elementary knowledge of the Jack Benny Radio Show!

6. (**$2000**) How many of the regular cast members of the early 1950s appeared with Jack on his very first show?
   A) zero
   B) one
   C) two
   D) three

7. (**$4000**) Which of the following was never mentioned as a member of the house band?
   A) Sammy
   B) Peter
   C) Bagby
   D) Frankie

8. (**$8,000**) What period of time did Larry Stevens substitute for Dennis Day?
   A) 1943-1945
   B) 1944-1946
   C) 1945-1947
   D) 1942-1946

9. (**$16,000**) Who was responsible for stealing Ronald Colman's Oscar from Jack Benny?
   A) Benita Colman
   B) Jack Warner
   C) Ronald Colman
   D) Darryl Zanuck

10. (**$32,000**) Although Rochester joined the show in 1937, he did not get billing at the top of the show until

  A) 1940   B) 1941
  C) 1942   D) 1943

If you made it to the 32,000 level without error, you can be very proud of your better than average knowledge of the Jack Benny Radio Show.

11. (**$64,000**) In response to Rochester's inquiry about a letter regarding a bank loan, what did Jack say?

  A) Jack was not going to take out the loan.
  B) Jack wasn't going to pay the loan.
  C) Jack said that he wouldn't hold the bank to the loan.
  D) Jack said that he wasn't going to give the bank the loan.

12. (**$125,000**) How many times were the Colmans appear as guests on the show?

  A) 15   B) 20
  C) 25   D) 30

13. (**$250,000**) In addition to Carmichael, the bear, and Polly, the parrot, which of the following animals is mentioned in at least two consecutive shows?

  A. Camel   B. Cat
  C. Snake   D. Elephant

14. (**$500,000**) Between 1946 and 1954, Jack bought Don Wilson a gift on the annual Christmas shopping show. Put the following four gifts in the order they were received, starting with the earliest.

  A) Wallet, Shoelaces, Cuff links, Oil paints
  B) Shoelaces, Oil paints, Wallet, Cuff links
  C) Shoelaces, Wallet, Oil paints, Cuff links
  D) Shoelaces, Wallet, Cuff links, Oil paints

15. (**$1,000,000**) Whose aunt lived in Doo Wah Ditty?

  A) Dennis Day   B) Phil Harris
  C) Rochester   D) Don Wilson

If you were able to make it to the $1,000,000 correct answer, you are a truly amazing Jack Benny Radio Show fan! You can go inside Jack's vault, on display at the Museum of Broadcast Communications in Chicago. (Answers on page 19.)

Jack Benny: A Man with a Heart
By Scott Ferguson Greene
(Excerpted from his 12/18/00 speech at Palos Verdes Estates, CA)

In a world marked by so much unrest, people continuously look for an escape. One of the most popular means of escape is entertainment. When we look at the surface of entertainment today, we see all sorts of liberties being taken. Nothing crystallizes that more than in the world of comedy. In both television and film, some writers, producers, and performers have resorted to "bathroom humor" and four-letter words for laughs. But what is funny about bathroom humor and four-letter words? How talented are people if they have to resort to such lowbrow humor? Why do I ask these questions, you say? Because the precedent has already been set as to what pure comedy really is. And I can name it in two words: Jack Benny.

Think about it. Jack Benny made his first radio appearance in 1932. It wasn't long before "The Jack Benny Program" had an audience that was equivalent to the Academy Awards and the Super Bowl combined! Do you realize how large of an audience that was? And that was every Sunday night. Did America think he was funny? Obviously. And think of the times that Jack Benny was on the air, making people laugh. First, there was the Great Depression, then World War II, finally the Korean War. During those hard and sometimes sad times in America, people really needed to laugh. And Jack Benny delivered.

In all that time, did Jack or his writers, or Mary Livingstone or Don Wilson or Eddie "Rochester" Anderson or Kenny Baker or Dennis Day or Phil Harris EVER resort to four-letter words or bathroom humor to be funny? Absolutely not. Jack Benny, the man-in-charge, was the epitome of pure comedy. If you listen to tapes of his radio show or watch reruns of his television show, you will learn that Jack was CONSISTENTLY funny, which is an amazing feat, considering he had to be funny over a span of four decades. That is a lot of pressure on one man. But once again, history shows that Jack Benny delivered.

On a personal note, I remember a commercial Jack Benny did for Gulf Western Oil Company in the mid-1960s. I was only about five or six years old. In that commercial, Jack was "driving" his [Maxwell], trying to get to a gas station. But he used wind sails from a boat for his car to get from his house to the gas station. Finally, Jack "sails" into the gas station and quickly puts the sails away. When the gas station attendant walks up to him, Jack asks the attendant to "Fill 'er up." The attendant turns to Jack and says, "But the tank is filled, Mr. Benny." Using perfect timing, Jack turns to the camera with this incredible satisfactory smile. I laughed and laughed and laughed. Even at age five or six, it was Jack Benny who made me laugh, not just cartoons. But that commercial was so Jack Benny.

Jack was so popular that major movie stars wanted to be on both his radio and television shows. From Edward G. Robinson and Groucho Marx to Gary Cooper and Jimmy Stewart, these stars knew that being on the air with Jack Benny was going to be an experience that they would remember for a lifetime. And, of course, Jack's spontaneous improvising made his funny show funnier. Jack had a way of saying nothing, and getting more laughs than anyone. I remember having tears roll down my face from laughter watching Jack trying not to laugh at one of his guests—especially the priceless George Burns, who could always make Jack laugh.

Everything about Jack's on-air persona made me laugh—his vanity, his stinginess, his egotism, and being eternally 39. And yet, in reality, Jack was one of the most generous and modest people in show business. America and the world embraced Jack Benny. Performers in the world of comedy, as well as entertainers in general, should take a cue from Jack Benny—a man with the gift of comedic talent. But more importantly, he was a man with a heart.

The Tale Piece

From William Murtough, retired CBS engineer (thanks much, Bill!):

"Joan Benny told about this incident at breakfast at Friends of Old Time Radio several years ago. Apparently Remley was a frequent visitor at the Benny home. During one of his visits the subject of the feud between Jack and Fred Allen came up. It seems that whenever Jack would phone Fred, Fred would hang up on him. It resulted in a bet; I think it was a hundred dollars. Remley betting that Jack wouldn't hang up, Jack, betting on a sure thing, wagered that Fred would hang up. When Jack got Fred on the phone, Fred stayed on with him endlessly. Finally Jack asked Fred why he didn't hang up as he usually did. Fred replied it was because he had half the bet.

"Jack came to CBS from NBC about 1949, as I recall. His one request was that his NBC engineer (George Foster) come with him. He was dedicated to his people. The program originated from one of our theater studios at Sunset and Gower. The first broadcast was live at 4:00 PM Pacific time and was fed to the full network. It was followed at 4:30 with a split network, Red Skelton going to the transcontinental network, and Corliss Archer going to the Pacific Network. I would be the engineer in the KNX master control room quite frequently. As the Benny show would run over 30 or 40 seconds it would throw the following shows out of synch, meaning that I had to coordinate the following two shows so that they came out even. I would first call the lady director on the Corliss Archer show, who always would agree to make up the time and get off on schedule. Then a call to the Skelton director, who also would make up the time, This meant that the following show, which was full network, could start on time. I never got to know the lady director but we had a great telephone relationship.

"The Benny show was recorded on acetate disc at Radio Recorders for playback to the Pacific Network and KNX at 7:00 Pacific time (I don't recall whether we played it back from the studio or a CBS engineer went over to Radio Recorders on Santa Monica Blvd. for the playback. We did it both ways. I regularly went there on my way home Sunday nights to play back the Whistler at 9:00 to the Arizona Network. This makes it obvious that there could be no difference between the original broadcast and the repeat.

"We had normally four outgoing channels at KNX master control. KNX (AM & FM), the transcontinental network (TC) to Chicago, the Pacific Network (PAC) to San Francisco, and the Arizona Network, feeding the Arizona stations. The PAC and TC were reversible with an eight second delay. These reversals were controlled by the master control engineer at each of our owned and operated stations.

"I have made some progress in writing a book about my career and activities in broadcasting. My interest in broadcasting began in 1924 at the age of 8 years when my family got their first one tube radio. I started working as a broadcast engineer at WHN in New York in 1936. I retired from CBS in the fall of 1981 after lousy trip to Cancun, Mexico, with the president. After being widowed for a number of years, I moved from the New York area to Florida, met Lucille, a retired schoolteacher turned author, and married her. She keeps on my tail to write a book about my broadcast career. I am on my sixth chapter."

Jack and the Smuggling Case

I get asked about Jack's mix-up with smuggled jewels a lot. Elizabeth McLeod, a veritable encyclopedia of radio knowledge, wrote this excellent summary for the OTR Digest:

"Jack and Mary visited Europe during their 1937 summer vacation, and while in France, they met a man by the name of Albert Chapereau -- a sleek, well groomed gentleman who gave his occupation as 'diplomatic attaché.' George and Gracie knew Chapereau as well, having encountered him during a prior European vacation. In reality, Chapereau was no diplomat at all -- and was in the habit of carrying more than just papers in his so-called 'diplomatic pouch.'

"Federal agents first learned of Chapereau's European adventures in October 1937, when they were tipped off by a wealthy New York couple's German housemaid, who had become aware that Chapereau was smuggling valuables for her employers. Investigating Chapereau turned up a number of interesting facts -- he had nothing to do with the Department of State, and he apparently had some pretty famous friends, having been seen in New York nightclubs on several occasions with George Burns or Jack Benny.

"A search of Chapereau's apartment turned up additional links to the comedians -- an autographed photo of Burns inscribed to Chapereau 'to Nate from Nat.' This puzzling inscription soon became clear when Chapereau's true identity was revealed: he was actually an adventurer named Nate Shapiro, with an extensive criminal record dating back more than twenty years. That Burns knew Shapiro well enough to sign the photo with his given name -- only his closest friends called him 'Nat' -- gave authorities an incentive to dig further. In doing so they found an enigmatic personal note from Burns: 'G. is crazy about the bracelet.' And, in the same stack of papers, a scrawled memo in 'Chapereau's' handwriting: 'See J. B. re clips for M. L.' The G-Men were suddenly *very* interested in just how well 'Chapereau' knew the Burnses and the Bennys.

"Making inquiries on the west coast, the Feds soon learned that Mary Livingstone and Gracie Allen had been seen in nightspots flashing impressive new jewelry -- Mary a set of diamond dress clips and ring, and Gracie a diamond bracelet and ring. Further, both were first sighted with the gems in early October -- coinciding with Chapereau's return to the States from Europe. Based on these facts, agents of the Customs Service were dispatched to have a little talk with George Burns.

"Three days after his chat with the agents, Burns was in New York -- telling all to a federal grand jury. He admitted knowing Chapereau/Shapiro, and that he had taken the 'diplomatic attaché' up on his offer to bring in some duty-free jewelry from Europe. Further, he admitted that he had met Chapereau in New York to pick up the goods -- along with some additional merchandise that had been ordered by his best friend, Jack Benny. On the strength of this confession, Burns was indicted on federal smuggling charges. He pleaded guilty, was fined $8000, and received a sentence of a year and a day in prison-- which was suspended in favor of a year and a day on probation. And Federal agents headed out to Beverly Hills to have a few words with Jack Benny.

"Jack fought the charges at first, refusing to admit anything to the grand jury-- but he was nonetheless indicted on three counts of smuggling. Federal agents got in touch with French authorities, and began tracing Benny's movements in Paris -- and soon had documentation of where the jewels had been purchased. Benny had strenuously denied knowing Chapereau at all -- but this was revealed as a false statement when investigators located a photo of Jack in a bathing suit, apparently taken in the French resort of Cannes -- showing the comic in a friendly pose with none other than Albert Chapereau/Nate Shapiro. Further investigation in Cannes documented several meetings between the two men -- and that Chapereau had actually seen the Bennys off when they left Cannes.

"Benny was in serious trouble. He had been caught lying to a Federal grand jury in connection with an investigation of a Federal crime. If he fought the case, and was convicted, he faced a Federal prison sentence. He was worried also about the effect the publicity would have on his sponsor -- even though he had one of the only 'non-cancelable' contracts in radio. But General Foods reassured him that it would stand behind him, come what may -- and Jack bit the bullet. On April 4, 1939, Jack Benny appeared before Federal Judge Vincent Liebell to take his medicine.

"The case was prosecuted by U. S. Attorney for New York John T. Cahill -- who harshly denounced the comedian, and on one occasion snapped at him to 'sit up straight' as Benny slouched shamed-faced in his chair.

"Jack pleaded guilty to all three counts, and received further words of rebuke from Judge Liebell. Benny was slapped with a $10,000 fine, and drew a suspended sentence of a year and a day in prison, along with a year and a day's probation.

"Following the sentencing, Benny released a statement to the press:

"'I want to take this opportunity of assuring my friends and fans of the radio and the screen that while I know this is a technical violation, I had no guilty knowledge that a crime was to be committed or was being committed. I regret most deeply that thru a stupid mistake on my part, however natural and honest it may have been under the circumstances, I have offended against the laws of the United States.'

"And life went on. Many radio fans found the case amusing more than anything else -- in keeping with Jack's cheapskate air personality. But it was no joke to Jack -- and he remained sensitive about it for years thereafter.

Two articles were published in Time magazine pertaining to the case. One from 4/17/39 was published in the last Jack Benny Times and attributed to Time Capsule 1939. Here is the other:

TIME, December 19 1938

"CRIME Chapereau's Way - Albert Nathaniel Chapereau (nee Shapiro) was a poor boy, and had to make his own way in the world. His way led him from Poland to Philadelphia, Manhattan, London, Paris, Brussels, Australia, and Hollywood. It frequently brought him into contact with police and prison keepers, and last week it led him into U. S. District Judge William Bondy's Manhattan courtroom. There three indictments were read to blond, buttery Albert Chapereau. Having heard himself charged with conspiracy, smuggling, faking a passport and fraudulently claiming U. S. citizenship, unperturbed Mr. Chapereau observed: 'My past is not a phonograph record to be played over and over again.'

"His immediate past interested not only U. S. authorities but respected people in Manhattan and Hollywood. Most interested was Mrs. Elma N. Lauer, wife of New York Supreme Court Justice Edgar J. Lauer. She was indicted along with Albert Chapereau for conspiring to smuggle $1,833 worth of Paris finery into the U. S. If convicted on all counts, she might have to go to jail for eight years, pay $25,000 in fines.

"'I blame it all on Adolf Hitler,' said Chapereau. The Fuehrer's connection was via one Rosa Weber, until lately a maid in the Lauer household. According to Albert Chapereau, she overheard much anti-Nazi conversation while she was serving Mr. and Mrs. Lauer, Chapereau, Publisher William Weintraub of Ken, 'a London and Paris financier' named Serge Ruben-stein, and three other guests at dinner in October.

"'Ladies and gentlemen,' Rosa Weber is supposed to have announced, 'I am a true German. I love Adolf Hitler. If you don't stop talking against him, I will stop serving the dinner right now.' Justice Lauer then and there fired Rosa Weber. She went to customs authorities with a story about Mrs. Lauer's new 'clothes. Albert Chapereau explained that he liked to bring in gifts for his friends. Acquaintances of Mr. Chapereau were called upon to explain that they accepted his gifts in good faith. Among the embarrassed donees were Comedians Jack Benny and Jack Pearl; Cinemactor Wallace Ford, Hotelman Ralph Hitz, Twentieth Century-Fox Executive Joseph Moskowitz. Professing great 'amusement' over it all last week, Albert Chapereau cracked: 'I smuggled in a dwarf for Snow White, a wig for Shirley Temple, shoes for Garbo, size 9, a necktie for Charlie McCarthy, a rattle for Mickey Mouse and a corncob pipe for Popeye.'

"Shortly afterward Albert Chapereau ceased to be amused. He was twice more indicted along with Comedian George Burns (sidekick of Gracie Alien) for smuggling $4,885 worth of diamond bracelets and a ring. To make matters worse, jolly George Burns admitted making payments to Chapereau, pleaded guilty to nine counts, laid himself open to a maximum sentence of 18 years in prison and a $45,000 fine."

Do You Know?

Russell Myers sent me a Yahoo map of Rochester Circle in Los Angeles. "It is said that the little cul de sac where Rochester lived was renamed in his honor after his death. It is around a mile west of USC," and near the intersection of Arlington Avenue and Exposition Boulevard (also a few major blocks from the intersection of routes 10 and 110). Can anyone reconfirm this, or provide any additional information about the street renaming?

Alan Grossman asks about information on Blanche Stewart. "I think she was with Benny longer than anyone except Mary and Don, and she would have small or bit roles, and—at times—a continuing role (the "Blue Fairy" in the early 40s). [EN: I've heard the "Blue Fairy" attributed to Mary Kelly, Jack's love from the 20s…any thoughts?] I think her real name was only mentioned once, but I've heard her in 1935 and 1936. She and Elvia Allman (someone should write about her and Benny) were most famous as Bob Hope's Brenda and Cobina…And the name that is overlooked is Cliff Nazarro, who must have been on at least two dozen shows. He was also on other shows and was hilarious."

If anyone has any information, or even better, would like to write an article about either or both of these actors, please drop me a line or E-mail to the address at the end of this newsletter.

Scripts from members' favorite scenes were a mainstay of the Times in past years. If you have a favorite scene, please transcribe it and send it to me at the address at the end of this newsletter.

Marcia Borie—she authored one of the major biographies on Jack Benny, and now there's not much information about her. Per Christine K., "In l955, she was managing editor of Movie Time Magazine. In 1963, she wrote a book called Famous Presidents of the United States. In 1966, she wrote articles for fan magazines UK Photoplay and TV Radio Mirror. In 1984, she wrote a book with Tichi Wilkerson called The Hollywood Reporter: The Golden Years."

What other work has she done, how did she connect with Mary Livingstone for the book, and is she still with us?

Bill Powers asks, "Who were the Beverly Hills Beavers. Does anyone know whom the kids were that did the Jack Benny Broadcast parodies? Does anyone know their backgrounds or what happened to them subsequent to their radio appearances? Would we recognize any of them today?"

A 1954 television appearance has the Beavers listed as: Harry Shearer, Ted Marc, Stevie Wootton, Jimmy Baird. Who else may have played the roles, and where are they now?

You Do Know!

Per Tanya Shaw's question in the last issue, Carmichael ate the gasman on the 4/6/41 show.

Per Mike Martini's questions about John Tackaberry, I am happy to say that I have had the pleasure of interviewing Stace Tackaberry, John's son. A transcript will be appearing in an upcoming issue.

Etcetera

From Teresa Brand, a deaf IJBFC member:

"You are curious as to how I got into Jack Benny. Well, until recently I was married to a wonderful, wonderful man (he recently passed away). My husband was an old time radio fanatic. He recorded everything he could get. I have a little over 10,000 shows that he collected. Somehow I stumbled upon Jack Benny. David, being a fan of Jack's told me about the show and some of the details of Jack's life. I was fascinated. I had this desire to hear the famous 'your money or your life' episode because after hearing about Jack, I developed in my mind what I thought Jack might sound like. From that time forward, I would seek and devour everything I could find on Jack. I don't recall how I found out about the IJBFC, but as soon as I did, I joined. From that moment on, I've searched for captioned videos and scripts. I'm still on the look out for videos and scripts, and I hope one day I'll be able to hear the many tapes my husband collected.

"So, that's how I developed my interest in Jack Benny. I am just now beginning to realize that I may be the only deaf club member around. But I have a great respect for Jack and his work. I definitely look forward to the day that speech recognition of musical equipment becomes available. What joy that will be for me."

From Walt Pattison: "Just ran across an obscure reference to Jack. In 1943, Spike Jones & the City Slickers recorded a song called It Never Rains in Sunny California. The verse is:

There are some things which never will happen
I'm sure you'll agree
Like Crosby's horses winning races
And Benny playing The Bee"

From Maria Scarvelis, Barbara Thunell, and the OTR Digest:

Phil Harris' first wife was an English actress by the name of Marcia Ralston. She and Phil were married for about 10-11 years and they adopted a son, Phil Harris, Jr. Marcia Ralston appeared in a movie called The Singing Marine with Dick Powell in 1937.

"Phil Harris Jr. of Keller, TX died Thursday, March 13, 2001 at a hospital in Kilkenny, Ireland. He was 65. A memorial service will be held March 24 at the Ann Seton Catholic Church in Keller. He was born March 18, 1935 in Los Angles, California. After completing four years of military service in the U. S. Air Force, he joined the Federal Aviation Administration as an air traffic controller. He was currently the program manager, Systems Requirements Office at the Fort Worth Air Route Traffic Control Center. He is preceded in death by his parents, Phil Harris and [Marcia Ralston]. He is survived by his wife, Joan C. Harris of Keller and two daughters, two sisters and several grandchildren."

Jack Benny Classifieds

§§§ Mary Livingstone photograph and autograph. Estimated 1940s, asking $30.00. Contact Sue Kesler, 1516 North Buena Vista, Burbank, CA 91505, bennybabe@earthlink.net

 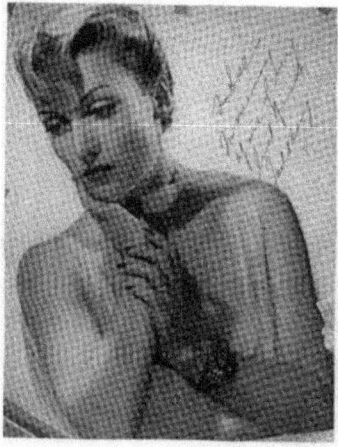 

§§§ (Above left) Four stamps w/ Jack Benny on them. Two USA 29 cent stamp not cancelled and two 35-cent Benny stamps from the country of Grenada not cancelled. I'd like 20 dollars for the set. Contact Sue Kesler, 1516 North Buena Vista, Burbank, CA 91505, bennybabe@earthlink.net

§§§ (Above center) I want to sell this unique autograph of Jack Benny. I bought it at an autograph show from a dealer that I have done business with for a while. It is a picture of Carol Lombard and Jack himself signed it. The story of this picture and autograph is that there was this doorman at a famous hotel in New York and he would get autographs of all the famous stars that stayed there. He had quite a collection and when he died, this dealer acquired all the pics and autographs. This is one of them. The picture of Lombard is from a movie magazine so it is on newspaper stock. This doorman asked Jack to sign it and he wrote the following inscription: "To Sel- In memory of one of my best friends Jack Benny." This autograph was given sometime in the late 40's or early 50's. Scan is not great sorry. I am a big Benny collector and I am clearing out some of my collection. If anyone is interested in something specific email me and I will let you know what I have. I am asking $85.00 for this item. Contact Sue Kesler, 1516 North Buena Vista, Burbank, CA 91505, bennybabe@earthlink.net

§§§ (Above right) Original picture professionally framed and matted that has Jack with Ken Murray. Picture is sharp and is from the late 40's or early 50's. I am selling it for $25.00. A great deal when you figure the framing alone is worth $50.00. Contact Sue Kesler, 1516 North Buena Vista, Burbank, CA 91505, bennybabe@earthlink.net

§§§ In 1984 The Jack Benny commemorative stamp committee was created to honor Jack on a stamp. The committee included Norm Crosby, George Burns and Irving Fein. A form letter was sent to many celebrities for them to sign their names and send to the stamp advisory committee chairman.I have a 3 form letters signed by Joan Benny, Phil Harris and Dennis Day.(I sent one as an example: click to enlarge) They all say the same thing. Along with the signed letters comes a form letter also sent to each honorary member of the stamp committee. The autographs come with a COA from the autograph shop I bought them from. I'd like them sold as a set for $40.00. Contact Sue Kesler, 1516 North Buena Vista, Burbank, CA 91505, bennybabe@earthlink.net

The Yeeeeesssss Man: Frank Nelson

I had the great privilege of interviewing Frank Nelson in 1985, one of the very first interviews I ever did for the IJBFC. Frank passed away in 1986, and I recently realized that I had never published the transcript. Apologies for the little room here for the interview, so I will include as much as possible and continue it in an upcoming Times.

L: How did you get your start in radio?

F: Well, I actually started at KOA in Denver, Colorado while I was still in high school, and the way that happened, somebody said, "They're having an audition out at KOA. Why don't you go out and see if you can get something?" I was doing nothing except amateur theatricals in school, and doing a few things with various clubs and little theatre organizations in Denver. So I went out and walked in, and this gentleman looked at me and said, "What are you here for?" I said, "Well, I understood you were having some kind of an audition for some kind of a series you were going to do." And he said, "Oh, good Lord…this is a man who's 35 years of age and he's married to a lady who is about 30, and it's their adventures and we're going to do it for a bank in Denver." And I said, "Oh," and I started to leave. And he said, "Wait a minute, have you ever read on a microphone before?" And I said, "No, no, I haven't." And he said, "Well you made a long trip out here," because KOA at that time was out on the edge of Denver, and he said, "Maybe you like to just stay and read just, you know, to see how your voice sounds over the radio." And I said, "Well, yeah, sure, why not?" So I read that day with about 30 other gentlemen, and the next day they called back 12 of us, the next day they called back 4 of us, and the next day they called me up and told me I was doing it. So I was, I guess, about a quick 15 at the time, and I played that series with the most gorgeous 30-year-old redhead I ever saw in my life. But I didn't know very much, so I didn't profit much by my experience. But that's the way I started, that was my beginning. That was in 1926.

L: When radio was really in its infancy.

F: Yes, it was.

L: So you were a regular on at least four shows: Jack Benny, Eddie Cantor, Blondie, and Meet Me at Parky's…

F: Yes, I did Blondie. I did the next door neighbor, Herb Woodley.

L: Which of those was the first one?

F: Actually, the first thing that I did…you see, transcontinental radio was coming out of Chicago and New York, but not out of Los Angeles. I had worked out here in Los Angeles for a gentleman by the name of John Swallow, and two radio stations in town which were sister stations called KFAC/KFED. And I had worked for him there for a couple of years, and finally, he was appointed the head of NBC. Well, NBC at that time consisted of one show that was done on the RKO Studios lot. That was the motion picture studio lot of RKO, and it was a sustaining show that advertised RKO pictures, and it was called "The RKO Theatre of the Air". And so John said, "How would you like to announce this thing?" And I said, "Well, sure, why not?" I think I got a quick $10 for announcing a transcontinental show, which was not sponsored by anybody. And then finally we did one sponsored show, which was called "Flywheel, Shyster, and Flywheel", and that was with Groucho and Chico Marx. And we did that from a soundstage on the RKO picture studio…Kind of an interesting thing happened to me on that. About four or five weeks into the series, they begin talking to each other in Jewish [Yiddish], and I knew they were talking about me, but I didn't know what they were saying. And that went on for a couple of weeks, and finally Groucho came over to me and he said, "Frank, can you sing?" And I said, "Oh boy! I couldn't carry a tune in a bucket…I'll give you an idea how bad I am. Last week, we were doing a serious drama down at KHJ, and at one point, the family sang Happy Birthday to George. And the director said, 'But Frank, you lay out.' That's how bad I was. I couldn't carry a tune." He says, "That's too bad, because we wanted to put you in our next picture." And that happens to be the picture that Allan Jones did Donkey Serenade in. That was what they wanted me for, but I couldn't sing, so I didn't do it. [EN: Allan Jones didn't sing Donkey Serenade in a Marx Brothers movie, but FSF was done in 1932-33. So the film in question must have been A Night At the Opera (1935).]

So then, I'm getting to this the long way, but I will answer the question, I'm actually going to get to it. So one day, Jack [Swallow] called me and he said, "Look, Jack Benny is coming out from New York to see about doing something in a movie [EN: based on the time this was probably Transatlantic Merry-Go-Round], and they want to keep him alive in the New York show, so we're going to do a five-minute insert from here, and I want you to work with him." So that was the first one that I worked with, that was Jack in 1934 [6/1/34]. And what we did, it was a little sketch on the train coming out from New York, and Jack is talking about how he's going out to Hollywood, and what a smash he's going to be, and how great he's going to be, and I'm non-committal but very polite to him, and he finally…says, "Well, you know, I think you're a very personable-looking young man, and possibly I might be able to do something for you. My name is Jack Benny, what is your name?" And my answer was, "Clark Gable." That was the joke. So we did that five minute insert, then we did another one about a week later, again a five-minute thing, and after that, Jack

75

went back to New York, and I think it was about a year before he came out to Hollywood. And as soon as he came out, he called me and I began working with him, but just in casual parts. So that was really the beginning of those shows that you spoke about. That was the first one that I did…

L: So how long was it before you started that familiar character?

F: Well, I guess I had worked for Jack now for several months, just doing casual things here and there, and one day, the writers [probably Bill Morrow and Ed Beloin] said, "We're going to try that again." And I said, "Try what again?" They said, "Well, you remember last week, you stretched the 'yes' out, and it got a big laugh." And I had to think for a minute, and I said, "Oh yeah, and I don't even really know why I did it." And they said, "Well, we're going to try it and, you know, see if it goes again." So they wrote it a second time, and it played again, and so that became the beginning of the character. But it just kind of grew like Topsy. Nobody told me to do that or how to do it, I just happened to do it and it got a laugh, so it developed into that character. And of course the first time we ever did the "Oo", I absolutely destroyed Jack on the show, because I held back on it…Finally, we were in this fight about something, and Jack said, "You really hate me, don't you?" And I said, "OOOOOOO, do I!!!" And he went right on the floor! He fell right down on the floor began to laugh. So he was a great audience you know…[TO BE CONTINUED!]

Answers to the quiz (and a few dates)

1. B (5/2/32)	6. A	11. D
2. B	7. B	12. B
3. A	8. B (11/5/44 to 3/10/46)	13.A (2/13/44 and 2/20/44)
4. D	9. C (5/9/48)	14.D (1946, 1948, 1951, 1954)
5. C (1/2/49)	10. C (10/4/42)	15.C (2/29/48)

Man About Town premiered in Waukegan, Illinois at the Genesee Theatre…
Come in September to see where it all began!

The Jack Benny Times

January – April 2002[1] Volume XVII, Numbers 1-2

---
[1] There is a date gap from October to December 2001. The dates were jumped to align the newsletter dates with the calendar year.

President's Message

Hello again, folks! The IJBFC is roaring along and nearing 1,000 members. I remember saying in 1987 that my ultimate goal was to have 200 members in the club; I never anticipated the impact of the World Wide Web. I have had many people E-mail me with comments of, "I'm so glad I'm not the only one who remembers Jack Benny."

Please help us clear out our inventory! We have many extra copies of all three 2001 issues, which include
- IJBFC exclusive interviews with Fred deCordova, Larry Adler, and Frank Nelson
- Articles on Jack's smuggling scandal, Jack's relationship with Groucho, and Kenny Baker
- Tons of trivia, stories, and Benny information

You can now have all three issues for $8.00. Checks should be made payable to IJBFC, and sent to: P.O. Box 11288, Piedmont, CA 94611.

Now on with the show!

New Members

**** Mike Allen **** Ken Behrens **** Randy Berg **** Chris Burns **** Elizabeth Evans **** Thomas Foley **** Drew Gloede **** Chris Gumprich **** John Guthrie **** Jeremy Hamilton **** David Holley **** Gary Horne **** Arti-Rene Knight **** Loren D. Lodge **** Harry McClellan **** William Rompala **** Philip Russell **** Jorge Velazquez Vergara **** Keith Wissman **** Anthony Bauman **** Ray Bidowski **** Mike Blakesley **** Dave Bradley **** Rob Caetta **** Terry Capps **** Emily Chayka **** Katie Chayka **** Adam Christing **** Mary Cooper **** Scott Day **** Don Fado **** John Gardner **** Brian Graves **** David A. Hazard **** Peggy & Steven Kolber **** Jim Lockhart **** Michael S. Ludlow **** John Matthews **** Larry Mayer **** Burton I. Meyer **** Gary Miessler **** Matt Padgett **** Mark Reed **** Michael Scott **** Stephen T. Smith **** Mrs. Larry Stevens **** Thomas McConn **** David H. Weiss **** Sam White **** Katie Wiemerslage **** Robert M. Baker **** Dennis W. Campbell **** Jennifer Jacobson Carew **** Mike Champion **** Christine Cornish **** James Crookes **** Jean Cullitan **** Dave Dawes **** Michael S. Eckles **** Andrew E. Galayda **** Scott Goldner **** Elizabeth Goryunova **** Rhys Haug **** Gary L. Meissler **** Stan Pinkowski **** Keith Pizzo **** Howard and Gail Rogofsky **** Tony Scotino **** Tom Smith **** Timothy W. Southern **** Robbie Strauss **** Lou Valentino **** Bob Valvano **** Neil Wadleigh **** Linda J. Charles **** Behn Israel Gonzales **** Anne Hockens **** Robert Kempf **** Daniel Lander **** Romy Marcus **** Richard Maro **** Ronald L. Mason **** Brian McQuaig **** Robert Pugh **** Mark G. Pysick **** Brendan Scherer **** Ryan Schroer **** Keith Segovich **** Barry Wanamaker **** Susan C. Wilson **** James Wine **** Brad Roberts **** Steve Dunnington **** Jeff Hawkins **** Sun Lim **** Kerrie McKeon **** Jack Benjamin Moskowitz **** Howard Mostovy **** Jay Ogletree **** Gerry Orlando **** Stephen Phillips **** Doug Shafer **** Ron Vickery **** Amanda Ward

***** Betty Hutton ***** Mimi Hines ***** Phil Ford ***** Gisele MacKenzie ***** Marvin Meyer

Waukegan's Jack Benny Statue – UPDATE

As most of you know, the Waukegan statue celebration was delayed until next year. The statue has been installed in the plaza diagonally across from the Genesee Theatre, with Jack "looking" at the theatre. The official dedication and celebration is being planned for early June. We will provide you with a full update in the next issue.

The National Comedy Hall of Fame induction of Jack Benny, originally slated in conjunction with the Waukegan celebration, is being planned for a separate date and venue. It is anticipated that it will be in mid-February around Jack's birthday. Please stay tuned to our Web site for the latest details as they become finalized.

In Memoriam: Larry Adler, Frederick DeCordova, Isaac Stern, and Ralph Levy

It has been a difficult few months for the IJBFC, with the loss of four of Jack's associates. It has also been personally difficult to write these memorials, as two of these gentlemen were friends of mine for nearly 20 years. Another I met earlier this year after 15 years of correspondence. I miss them very much. They left the world a more beautiful place than they found it, and they brightened mine personally.

Larry Adler

Larry Adler was reknowned for his virtuoso harmonica (or as he preferred to call it, mouth organ) work on stage, screen, and recordings, plus his work behind the scenes of movies such as <u>Genevieve</u>. He worked with Jack in many venues: appearing in <u>The Big Broadcast of 1937</u>, appearing on several radio programs (2/13/44, 2/27/44, 11/19/44, 5/20/45, 5/27/45, 10/14/45), and navigating the globe to play for military stations during World War II.

To quote Larry's words about preparing for the WWII shows (from my talk with him at his apartment in London in 1998), "I went to New York and was introduced to Jack Benny,

Martha Tilton, and Marie Shaw...no, it was Anna Lee. And Jack and I got on right away. It didn't take any time to know him, we fit as if we had been brothers for a long time, and we did these shows. Working with Jack, for me, was like going to a university of show business, because that man knew, but not only knew, but was generous in imparting what he knew. There was no jealousy in him, there was no envy."

It was through his work with Jack that Larry met Ingrid Bergman, who was appearing with the show in Germany. Larry and Ingrid would develop a deep and lasting attachment that nearly resulted in marriage. Bergman also prompted Larry to learn to read music, which led to his writing scores for many movies.

Larry recalled, "Jack would never ask for a favor for himself. I started to tell you that I wrote this sketch for Ingrid and Jack, I based it on Casablanca, and at one point Ingrid is trying to get Jack to leave his wife and run away with her, and she's shaking him, 'Don't you realize this thing is bigger than we are?' And he's supposed to say, 'You're bigger than I am!' He couldn't say it because she *was* bigger than he was, and the ridiculousness of it made him laugh, so when he got to that line he couldn't say it. The only time it got said was when Jack had a cold and I did the sketch with Ingrid."

On a more personal note, Larry was a phenomenal letter-writer. For a few years we sent puns (a personal passion for both of us) back and forth, but I was completely out of my league. Larry had been an occasional attendee of the Algonquin Round Table, and could easily recall bon mots spun by some of the sharpest wits of the 20th century. He also had been acquainted, and often friends, with most of my major "heroes" (Jack Benny, George Gershwin, Al Jolson, Ralph Vaughan Williams, etc.) To talk with him was to be in the audience of a living encyclopedia of 20th century show business. I have no doubt that he is once again verbally matching with Dorothy Parker, and discussing musical arrangements with Maurice Ravel.

Larry Adler passed away on August 7, 2001 at the age of 87.

Frederick DeCordova
Frederick de Cordova was an instrumental man in show business through seven decades. He worked in theatre in the 1930s, directed movies in the 1940s, and television through the rest of the century. He is best-known for his work as the Executive Producer of <u>The Tonight Show</u>, where Johnny Carson would occasionally reference him from a dark section of the wings.

Fred was the producer/director of The Jack Benny Program in the late 50s and early 60s. He had known Jack and Mary since 1936, and they spent a great deal of time together through the years, on and off the set.

One of Jack's favorite expressions, in Yiddish or English, was "kiss my ass". One Christmas, he presented Fred with a barrel of liquor with the expression engraved on it. I asked Fred in 1995 if he still had it, and he said, "The barrel is tucked away near my swimming pool with the brass plate on it: 'Love and kisses and kiss my ass, Jack.'"

Fred also recalled, "Over a period of time, and God knows I've been over a period of time, somebody asked me—lots of people asked me—about all the people I've worked with, and that goes back forever and ever, people like Bea Lilly and Fanny Brice and Bert Lahr and Durante and Bolger in the New York days and all the people in pictures and 22 years with Johnny Carson, who was my favorite person? And it is a good but absolutely honest answer that both on and off stage, the one person I miss most is Jack. I continue time and time again to, something will remind me of something about Jack that again will bring back that feeling that there was nobody like him. And Mrs. Benny and Mrs. deCordova became close friends, so we had a great deal of on stage and social evenings. I don't mean necessarily big social evenings, although Mary was a wonderful hostess. He was the kind of a man that if he went out to buy a tie, he bought a tie for other people who were close to him, with a note that would say on it 'Kiss my ass.' So anyway, any memory of the time I spent with Jack comes under the heading of just about the nicest times I ever spent."

Again on a personal note, Fred was one of the first honorary members of the IJBFC. He was always tremendously supportive and generous, putting me in touch with Mary Benny and many others. Although I was in awe of his work in show business and the people he had known, he had a way of always making me feel personally special. Everything that you'd want to attribute to classic stars on the big screen: class, suaveness, charm, elegance...Fred had all these qualities, and they came naturally to him. He was a beautiful human being, and I will miss him for many, many years to come.

Fred de Cordova passed away on September 18, 2001 at the age of 90.

Isaac Stern

I think that Isaac's own words (and Jack's that are quoted in the interview) are the best tribute to him. Isaac Stern passed away on September 22, 2001 at the age of 81.

Ralph Levy

Ralph Levy was the Executive Producer-Director of <u>The Jack Benny Program</u> on television for 1951 to 1957, directed <u>The George Burns –Gracie Allen Show</u> until 1953, and also directed the TV pilots for <u>I Love Lucy</u> and <u>You Bet Your Life</u>. Levy had his hand in the directing of many other notable shows on CBS through the 50s and 60s.

When shooting the Jack Benny programs on location in Europe, Levy cast Sean Connery in his first acting job, playing an Italian porter in Rome with one line. He also cast Peter Sellers (then still a minor) in the London show, but was later dropped because Jack felt Sellers' timing and delivery was too similar to his own.

In 1957, Levy became ill before a <u>Shower of Stars</u> program, and was replaced by <u>Studio One</u>'s Ralph Nelson. Levy directed a few more half hour shows, but owing to his health problems, was shortly thereafter replaced by Seymour Berns. Levy later directed two 1959 <u>The Jack Benny Hour</u> specials, which earned him an Emmy; and the 11-3-65 <u>The Jack Benny Hour</u>, with Bob Hope, Elke Sommer, Walt Disney, and the Beach Boys.

Ralph Levy passed away on October 15, 2001 at the age of 81.

You Do Know!

W. Gary Wetstein noted that the story in the last issue that attributed the quirk of always hanging up the phone on Jack was George Burns, not Fred Allen. Thanks, Gary, I should have caught that myself!

Bill Powers had asked who played the Beverly Hills Beavers. In a 3-6-55 TV episode where Jack takes the Beavers to the fair, they were played by:

- Harry Shearer (currently playing many characters on <u>The Simpsons</u>, including Montgomery Burns and Smithers)
- Ted Marc
- Stevie Wootton
- Jimmy Baird

Christine K. provided this additional information on Marcia Borie, author of one of the Jack Benny biographies:

"In 1955 she was managing editor of Movie Time Magazine. In 1963 she wrote a book called Famous Presidents of the United States. In 1966 she wrote articles for fan magazines UK Photoplay, and for TV Radio Mirror. In 1984 she wrote a book with Tichi Wilkerson called The Hollywood Reporter: The Golden Years."

Isaac Stern: The Man Behind the Music

I had the incomparable privilege of talking with Isaac Stern at his Nob Hill hotel on April 25, 2001. We sat in the restaurant by the fireplace, having breakfast and reminiscing about Jack. Isaac was one of those rare people with whom you were always aware that you were in the company of a legend and a genius, but he was so genuine that you were immediately at ease. Enjoy.

L: Well, let's start at the beginning. You met Jack…how?

I: Jack and I first met…was it Hollywood? I'm trying to remember precisely. We were introduced by someone else, I think Danny Kaye…So Danny used to come to concerts and Jack was interested, with the fiddling, so one thing led to another. And we met, and we became very, very good friends. He was one of the most generous men I've ever met, and I sort of became his manager, arranging his benefit concerts all around with orchestras and conductors. I was very fond of Jack because he was as gentle and generous a man I think I've ever met, and who had no bit of show business blown-up self esteem. He would have loved to have been a fiddle player, and I once said to him, "You know, Jack, if you worked a little bit, you could play a lot better." He said, "It wouldn't be funny." And he was right.

L: I remember he said that if he had one wish, it would to become a concert violinist.

I: Yes, but then when he realized what the limitations were, he said, "Well, look at it. Now people pay more money to sit as far back as possible." And he was very generous, and I sort of helped out when he did benefits for orchestras and various things, I helped make the arrangements.

L: Knowing the disposition of musicians and knowing Jack...I know that his mother wanted him to be a violinist, but what do you think it was that inspired that passion to be a violinist?

I: I have no idea. He liked music to some degree. He wasn't very well-versed in it, but he did like music, and I think it was part of the early training and some background that his parents—European background where kids were educated with music. They weren't educated unless they studied something. And he got the violin, and...where and when he knew very quickly that he wasn't going to be a fiddle player and then went into show business, I don't know. I don't know that early part of his life that intimately...But we met through his love of music and through mutual friends in Hollywood, and one thing led to another, and he did, in his own way, raise so much money for orchestras.

L: Almost six million dollars.

I: That's right. And it was quite, it was adorable the way he did it. He really cared.

L: Tell me a little bit more about the structure of the concerts. You listen to him scratching through "Meditation" from Thaïs, and how could you sustain that for an hour or more?

I: Well, first of all, the playing occupied, I would think, probably less than 20% of the time he was on stage. The rest was all talk. And he was very comfortable, he could make fun of himself without meaning to, but in the best possible way. Some of his deadpan looks, as if to say, "That wasn't so bad, was it? I could..." and everyone would break up. But I loved working with him because, first of all, he was a wonderful friend, and Jack never made fun of anybody. Only himself. And in that, there was another thing too that he adored classical musicians and he respected them. And he didn't find it necessary to either play them down and say, "Well, that's a little bit above my head," it wasn't, but his whole attitude towards music and musicians was extremely healthy. There was nothing neurotic about the way he felt about music or about himself in relation to this. I think in a way, I think I knew Jack for twenty years or more, and I never in that whole time heard him say a bad word about anybody, or gossip or be mean. He just couldn't do it. That was not his way. And that's in a town where they live on gossip and badmouthing people. No, Jack was a unique character and when I think of Jack, the words that come into my mouth are gentle, generous, and some way, adorable.

L: It even says right on his grave "A Gentle Man". A perfect epitaph for him. I've heard people say everything from one extreme to the other about how well Jack truly played the violin. Now, you're the master...

I: He played no better than what you heard. And as he said, and as I told you, when I said to him, "you know, a little work and you'd play a lot better," he said, "The better I play, the less funny it gets." And he was perfectly right. He had this extraordinary ability to see himself in the third person from a distance, without any excuses. Very few people have that measure of honesty with themselves, and then put it in relation to the work they're doing and what they're involved with. But he had it.

L: What do you think the philosophy is that people would pay so much more to come and hear Jack?

I: They didn't come to hear Jack, they came to hear him talk, not play. He was one of the great, great standup comics. And for that, people pay money. The rest was icing on the cake. And he used his apparent fiddle playing, which is the most you could say for it, and he was unafraid to make fun of himself. And there was something so ingenuously endearing about the way he tried, made fun, and always he was the loser, nobody else. So he had a very rare character....He and George Burns did routines after routines that [made fun of each other], and he had another partner, who was the other comic...trying to think, he was an acid-faced...Fred Allen. But Fred and he played off each other, they knew exactly what they were doing. Fred loved to work with Jack, and they made an incredible team.

[Isaac asks me about how I got started with the fan club, and I we talk a little bit about it.]
L: I was looking at some things in preparation for the interview, and I came across this paragraph—maybe you've heard it before...this is Jack from his autobiography:

> I just worship Stern, who is not only one of the greatest virtuosos now living, but who is also a man with a passion for life and eating and humor. He is wonderful company. And he became my friend. Can you imagine what it would have meant to my mother if she could have known that someday a man as great as Isaac Stern, a musician like him, would accept her son as a friend?

I: [surprised and complimented look] Good God, I've never...I never knew that.

L: It's just kind of amazing to me that…we have almost 800 members worldwide, some of whom would practically prostrate themselves in front of Jack if they had the opportunity, and Jack would have gladly done the same for you. I don't know if you ever had a concept of that.

I: [still taking in Jack's words] No, I knew that he respected…the world in which I lived as a concert violinist, and he was delighted that he could sort of fit in at the edges the way he did, and I…I just accepted him as a dear and adorable friend. That was the way it was. We didn't do anything unusual to play the game for him, and I didn't have to. There were no games with Jack. He was very straight. But…I remember that every time there was an opportunity for us to be together, I was looking forward it, to help arrange which orchestras, he would check with me which orchestras needed him, how it was, and what to do. And then with the orchestra, I would sometimes help in arranging that the orchestra people played into his hands in the right way. And once you began, once he started doing whatever he was doing in that set, wherever or whatever city it was, they relaxed and didn't become, "What's this outside amateur doing in our profession?" They went along with him, and they just sat back and you could see them visibly relaxing and becoming his gang around him. And that was wonderful. He had this ability to sort of look at people and, in a way, psychologically put his arms around them, and they became his immediate family right there. And that's an extraordinary ability for someone like that. He stripped everybody of their fears and of their stiffness and of their worry about "quite how will this go?". Everything went. Around Jack there was no paranoia. It was wonderful.

L: How did it happen that you became his "agent"?

I: Because I knew what he could do, and it struck both of us that doing his act in front of an audience of an orchestra as a benefit would be a tremendous help to the orchestra. This was something where EVERYBODY would want to go and get involved. And it worked out very well that way. I think it started…shortly after we met, and he got to Philadelphia or some other orchestra, thought maybe they would like to do something, he asked me, and we started to talk about it, how to structure it so it would work. From then on, I sort of suggested, sometimes I'd suggest to conductors or to orchestra managers, and I'd say to Jack, and I would sort of be the guy in the middle, helping them get together. And it was a happy thing to do, because it made everybody happy. He was happy to do it, and they were happy to have him, so it was one big smile from the beginning to the end. It's very rare that you get a situation where you can honestly do that sort of thing, and with an open heart and gladly.

L: In 1961, you arranged a tribute called "Carnegie Hall Salutes Jack Benny". I've heard conflicting things if the money raised from that was what put Carnegie Hall over the top and saved it, or if it was already taken care of.

I: No, it was in addition to what we were doing. It worked out to be a major help at a very important time. It was as important that people saw that he was doing it for Carnegie…because Carnegie has a worldwide and…about a 100 year old reputation. Actually we only found out the other day that it's the second-most recognized symbol of the United States, in America and around the world. Instant recognizability. The only thing in America that in some areas and certain ages that's a little bit more recognizable is Microsoft. Otherwise, Carnegie Hall passes everything. In every area, in all parts of the country and parts of the world.  Compared to even when people think of America, they know the Statue of Liberty, the Washington monument—Carnegie Hall is instantly recognizable to everybody. And we didn't realize to what degree its recognizability is taken as a matter of fact by people all over the world. It happened in a survey not long ago, one of our board members commissioned a survey and we found out that we're really the, in some ways, the most recognizable American object to people everywhere, which is nice to know. And Jack recognized that. In his heart, maybe his inner heart and his mind and his mother would have loved to have him play a debut concert at Carnegie Hall, because it was already in business in his lifetime. And the fact that he came and did some special things there, that was…it meant a lot to him. And it meant a lot to me.

L: You did this record with him [handing Isaac the LP of <u>Jack Benny Plays the Bee, Ably Assisted by Isaac Stern</u>]…How did that come about?

I: I can't remember…His agent or mine, my recording people, somebody…somebody thought it would be a good idea because the TV shows were doing nicely. This record was made, and I must tell you that as far as I can remember, I don't think it did very well.

L: It seems to be geared for getting kids to appreciate classical music.

I: Yeah. I don't think it was a great business success.

L: You were on the TV pilot that Jack did in 1949, and he had the Andrews Sisters and Lum and Abner and a variety of different people on that. Do remember anything about it?

I: You're telling me something I don't remember. That's great!

L: No one ever talks about it because they remember Jack's debut in 1950, but I haven't seen it and don't know if a copy exists.

I: I can't help you on that. I wish I could.

L: You also appeared on a couple of the radio shows and a couple television shows.

I: They were fun. I had a great time making some jokes. And I remember once we were rehearsing, and I was doing that silly one hiding in the closet [television]. And the scene called for him to open the door and see me as a surprise, and I think that I come out of the closet and instead of saying what I was supposed to say, I said, "You were expecting maybe Jascha Heifetz?" And he broke down completely. It was a great time.

L: Do you know if you did that routine twice? There was one where Rochester was pretending that he was recording you…

I: Yes, there were different versions. I remember that when my concert visits took me to Los Angeles, we always had an evening together. Very relaxed and very nice.

L: Did you talk about music, or…

I: No, nothing specific. We talked about whatever the moment was about, whatever was going on, or between ourselves. No specific subjects. One thing…in all the time, he's the only person in Hollywood from whom I never heard a word of gossip or criticism of someone else. He just couldn't take that. He didn't want to listen to it, and he didn't do it…If someone starts, "Well, have you heard that?", he'd get sort of a pained expression and say, "Well, I really…I happen to like that person very much." He would fend it off completely. He didn't want to hear gossip, and he didn't repeat gossip. But in a town like Hollywood, that's something. It makes him stand out in an extraordinary way.

L: There are two people in Hollywood that no one ever said a bad word about: Jack was one of them, and Jimmy Durante was the other. Out of curiosity, another thing you might not have been aware of was that the first time you were going to be on Jack's radio program, they had a certain budget for the guests. They only had $4000 for you, but at the time your fee was $5000. Jack actually paid the remainder out of his pocket to have you on the show.

I: [again surprised and complimented] Really? Now you're telling me something that I'd forgotten completely. Did I know about that?

L: According to [Jack's autobiography], he made a point of not telling you. I hope he'll forgive me for telling you!

I: I didn't think so…That's alright! I would have remembered. Because I don't remember any discussion. I had been asked to be on one of the radio shows. It was only with Jack that

I was comfortable, because he never denigrated either classical musicians or spoke about music as if it were an occult device that was given to a few other people but not them…I was comfortable, being who and what I represented and classical music, I was comfortable with Jack either on radio or television…He had a healthy, wonderful, and adorable way…I had the sheer pleasure.

L: Had you had any bad experiences performing with other comedians?

I: No, but I had watched them, and in their mouths, any word about classical music sounded like a language from Mars. They were uncomfortable with it, and they didn't feel at ease. Jack was completely normal. The only two people who really weren't too big, Hollywood people who I knew at home and who came to concerts, the other one was Danny Kaye, who would show up at the concerts offstage and…walk in after the concerts or intermission in his open shoes and his hat and make funnies around and have a good time. He was a very, very good friend; also, [Danny Kaye] was a very good cook. I had some of the best Chinese food ever at his home. He was a fabulous cook. He loved it, and he, typical Danny, when he was in Hong Kong he found out the right person to get the right condiments and everything, he had it all at home, and he had his staff preparing it exactly the right way, and he'd come and put it all together in two minutes, and it was great. He had two big woks built into his kitchen, and it was wonderful.

L: You had some correspondence with Jack.

I: There was one that was very funny…I can't remember…I saw it by chance because my office had received an inquiry from the Library of Congress, wanting to go through my letters, and…after my kids get first grabs, I'm going to leave a lot of my personal items to the Library of Congress. And in the course of that, they came across a couple of very funny letters. And I can't remember them specifically now, but in reading them they made me laugh.

[At this point I asked if Isaac would consider sharing the letters for publication, and we discussed it a bit. Happily, I received a package of copied papers from his assistant shortly thereafter.]

I: [I'm] flying on Sunday to Japan.

L: So you're still keeping a very busy schedule.

I: Well, sometimes. The Japanese is because I teach there and in Europe, and it's a nice visit and I'm there for about a little over two weeks. Then I'll stop off a day in Korea for a day or two more, there's something I want to investigate for myself, then back to New York to continue the same teaching at Carnegie Hall, except in Korea I'll be listening to four groups, and in Carnegie twelve.

L: Are you doing any performing now?

I: I'll be playing a chamber music concert in Japan at the end of my stay there.

L: Who do you learn from, how do you develop as a performer nowadays?

I: Who do I learn from? I don't learn, I teach. No, I always learn because I'm curious. You know I have never…actually, I had any number of influences, and very few of them were on the violin, because I grew up here in San Francisco listening to the opera and the symphony orchestra, and I was allowed to come to rehearsals. I heard the whole Ring Cycle [Wagner operas] by the time I was 15, and I was invited to symphony rehearsals. So I grew up with all the great artists of music in San Francisco, and there was the Budapest Quartet who were very close friends of mine…I heard their Beethoven and Bartok cycle in Mills College when I was about 15, and that has remained for me apparently a subliminal memory that I have to this day. You know, I was lucky. It wasn't one person, but a combination of so many people in this city, who visited and I had a chance to meet and listen and learn. Not in the way of going to class or asking questions, but more or less by, I could think by osmosis."

At this point, Isaac needed to meet some friends for lunch, so we got into my Miata and I drove him to the restaurant. During the drive, I asked about the time that he had invited Jack to play second violin in a string quartet with him, Leonard Rose on viola, and Gregor Piatagorsky on cello, at Piatagorsky's home. He said that he'd done it because he wanted Jack to experience what it was really like to play serious chamber music with professionals, and that Jack loved every moment of it. He also recalled that Jack sight-read the music very well, and that although he played "in the general vicinity of the notes", the performance was well-received.

We thanked each other, and I watched him walk off into the crowded sidewalk. His pleasure and surprise at hearing Jack's words about him still stayed with me, and being able to convey them to him was one of the greatest privileges that I will ever know.

Benny and Stern: The Papers

The first item was a formal invitation on a 4 x 6 card:

Mr. Jack Benny
requests the pleasure of your company
at Cocktails, Dinner and Dancing
on Thursday evening, November tenth
at eight o'clock
The Automat
Five hundred forty-five Fifth Avenue
Entrance on Forty-fifth Street
New York, New York

R.S.V.P. Black Tie
Plaza 9-6272

The second was the text of a speech Isaac Stern gave during a Jack Benny Testimonial by the Friars' Club at the Beverly Hilton, 2/14/57:

Ladies and Gentlemen: I am indeed very happy that my concert tour has been so arranged—making it possible to be here for the Heart Fund Dinner—and for my friend and colleague…Jack Benny.

I have appeared with Jack on several of his television shows—and I have never had any hesitancy in accepting these engagements because I know they are always in good taste.

Of course, one of the reasons I am glad to be here tonight…Jack has been talking all these years—and getting laughs—then successfully deciding to butt into my field—and give concerts…I don't say that this hurts us exactly—but I can't see how it can help us…Therefore, I felt that I should be here tonight—and butt right back by not bringing my violin—just talking. This is my opportunity and I wouldn't want to miss it…and at least I have one advantage on Jack…to just talk…I don't have to practice—fruitlessly—for hours.

Now I must tell you what happened recently on two concerts that Jack gave in the East…His first one was at Carnegie Hall—in which he played "Gypsy Airs by "S"…This was done to save Carnegie Hall—with the result that they have sold the site…and are going to tear it down.

The next concert was about 3 weeks ago at the Academy of Music in Philadelphia in which he played "Mendelsohm" [sic]…Mandelsohm [sic] lost.

Now I would like to tell you about an incident that happened while Jack was at Carnegie Hall…I knew that even though he was giving this concert for charity and for comedy purposes—that he would be nervous…He would <u>have</u> to be nervous—standing in front of 90 of the finest musicians in New York—and directed by Alfred Wallenstein…So I thought I would be with him back-stage and try to calm him down…

Before Jack made his appearance—he kept walking up and down…practicing scales—fooling with his fiddle—and when I spoke to him—he didn't answer…Finally I said to him, "Jack sit down a minute…I want to talk to you"…I said, "Jack I can understand your being nervous if you were doing a television show…That's your business—your livelihood…But why should you be nervous giving a concert when this is not your business, and the audience really doesn't expect you to play well? After all—you are not a great musician if you just get through and finish in reasonable proximity with the orchestra—but <u>you</u> are <u>one</u> of America's greatest comedians"…Jack looked up at me and said, "What did you say, Isaac?"…I said, "you are <u>one</u> of America's greatest comedians"…So Jack looked at me and said, "You want to know something, Isaac?"…"Many times when I rehearse my television show all by myself—I do it in front of a mirror…and I say to myself—'Jack Benny, <u>you</u> <u>ARE the greatest comedian in America</u>'…But I don't believe me."

In a way, this is a measure of the warmth—the graciousness and the modesty of a good friend—whom I am privileged to be here tonight to honor…I want to thank the Committee for inviting me.

Then followed a series of correspondence:

6/6/57

Dear Jack:

I had planned to write this some time ago when I first heard the good news that you had acquired a fine Stradivarius violin. But, as usual, the pressure of events here kept me from attending to this pleasant idea until now.

I was very happy to hear that you had finally chosen a good instrument, and I hope you will have as much pleasure using it as I have from mine. I know what fun at least <u>you</u> get out of the violin when you play, and for anyone who has been as faithful to his first love as you have been to violin and music deserves a fine instrument.

Vera and the baby are flourishing. We recently returned from a very exciting and happy three weeks in Puerto Rico during the Casals festival. We are home now for a while, although I am going to Europe for a short ten-day visit—on pleasure, not business. In July and August, I begin doing the summer circuit—New York, Chicago, Tanglewood, etc. Between August 10th and 22nd, I will be on the West Coast a good part of the time, staying at the Beverly Hills Hotel. I am playing in San Diego on August 31th [sic] and at the Bowl on August 22nd, with a trip to San Francisco in between. Perhaps you will be there at that time?

In any event, Vera joins me in sending you and Mary our fondest greetings.

Cordially, as always,

6/10/57

Dear Isaac:

I received your letter and was very happy to hear from you as I always am.

Yes—I finally bought a Stradivarius and I think it is a real good one. I used it for my concert at the Philharmonic here which I am happy to say was a very big success. The laughs seemed to be bigger than ever, and believe it or not—I even played better. Of course, you could have shut your eyes, and still have known that I wasn't Stern or Heifetz, but it was a little smoother than usual. This is either because I have been practicing or the Strad that I have—played a little easier than most of them. Am very anxious for you to see it.

My next two concerts will be in Chicago and Toronto sometime in the fall, and if you and Vera can possibly make it—I want you both to be my guests from the time you leave your house in a taxicab until you get back home. Naturally I'll appreciate it if you will use the bus.

Glad to hear that Vera and the baby are fine. I expect my second grandchild in August.

I open at the Flamingo Hotel in Las Vegas for three weeks—starting the 20th of this month. After that, Mary and I are going to Europe for a vacation until the end of August. So am afraid we will not be here when you play the Hollywood Bowl. When people ask me why I am playing Las Vegas—I can only give them one answer. I am like an over-sexed dame who has to try everything once.

Thanks again Isaac for your letter, and I would like to add, I am very proud of our friendship. Mary joins me in love to you and Vera and all good wishes—always

Jack

[Handwritten in the margin] P.S. By the way the TV show we did together will be repeated next Sunday.

[Handwritten by Jack on the back of a one-sheet advertising Stern's appearance at Los Angeles Philharmonic Auditorium on 2/25/58. The front shows Stern playing.]

Dear Isaac,

I can tell from the picture on the other side exactly which concerto you are playing—and I have a feeling that your third finger is a little too high—unless you are goosing some one.

[Written after the printed text "Stern's big repertoire (he is equally at home in Baroque, Classical, Romantic, and Modern works)"] I am equally at home with my wife—the cook—the Butler and the maid, etc.

Jack

[Telegram 1/14/61]
DEAR ISAAC   TODAY IS MY WEDDING ANNIVERSARY SO FOR AN ENCORE PLEASE PLAY THE ANNIVERSARY WALTZ STOP THAT THE LAST [sic] YOU CAN DO
JACK BENNY

[Telegram 2/28/61]
ISAAC STERN
GOOD LUCK TO US GIVE THEM MY BEST OR YOUR BEST AS YOU PREFER STOP I MIGHT HAVE A LITTLE TROUBLE HERE AS THE STAGE IS IN DALLAS AND THE AUDIENCE IN FT WORTH STOP PLEASE GET WORD TO CASALS THAT I WILL BE IN PUERTO RICO IN A FEW DAYS LOVE
JACK

[Telegram, 11/22/??]
DEAR ISAAC, AREN'T YOU GLAD I HELPED YOU SAVE CARNEGIE HALL? IF NOT, WHERE WOULD YOU BE PLAYING TONIGHT? LOVE
JACK

12/26/62

Dear Isaac:

Even though we are constantly in competition as violin soloists, I think it only fair that you have a biography of my musical career—so I am enclosing same.

Love,
Jack

[Bio is a joke patterned after Stern's own bio. From the looks of it, I think Jack may have typed it himself.]

JACK BENNY
Nee
BENNY KUBELSKY

Benny Kubelsky was born in Kriminiesz, Illinois. His parents brought him to Waukegan when he was one year old. At six, Kubelsky began studying the piano. Two years later, he switched to the violin.

He is one of the few great violinists who is entirely American, even to his musical training, obtained in the Illinois city from Naoum Blinder, and in New York from Louis Persinger.

In 1930 at the age of eleven, he made his debut with the Waukegan Symphony, conducted by Pierre Monteux. At this concert, the young Kubelsky was such a big hit that he played four encores and took seventeen bows while peeing in his pants.

The most rewarding adventure began when the Juilliard School Of Music in New York invited Mr. Kubelsky to play at the Hindemith Festival in honor of the distinguished modern composer's Fiftieth Birthday. For this occasion, Paul Hindemith conferred on him and Mr. Merrick, his accompanist, the privilege of playing the world premier of his unpublished, "Sonata-1939"—for violin and piano.

After Benny Kubelsky had played "Prokofieff's, "First Sonata" with the New York Philharmonic Orchestra under the baton of Efren Kurtz—Louis Biancolli wrote in the New York Telegram—"If there was an Oscar for the season's best solo fiddling, my nominee would be Benny Kubelsky at yesterday's Carnegie matinee. I was ready to concede if there was one violinist inching up close to the great Isaac—his name is Benny Kubelsky."

Two years later, Kubelsky played the Brahm's [sic] Concerto at the Lewisohn Stadium under the baton of Fritz Reinee. He played it superbly. The noted critic, C.H., wrote in the

New York Times—"Mr. Kubelsky's rendition of the Violin Concerto was immediately and unceasingly impressive for it's impeccable intonation."

By this time, Mr. Kubelsky was rapidly becoming such a great violinist, that he was overshadowing Stern, Heifetz and Milstein. Being very modest and unassuming, he did not want to do this as he loved these three great artists. It was then that Benny Kubelsky changed his name legally to Jack Benny.

I would like to add that Mr. Benny being a true interpretive artist, when he played Brahms, he made you forget all about Mr. Benny—and concentrate on Brahms. He seemed to be acting like some chivalrous go-between saying—"Ladies and Gentlemen, I give you Brahms."

At Thirty-Nine—Jack Benny is regarded as one of the world's finest violinists. His soundtrack performance and the beautiful photography of his fingers in Warner's Hollywood picture, "Son Of Humoresque"—brought his magnificent playing to the attention of movie goers as well. You will soon hear Mr. Benny again in Warner's new picture—"Shmuck Takes a Holiday."

[Telegram 12/27/62]
ISAAC STERN
IMPORTANT ERROR IN MY BIOGRAPHY THAT I SENT YOU YESTERDAY SPECIAL DELIVERY. ON PAGE ONE PARAGRAPH SIX PLEASE REPLACE THE NAME FRITZ WITH LOUISE. HAPPY NEW YEAR
JACK

[Telex 12/01/72]
DEAR ISAAC I AM MERELY SENDING YOU THIS WIRE TO LET YOU KNOW THAT I KNOW WHERE THE HELL YOU ARE LOVE
JACK

12/7/72

Dear Jack:

Got your wire. Very glad to receive it, because it made me look up where I was. Sometimes I feel you've seen one hotel, you've seen them all.

Spoke to Hurok today about your future career as a child prodigy in concerts. For some reason he's interested and would like to discuss it with you in detail when he comes to Los Angeles. He will be there—at the Beverly Hills Hotel—between December 21 and January 1.

Keep in touch and love from house to house.

As ever,
Isaac Stern

5/29/74

Dear Isaac,

I was so sorry I had to miss your recital in Los Angeles, particularly because it was a recital instead of a concert.

Now I know you must have seen this review by Albert Goldberg but I liked it so much I thought I would send it to you anyway in case you missed it. You probably need another good review like you need an extra F-hole on your violin.

When you explained to me about Mrs. Feline's orchestra in Washington, D.C., I realized that was the kind of a concert for which I get paid for a change. You also told me to be careful and see to it that that particular orchestra plays better than I do, so I have a rough idea of the kind of musicians they are.

However, I believe I know how to handle it. I'll play the Paginini Concerto which I cannot play, nor even spell…and for an encore, instead of playing "The Bee," I'll play "The Flight of the Bumble Bee," which I also cannot play. In other words, even if I could play "The Flight of the Bumble Bee," it would take me forty-five minutes. [handwritten] when it should only run 45 seconds!!

This is just a silly letter that I felt like writing to you.. and Mary and I send love to you and Vera and your family. Hope to see you soon –
Much love,
Jack

6/7/74

Your letter of May 29 was a distinct pleasure. Whether or not I need an extra F-hole, pleasant words from you are always welcome. What I'm really wondering about it why four or five different people, all clipped out that review and sent it to me. It makes me wonder if they are so surprised that I got a good review for a change. I have had one or two in my time, but I guess the recent experience of visiting artists with the local cut-ups on the paper have been so bad that a good review about anything comes as a welcome change.

I must agree with you, you don't know how to spell. But I hope that whatever I had to say about the orchestra in Washington will be helpful. I wouldn't worry too much about your playing. I'm sure that your usual standards will be in full evidence and the difference between you and the orchestra will be apparent. As you see, I am one of your most ardent admirers and I always believe in helping a colleague's moral [sic]!

Take care of yourself and most affectionate greetings to you both from Vera and myself.

Yours as ever,
Isaac Stern

My very sincerest thanks to Carl Samet for all his hard work and patience in arranging the interview and providing me with copies of these priceless documents.

The Jack Benny Times

May - August 2002   Volume XVII, Numbers 3-4

President's Message

Hello again, folks! The IJBFC has now reached 1,082 members and 13 countries: United States, Canada, Mexico, England, Scotland, the Netherlands, Sweden, Germany, Spain, Israel, China, Japan, and Australia. Plus, you wouldn't believe the number of countries that hit our Web site; for instance, I never knew Jack was so popular in Iceland. Or Nepal. It's amazing what international appeal his work has.

I am happy to say that I spent three fantastic days in March at the Boston Public Library going through their Jack Benny collection. Some of you may recall that the BPL purchased a number of letters from Jack to Frank Remley. Many of these are "Ripley letters", where Jack clipped an item from the Ripley's Believe It or Not! column and then wrote an extended commentary on it. I was able to date a number of undated items, reunite clippings with letters, and similar things. I also looked at part of the Fred Allen collection, and hope to do more in the future. It was a real thrill, and the staff of the BPL was helpful and friendly. Some have reported issues in the past of dealing with the BPL over the Allen collection, but I can confidently say that my experience there was completely positive. The article here on the start of the feud is based on my work there; I look forward to bringing you more information in the future.

You can still get all three 2001 issues for $8.00. Checks should be made payable to IJBFC, and sent to: P.O. Box 11288, Piedmont, CA 94611.

Now on with the show!

New Members

*** Larry Cohen *** Michael Dineen *** Joseph A. Greco *** Errol Helbling *** Neil Helgeson *** Bruce Hoddinott *** Michael E. Landau *** Christopher Lewis *** James and Agnes Lewis *** Kelly J. Lewis *** Ramesh Murthy *** Joel Neimeth *** Mark Norris *** Joseph M. Piotte *** Christopher Pizzo *** Scott Rowland *** Gerald Ryalls *** John Sloan *** Jack Strong *** Kennth Studdart *** Jerry Taft *** Linda Thuringer *** Donald W. Urbancic *** Jerry Williams *** Thomas Lininger *** John and Laura Rousseau *** Thomas Hardiman Jackson, Jr. *** Lyndon Ware *** Jeff Stutsman *** David Shurtz *** Steven Poole *** Sheree Smazik *** Lew Elliot *** Ben Thum *** Ann Leef *** Charles E Verhoeven *** John P. Laurenzano *** Jeffrey Chase *** Mr. Theron P. Carson *** Richard S. Perry *** Janet Maday *** Arthur R. Spafford, Jr. *** Christopher L. Stamper *** Michael Amowitz *** Sidney Berkowsky *** Anne Hodgins *** Fred Velez *** Michael Franden *** Randy Bruno *** James M. Forni *** Janet C. Moore *** Davy McGlawn *** Clint Brown *** David Cooper *** Thomas P. Lydon *** Paul J. Hoover *** Danny Box *** Brian Richey *** Katie Dunn *** Terry Morin *** Jeff Sparkman *** Jose A. Celis *** Judy Newman *** Larry R. Bernard *** Bryant White *** Trent Clifton *** Brian Cruz *** Rodney Keller *** John Doodigian *** Jeff Grapevine

*** Hugh Paxton *** Steve M. Thompson *** Ben Ohmart *** Steve Lund *** James Conahan *** Bruce Crowley *** Greg Jacobs *** Rachel Waters *** Dave Neufer *** James W. Page, III *** Richard Presutti *** Greg Van Beek *** Mitchell Wilyman *** Michael Schlorke *** Lorraine Kotler *** Laurie Heupel *** Dr. John Holman *** Richmond K. Shields *** Samantha Himmelstein *** Jeffrey P Burkett *** Stephen Neafcy *** Tony Baltulis *** John Dial *** Ann McTeer Davis *** David Gow *** Richard Gregg *** Karl Hinkebein *** Jim Kempton *** Rick Bernier *** K. Brogdon *** Gilbert A. Cherryhomes *** David Higginbotham *** George A. Menghi *** Frank Swiezy, Jr. *** Toccoy Dudley *** Doug Gerbino *** Aaron Montgomery Ellis *** Lloyd Cohn *** Mary Poehler *** Francis Chan *** Thomas Anglum *** Jeff Allen

Waukegan's Jack Benny Statue Celebration

Friday, June 7

6:00 to 10:00 PM - Benny Benefit Dinner
Bonnie Brook Clubhouse at the Bonnie Brook Golf Course
$39 per plate and the proceeds will benefit the Friends of Jack Benny Center's Scholarship Fund. Cash bar with hors d'oeuvres, and a buffet dinner of beef or chicken, salad, potato, side vegetable, roll and butter, dessert, milk/tea/coffee.

There are a limited number of seats available so please reserve early. Call the Benny Center at 847-360-4740 and ask for Claudia. VISA and MasterCard accepted.

Saturday, June 8

Ongoing – Self-guided Benny tours
Brochures will be available to guide people to a variety of Benny-related places, including the site of Jack's boyhood home, the Great Lakes Naval Center (where Jack was stationed in WWI), and Jack Benny Middle School.

Noon to 5:00PM - Downtown stage
Various musical acts will perform, and **the IJBFC will stage a recreation of the 9/23/51 Jack Benny radio program, featuring Eddie Carroll as Jack Benny.**

5:00 to 5:30PM – Statue dedication
The Jack Benny statue will be officially dedicated.

Evening, time and location TBD – Kibitzing
IJBFC members and Benny fans are invited to an informal get-together at a local restaurant. The time and location will be distributed by E-mail before the event, and will be made known to the concierge of the Waukegan Ramada.

Sunday, June 9
1:00PM - Museum of Broadcast Communications, Chicago
A trip to Chicago's Museum of Broadcast Communications to see the Jack Benny vault exhibit, and other radio show recreations.

WHERE CAN I STAY?
I have negotiated a group rate of $80 a night plus tax at the Waukegan Ramada. This is one of the newer hotels in Waukegan, and recommended by the city. Call them at 1-847-244-2400 and ask for the "Jack Benny Fan Club rate". **ROOMS MUST BE CONFIRMED WITH A CREDIT CARD.** For more information on the hotel, please see their Web page at http://www.the.ramada.com/waukegan01082.

THE IJBFC COMMEMORATIVE T-SHIRT – ORDER NOW!
Special IJBFC limited edition commemorative T-shirts will be ordered by April 26. ORDER **NOW,** as the quantity will be based on response and very few extras will be available. These are yellow shirts with the Bouché line drawing of Jack Benny, the club name, and commemoration. Available in adult S, M, L, XL, XXL. Wear your shirt to the celebration as a proud IJBFC member and to connect with other members—or wear it at home and be there in spirit. The cost is $16 per shirt, $4 postage for the first shirt, and $2 postage for each additional shirt. Please send checks (payable to IJBFC) to: P.O. Box 11288, Piedmont, CA 94611.

The Start of the Benny-Allen Feud

Elizabeth McLeod wrote an excellent analysis of the start of the Benny-Allen feud for the Old Time Radio Digest:

"The common explanation is that the feud had its origin on Allen's "Town Hall Tonight" broadcast of 12/30/36. During the "Town Hall Varieties" segment in the second half of the show, one of the performers was ten-year-old violinist Stuart Canin, who performed Schubert's "The Bee." Following Canin's virtuoso performance of the piece, Allen inserted an ad-lib comment along the lines of "Jack Benny should be ashamed of himself." Benny responded to this comment on his show the following Sunday, and thru the first three months of 1937 the performers exchanged verbal thrusts, culminating with a face-to-face mock confrontation on Benny's program of 3/14/37. From then on, the feud became a running gag, which continued until Allen's death in 1956.

"There are a few myths surrounding the feud, the foremost of which is that it began spontaneously with Allen's comment to Stuart Canin. In fact, Allen had been ridiculing Benny's violin playing as far back as the fall of 1935 -- and the two performers had shared the microphone for the first time on Allen's show of 2/26/36. Benny, for his part, directly mocked Allen with a parody sketch entitled "Clown Hall Tonight" on 4/5/36. It's evident from these examples that the foundation for the feud had been laid well before the Canin broadcast.

"Another myth is that Allen's comment to Canin about Benny was an elaborate, clever insult. Allen himself created this myth in his 1954 book "Treadmill to Oblivion," when he declared that he had started the feud by commenting "Mr. Benny should hang his head in symphonic shame and pluck the horsehairs out of his bow and return them to the tail of the stallion from which they were taken." Benny, on the other hand, in a 1956 interview remembered the trigger line as being simply "'Jack Benny should be ashamed of himself.' That's all he said."

"The problem here is that there is that no recording exists of the West Coast broadcast of the 12/30/36 "Town Hall Tonight" -- the broadcast that Benny, in Hollywood, would have heard. The Town Hall Varieties segment was entirely unscripted, and it is likely that Allen's ad libs varied between the early and late broadcasts.

"Without a recording, the best contemporary source on the Canin broadcast is a piece by Ken W. Purdy in the 2/27/37 issue of Radio Guide, entitled, naturally enough, "The Story Behind The Benny-Allen Feud." Writing just two months after the commencement of hostilities, Purdy states that on the 12/30/36 "Town Hall Tonight" program, Allen ad-libbed that "a certain alleged violinist by the name of Benny should be ashamed of himself."

"This version of events squares pretty closely with what Benny himself remembered hearing, and given how soon after the original event this article was written, I'm inclined to accept it as a more reliable source than anyone's reminiscences twenty years after the fact. Until and unless a recording of the West Coast feed of this show appears, this is probably the closest we'll ever come to positive documentation. Apparently, when Fred recounted his version of events in "Treadmill To Oblivion," he couldn't remember exactly what he had said -- or he just couldn't resist the temptation to revise history and embellish his remarks.

"In the course of researching this subject, I took note of John Dunning's account in his Fred Allen entry in "The Encyclopedia Of Old Time Radio." He gives a much more elaborate quotation, and implies that Fred's comments were made in reaction to a prior promise by Benny to play "The Bee." This is completely at odds with all other accounts of the incident, as well as with existing Benny shows from the period -- which only mention "The Bee" *after* Allen's initial comment.

"A bit of further research explains this discrepancy: Dunning's quotation doesn't come from the 12/30/36 show at all. It comes from Stuart Canin's *second* appearance on "Town Hall Tonight," on 2/3/37. Unlike the original December appearance, which was completely unscripted, this February appearance was fully scripted -- enabling Fred to be much more precise in his comments about Jack. Purdy mentions this appearance in the Radio Guide article -- and in fact, cites it as the "high point of the feud to date."

"Town Hall Tonight was in the midst of a steady ratings droop when the feud got started -- the program's Hooperating for the first week of January 1937 had dropped to 20.6. While the show was still in the top ten, the rating wasn't as healthy as it had been a year earlier, when it scored a 22.6. Part of this decline may be attributed to the fading of the amateur craze -- the Town Hall Amateurs had been the show's major attraction during 1935-36 -- and Allen constantly tinkered with the show during 1936 looking for a fresh angle. As related in "Treadmill," he tried very hard to come up with a "running gag" that listeners would get interested in following from week to week, with the "Talking Mynah Bird" appearances of February 1936 his earliest attempt -- will the bird talk or not? Tune in and see! This bit was squelched by the agency just as it was taking off -- and other experiments didn't seem to make much difference. Indeed, the most effective running gag on the "Town Hall" show during 1936 had nothing to do with Allen -- it was the "Keep Him Out Of The White House!" anti-Presidential campaign run by Stoopnagle and Budd when they filled in for Allen over the summer. This bit was so effective that Fred himself riffed on it when he returned to the Town Hall that October.

"Clearly, the feud came along at exactly the right time for Allen – the idea fit in exactly with what he was trying to do, and it certainly brought his show the most publicity it had ever received. Whether it actually accomplished the results he believed it accomplished is debatable -- while there were month-to-month spikes in the rating, the overall Hooper trend for "Town Hall" was downward all thru the late thirties. Thus, there was constant incentive for Fred to keep the feud alive, and an examination of broadcasts from the late thirties will reveal that Allen was usually much more aggressive in promoting the feud than Benny.

"For me, the feud reached its absolute peak on Allen's 5/7/41 program, styled "A Salute To Jack Benny." The entire hour is set aside as a tribute to the start of Benny's tenth year in radio -- but Allen goes to absurd lengths to avoid actually mentioning his name. The highlight of the show is a guest appearance by Amos 'n' Andy, who are recruited by Allen to contribute to the dedication of an equestrian statue of the "star of the Jell-O Program" -- Rochester!

"Comic feuds were a longstanding tradition carried over from vaudeville -- in those days, rival performers would exchange thrusts by means of ads in theatrical journals. Allen himself had engaged in such a feud with a smalltime comic named Harry LaToy, who had been a former mentor of his in Boston around 1912, and who went on to swipe much of Allen's act – and the tone of Allen's comments in the LaToy feud set a clear precedent for the Benny insults of later years.

"On radio, comic feuding went back as far as the gibes exchanged by announcer N. T. Granlund and Broadway musical-comedy star Harry Richman in the twenties - but the outstanding pre-Benny/Allen feud was the Walter Winchell-Ben Bernie pairing. Winchell and Bernie were both old vaudeville hands who knew how the game was played, and their feud reached its peak from about 1932-37, during which time the two made a couple of very amusing movies, "Love and Hisses" and "Wake Up and Live," and succeeded in generating a lot of publicity for each other. Their "feud" continued until Bernie's death in 1943 -- and its mid-thirties success can probably be considered the major inspiration for Benny-Allen." (Thanks, Elizabeth for another great analysis. – LL)

Many accepted that Fred started the feud on his show of January 6, 1937, since Jack's show of January 10, 1937 was the one where the cast focused on the feud for almost the whole first half of the program. However from the scripts and audiotapes in the Boston Public Library collection, Elizabeth is correct that the show where Stuart Canin first appeared is definitely December 30, 1936. This is also confirmed by Jack's program of March 7, 1937, where he mentions the December 30 date of Canin's appearance. My theory is that by Thursday, the script of the January 3 Benny show was fairly set (featuring another in the Buck Benny series). Since Fred's comment was fairly brief, it may have taken a day or two to suggest that Jack should respond. Thus they decided to devote the following week to it.

The Marcia Borie Benny biography has an extended Allen-Canin exchange it claims to be what started the feud. In it, Allen is in open attack and it sounds very scripted. I am unsure of its source, but I compared it to the script of Canin's 12/18/40 appearance on Fred's show and it does not match. This may be from the 2/3/37 show.

The "Town Hall Varieties" was indeed unscripted, simply indicated as "[VARIETIES]" in Fred's own script, although a young man named Murray Wood from Brooklyn, New York, emcees the Varieties segment and sounds partially scripted. The segment features young talent, including the DeMarco Sisters immediately preceding Canin. Below is a direct transcription of the dialogue from the NBC copy of the show that resides at the Boston Public Library.

Mur: Well, it's quite alright as the next one is Stuart Canin, he's a violinist, and he's from Edgemere, Long Island. Believe me, ladies and gentlemen, you haven't heard anything yet. He's really marvelous. (fades…line guessed) And this night he's playing … (consults Canin)

Can: The Bee by Schubert.

Mur: The Bee by Schubert. Ladies and gentlemen…

Allen: Well wait a minute, wait a minute, Murray…I'm running an orphan…I don't want to butt in, but…

Mur: (unknown)

Allen: …because this is…

Mur: Well, just how old are you?

Can: Ten and a half.

Allen and Murray: (almost in sync) Ten and a half.

Allen: This is the first time probably where you've had a double-talk emcee…

Mur: I still think I can take him over, though.

Allen: Not without the violin. Well you go right ahead there, Murray.

Mur: Well, all right now. You just give it to them.

(Canin plays The Bee)

Allen: Stuart, I think it's too bad, Stuart, that we haven't time to ask you to play an encore. You are without a doubt the most remarkable child violinist I have ever heard. Am I right, Murray?

Mur: I should think so.

Allen: How long have you been studying?

Can: Five years.

Allen: Five years, huh? And you're ten years old?

Can: Yes, sir.

Allen: That isn't a full-size violin, is it?

Can: No.

Allen: Did you start on that at five years, or smaller?

Can: No, smaller.

Allen: Smaller than that, huh?

Can: Three-quarters.

Allen: That's a three-quarters, isn't it?

Can: Yes.

Allen: Imagine if ten or fifteen years from now and you're playing the cello up on the (???)…What grade are you in at school?

Can: Public school?

Allen: Public school, do you go to public school?

Can: Yes, Five B.

Allen: Five B? Where do you live, Edgemere?

Can: Edgemere.

Allen: And you're in Five B, huh?

Can: Yes.

Allen: What do you know, Murray? A little fella in the fifth grade at school and already he plays better than Jack Benny…(4 second burst of laughter)…Well, we want to thank you very much, Stuart, and it's certainly been a pleasure to have you here, and I'm still, I'm convinced. I'm going to watch you play again, I think you've got another arm comes out of your sleeve there. I don't think you were doing that all with two arms. And thank you a lot.

Can: Thank you.

(APPLAUSE)

Bea Benaderet
By Lynn Wagar

Buzz! Buzz!
Mable: Oh Gertrude.
Gertrude: Yeah Mable.
Mable: Mr. Benny's line is flashing.
Gertrude: Yeah. I wonder what dial "M" for money wants now?

The comic banter between these two telephone operators made millions of Jack Benny fans fall off their seats in laughter. Bea Benaderet played Gertrude Gearshift on Jack's show, and Sara Berner played Mable Flapsaddle. Bea joined the show as a semi-regular cast member playing Gertrude, and taking bit or one-line parts as needed. While Bea's roles were small, she always got big laughs. Her bubble gum Brooklyn accent brought us the picture of a cheap date. When Jack would date Gertrude off and on, she never missed an opportunity to make fun of Jack's closeness with the dollar. On the 4-17-55 program, we find Jack and Bob Hope dating Gertrude and Mable in a classic cheapness episode.

Bea Benaderet was born on April 4, 1906 in New York, and her family moved to San Francisco soon after. Bea's career started at radio station KFRC as a singer, announcer, writer and producer. In 1936, she moved to Hollywood to make her dream of being an actress come true. Bea would spend the first few years of her career doing voiceovers and any bit parts she could find. During one of her evening performances, Orson Welles was in the audience, saw her talent, and gave her several guest appearances on <u>Campbell Playhouse</u>. She soon had no problem finding work, and was named "Radio's Busiest Actress".

In 1938, Bea married Jim Bannon, an actor famous for his movie roles as the cowboy Red Ryder. They had two children, Jack and Maggie Bannon. They would divorce in 1947, and Bea would marry sound engineer Gene Twombley.

During her career in radio she had regular or semi-regular roles on the following shows:

A Day in the Life of Dennis Day	Fibber McGee and Molly
The Great Gildersleeve Show	Glamour Manor Variety Show
The Ozzie and Harriet Show	My Friend Irma
The Mel Blanc Show	The Burns and Allen Show
Blue Monday Jamboree	A Date With Judy
Maisie	The Penny Singleton Show
This is your FBI	The Twelve Players Show

While she had steady work on these shows, she always found time for guest appearances. Just a few to her credit are:

Campbell Playhouse	Lights Out	Arch Oboler's Plays
Escape	Suspense	Sam Spade
Lux Radio Theater	G I Journal	Mayor of the Town

Like many of the stars of radio, Bea made the jump to TV with great success. She decided to stay with The Burns and Allen Show in her role as Blanche Morton, Gracie's best friend and neighbor. Bea played this role for more than 20 years on radio and TV, and received two Emmy nominations for Best Supporting Actress in a TV Comedy Series.

Lucille Ball wanted Bea to play the role of Ethel Mertz, but she turned it down because of other commitments. Bea auditioned for the role of Granny on The Beverly Hillbillies, but the producers thought she was right for the role of cousin Pearl Bodine. Besides her successful TV career, she also did extensive cartoon work with Warner Brothers, including the voice of Betty Rubble on the Flintstones.

In all of the 32+ years Bea was in the entertainment industry, she would only have one staring role: Petticoat Junction, a down-home family show about life in "Hooterville" during a simpler time. Bea played the Shady Rest Hotel owner and mother of 3 teenage daughters.

While Petticoat Junction was on the air, Bea developed lung cancer from years of heavy smoking and hard work. She fought the disease and returned to the show, but cancer had a way of coming back. On October 13, 1968, it would claim her life. Devastated by his grief,

Bea's husband Gene Twombley died just 4 days after Bea. Ironically, Bea's father, Sam, owned Benaderet's, Inc.--a manufacturer and retailer of tobacco products.

For fans of <u>The Jack Benny Show,</u> we will always remember her as the smart, wisecracking telephone operator whose jokes about Jack's cheapness gave us the gift of joy and laughter.

Author's Note: Bea also had an outstanding career in the movies and sound recordings. If you would like more information on Bea's career, visit http://exx.hypermart.net/exxy/benaderet%Bea.html or search at www.google.com, keywords "Bea Benaderet".

Do You Know?

The National Lum and Abner Society is having Ginny Tyler as a special guest at their June convention. Ginny says that she filled in as the voice of Polly on the television show after Mel Blanc's car accident. She also notes that when playing Polly, a director heard her and she was cast as Polynesia the parrot in the 1967 Rex Harrison version of Dr. Dolittle.

Does anyone know what show(s) she was on, or have a copy? Please send any information to the address at the end of this newsletter.

According to Lee Musnick, Frank Parker—vocalist on the Benny program during the early 30s—is still alive. He is believed to be living in Florida. Please let us know if you have any information on his current address or how to reach him.

Bryan Guinn reports seeing a cartoon (but not in time for the title card) with a Benny cameo. "This one takes place inside a small grocery store, and all the labels come alive—a typical theme back then. Unfortunately one of the animal cracker gorillas escapes his cage and begins menacing the label folk. Jack "Bunny" is among the denizens and calls on his "Buck Bunny" character and rides off to save the town. Unfortunately his horse is quite afraid of the gorilla, and our fearless hero gets backed into a corner when his gallant steed throws him. But all is well when the gorilla's mother comes along bellowing 'Hen-REE! HEN-ree APE-rich!" Any ideas as to the title of this cartoon?

From Ben Schwartz (benjy@earthlink.net):
"As a side article for the Writers Guild web site, I'll be writing up the 1936 split between Jack Benny and Harry Conn. I've got never before published information on it but we have no photos of Harry. If you have one that we could borrow or copy on computer, please let me know. I'd be happy to send out a copy of the magazine and reimburse for any costs."

From member Gerry O.:
"Around 1965 Chase & Sanborn sponsored a NBC Radio special, hosted by Edgar Bergen & Charlie McCarthy and featuring excerpts from Bergen's old Chase & Sanborn-sponsored radio programs. I have this retro special on tape, and one excerpt is particularly funny...It features Jack Benny as a guest, and the show's story has Jack losing his wallet. Charlie and Edgar find it and return it to Jack...but before they do Jack must identify the wallet's contents. Jack knows every bill denomination that was in the wallet...and even rattles off each bill's serial number! (Plus Jack says that there was a photo of silent-screen star Pola Negri in the cardcase!). I would LOVE to get my hands on this complete show, but I haven't seen it listed anywhere....Does anyone have any info on, or access to, this Bergen & McCarthy episode with Jack?"

From Elizabeth McLeod:
"There's a little known bit of information regarding the famous "J-E-L-L-O" musical signature. It was created by Don Bestor, the original musical director for the Jell-O Program, in 1934 - and continued to be used on the program even after Bestor left the series the following year.

"Several years later, Bestor filed a lawsuit claiming that he held the copyright on the musical progression -- and that it was being used without his permission. His action named General Foods, Young and Rubicam, NBC, and Jack Benny as defendants. I've never seen anything published to indicate what happened with this case, but I presume it was settled out of court. Since the progression is still used in Jell-O TV commercials, perhaps the Bestor heirs are still getting a cut from it?"

From Bruce Milne:
"A long time ago when I was very young, my father and I went to LaGuardia airport in New York to pick up my aunt. While there a young blonde-haired boy had seen Jack Benny coming toward the baggage area. While passing, this young boy yells out for all to hear, "Hi Jack!" A few minutes later, I was brought into a room where Mr. Benny sat. I was ask by him to sit on his lap. He then started to play his violin. At that point I placed my hands over my ears, and all I ever saw after that was flash bulbs going off. I know there is a picture some where out there, either in the Daily News archives or somewhere. Hoping you can or direct me in the right area."

OK, it's an old question, but no one has yet answered it conclusively. It comes up constantly. Was Mary Livingstone related to the Marx Brothers? Her maiden name was

Sadie Marks. It says explicitly in the Benny biography co-authored by her that she is not related to them. The circumstance of Zeppo Marx bringing Jack to their seder (Passover dinner) was a matter that the Marks family often entertained Jewish entertainers passing through town. However, Jack's autobiography says that she was a distant cousin of theirs. Was this just a reference to the old joke about all Jews being sixth cousins? Has anyone charted the tree far enough to find a connection? If you have any information, please send it to the address at the end of this newsletter.

You Do Know!

Some time back, Jack's New York address (before the move to Beverly Hills) was requested. The answer: 55 Central Park South. George Burns and Gracie Allen reputedly had the apartment above theirs, and many other noted comedians (including Fred Allen) lived in the same neighborhood.

W. Gary Wetstein provides a few thoughts on previous "Do You Know" questions.

"You asked who played the blue fairy, and I know that it was Mary Kelly. This is not from any documented source, but from having listened to the show myself. Her voice is absolutely unmistakable.

"I can't recall ever hearing Elvia Allman on the Benny show; she was on Burns and Allen quite a bit in the 40s, and even appeared on the Burns and Allen TV show quite a few times. I'm nowhere near as certain about this as I am about Mary Kelly (I'd have to have listened to every single program to know that she *never* appeared), but I certainly wouldn't consider her a recurring bit player.

"As for the Beverly Hills Beavers, again I can't be certain about this, but I would wager that most, if not all of them, were played by adults. Just an educated guess on my part, but I understood that children's parts on radio were usually played by adults, and they don't really sound like children to me. Besides, they were on the show for many years and their voices never changed? That would seem unlikely. . . and in the days before the show was transcribed, would kids really have been allowed to perform at 10pm for the east coast rebroadcast?"

Of course in the TV years, the Beavers had to be played by child actors, including Harry Shearer. But are there any thoughts about the actors from radio?

I can't remember who provided this to me, but in answer to the question of who played the "double talker" in the 1930s (appeared in Snow White and the Seven Gangsters, among others)—it was Cliff Nazarro.

Etcetera

There is construction being done on Jack's long-time Beverly Hills home, 1002 North Roxbury. The house was designed and construction overseen by architect Carlton Burgess. According to the Marcia Borie biography, the steel beams of the foundation were covered in character and actor names from the Buck Benny series, which was a regular fixture of the show at the time. There are plenty of stories about the house itself. One that is often told is Joan being afraid of the eyes of a tile octopus at the bottom of the swimming pool, prompting Jack and Mary to have the pool drained and the eyes removed.

While much of the inside is being redone, many features (such as the tiles and paneling in the library) are being retained. The facade will have minor changes, as the bay windows are being enlarged. As you can see in the pictures, the roof has also been removed. I have no ETA on the completion of the work, but will bring you updates as information becomes available. Thanks to Tom Williams for photos of the work in progress.

What car did Jack have before the Maxwell? On the 10/24/37 show, he says that he got the Maxwell when he traded in his Stanley Steamer.

From William Hardie:
"I found the episode where Phil Harris introduces his song "That's What I Like About The South". It is the show "Herbert Marshall Hosts The Show" airdate; 41-02-02. In case you don't know, Phil's other song that Jack got some mileage out of, "The Thing", was first sung on the episode "How Jack Found Rochester" with Mary's blooper "Grass Reek" airdate 50-12-03."

I have gotten many questions over the years about the Si-Sy routine, and when it was done. Ironically, Mel was not the first person to play the Hispanic part of this exchange--it was Mary posing as an entertainer in her brother's saloon. It was also used multiple times on television, and in the Twentieth Anniversary Special. If you know of any radio shows were it was done that are not listed, please let me know.

9/24/50   5/6/51   9/23/51   12/9/51   9/28/52   10/18/53   4/4/5

From Jim Wider, via the Old Time Radio Digest:
"This reminds me of my awareness of changing times related to OTR. There is a cafeteria chain in the eastern Midwest (Indiana, Ohio mostly) that used to have a dish special called a "Jack Benny" that was a lower cost entrée that came with smaller portions. Recently, they began to sort of upscale their image to appeal to younger people too (the chain has good food, but a reputation as "appealing to older folks"). In doing so they renamed their Jack Benny special to a non-descriptive "value plate." I guess some people did not understand the reference. Too bad..."

Jack Benny Classifieds

§§§ From Norma Stevens, widow of Larry Stevens. Larry was Dennis Day's replacement from 11-5-44 to 3-10-46 while the latter was in the Navy.

"Larry passed away in April 2000 but before his death, he made several appearances on the East Coast for OTR. Two years before his death, he made a singing comeback at The Cinegrill in the Hollywood Roosevelt Hotel. Larry followed this performance by making a CD of many of
his favorite songs, some of which he had sung on The Jack Benny Show. His death occurred before his CD could be distributed. If anyone is interested, it is a beautiful album and can be obtained by e-mailing me at
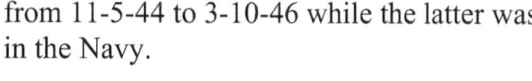
SongsbyL@aol.com. His voice was as beautiful, if not more beautiful at the age of 77 as it was when he sang on the show in 1944-46."

§§§ Member Al Baggetta is providing a valuable resource for all members with Pocket PCs:

"I have also been recently programming for the new handheld devices known as Pocket PCs, available through many companies and supported by Microsoft software. I just finished a program which I call The Jack Benny Show Radio Logs. Users of the Pocket PCs can carry the logs around with them, scroll through the contents of the file, or (very handy) search the logs by keywords or dates. I'm offering this to all Jack Benny fans who have the Pocket PC for FREE. They can download it directly from my website at http://www.baggetta.com. Click on the Jack Benny icon at the top of the page to go to the download page. Users will have to have a Windows PC with their device attached using ActiveSyn (pretty standard) to install the program on their handheld device. Please visit the site and check out this handy program."

§§§ **WANTED** – Will buy or trade for three rare Jack Benny films to complete my collection.
- Bright Moments (1928), Jack's first appearance on film
- The Songwriters' Revue (1929), a Metro Movietone 2-reeler, and
- Mr. Broadway (1933), co-starring Jack Dempsey, Bert Lahr, and Ed Sullivan.

If you have one or more of these, or have information as to where they can be located, write or call Gary Smith. 117 Smith Road, Hermon, Maine 04401; (207) 848-7735.

§§§ Dick Hill is thinning his book collection and offering the following titles:
- The Jack Benny Show, Milt Josefsberg (1977, Arlington House) – Good condition, except dust cover is frayed. $20.00
- Jack Benny: An Intimate Biography, Irving A. Fein (1976, G.P. Putnam) – Good condition, except dust cover is frayed, torn, and taped. $20.00
- Sunday Nights at Seven, Joan Benny (1990) – Excellent condition. $15.00
- Jack and Mary's Jell-O Recipe Book (1937) – New condition. $5.00
- Fred Allen – His Life and Wit, Robert Taylor (1989) – Excellent condition. $10.00

I will take offers, and I would like to have a copy of the movie (on video) that Jack and Fred Allen were in together, Love Thy Neighbor. I would be glad to trade for or pay for the video. Dick Hill, 1802 Bateman, Hastings, NE 68901.

§§§ For a book on the life and career of Buddy Hackett, I would appreciate hearing from anyone who saw Mr. Hackett perform live, met him, corresponded with him, or who has any memorabilia regarding his life or work. Any material lent to me will be treated with the greatest care, and returned immediately after copying. Any assistance which proves beneficial will be credited in the book's acknowledgments. Jay Ogletree, Hackettman1@hotmail.com

§§§ Michelle Varteresian is looking for the following (use address at the end of this newsletter):
- This Way Please, movie costarring Mary Livingstone
- Movies Mr. Broadway and Bright Moments
- The television program "Jack Dreams He is Married to Mary"
- Any memorial tributes paid to Mary at the time of her death

§§§ From the Boasberg Institute (and Ben Schwartz):

After nine long years, my essay "The Gag Man," the never-before-told, 15,000 word epic study of vaudeville genius Al Boasberg (1891-1937) is finally in print! Boasberg was the guru, mentor, and comedy writin' genius who created the stage characters Jack Benny, Bob Hope, and Burns & Allen all played. Boasberg invented stand-up with Benny and sent a 16-year-old Milton Berle out on stage telling him it would be funny if Berle said he'd been accused of stealing gags. Boasberg co-wrote Buster Keaton's The General and Battling Butler, saved the Marx Brothers' careers with A Night at the Opera and A Day at the Races, did punch up on Freaks, directed the Three Stooges in their first starring feature Myrt and Marge, and the last day he wrote a joke, introduced Rochester on the Jack Benny show. Groucho called Boasberg a comic genius. Benny thought him the greatest joke writer in the world. And did I mention nine years? He was o.g. - the original gagster.

CENSORED BY PRINTER

Megastore and in LA at Book Soup. Besides me, the book also sports essays by J. Hoberman, David Thomson, Frank Capra, Leo McCarey, as well as stuff on everyone from Edgar Kennedy to Woody Allen, and was edited by Gregg Rickman.

Also, if you get the Writers Guild of America magazine WRITTEN BY, there'll be an excerpt article on the Boasberg-Benny partnership published in the April comedy issue.

Jack Benny Talks About Comedy

Motivational Humorist Larry Wilde's 53rd book Great Comedians Talk About Comedy contains interviews with seventeen of the funniest people of the 20th Century talking about how they make people laugh. And of course, includes a fascinating dialogue with Jack.

Each engaging interview was painstakingly elicited by Larry, who spent years researching, collecting the material and recording these intimate one-on-one conversations. It is a fascinating compendium of life lessons, wit, motivation and inspiration that can be used to revitalize our own lives and careers.

Here are the big time performers who star in this book: Woody Allen, Jack Benny, Milton Berle, Shelley Berman, Joey Bishop, George Burns, Johnny Carson, Maurice Chevalier, Phyllis Diller, Jimmy Durante, Dick Gregory, Bob Hope, George Jessel, Jerry Lewis, Jerry Seinfeld, Danny Thomas and Ed Wynn.

Larry has graciously permitted us to include these excerpts from his conversation with Jack Benny. You will soon be able to hear the actual interview when it is released on a CD from laugh.com. For more information, please see www.larrywilde.com.

This meeting took place in Mr. Benny's Beverly Hills office. Most of the five rooms contained filing cabinets of past radio and television scripts. The walls of each room were decorated with plaques, pictures, awards, tributes, citations, copies of newspaper and magazine articles, even a photograph of Salisbury and Benny, his first act.

Fifteen minutes passed while Mr. Benny worked on some material with his writer for an upcoming Lake Tahoe appearance. Suddenly, the door to his private office opened and my idol, the man I admire and respect most in my profession—Jack Benny stood before me. A mortal. Wearing a gold-colored sport shirt, tan slacks, a yellow and black sport coat and smoking a cigar.

As we chatted, it became increasingly difficult for me to believe that the man sitting behind the desk was in his seventies. He looked fifty-five sharp, alert, handsome. I sat enthralled and nervously began the questioning.

>WILDE: To kind of get started, Mr. Car...eh, Mr. Benny, I would...

BENNY: As long as you're gonna make a mistake with my name, call me Jack!

>WILDE: All right, Jack! How many years did you play the violin before you decided to become a comedian?

BENNY: We-e-ll...when I was about fourteen, fifteen years old in Waukegan, I used to play with dance orchestras. We would play in stores on Saturdays and maybe get a dollar and a half for the day. Then I studied and I went in to vaudeville as a violinist. There was a woman pianologist—or whatever they called them—who sang and did talking, comedy songs. Her name was Cora Salisbury. She took me with her on the road. We did a violin and piano act—Salisbury and Benny.

    WILDE: Did you do any comedy?

BENNY: No, only a little bit of kidding with the violin, but I never talked.

    WILDE: What happened to make you give up being a musician and become a comedian?

BENNY: Well, Cora's mother became very, very ill and she had to give up the stage. Soooooo…I found another partner, a fellow by the name of [Lyman] Woods and I called the act Benny and Woods. That's how I have Benny as my last name—Benny is my right first name. We stayed together doing a violin and piano act until the First World War and then I joined the Navy.

    WILDE: Until then, you still had not done any comedy?

BENNY: No comedy at all. Then in the Navy at Great Lakes, David Wolfe, who became a very dear friend of mine later, was the author of a couple of sailor shows for Navy Relief. And in this show I did my violin and piano act with Zez Confrey. But David Wolfe needed somebody to play the part of an admiral's orderly, who only had one or two comedy lines. He happened to see me and said, "Hey, young fella, come over here!" (I was a young fella then.) And I read a couple of lines and he liked it, because the next day he added lines for me and by the time the show opened in Chicago in the Auditorium I had practically the comedy part of the show. Then I realized I could talk and get laughs. When I went into vaudeville again, I went back as a single act. But I always held the violin…did a lot of violin playing and just a little bit of talk. And then gradually I kept talking and less violin, until finally I dropped the violin entirely. If I wanted to have a finish for my act I borrowed a violin from the orchestra.

    WILDE: How many years did you continue to carry the violin on stage?

BENNY: I carried it until one week I played the Palace Theatre in New York, which was the acme—you know, the highest—Jake Shubert came in to see me…but he felt because I held the violin it classified me as a violinist. So the next time I went to the Palace I dropped the violin but I tried it in other towns first.

    WILDE: Even though you stopped playing the violin, why did you still hold it? For security?

BENNY: Yes, for security. Also, it made all my jokes sound impromptu—when you hold an instrument, they always think you are ready to play.

    WILDE: How long was your spot?

BENNY: Around fifteen minutes.

    WILDE: Where did you get the material you used?

BENNY: I would get help occasionally from writers and I would pay them for that particular routine—thirty-five or fifty dollars—but I wrote a lot for myself. In those days I was able to write because I had to. The only trouble…was always walking down the street and staring and people would pass me and say hello and I would not even know who they were. I was always thinking of jokes.

WILDE: Was your delivery basically the same as it is today—that is, leisurely, unhurried?

BENNY: Basically the same, but I was always nervous, the first few years, when I talked. I wouldn't gesticulate enough…and though I work easy and smoothly now and I put something into it, in the old days I was afraid to. When I was a hit in those days, I was a big hit because I worked so easy and smooth, but if I flopped I was a big flop for the same reason. You see, there's such a thing as being too nonchalant on stage. It looked as though you were…

WILDE: Too well rehearsed?

BENNY: Yeah. It looked as though you were over-acting and under-acting at the same time. Trying too hard to be smooth and easy. I learned since then I have to have a little action. I learned that later in radio and television.

WILDE: In the beginning of your career, did you sit with other comedians and discuss jokes and audiences and comedy in general?

BENNY: Yes. Most comedians, strangely enough, are very good friends. It doesn't always happen in other branches of our business…for some reason or other, actors…although I do think in our business people are very, very close, and even though there is competition and you have rivals or you try to reach a point where a friend of yours has already reached. Like Phil Baker never thought I would get any place. He thought I worked too blahh! But we were all pretty good friends. Maybe some of them in their hearts would not like to see others do well, but…comedy is not the easiest form of entertainment. That is, to reach a point in your career where you become a star or an institution or a household word—there are some great comedians now who won't make it, but they are great comedians—see, there has to be something more than just getting laughs. Laughs are not everything. People can scream at a comedian and yet can't remember anything afterward to talk about.

WILDE: What qualities are required, other than being able to make people laugh?

BENNY: In the first place, to become real successful they must like you very much on the stage. They must have a feeling like: "Gee, I like this fella"—"I wish he was a good friend of mine"—"I wish he was a relative." You see, it's like a television show—if they like you, you may think sometimes you are doing a bad show and you're not at all. But if they don't like you, you cannot do a good show. Of course, we had great schools in those days—vaudeville and burlesque, which they haven't got today. That's why I give all the new comedians a lot of credit for making it as quickly as they do and actually getting big laughs. For instance, I can walk on stage and if I want to be secure I can open up with a stingy joke and everybody screams. Well, a lot of comedians who haven't got those characterizations have to actually make good as comedians, not as institutions—household words. Not that I'm bragging that I'm an institution, I'm just trying to explain…

WILDE: When you started, were there any comedians you admired or patterned yourself after? You said Phil Baker was your idol—

BENNY: It was not so much that Phil Baker was a great comedian—he was a great personality. One of the handsomest fellas you have ever seen and people loved him. He would always have somebody working with him to get laughs, like I do on television. I used to like Frank Fay very much. I was never a very good friend of his, but on the stage I admired him. Al Jolson was the world's greatest entertainer. I don't think there's been anybody since then that has his magnetism, and particularly when he was in blackface. He had a sympathetic quality. I have always thought Ed Wynn was the world's greatest comedian, and I still think there is nobody that has ever been as funny, or will be, in my time as he was in his heyday.

>*WILDE: Most comedians work for a period of years before they "find" themselves; that is, before they discover the kind of material, attitude, and delivery that's right for them. How long did it take you to acquire this self-awareness?*

BENNY: It took me a very short time when I was a monologist. It took me quite a while to *perfect* it—to get to the point where I wasn't static. In those days everything had to be set. Every word had to be set. If we wanted to change something we had to go out of town and break it in, that's how nervous we'd be. George Burns talks about things like that. But…let me explain something…once I have the right wording and the jokes in the right place I try to keep 'em there, because I find that a certain joke is better second or third or fourth or fifth.

>*WILDE: Do you get that by trial and error?*

BENNY: By experimenting and trying. I try to get from one subject to another gracefully so that the audience doesn't realize I have made the change—they think I'm on the same subject for twenty minutes. I don't tell a joke about my uncle and then the next one about a saxophone or something.

>*WILDE: They kid Henny Youngman about that.*

BENNY: Yes, but then that's his style and it's good.

>*WILDE: Jack, has what people laughed at changed much through the years?*

BENNY: I don't think so. I think they laugh at the same things. Years ago you could do some corny things and be funny. I can look over what I used to do many, many years ago and pick out things to use now. The only thing is if you are working on characterizations, things that were funny thirty years ago have to be embellished—have to be smarter—wilder. Like, if I do stingy jokes I can't do an ordinary joke about leaving a guy a nickel tip—that's not funny any more. Now you have to be more wild. Maybe the waiter leaves me a dime tip knowing how cheap I am. It would have to be crazy, you see, in order for it to be funny. Today, it has to be actually funnier.

>*WILDE: Many comedians earn an excellent living doing club dates, conventions— some as much as twenty-five thousand dollars a year or more—but the world will never hear of them. Some are very content with this anonymity while others are still striving to reach the top. Was it always your goal to become a star?*

BENNY: I would think so, and I think nearly every comedian wants to be…just like a politician would like to be President of the United States. And I don't care who the Politician is—he might be the mayor of Carson City, but if he's in politics, he would like to end up being President. I think every dramatic actor, every singer, would like to be among the top few. Every concert musician would like to be considered among the top half-dozen. But when I saw "would like to be the top"…you see, we didn't demand too much in those days. For instance, when I played the Palace in New York, which was the theatre every actor was nervous about, and I was a big hit…you had the feeling that everybody in the world knew about it and you didn't have to go any further. And the same with money. When I got to the point where I was getting four hundred and fifty dollars per week, I thought I was quite a rich man. I started to move in the first-class hotels…oh, my goodness, I thought, if I could ever make a thousand dollars a week, brother, then I'm ready to call it a day—this is it.

> WILDE: *So you really didn't wake up one day and say, "I want to be a great comedian"? It was a step-by-step process?*

BENNY: Yeah, but I think everybody does feel that way, because if they don't, it's not good—it's better to feel that way. But mine has been, fortunately so, a step-by-step…not only in recognition, but in improvement in what I was doing. If you get up to the top step-by-step, you don't drop so fast. Some people are overnight sensations and then stop the same way.

> WILDE: *Could you pinpoint the specific steps you've taken to remain a star all these years?*

BENNY: I think I have had, through my years of radio and television, almost always a very, very good show. I can't stand *bad* shows—I get embarrassed. I was the comedian, of course, but I think I was almost a better editor. Most comedians give me credit for being not the best comedian in show business, but the best editor—which is as important as being a comedian. It's not that I am such a particularly funny man. It's the things I do in routines. People will say to me, "Did you study the pauses in the tape?" This all comes as you go along, but there is nothing as important as editing.

> WILDE: *Were you born with this talent for editing or do you feel it came about as a result of years of analyzing yourself and your material?*

BENNY: The latter—I don't think I was born with it. It was important to me never to have a superfluous moment in my act or in my radio or television shows.

> WILDE: *How did all the Jack Benny trademarks come about? Thriftiness, bragging, playing straight to the people you work with, etc.?*

BENNY: All these things happened by accident, with one show. Now how I probably became a stingy character happened because on one show I did some jokes about my being stingy…

> WILDE: *This was in radio?*

BENNY: Yes. Then we did it again and again, until suddenly by accident it became one of my characterizations, and it's the easiest one to get laughs. My feud with Fred Allen was an accident. Fred said something one night, I answered him—he answered me—I answered him, and it went on and on. We never got together and said, "Let's have a feud." If we did, the feud would have flopped, because it would have been contrived. We would have worked so hard at it, it would have been lousy.

> WILDE: *Why was Fred Allen considered the comedian's comedian?*

BENNY: Because he was a great writer. Fred was a wonderful humorist. He wrote funny letters. He wrote funny books. He wrote great shows. I don't know whether he was altogether a great editor, because sometimes he would have sensational shows and sometimes they wouldn't be at all. They would be far from it. I always blame it on editing. Let's take you...you are preparing this book, you gotta edit it, right? They say a play is never written, it's rewritten. Well, the same goes for an article in the paper, or a monologue for a show—everything. My four writers and myself sit down and argue and discuss whether the word "but" helps or hurts a joke. That's how important editing is.

> WILDE: *Your writers have worked for you many years. What does it take to have a successful relationship with the men who provide the comedian's material?*

BENNY: First of all, you should have faith in them. You should feel that one is just as good as the other. Never let any of your writers feel that one person is doing the big job and the others aren't. You usually find through the years that one week one fella has delivered the best and another week another fella has. I don't try to remember who gave me any particular joke. I don't remember if it was my idea or theirs. I don't care. I only care about the results. Some writers think fast—ad-lib fast. Others think first before they talk. Others are better for continuity. I can't tell you how many times I have felt some of the material they brought in would not make a good show, but it did, and I always wind up apologizing. I'd rather apologize than have a bad show. I learned something that was very, very important after being on television a few years: I must never be angry with writers. If you become angry it becomes difficult for them to work. I found out the happier we are as a combination, the more fun we have, the greater shows I have. My writers and I get along like four intimate friends who are having a good time and that's how we write scripts.

> WILDE: *What percentage of your total performance is the writers' contribution?*

BENNY: Well, let's start with the ideas. In radio and television maybe thirty-three and a third percent came from me—the theme of the shows—and two-thirds from them. I have always come up with ideas. Sometimes they were good and sometimes they weren't. Sometimes they were good ideas but my writers felt that they were one-joke ideas and they couldn't get enough out of it, so I would say, "Drop it." When it comes to actual jokes they would contribute ninety or ninety-five percent. When I would see the script, I would add a line or two. Now when I give stage appearances or when I speak at a dinner...a lot of the jokes, I prepare. If it's weak, I give it to my writers.

> WILDE: *How did the final scripts for your television shows come about—the step-by-step process?*

BENNY: Well, we never stopped. In radio we wrote right up to air time, because all we had to do was read it. Now on television we had to naturally do it before—so we could learn it. But it never stopped until the last minute of the time allotted to us to have it ready, because we were always changing, always editing—like I told you before.

> WILDE: *When you got together for the TV show, getting back to that for a moment, let's say the idea for that particular show that week came from you. What was the next step?*

BENNY: We have a meeting with the writers. My writers had a wonderful way of working. They didn't just sit down and put stuff on the typewriter. They would go home and make notes about where they can go with this idea of mine and suddenly I would get a call and they'd say, "Jack, your idea is great, we're gonna have a wonderful show." Or

"Jack, we're afraid that we are not going any place with it—it doesn't spread enough. It's a one-joke idea and is only good for a couple of minutes." So I would say, "Drop it! You figure which way you want to go!" Later they would call and say, "We got a great idea about so and so," and they would write it. Then they came in with the script and we would sit down and edit it and we would work on it.

> WILDE: *How did "Love in Bloom" become your theme song?*

BENNY: Quite by accident. "Love in Bloom" is not a theme song I particularly like. It has no significance with a comedian. It happened that I was fooling with that number thirty years ago, and before I could do anything about it...it was an avalanche, and it became my theme song.

> WILDE: *It's amazing how so many elements of your comedic character...the comic-attitude...your theme song...have all come about without being planned.*

BENNY: That's why it was good. There's no reason for "Love in Bloom" being my theme song. I couldn't stop it.

> WILDE: *Mr. Benny, eh, Jack...you are considered to have the best timing among comedians. What exactly is timing?*

BENNY: Sometimes I think I have been given more credit than I merit in that, because every good comedian has to have, right off the reel, good timing, otherwise he can't even appear anyplace. I think the reason other comedians [feel this way] and maybe the public, who are gradually getting to know about timing, they know the words now...because I talk very slowly and I talk like I am talking to you...I might hesitate...I might think. Everybody has a feeling, at home watching television or when they come to a theatre, that I am addressing him or her individually. They feel that I am doing it for them, and because I talk slowly...I make it a point to talk like I would in a room with fellows. So they think my timing is great for that reason. Other people have great timing but they talk very fast. It would be tough for them to talk slowly and it would be tough for me to talk fast.

> WILDE: *Could you define timing?*

BENNY: It's tough to define.

> WILDE: *Do words like "rhythm"..."pause" help describe it?*

BENNY: Well, my pauses fortunately went over even in radio, when you couldn't see me. The audience *felt* the pauses, but pauses make an audience think you are thinking. Sometimes I might do a monologue three or four nights and not change a word and an audience sitting out front will think I am ad-libbing a lot of it because I hem and haw around. But how do you define timing? It's a necessity. It's something everybody has to have. A good joke without timing means nothing—except you can help a bad joke with timing where you can't help a good joke with bad timing...I don't know how to define it.

> WILDE: *Is it a question of an easy flow...?*

BENNY: That's right—one word or one syllable too much, can throw it off completely. I had an experience once...I was playing Las Vegas...wonderful audience every night and I knew that my very opening line would be a big laugh, and every night it was a big laugh, and I knew just how that laugh would hold...and then I would continue. One night I walked out and the laugh was good but not as long or as big…and that performance knocked me off my timing for about two minutes. I couldn't get back into the swing and rhythm.

WILDE: Can anyone learn timing?

BENNY: I think so, but innately he has to have something.

WILDE: It has been said that instead of being a comedian you are the world's foremost comedy actor. Do you agree?

BENNY: I don't agree on being the world's foremost comedy actor. I *could* be a very good actor, and I think I am. I think Jackie Gleason is a great actor. Red Skelton does pathos very, very well with his face and gestures…and his mimicry.

WILDE: Is there a difference between a comedian and a comedy actor?

BENNY: Yes, you can be both, but you can also be a fine comedian and not be a good actor, and you can be an actor and not a comedian. I don't know if you ever noticed it, but I always get the greatest results in comedy with a dramatic actor. I had Ronald Colman [as a guest] for years and I asked him, "to read the lines that we have written for you as though you were reading a dramatic scene." Every good actor is a good comedian.

WILDE: Aren't men like Cary Grant and Jack Lemmon comedy actors rather than comedians?

BENNY: That's right, but they are great comedians. Cary Grant is one of the finest comedians we have ever had in motion pictures. He knows what to do with a comedy scene. Jimmy Stewart is great.

WILDE: Jack, which medium—radio, television, movies, night clubs, or the stage— do you prefer to work in?

BENNY: The stage—and my concerts. They're all charity, you know, I enjoy playing with the big symphony orchestras…Carnegie Hall. A concert is the finest background a comedian can have. I'm dressed in tails as though I were the world's greatest violinist. The musicians behind me are ninety or a hundred of the greatest musicians—Leonard Bernstein, George Szell, or William Steinberg, Alfred Wallenstein, or Zubin Mehta are conducting for me like they would for Heifetz.

WILDE: Do you find that the laughs come more easily when you are doing a monologue or when you are involved in a sketch?

BENNY: They might be…they could be oftener in the monologue. However, there are certain jokes I like to tell that are very smart and very clever that do not get the laughs some of the others do, but they will be the kind of joke the audience will remember. There will be the kind of joke that will only call for a *nice* laugh, and you don't want to leave it off. You don't have to get a laugh every second.

WILDE: Any average, intelligent person with practice and hard work can become a lawyer or a CPA. Is it possible for someone to put in the same amount of effort and become a comedian?

BENNY: Only if he has something. Only if there is a spark that can develop into a flame. In the first place, he has to have a great sense of humor. Everybody should have a public and high school education. I never had a high school education and I never was good in public school, but the fellow who thinks he is going to be a comedian—be in show business—I think a college education can hurt him. He knows too much. He knows too many fine words. His vocabulary is too good. I have a fine vocabulary, but I never use it. He doesn't get down to earth. You look back and see who are some of the fine comedians, you will find usually that they are people without college educations. College does something to you. It makes you feel that you know a little bit too much and you do not then consider an audience your equal—while if you haven't had that college training you are very careful about what you say and how you say it.

> WILDE: *A certain amount of capital is required to start in any business. How much would you say is needed to start as a comedian? And what would you use it for?*

BENNY: Well, I wouldn't know how much capital, because I never had any. But I would use it to buy material, buy jokes. If you don't know now to routine the jokes…if this doesn't come easily to you, maybe you have someone help you who knows how. I will go to a young comedian that I like, and I say, "You do a fine act but you open badly." They say, "What do you mean?" I say, "You open like an act. If you would come out and say, 'Well, ladies and gentlemen, it's great to be here in Plainfield and you know, I haven't been in Plainfield in years' and you have a joke about it and *then go* into your routines. When you come out and start right off and say, 'I want to tell you, the way children are today'…they know it's a set act. They know immediately this is a routine you do every night. And even though they will laugh and everything, you have no rapport with an audience."

> WILDE: *What advice would you give to a comedian just starting out?*

BENNY: This has been asked me, Larry, many, many times. And it's the toughest question in the world to answer. You can't tell a fella where to go today. The minute he's any good he's thrown to the wolves, which means television. He hasn't had a chance to work out any background. It's a very difficult question to answer. More difficult than trying to explain timing. I never got advice and most of the fellas today never got advice…Joey Bishop…he's one of the funniest men I have ever seen. He's just naturally a funny man. Great ad-lib comedian…thinks fast. A lot of people think he worries too much…I think so too, but then this you can't stop…that's his style but he's great. What would you advise somebody to do? You see, in the old days there were schools…vaudeville…then I would say: Start out on small time, play Kokomo, Indiana. If you are a flop there, the only people that will know live in Kokomo. And then only the people in the theatre or who read the paper. By the time you get there next year you might have improved a lot. By the time you get to the Chicago, you have improved. Maybe it will take a couple of years. I played all the small little theatres.

> WILDE: *Is there anything specific you have done to stay healthy and in good physical shape?*

BENNY: Everybody thinks I take such good care of myself. Actually I do not. I watch food because I want to look good at my age. If I intend to work, I intend to look good. I know I am at an age where a lot of people could look very old. I think it is better if I look young; otherwise my "thirty-nine years old" gag wouldn't be funny at all. It would be sad. If I actually looked my right age…people say to me all the time, "We know you are older than thirty-nine, but you certainly don't look your right age." So then I can have fun with the gag.

Please send all questions, comments, corrections, and additions to:
International Jack Benny Fan Club
P.O. Box 11288
Piedmont, CA 94611

JackBenny@aol.com
www.jackbenny.org

Please, friends, send no bombs.

The Jack Benny Times

September - December 2002   Volume XVII, Numbers 5-6

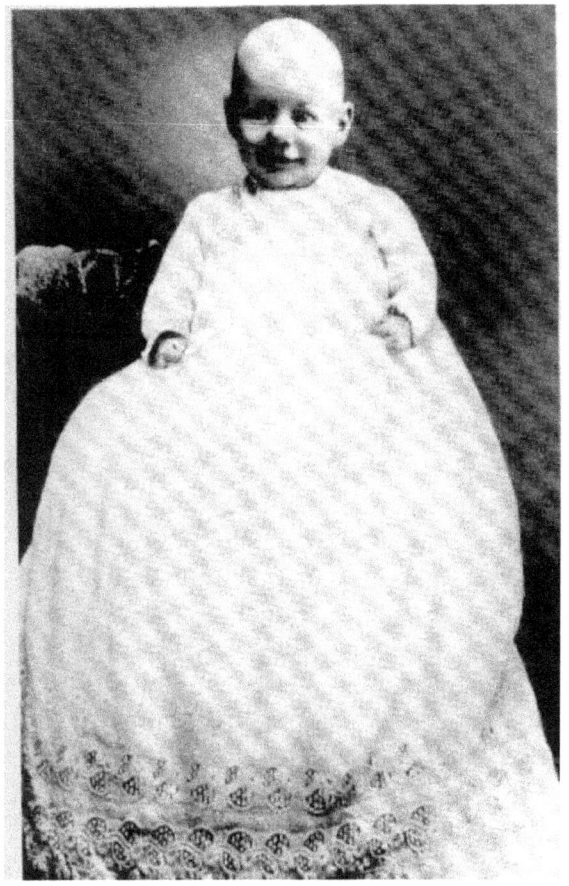

Waukegan Honors its Favorite Son…

Benny Is Back Celebration
June 7-9, 2002
Waukegan, Illinois

President's Message

Hello again, folks! What can I say about Waukegan that hasn't been said? I hope you'll indulge me a little space for my own personal thoughts. It has been a privilege and pleasure to work with David Motley and the City of Waukegan to bring the event to reality. It has also been a kick to work with the recreation cast, meeting timing and technical challenges to arrange rehearsals through Yahoo Chat. It was a blast working with and learning from Eddie Carroll. There was a great sense of personal pride in seeing people on Saturday in their bright yellow IJBFC T-shirts, remembering the night that I folded and packaged all of them. It was also humbling to be able to help put together an event that literally brought people together from coast to coast.

And it was wonderful sitting at dinner with so many IJBFC members and fans, everyone talking, smiling, making new friends, and having a good time. In this world of uncertainty, it was a little pocket of warmth and conviviality. As I have said many times, Jack Benny fans are just good people.

And we're going to do it again in Los Angeles in February. Now on with the show!

New Members

**** Howard M. Shryock **** James Koski **** Richard Cline **** Edward J. Szewczyk **** Walter Arriola, II **** Leslie D. Martin **** Pernilla Foran **** Nathan Grove **** Don Ellison **** Ludwig van Catt **** Steve MacDonald **** Katie vanMeter **** Lisa Marie Collins **** Mark Addison **** Jessica Mila **** Alan Magill **** Becky Dietz **** Qiana Stewart **** Deborah Anderson-Gaiser **** Nancy Fuller **** Dean Bailey **** Bob Sebring **** Daniel Brown **** Ronald J. Elersich **** Ronald Pelletier **** John E. Clifford **** Midge Evans **** Steve Goodger **** Philip Stromer **** Ed Hanson **** Carol Wolf Britton **** Harry Major **** Bobby Donovan **** Sarah Hamarain **** James Updike **** Alan Smith **** Marty Artz **** Barbara Googins **** Adam Burke **** Phoenix Producers Group **** John B. Sientz **** David LeMunyon **** Bruce Young **** Fred Fagal **** Bill Herzler **** Mark Pighin **** Russ Ross **** Scott B. Kelly **** Brian West **** Kevin Trudeau **** Scott Gutmann **** Perry Huntoon **** Howard Elliott **** Ted Bleiman **** Marcus Downing **** Stephen R. Balmes **** Joseph Zdenek **** Tim Carvis **** Bill McGuire **** Matthew Sanfelippo **** Ron Sayles **** Arthur Edivan **** Ginger Ross Delachler **** Kevin Johnson **** Patricia A. Olean **** Tom Franz ***** Eddie Carroll **** David Motley **** Darlene Lattimore **** Katie Costello **** Paul Wattson **** Joe Daniel **** David Mink **** Andrew Clarke **** Aaron Harris **** Yvonne Mikulencak **** Richard Briggs **** Michael A. LaRue **** Jessica Smith **** Mark Stroman **** Stephen Carter **** Jennifer Sica **** Nancy Paulette

Waukegan Diary

Thursday, June 6

Arrived in Waukegan. Saw a copy of a big article in the Waukegan News-Sun tacked on the wall of the Ramada. Saw the statue in person for the first time. I have to say I'm very impressed. The statue is lovely, and captures Jack well. The base has a variety of different etchings of related people and items (a violin, Mary, a pair of glasses, Jack's vault lock, etc.). It's on a beautiful granite base with "Jack Benny" engraved on it. The park itself is also lovely, and the period-style streetlights make it very bright after dark. The Genesee marquee (diagonally across the street) was also brightly lit, which did my heart good (remembering when there was question as to whether it should be torn down). Had dinner with the sculptor, Erik Blome, who is a well-spoken and insightful gentleman.

The NPR focus on the Benny statue is going to be on the Chicago NPR affiliate (WBEZ, 91.5) at 10:00AM on a show called "848".

Tomorrow brings photographs at the statue in the morning, then setup and rehearsal for the recreation, and the Benny Benefit dinner in the evening, with Eddie Carroll's one-man show. Must find good, strong coffee in the morning.

Friday, June 7

Today started with a gathering of some of the key people at the statue around 10AM. I got there early and walked around the pathways, looking at the names of various people who sponsored bricks (including some of our own members). Met up with our sound effects man (Charlie Willer), the Direction of Public Relations for the City of Waukegan (David Motley), and then Eddie Carroll and his wife arrived. Charlie asked Eddie if he could take a photo of him with the statue, and Eddie climbed all the way up on the base so that he was standing right next to it. Eddie removed his glasses and mirrored the statue's pose. I involuntarily drew in a sharp breath, as the startling likeness sent shivers down my spine.

We all walked over to the Genesee Theatre, and Peggy Kolber was kind enough to let us inside. The renovation is fully underway. The work crews had been peeling the paint from the lobby walls and cleaning the silver leaf of the ornamentation with wax. A large chain hung from a ring in the ceiling where a large chandelier had once graced the entrance. There are mixed stories, varying from mysterious to tragic, about how the original chandelier disappeared. However, they had now ordered a Baccarat crystal chandelier. Its weight was two tons, so the chain was for the stress test of the ceiling to insure no unfortunate accidents! The seats are still out of the theatre itself. We walked down the aisle and up on the stage, where we surveyed the fly cables, light board, and general layout. The ETA for completion is Fall 2003.

Afterwards, we walked up to the City Planning Commission, where the original Genesee organ was on display. Steve and Peggy Kolber, along with everyone there, were very kind and helpful to us. We also met the Mayor of Waukegan, Richard Hyde, along with Laini Zinn, one of the originators of the Benny statue effort.

Sound effects setup and rehearsal took up a good portion of the afternoon. The cast is very enthusiastic, and getting everyone in the same room for the first time really pulled together the team dynamic. We did two run-throughs, and everyone did very well. Charlie Willer has done an unbelievable job of pulling together all the sound effects equipment.

A short break and then on to the Benny Bash annual benefit dinner for the Jack Benny Center for the Arts. The feature attraction was an abbreviated version of Eddie Carroll's one-man Benny show. As an introduction, some video outtakes from Jack's TV shows were shown. At some point, I turned around and looked out toward the foyer. I could see a person's silhouette, which gave me a small gasp as it looked exactly like Jack Benny in one of his famous poses. Of course, it was Eddie awaiting his opening cue. He even worked my name into one of the jokes, which gave me quite a surprise. An excellent show enjoyed by all, and received a standing ovation.

Tomorrow is the big day, starting with final run-throughs at 8AM. It is now approaching 2AM. Must find more good, strong coffee in the morning.

Saturday, June 8

The fateful day has come at last! We had an early morning with an 8AM rehearsal. Eddie did not attend this rehearsal, but after 15 years of doing a Jack Benny one-man show and two run-throughs with our cast, he certainly didn't need it. Thanks to long-time IJBFC member Hal (a.k.a. "Humphrey") Bogart for standing in as Jack Benny. The CD of piano accompaniment for Dennis' "Clancy Lowered the Boom" developed technical problems on Friday, and he opted to do it a capella. I should note that our Dennis learned to sing from Perry Como (another story), and it shows.

At 10:00 after two run-throughs, we called it good and disassembled all the sound effects equipment (no small task), carried it all down to our vehicles, and transported the show to the downtown stage. The blocks around Genesee and Clayton had been closed to traffic, and 20' by 40' stages were set up across Genesee on the south side of the intersection (our stage), and Clayton on the West side (for the symphony and band). This put the statue between the two stages; it was covered with a magnificent royal purple satin, which shined in the morning light. The weather could not have been better--warm with skies as blue as Jack's eyes. We proceeded to scope out the space and set up shop.

As we worked, some of the media arrived. A local cable producer set up his camera, and Chicago Land Television (CLTV - affiliated with WGN and other Chicago area stations) asked to interview me. By 12:00, the sound effects were set, the microphones and audio connections were done, and sound checks completed. We all had been sweating it out, and ran back to the hotel to clean up and change into more formal wear for the performance. We reconvened at 12:45 in Paradiso Perduto, a downtown restaurant that served as a green room.

Bill DeVore, a Waukegan media personality and entertainer, emceed the show. He introduced Chuck Schaden, a legend of Chicago radio and the host for 30+ years of "Those Were the Days", a show devoted to old radio. Chuck kicked off his broadcast, and segued into a Jack Benny program that was to be played on air. The entire event would be recorded and edited down for broadcast at a later date, probably next February. Bill then introduced me, and I talked with the crowd about the Benny show and hoped to educate any "newbies" about the characters. Our sound effects man helped with a demonstration of various techniques, including the squeaking of a ship and the sound of Don Wilson falling overboard. I then introduced the cast in this order:

Sound effects and Mel Blanc	Charlie Willer
Rochester Van Jones	Dan Leff
Don Wilson	Bill Powers
Phil Harris	Eric Brolund
Dennis Day	Tom Trethewey
Mary Livingstone	Maria Scarvelis

"and the star of our show, the one and only...MR JACK BENNY."

Eddie Carroll then strolled out to center stage. He interspersed jokes from his one-man show with comments about Jack's history and connection to Waukegan. I've heard many people say how eerie it is to watch him work because he has the Jack Benny persona down so perfectly. I never completely believed it until finally working with him. In fact, an

audience member familiar first-hand with Jack Benny's work was moved to tears by his convincing performance. I also must note that he was always a complete professional in working with the cast, providing valuable coaching, and although he has ten times more years in show business than all of us put together, he treated us as equals.

Eddie then segued into the radio show recreation. Energy was high, and you could feel the electricity in the air on stage. Everyone gave a fantastic performance. Just one flub, when Phil called for an 11-gun salute (one of only two recorded sound effects) to welcome El Supremo on board Captain Horatio Hornblower's ship, he got a rousing chorus of "Rule Britannia" instead. We all cracked up and Eddie immediately jumped in with ad libs; it felt as though we had just created another "chiss sweeze" or "Drear Pooson" moment. I'm sure Gene Twombley (one of Jack's sound men) was laughing at us, somewhere! It ended up being handled so well that several people thought it was an intentional gaff; it ended up giving us some of the biggest laughs in the whole production.

Afterwards, Eddie stepped out of character to bring several people up in front of the statue. These included the Mayor, a State Senator, Laini Zinn, myself, and two of Jack's grandchildren: Maria Rudolph and Joanna Meiseles. A bronze plaque listing the major contributors (including the IJBFC, which really took my breath away) was read. Then the rope tying the satin was pulled, and all the people who had been introduced reached forward to pull the glistening material off the statue. The crowd applauded enthusiastically, and pressed forward to shake hands and have their picture taken with Eddie and the statue.

After talking with various people and meeting several members of the IJBFC, I went back to the green room and had lunch with the cast. Eddie stayed with the crowd, shaking hands, signing autographs, and posing for pictures. At 3:10, I went over to Chuck Schaden's tent. Eddie was at the microphone, trying to talk above a very loud (and very good) performance of "Johnny Comes Marching Home Again" by the Waukegan Symphony Orchestra. Chuck then interviewed me for a few minutes. It was a real pleasure to finally meet him.

Eddie and I went back to the restaurant. The cast passed around scripts and we all signed them. Charlie had retrieved a tape of the performance, and we sat down and listened to it. We were finally able to hear how we sounded (it's almost impossible to know that when you're performing, because you're concentrating on the task at hand), and we laughed at the show, ourselves, and the ad libs all over again.

Someone suggested that we take a cast picture, so we stood for a few in the restaurant. One person had a camera without a flash, so we had to go outside. We debated about the best setting, and decided to walk back down in front of the statue to pose. After many people decided to snap our picture, Eddie's wife, Carolyn, said, "OK, let's take a crazy one." In a fit of spontaneity, I climbed up on

L to R: Dan Leff, Eddie Carroll, Laura Leff (by statue), Bill Powers (on knee), Maria Scarvelis, Eric Brolund, Tom Trethewey, Charlie Willer

the granite base and stood next to the statue. After a fall a couple years ago that almost broke my nose, I had developed a minor fear of falling. So here I was, on a small patch of granite about four feet above Waukegan pavement. I put my hand around the back of Jack's leg to brace myself. Fortunately, Carolyn quickly stepped forward and told me to move my hand, as it looked like I was getting VERY personal with Jack!!! I finally got comfortable enough to let go and strike the classic Benny pose, and was snapped by about 10 cameras. Eddie was also persuaded to climb up on the base and do the pose. Can't wait to see those pictures.

It was getting toward 5:00 and we finished disassembling and packing the equipment. The cast went back to the hotel to relax and change, and I stayed downtown to talk with the two unsung heroes of the day, David Motley and Kelly Link from the Public Relations and Special Events department of the City of Waukegan. Every event has someone who is the mortar between the bricks, the one who holds everything together, and David, Kelly, and Claudia Petrusky of the Jack Benny Center for the Arts were just that. Tom Gillette, Director of the Waukegan Municipal Band was kind enough to give me a lift back to the hotel.

L to R: Joanna Meiseles, Eddie Carroll, Maria Rudolph, Brad Meiseles, Maureen Finn

I arrived just in time for the 7:00 gathering in the lounge. Bill Powers generously bought the first round, and afterwards the group of about 30 people went to the restaurant. The youngest attendee was about 10 years old (there were at least 3 under 20), and the oldest was in their 80s. Although Eddie and Carolyn Carroll had originally intended to join us for just one drink, they graciously stayed through the whole evening and enthralled everyone with stories about Jack and other celebrities, plus a discussion of the challenges of perfecting and performing Jack's character. He commented that he hadn't intended to stay with the crowd so long that afternoon, but if people are enthusiastic and interested, it is worth it to be able to create more positive feelings around the image of Jack Benny.

Three of the grandchildren (Maria, Joanna, and Bobby Blumofe who had arrived after the festivities) joined us for dessert. We rearranged the tables to accommodate them. The conversation continued with plenty of stories, trivia, and reminiscences. Several members commented that they sometimes feel a little isolated as Jack Benny fans, but it was wonderful to be with a large group of people where you can discuss Benny trivia and tell stories...and everyone "gets it."

The evening ended about 11:00. Most of the recreation cast decided that we wanted one more opportunity to discuss the events, so we went back to the rehearsal room to chat over some beverages and potato chips. A good time was had by all.

Sunday, June 9

Several members went to the Museum of Broadcast Communications in downtown Chicago in the afternoon. It's a great place in the Chicago Cultural Center, which I recommend to anyone visiting the area. It includes a replica of Jack Benny's vault, which has a motion sensor that sets off the alarm when you go through the door. Here's the ironic thing...I saw several people go in and out and set off the alarm each time, and someone said, "Go in Laura, and set off the alarm." I walked in...and no alarm. I moved around, and nothing. The person who sent me in had a very confused look. I walked out...and no alarm. I said, "You see, *I* know the password."

Many goodbyes, well-wishes, and looking forward to the opportunity to see each other again. It will be good to get home (and sleep for about a week...writing this on the plane), but this weekend was definitely the IJBFC's proudest moment.

Waukegan Memorabilia

There are a few items available as mementos of the Waukegan celebration (first three available through the address at the end of this newsletter).

¼ Scale Replica of the Waukegan Benny Statue: Waukegan Benny sculptor Erik Blome has extended a fabulous offer to the IJBFC (and anyone else who is interested). He has the mold for the bronze miniature of the Waukegan Benny Statue, and is making a limited edition of 39. $1,800 plus shipping. Please contact me at the address at the end of this newsletter for more information.

"Benny is Back" Poster: Beautiful 11 x 14" full color poster in heavy laminate. See image at left. Quantities are very limited, so order quickly! $10.00 plus $1.00 postage.

Jack Benny Commemorative Book: 24-page booklet telling the story of the statue, local memories of Jack Benny, and a listing of statue donors. $2.00 plus $1.00 postage.

Waukegan Historical Society CD: The Waukegan Historical Society is offering a CD of Jack Benny's two Waukegan-related shows: June 18 and 25, 1939. These have been digitally remastered from transcription disks into WAV format, so it can be played in your car or any regular CD player. Even if you already have a copy of these shows, you can feel good knowing that you are supporting a good cause and improving the sound quality of your collection. $10 plus $3 shipping. Please make checks payable to the Waukegan Historical Society, 1917 North Sheridan Road, Waukegan, Illinois 60087, (847) 336-1859.

BACKSTAGE with Eddie Carroll
Notes from Waukegan

Having performed my one-man show, <u>JACK BENNY: Laughter in Bloom</u>, in theaters across the country for the past fifteen years, I needn't tell you how meaningful it was to be invited to the recent "Benny Bash" in Waukegan. Performing my show the first night for The Jack Benny Center for the Performing Arts was a personal fulfillment. But the next day at the celebration in the town square, I had the added privilege of representing Jack Benny in a re-creation of an authentic radio show as well as introducing the honored guests and taking part in unveiling the new bronze statue of Jack Benny. The statue is diagonally across the street facing the old Genesee Theater where Benny appeared, and is currently being restored to its original elegance. It should be ready to open next fall, and I hope to be the opening performance.

What made the events in Waukegan such fun was meeting so many enthusiastic members of the Jack Benny Fan Club, who traveled long distances to be part of the celebration.

In particular, I would like to single out several members for their contribution that made it special. First to our lovely "leader" Laura Leff, who did an outstanding job in organizing and planning all the details, plus providing and sending out the radio script, writing the revisions, choosing the radio "cast" from the membership,

L to R: Eddie Carroll, Charlie Willer, Bill Powers, Tom Trethewey, Maria Scarvelis, Dan Leff, Eric Brolund arranging and overseeing the rehearsals on a tight schedule and all of it done with professional skill and polish. Bravo!

Second…to all of those special members who were in the radio cast, if any of you had apprehensions about your performance in the show, they certainly disappeared once we were all on stage. From Maria Scarvelis, who portrayed a delightful Mary Livingstone…to "dapper" Bill Powers who sounded and <u>looked</u> like Don Wilson…Laura's husband, "dandy" Dan Leff who physically stretched the credibility gap by playing Rochester, but vocally did a journeyman's job…(as did Laura with a sexy one-liner as Rochester's girlfriend)…the "big noise", Charlie Willer who hauled a truck-load of sound effects from Indiana and did double duty as the voice of Mel Blanc (Si!!!)…Tom Trethewey who played ditzy Dennis Day and not only had the courage to sing an entire song as Dennis, but had double the courage to sing without any music accompaniment…WELLL…!! And finally to our fellow Canuck from Winnipeg (and Calgary) Eric Brolund who played a smooth Phil Harris. (Eric discovered, to his delight, that when rehearsing to play Phil Harris, first you order a double bourbon on the rocks!)

It was great fun to share the stage with all of you. My thanks and applause for a job well done! To all of the IJBFC members, the schedule of my show bookings will be continually updated on the Web site. If I'm appearing in your area, please come by and say hello. Meantime, my best wishes and may you all stay 39 forever!

Waukegan Memories

In the process of arranging the event, I had the pleasure of talking and corresponding with several people from Waukegan who shared their personal memories of Jack.

Gordon Ernst

"I thought you'd be interested in a Jack Benny anecdote about the Ramada Inn on Green Bay Road in Waukegan. In early April 1974, my parents and I returned to Waukegan after living in Northern Ireland and were staying at the Ramada (in those days, the Sheraton I think…it's gone through a few name changes). Mr. Benny was in town to give a benefit concert with the Waukegan Symphony [LL: Saturday, April 20, at 8PM; Dudley Powers, conductor. Tickets were only $7.50 for the main floor or $5.00 for the balcony; for $25 you could attend a champagne reception with Jack afterwards!]. We had a room on the ground floor in a wing on the left side of the hotel (near the lobby, I'm sure the layout of the hotel has changed since then). Mr. Benny had a room on the floor above us (I think the second, I can't remember whether or not there are more than two floors to the hotel) [LL: Just two.]. One day my mother saw Mr. Benny from the window walking to his room (through a glass walk way that connects the lobby with the wing on the left). I walked upstairs and walked past his room. The door was open but I was too shy to look. When I walked back past his room, someone has shut the door (they had seen me walk by, I was only 14 at the time).

"One morning, my mother and I had finished breakfast and were leaving the dining room. We saw Mr. Benny walking down the hall (in the front part of the hotel next to the parking lot) toward the dining room. As we passed him, my mother said, 'Hello, Mr. Benny.' He said, 'Fine, thank you,' (he hadn't heard what she had said, he was 80 years old after all). After we passed him, a woman came running toward us, yelling, 'Mr. Benny! Mr. Benny!' He turned around and said, "Whaaaat?' (just like he would have on radio or on television). I had been too shy to speak to him or to ask for his autograph. So when you are staying at the Ramada, you will know that Jack Benny slept there."

Jack Blumberg

Jack Blumberg had many unique memories of Jack Benny. Blumberg's uncle played in the Barrison orchestra with Jack, and they would reminisce about their "violin days." Blumberg's father was in the furniture business, in competition with Cliff and Ben Gordon, Jack's cousins (see memories of Marvin Gordon for full family information). Despite this, Jack posed with the senior Blumberg for a full-page ad for Simmons that appeared in trade magazines in the late 1940s.

You probably know that Jack's father, Meyer Kubelsky, was in the clothing business. Julius Sinykin was also in the clothing business, and is often mentioned as one of Jack's earliest friends. There are stories in the Marcia Borie biography of how Jack would send him a portion of his pay, which Sinykin would hold for later use. It was in Sinykin's apartment at the Clayton Hotel (now razed, which stood at the southwest corner of Clayton and Sheridan, one block east of the Waukegan statue) that Jack and Mary were married.

Blumberg took a train to Chicago to see a performance of Jack's radio show. One of his friends was with him and asked Blumberg to introduce him to Jack Benny, since he knew him. Blumberg begged off, but Jack came through a back door from the bathroom and overheard the exchange. He walked up to the table and said, "Why don't you introduce me to your friend?"

Blumberg also took Jack out to dinner when he was performing in Cleveland. After Jack switched networks in 1949, Blumberg attended one of the radio shows in Los Angeles. Jack didn't see him, and didn't say anything to him. Blumberg thought that he had become a big star and was "stuck up." When Jack found out he had been there, he called Blumberg immediately and sent a car to bring him to the Roxbury house. Jack took them to the Brown Derby, as they were preparing for a party at the house that night.

When Jack was filming his television show in Waukegan at the Jack Benny Junior High School, he heard that Blumberg's father was there. Jack insisted that the senior Blumberg be brought up to the front row, or he wouldn't do the show. Jack also called Blumberg when his father passed away. He didn't want to come to the memorial service, because he felt that his presence would distract people. This was the same reason that he didn't attend the funeral of his brother-in-law, Leonard Fenchel.

Blumberg recalled that Jack always visited two places in Waukegan: Am Echod and the cemetery. He would look at the memorial board at Am Echod and say, "This is so sad...all my friends are here." He would then go to the cemetery and say, "I don't think I can come back, because all my friends are here now."

Marvin Gordon

I am sorry to say that Marv has passed away since I spoke with him, but I am eternally grateful to him and his wife for generously sharing their time and stories with me. As you will see, they are absolutely priceless.

First, the family tree. Meyer Kubelsky had three sisters: Claire, Becky (Chicago), and (name unknown) (Arizona). Claire Kubelsky married Charles Gordon, and gave birth to Cliff (in 1895) and Ben Gordon.
Cliff Gordon married Sudie Sachs, who was the niece of Emma Sachs (Meyer Kubelsky's wife), and gave birth to Marv Gordon. So...Cliff and Ben Gordon were first cousins to Jack Benny. Marv Gordon is the first cousin once removed to Jack, and Joan's second cousin. Claire, Charles, Cliff, Sudie, and Ben are all buried in the Am Echod cemetery, just in front of Meyer, Emma, and Florence (whose grave is unmarked) Kubelsky and Leonard Fenchel (Florence's husband). Note in the above picture that Emma is buried under the name Naomi, which is also Joan Benny's middle name (Jewish custom dictates that children are named after deceased family members).

When Jack and Cliff Gordon were about seven or eight years old, they decided to hike to Zion City (about seven miles north of Waukegan). When they got there, "their shoes were finished." They wired back to Waukegan for their fathers to send money for them to buy shoes. They got the money, bought the shoes, and returned home. Cliff got some "strong lip service" from his father for it, and "Jack got a licking!"

Meyer was a very strict man, with very little sense of humor and did not allow jokes. He would laugh at Jack's shows, but very little else. Meyer married a widow for a couple years later in life. Florence did not support this marriage, and eventually broke it up. Meyer's last Waukegan house was at 518 Clayton, when he co-owned a clothing store in Lake Forest with Cliff and Ben Gordon. Meyer vacationed in Florida every year in later life, and Florence sometimes went along to take care of him. Meyer went to see one of Jack's movies at a theatre there. Around 6PM, Florence started to wonder where her father was. They went to the theatre, and Meyer was still there. "I just had to see the movie three times," he kvelled. Proud Meyer would sit on a park bench in Florida and say to passersby, "Do you know who I am? I'm Jack Benny's father!"

Claire and Charles Gordon moved to Waukegan from Chicago, because the city was too much and they wanted to raise their kids in a small town. Charles Gordon was in the furniture business. Cliff took over the business when his father died. Ben took it over after Cliff died, Marv took it over after Ben died, and later sold it.

After three years in the Navy, Marv landed in San Diego and was discharged (about 1946). He went directly to Jack's home and knocked on the door. It was answered by a maid, who informed him that Jack was at home but asleep. Marv said, "Just tell him that his cousin, Marv Gordon, is here." She went up and told him, then came back down and said, "Mr. Benny says for you to come right up." They then spent the afternoon together. During this visit he also saw Joan. She was about 12, and was just walking down the street by herself. He thought at the time that she might not be safe and anyone could grab her, but "it was a different time."

Jack said to Marv, "How long has it been since you phoned your mother?" Marv said that it had been three years, since he'd been in the Navy. Jack said that he was going to phone her himself, picked up the phone and dialed. There was no answer. Jack said, "Damnit, she's probably out playing bridge again!"

Jack invited Marv to his radio broadcast the next day, and called him up onstage. He introduced him to Danny Kaye, who was one of the guest stars. He said, "I'd like to introduce you to my cousin, Marv Gordon." Kaye responded, "But I have no cousin Marv Gordon." "No, no, I said **my** cousin," Jack said. They then proceeded to banter for a few minutes. Van Johnson was also there, but talking with Mary.

After the broadcast, Jack said that they were having a party the next night with a number of stars, including Gregory Peck, and invited Marv. Mary said, "Jack, I really don't think that it would be very interesting to Marv." So Jack said, "Well, OK, maybe we can just leave it for next time, Marv." Unfortunately, next time never came. Marv also recalled that Mary would say that she was "very tired", as a hint to people not to stay too long. However over the years, Jack did introduce Marv to a number of celebrities, including Andy Devine (who Marv recalled as a "very nice man"), Dorothy Lamour, Gisele MacKenzie, and Jack Jones.

Marv was married in 1946, and Jack sent a telegram of congratulations. Marv responded with "Where's the check?"

Furniture was not Marv's first career aspiration. He was considering a career in announcing after his marriage in 1946. He had studied acting and public speaking at the University of Wisconsin. Jack got him an interview with NBC. The engineer said, "When the little red light goes on, start talking." His mike fright was very bad, and he did not do well. He brought back a recording from it, and Jack sat down to listen to it with him. Afterwards, Jack said, "Well, what do you think?" Marv said that he thought it was pretty poor. Jack said, "Well, it's not good." However, he committed to getting him something to get his foot in the door. He later called with an opportunity in Wheeling, WV as a beginning announcer for $40 a week. This was not enough money for Marv to support himself and his new wife, so he declined it saying, "I wasn't going to be a Don Wilson."

When Marv vacationed in California, he stayed at the Beverly Wilshire Hotel. When he went to check out, he was told that his bill had already been taken care of by Jack.

Jack stayed with Marv's mother (Sudie Sachs) when he was in Waukegan. He practiced violin in the bathroom. Sudie said to him, "Please, Jack, don't practice so much! My lease is almost up on the place and I don't want to have anyone complain about me!"

Later in life, Jack and his grandson Michael went to the Montreal World's Fair. Marv and his wife had moved there by that time, and it was Marv's son who looked after Michael during the visit. Marv summed up his fond memories of Jack with the words, "He was a real sport."

39 FOREVER CELEBRATION!

With all the enthusiasm from the Waukegan celebration, there was a groundswell of call to have an IJBFC convention. So that's exactly what we're going to do!

SCHEDULE OF EVENTS

We can't yet reveal all of stars that are being engaged for this event, but more details will be provided as celebrities confirm and contracts are signed.

Pre-Event
Script writing contest - entries posted on the Web and members vote on the winner.

Friday evening, February 14, 2003
Birthday party and radio show recreation - featuring EDDIE CARROLL

Opening night gala featuring Eddie Carroll, the world's foremost Jack Benny impressionist. This is as close as you can get to seeing Jack perform live. Plus a recreation by the "Not Ready for Sunday at Seven Players" of the 2/13/49 program where Jack turns 40...or does he? Hors d'oevres, birthday cake, cash bar.

Saturday morning/afternoon, February 15, 2003
The Jack Benny Marathon
A jam-packed day of Benny events, including:
- Jack Benny panels featuring those who knew and worked with him
- Jack Benny jeopardy team challenge
- Screening of Jack Benny television programs
- Jack Benny art show competition
- Auditions for and performance of the winner of the Jack Benny script writing contest
- Dealer area of memorabilia on Jack Benny and other favorite comedy and nostalgia personalities

---

Saturday evening, February 15, 2003
Jack Benny Banquet at the Beverly Hills Friars' Club

An evening of food, music, and comedy devoted to the legacy of Jack Benny. The evening will be capped by the formal induction of Jack into the National Comedy Hall of Fame, with awards being presented to Joan Benny and the family.

Sunday afternoon, February 16, 2003
Down Memory Lane
- Self-guided tours of area Benny sites, such as: his house in Beverly Hills, Graumann's Chinese Theatre, and Hillside Cemetery
- Memorial/Yizkor service at Jack Benny's grave at Hillside Cemetery
- Informal lunch at Canter's Delicatessen (near CBS Television City)

Prices
You can attend any or all of the events (but hey, who wouldn't want to attend the whole thing?). Individual event per-person prices are:
- $30 – Birthday party and recreation
- $50 – The Jack Benny Marathon
- $100 – Jack Benny banquet at the Beverly Hills Friars' Club
- Down Memory Lane – free

EARLY BIRD SPECIAL: People paying for all events before September 1 will receive:
- A free event T-shirt ($16 value), and
- A free year of The Jack Benny Times (a $12.39 value...price increase next year!)

We need to cover deposits for various things, so please send your checks ASAP to:
IJBFC
P.O. Box 11288
Piedmont, CA 94611

Sponsorship activities will begin soon, so please let me know of any groups, companies, foundations, or individuals who might be interested in sponsoring the event. See you in Los Angeles!

Congratulations to Bobby and Joanna

I am happy to report that the Benny clan is expanding, in more ways than one! Bobby Blumofe recently became engaged to Cynthia Breazeal, a professor at MIT, working at the Media Lab on social robots. She was at the Waukegan celebration, and is a truly lovely lady in every way.

Also, Joanna (nee Blumofe) and Brad Meiseles are expecting a third child in December! However, this did not stop them from climbing atop the granite base of the Waukegan statue for a few photographs. (Did anyone get one of them there?) Joanna's oldest son is named Benjamin, in memory of her grandfather.

Jack Bloom Pasadena Chapter

The Jack Bloom Pasadena Chapter was started in 1990 as an honorary society for IJBFC members who have been active for four or more consecutive years. Jack Bloom was a dedicated member of the IJBFC, doing extensive research on him for the Times and the original edition of 39 Forever, plus donating hundreds of shows to kick off the IJBFC tape library. Additionally, Jack and I kept a running correspondence for years, discussing Jack Benny and other shared passions, ranging from George Gershwin to bird watching to bad puns. His passing in June of 1990 was a tremendous loss for all the IJBFC members. I still miss him, and am grateful for the warmth and humor that he shared with me.

Below is the full JPBC membership, with members added this year indicated by an asterisk.

Jefry N. Abraham	Frank Gregory *	Kenneth Levites	Joel S. Rothman
David A. Adler	Joseph F. Gross	James A. Link	Rhiman A. Rotz
Michael Avedissian	Bryan Haigood	Patricia Link	Richard Rubenstein
Al Baggetta *	The Hardings	Mark R. Linke	John Saucinas *
Neil J. Baskin	Jon Heinz	Stephen H. Loeb	Rick Scheckman
Bernard Beckert	Tom Heathwood	Bobb Lynes	Clair Schulz *
Dennis Benedict	Franklin Heynemann	Howard Mandelbaum *	Scott Severson
Louis Bianco *	Jimmie Hicks	Hooman Mehran *	Mel Simons
Steve Brent	Richard Hill	Steve Metzger *	Gary Smith *
James G. Burke	Ellis Hogue *	Walt Mitchell *	Scott J. Smith *
Charles Burton	The Hornbergers *	Russell Myers	Steve Smith
C.A. Caramella	Bill Housos	George W. Nichols	W. Robert Smith
Rob Cohen	David Howell	Robert Nystrom	Helen Songer
Francis W. Daly	Connie Johnson *	Jack Palmer	Benjamin Spangler
Warren Debenham	The Jonases	Lewis Pearson	Bonnie Spangler
Anthony DiFlorio *	Margie Jones	Teresa Perry *	Gus Storm
Steve Dillie	Will Jordan	Paul Pinch	Gary Tallman
Matthew M. Drew	Larry Kampwirth	John Poole *	Barbara Thunell
Ray Druian *	Thomas Kessel *	Alvin Post	Eva Tintorri
Wayne Ennis	Nik Kierniesky	Frank Pozzuoli	Marion Tintorri
Charles Fair	Kenneth Klein	Richard Rieve	Bill Twillie
Don Friedrich	Kenneth Koftan	Clive Roberts	Larry Valley
J. Ed Galloway	Caroline Lake	The Robertses	Harvey Walker *
Robert L. Garland	Steve Lake	Elinore Rogers *	Mary Lou Wallace *
Joe Goff	Michael Leannah *	James Rogers *	Ken L. Yesson
Bill Graff *	Sam Levene	A. Joseph Ross	

Emeritus Members (15+ years)

Jack Abizaid	LeRoy Fillenwarth	George Lillie	Joyce Shooks
Bruce Baker	Marilyn Fillenwarth	Tom Mastel	David Spangler
Jack Bloom	Alan Grossman	Bill Oliver	Steve Szejna
Hal Bogart	Jay Hickerson	Robert Olsen	Barbara Watkins
Robert Duncan	Tim Hollis	Donnie Pitchford	Ken Weigel
Phil Evans	Saree Kaminsky	John Schlamp	Doug Wood

Tape Trading List

Rob Cohen, 1603 Harrison Pond Dr., New Albany, OH 43054; robcohen@ameritech.net - Rob is also interested in trading MP3s of other comedy shows (e.g., Fibber McGee, etc.)

George Grube, 6402 Rolling Greens Dr., Ocala, FL 34472; Ontime6402@aol.com

Laura Leff, P.O. Box 11288, Piedmont, California 94611, USA; JackBenny@aol.com

Janet Maday, maydaymayday@aol.com

John Matthews, glowingdial@yahoo.com

Jay Meade, 681 Straits Rd., Gloucester, NC 28528; jmeade@starfishnet.com

Jack Palmer, 145 N. 21st St., Battle Creek, MI 49015; vdalhart@prodigy.net

Brendan Scherer, goldenstar4@juno.com

Jeff Tanner, P.O. Box 65787, Vancouver, WA 98686, USA; TannerJeff@aol.com

John Tisinger, 1998 Clem-Lowell Rd., Carrollton, GA 30116-9253 jdtisinger@peachnet.campuscwix.net

Lynn Wagar, philcolynn@aol.com (cassette only)

Drew Wiest, 6109 NE 197th St, Kenmore, WA 98028, USA; dwiest12@hotmail.com

Ken Yesson, 4316 – 83 St., Edmonton, Alberta T6K-0Z5 Canada; yesandno@connect.ab.ca

The Review of the Revue

This article appeared in the November 1918 issue of <u>The Great Lakes Recruit</u>, a magazine that was published solely by and for the Great Lakes Naval Training Center where Jack was stationed during World War I. This tells the full story of the production where Jack had his first speaking role. My gracious thanks to Cary Wiesner for locating it before his departure from the GLNTC. We are all in your debt!

When the blasé metropolitan theatrical critics, hardened by the nightly jesting of the comedian or the warbling of the Prima Donna or still the gnarling of the mustached villain, calls it the best show in town, why it must be. Such was the honor that fell to the "Great Lakes Revue," which was acted entirely by Great Lakes sailors for the benefit of the Navy Relief Society and the Lying-In Hospital, for the wives and mothers of enlisted men at the Great Lakes Naval Training Station.

It was a farce cleverly acted, with a sprinkling of vaudeville thrown in. It was spicy enough to hold interest and it fairly oozed with songs that will be hummed with growing popularity for some time. The personnel of the cast of characters discloses a number of stars from "big time," who not so long ago had their names blazing in huge electric lights along the rialto in cities of some size. The effect of the show on the public can well be illustrated by a remark overheard on a street car in Chicago. "It's the best show I've seen for a dollar and a half for some time," said a middle aged lady. "In fact it can't be duplicated in town." So much for the success of the farce.

The story opens in one of the barracks at the Great Lakes Naval Training Station. It is after taps. Of course the men are in their hammocks. Enter the truculent God of War, shining majestically in his armor, who with low bass voice discusses martial problems confronting him. Few could be more sanguine than Duke Staples. But wait, hoary Neptune enters clad as the "Field Marshall" of the sea. He converses volubly with Sam Green (Bob Carleton), a rookie of five days, and before he departs, in confidential voice he informs the doubting "rook," still "shotless," that from that time on he is an Admiral. The fun starts almost simultaneously with the entrance of Issy There, the "Admiral's" orderly. Too much credit cannot be given to Benny Kubelsky, who played the orderly role. He is a laugh provoker who caused many to return to their homes still holding their sides. It's a delicate part to play, too. Yet there was nothing amateurish about the acting of this sailor who claims Waukegan for his home. He is a comedian of merit, whose clean, wholesome comedy is natural.

But on with the playlet. Admiral "rookie" Green, coached a bit by his overzealous orderly, with military precision starts to give orders. But first he must awaken the somnolent men in the hammocks. He has his uniform, the sleeves to the elbows glisten of gold. "Who wants a shot in the arm?" he inquires first. But the hammocks remain quiet. No one stirs. Interrogation number two is "Who wants some navy beans?" Still no response. Orderly and Admiral confer. Result is question number three. "Who wants a ten day furlough?" Pandemonium holds sway for some time. It goes over big. Quite realistic, eh?

But listen to the alleged Admiral's first mandate. In forceful tones, strutting about before the footlights, he arrogantly informs his "crew" that soon there is to be a "revue."

Not of the popular weekly affairs at the Great Lakes, but a R-E-V-U-E which will bring out all the thespian material. This is greeted with handclapping and shouts. With a few incidentals, snappy repartee and clever patter the vaudeville is on. This starts when the curtain arises on the second act.

Rupp & Linden start things. The do a piano and violin specialty and do it well. They span that big gap that separates the classical from the more popular raggy music with great success. There were many calloused hands after this choice act. Both participants are musicians of merit. The act would go well at any of the popular variety houses in any metropolis.

The Great Lakes Quartette harmonizes next and these four sailors with the pleasing voices sing well.

Duke Staples, with a clever impersonation of the internationally famous evangelist, Billy Sunday, follows. Those who have heard and seen the fighting preacher who indulges in acrobats and invectives in describing "Demon" Booze and the Kaiser received a perpetual laugh in "Duke." His lines are funny, his acting clever and in all it's a very good effort.

But without a scintilla of doubt, variety critics would select the Ja Da Trio as the headliner on any bill. The trio made up of Carleton, Rosenberg and Sobol are natural comedians, with a two fisted punch of honest to goodness comedy. They're original, these Ja Da boys, with a "jazzy" act that makes the most Puritanical matron sway her shoulders syncopatedly. Both Carleton and Rosenberg are delightful contributors to the entire show. There's a frolic or a laugh every time one or the other walks near the footlights and because they hold the stage continuously one need not explain further why the show was such a success.

The next act is billed as the Great Lakes Tumblers and this, too, proves interesting. They do the usual strong man stunts while large muscles bulge.

Then Benny (Kubelsky), with his trick violin, trips lightly on the stage. He has with him [Zez] Confrey, a piano player of merit, who is a good running mate with his inimitable partner. "Benny" plays the violin in a style all of his own. One might suspect that this team worked together for years. This act pleases and goes over "big."

A syncopated wedding which causes much mirth and is really ludicrous takes place near the finale. Admiral Green takes unto him one Clementine Speed (Chester Rosenberg). It was a snappy affair that caused the toe of the right foot to beat time to the extremely raggy melody.

But before the curtain is rung down and the Admiral exposed there are many deserving of creditable mention and words of praise for the part they played in the success of the Great Lakes Revue. Harry Fender, a former member of the Park Opera Company of St. Louis and who was sought by many of the most celebrated of producers, indeed aided greatly in the success of the show. He is an actor from the tip of his graceful toes to his neatly sleeked dark brown hair. He is as graceful as man can be and his voice is all that can be asked for.

Walter Peterson, who sang the opening number, showed ability, as did Clyde Olney, who took the part of a grouchy C.P.O. The chorus was a novelty. They danced and pirouetted with the ease and grace of the professional.

There are many others deserving of credit. Take for example James O'Keefe. Mr. O'Keefe wrote all the lyrics and music. Any man that can write songs like "When the Great Lakes Band Goes Marching on Parade," "Hija, My Pretty Nile Queen," "June Moon," "Good-Bye America," "Clementine," "Naughty Little Front Row Girl," "The Ragtime Wedding," and "I've Been Waiting for You," is clever. Every one is a gem in the music world. But take "When the Great Lakes Band Goes Marching on Parade." It's a haunting thing full of good melody. It should live for some time.

Then, too, there are many folks who are deserving of much credit, but who never showed before the footlights. Take for example the graceful Dolly Sisters. The two stars from "Oh, Look" came out to the Great Lakes on several occasions and taught the cast a few of the finer steps in Terpsichore. With them came the clever husband of "Dolly" Yansei, Harry Fox. Their work was appreciated by officers of the Navy Relief Society. But then Dave

Wolff, playwright and good fellow, must not be overlooked. Few worked as hard as Mr. Wolff. He was "on the Station" late evenings listening to rehearsals, coaching, persistent and confident. His work is appreciated by thousands of Station men.

There's no mistaking the prominent part the orchestra played. For what's a musical comedy without an orchestra? And what an orchestra! Gathered directly in front of the stage in that orchestra pit were many celebrities in the music world, now fiddling or saxophoning for Liberty. There's no way to get around that, the music was good and any show with pretty music well played is bound to go over. Hence the success of the Great Lakes Revue.

Debutantes, many of them of Chicago's four hundred, sold programs and stimulated the sale of Liberty Bonds, which was a nightly affair. They, too, deserve much credit for the ardent spirit they showed and their untiring efforts toward one of Uncle Sam's projects. Through their work many thousands of dollars of Liberty Bonds were sold.

Secretary of the Navy Daniels was a visitor for the show. He made a short talk and was accompanied by Captain Moffett.

IJBFC Members Coast to Coast
L to R: Gary Smith (Maine), Barbara Thunell (California) and Hal Bogart (Ohio)

Benny is All in the Family
L to R: Eddie Carroll, Benny Rothman, Jeri Rothman, Joel Rothman, and Michael Rothman

The Jack Benny Times

January – April 2003 Volume XVIII, Numbers 1-2

President's Message

This has been an unbelievably busy time for the IJBFC with preparations for 39 Forever, and lots of member activity and interest. We are currently launching our 39 Forever media campaign, so watch for us on the news and in the papers! If you know of anyone in your area who would be interested in getting more information about the event, please contact me by E-mail or regular mail at the address at the end of this letter.

The club has now grown to about 1,300 members in 15 countries: United States, Canada, Mexico, England, Scotland, France, Belgium, the Netherlands, Sweden, Germany, Spain, Israel, China, Japan, and Australia. Through the Web, we are getting an average of a new member every couple of days. Wonderful to see all the continuing interest, and all the different places that people have encountered the humor of Jack Benny (including through recent retrospectives of CBS Television City and Bob Hope).

Thanks to so many of you for your help, support, and encouragement during this busy time. I wish all of you a healthy and happy holiday season, and I hope to see many of you next February! -- LL

New Members

**** Tom Wagner **** David Wilk **** Chris McDonald **** Dan Eckelbarger **** Erica Fujiwara **** Jim Hilliker **** Lindsay Salvati **** Brandon Reed **** Cathy Rokicki **** Rick Clemons **** Steve Rodrigues **** Todd Dowell **** Dwayne L. Gobin, II **** Jack Richards **** Thomas Osborne **** Randy Larson **** David M. Lynch **** Lisa Stewart **** John Ambrose **** Rob Beaton **** Brian Tucker **** Mary Short **** Lizzy Barron **** Kevin Wierda **** Richard Carver **** Larry F. Herndon **** Chantell Richardson **** Jay Edwards **** Ralph H. Hall, Jr. **** Bob Wombacher, Jr. **** Terri Simon **** Steven Lewis **** Jerry McDaniel **** Anthony Miranda **** Chris Jackson **** John M. Brown **** Ralph Phillips **** Tony Ashlin **** S. Duncan Miller **** William and Patricia Lackner **** Will Stifel **** Richard Holland **** Jess Walker **** Dave Walker **** Paul Thornton **** Josef E. Silvia **** Chris Larsen **** Floyd Kirk **** David Lambert **** Nathanael Long **** Patrick Maue **** Len Winter **** Jeff Boldman **** Mark Stenger **** Art Leason **** Francis Hajash **** Jim Syoen **** Christine Schreiber **** Stephen Helfant **** Stephen M. Sipos **** Jay Ranellucci **** Evan Golding **** Colin G. Campbell **** Jennifer Morgan **** Ron Fleishman **** Mark Huffstutter **** Jerry Hippert **** Roger Weiss **** Steve Block **** Dave Hood **** Elisabeth Rossman **** David Law **** Carl Vitelli, Jr **** Chris Watkins **** Steve MacKay **** Paul J. Duggan **** Carol LeVan **** Frank Nova **** Matthew Bullis **** Edward Freeman **** Brian Gunther **** Mike Finger **** Marcus B. Johnson **** George Granger **** Lauren Rogers **** Gordon Stevens **** Deanna Nakashima **** Robert Cohen **** Andrew Godfrey **** Wesley Laverdure **** Andy Kasparson **** Vincent Spiteri **** Mark

Bobbitt **** Wayne Taylor **** Gabriella Guilfoil **** Jessica Diggs **** DJ MacIntosh **** Jules Young **** Shelly Lester **** Alan Glaser **** Ivan & Eva Ulz **** Len Klatt **** Jack Sobel **** Donald DuBrule **** Mark Solkoff **** Richard Erickson **** Berdetta Moore **** Robert Glenn **** Erwin L Nudel **** J Hicks **** Jeannette Burris **** Dale Newman **** Michael Simons **** John Wong **** Gary Crowe **** Anthony F. Baechler, Baechler, III **** Noiel Spearman **** Mitch Roberts **** Matt Collins **** Brad Vereen **** Lisa L. Moll **** Charles Sellers **** Robert J. Seiler, Sr.

39 FOREVER

Sponsored by JELL-O

And the Levine Communications Office

SCHEDULE OF EVENTS

Friday evening, February 14, 2003

Birthday party and radio show recreation – featuring EDDIE CARROLL and NOEL BLANC

Sheraton Gateway Hotel Los Angeles Airport, 7:00PM to 10:00PM

Opening night gala featuring Eddie Carroll (pictured at left), star of the long-running one-man Jack Benny tribute, Laughter in Bloom. This is as close as you can get to seeing Jack perform live. The "Not Ready for Sunday at Seven Players" will present a recreation of a program where Jack turns 40...or does he? Noel Blanc, son of legendary voice artist Mel Blanc, will reprise his father's role. Which one? Attend and find out!

Hors d'oevres, birthday cake, cash bar.

Saturday morning/afternoon, February 15, 2003
The Jack Benny Marathon
Sheraton Gateway Hotel Los Angeles Airport, 8:00AM to 4:30PM

- Jack Benny speakers featuring those who knew and worked with him, including:
  Daughter JOAN BENNY - hosted by writer and talk radio personality Michael Levine
  Manager IRVING FEIN
  Grandson MICHAEL RUDOLPH
- Jackpardy: the Jack Benny jeopardy-style team challenge
- Screening of Jack Benny television programs
- Jack Benny art show competition
- Auditions for and performance of the winner of the Jack Benny script writing contest
- Dealer room of memorabilia on Jack Benny and other favorite comedy and nostalgia personalities

---

Saturday evening, February 15, 2003
39 Forever Celebrity Banquet at the Beverly Hills Friars' Club
Cocktails 7:00PM, Dinner 7:30PM, Entertainment 8:30-10:30PM

A star-studded evening of food, music, and comedy devoted to the legacy of Jack Benny. The evening will be capped by the formal induction of Jack into the National Comedy Hall of Fame, with awards being presented to Joan Benny and the family.

featuring...the fabulous INK SPOTS!

The Ink Spots and the Manny Harmon Trio will share their extraordinary musical legacy at the 39 Forever banquet. The Ink Spots appeared on the Jack Benny program in 1948 and 1950, and continued to be one of Jack's favorite musical groups.

The Ink Spots have had 86 hit recordings ... many of them million sellers. "IF I DIDN'T CARE" (their "anthem") has sold 19 million copies. Some of their other million sellers are:

My Prayer
For Sentimental Reasons
Marie
and many more!

Whispering Grass
Maybe
We Three

Sunday afternoon, February 16, 2003
Down Memory Lane

- All-day Museum of Television and Radio Benny exhibits and screenings or rarely-seen Benny material, including Jack Benny's specials, <u>Shower of Stars</u> appearances, <u>Carnegie Hall Salutes Jack Benny</u>, and Jack Benny programs featuring guests such as Harry Truman, Fred Allen, Frank Sinatra, Groucho Marx, Ginger Rogers, John Wayne, Rock Hudson, and many more.
- Self-guided tours of area Benny sites, such as: his house in Beverly Hills, Graumann's Chinese Theatre, Hillside Cemetery, and more.
- 12:00PM - Memorial/Yizkor service at Jack Benny's grave at Hillside Cemetery
- 1:00PM - Informal lunch at Canter's Delicatessen (near CBS Television City)

ATTENDANCE FEES

$30   Birthday party and radio show recreation - featuring EDDIE CARROLL and NOEL BLANC
$50   The Jack Benny Marathon - featuring JOAN BENNY, IRVING FEIN, and much more!
$100   Celebrity banquet at the Beverly Hills Friars' Club - featuring THE INK SPOTS
$180   ALL EVENTS

Pay online with your credit card on our Web site, or make checks payable to IJBFC and mail

☆ BY DECEMBER 31, 2002 ☆

to IJBFC, P.O. Box 11288, Piedmont, CA 94611.

HOTEL INFORMATION

The Sheraton Gateway Hotel Los Angeles Airport, located at 6101 West Century Boulevard, Los Angeles, California, is the official hotel of the 39 Forever Celebration. All Friday and Saturday events (except for the Friars' Club banquet) will be held at that location. We have negotiated the following excellent rates:

Room	Single Rate	Double Rate
Nonsmoking King	$89 per night	$89 per night
Nonsmoking Double	$89 per night	$89 per night

These prices are exclusive of applicable state and local taxes.

How to Reserve
Please contact the hotel's reservation department at 310-642-1111 or through the Central Reservation Office at 800-325-3535. Identify yourself as being with the International Jack Benny Fan Club. **All reservations for these special rates must be made by January 24, 2003.**

Related Information
Shuttle service is available from Los Angeles Airport. All reservations will be held after 5:00PM and guaranteed for late arrival only if accompanied by a first night room deposit or guaranteed to a major credit card. Guests will be responsible for their own guest room, tax and incidental charges.

HOW YOU CAN GET INVOLVED!

Script Contest
Always envied George, Sam, Milt and Tack (or Hal and Al...or Morrow and Beloin...or, you get the idea)? Now's your chance to write your own Jack Benny radio program. Here are the rules:

- Entries must be a maximum of 15 minutes in length (approximately 11½ pages with 1½ line spacing). There is no minimum length.
- Entries must have a minimum of 2 and a maximum of 6 characters.
- Only sound effects that can be done with materials that can be readily found within the hotel should be included.
- Entries should not include language or references that would not be appropriate for performance before an audience that includes children. The IJBFC may turn an entry back to the author for editing if something is deemed inappropriate.
- Entries must be submitted via E-mail to jackbenny@aol.com no later than midnight, December 31, 2002.
- Entries must be in an MS Word-compatible format, rich text, or plain text. Entries may also be sent within the body of the submitting E-mail.
- Entries will be posted to the IJBFC Web page after January 1, 2003. The author's name and state/country will accompany the posting.
- Members will be invited to review the entries and vote on their favorite.
- Voting will be concluded at midnight, January 31, 2003. The results will be tabulated and reviewed by the IJBFC council to insure fairness and accuracy.

- The winning entry will be announced at the opening gala on February 14, 2003, and performed during the 39 Forever Celebration on February 15, 2003. Auditions will be held for all parts in the morning, and the performance done at approximately 4PM.
- No prizes other than the performance of the winning script will be awarded.
- All entries become property of the IJBFC, which reserves the right to publish any or all of the entries, in whole or in part.
- Entries must be original works, but may reference or use portions of scripts within the Fair Use Act restrictions. The IJBFC is not responsible for any copyright violations.
- The IJBFC reserves the right to refuse any entry that does not conform to these rules.

Art Contest

A picture is worth a thousand words...but our Jack Benny art contest isn't just limited to pictures. If Jack inspires you to draw, paint, carve, sculpt, or work in any visual media, you can be in the 39 Forever art contest. Here are the rules:

- Entries may be of any media that can be readily exhibited without requiring additional technology (e.g., no sound recordings, slide shows, etc.).
- Entries should not include any subject matter that would not be suitable for an audience that includes children.
- Artists will be responsible for transporting their work to the hotel and displaying it in a location to be assigned for art contest entries. No specific lighting or display supports will be provided.
- Artists may retain ownership of their entry after the contest, or donate it to the IJBFC. Items donated to the IJBFC will be auctioned off during the 39 Forever Celebration.
- Artists must make known their intent to enter the art contest via E-mail to jackbenny@aol.com no later than midnight, December 31, 2002. This E-mail must include: the artist name, address, phone number, a brief description of the intended work, and whether they are willing to donate it for the art auction.
- Artists must submit a photo of their work, by E-mail or regular mail, by midnight December 31, 2002.
- Entries will be displayed at the 39 Forever Celebration during the day's activities of February 15, 2003. Attendees will be invited to vote for their favorite via secret ballot, to be placed in a sealed box by the display area.
- Voting will be concluded at approximately 4:30PM, February 15, 2003. The results will be tabulated and reviewed by the IJBFC council to insure fairness and accuracy.
- The winning entries will be announced at approximately 5PM, February 15, 2003. The prizes will be as follows:
First prize   Five years of The Jack Benny Times ($62 value)
Second prize   A copy of the 1984-1995 back issues ($45 value)
Third prize   A copy of 39 Forever ($15 value)

- The IJBFC reserves the right to publish photographic or other reproductions of any work, in whole or in part.
- Entries must be original works. The IJBFC is not responsible for any copyright violations.
- The IJBFC reserves the right to refuse any entry that does not conform to these rules.

39 Forever T-Shirts

Back by popular demand, we are offering T-shirts commemorating 39 Forever. These sharp-looking shirts are black with the photo of Jack playing the violin that graces the cover of this issue. The shirts will also feature the fan club and event names, and the dates below the photograph. ORDER **NOW,** as the quantity will be based on response and very few extras will be available. Available in adult S, M, L, XL, XXL. Wear your shirt to the celebration as a proud IJBFC member and to connect with other members—or wear it at home and be there in spirit.

The cost is $16 per shirt. Shirts will be available for pickup at the front desk of the Sheraton Gateway Hotel. If you will not be at 39 Forever, include $4 postage for the first shirt, and $2 postage for each additional shirt. Please send checks (payable to IJBFC) to: P.O. Box 11288, Piedmont, CA 94611. **ORDERS MUST BE RECEIVED BY JANUARY 15, 2003.**

What's Up in Waukegan?

I am pleased and proud to announce that Eddie Carroll has been named Honorary Mayor of Waukegan. Here's the text of the official proclamation:

RESOLUTION 02-R-63

WHEREAS, on June 7th 2002 Eddie Carroll attended the Jack Benny Bash at Bonnie Brook Golf Course; and
WHEREAS, on June 8th 2002 Eddie Carroll attended the Dedication of the Jack Benny Plaza and Statue; and
WHERAS, Eddie Carroll entertained the audiences at both events with his wonderful impersonation of Waukegan's favorite son Jack Benny; and
WHEREAS, Eddie Carroll has dedicated a substantial portion of his entertainment career instilling the memory of Jack Benny into the hearts and minds of audiences throughout the world,
NOW THEREFORE, BE IT RESOLVED, that the Mayor and City Council of the City of Waukegan recognize Eddie Carroll as HONORARY MAYOR of the City of Waukegan.
BE IT FURTHER RESOLVED, that a suitable embossed copy of this Resolution signed by the Mayor and City Clerk be presented to Eddie Carroll.
DATED THIS 15TH DAY OF JULY, 2002 – Richard Hyde, Mayor of Waukegan

The renovation of the Genesee Theatre is moving along even more quickly than expected. The opening, originally planned for Fall of 2003 may be as early as the Spring. We will keep you informed of the official dates and planned events as they unfold. You can find more information at www.geneseetheatre.org.

I recently received a beautiful banner that was the prototype for several such banners that have been hung in downtown Waukegan around the Benny Plaza. These banners are purple and turquoise, and feature the face of the famous Bouché line drawing (pictured at left).

The IJBFC has also donated a copy of our entire MP3 library to the Waukegan Public Library. We are proud to be able to bring a full collection of Jack's audio work to his hometown, so that Waukeganites can learn more about their own famous son. We encourage members in the Chicago area to go to the Waukegan Library (just a block West of the statue) and enjoy the collection.

The Tale Piece

Here's one from Hal Stone, author of the recent release <u>Aw...Relax, Archie! Re-laxx!</u> about his work in radio (best known as Jughead in <u>Archie</u>) and as a television director. The book is available for $26 from Bygone Days Press, P.O. Box 4418, Sedona, AZ 86340 (and Hal's not even giving me a percentage for that plug). This story is from the OTR Digest, to which everyone OTR fan on the Web should subscribe (see the bottom of our Links page for help in doing so).

"I met Jack Benny once. I didn't work for him, but does 'auditioning' for him count?

"Benny had to be in NY for some reason, and was arranging to originate his program from there. (For how many weeks I don't remember). It seems a young kid was needed on the show in a small part. I was called to go read for Jack Benny personally. It was the first and only time in my career that I auditioned outside of a radio studio. I had to go to the Plaza Hotel where Mr. Benny had a suite of rooms. I knocked on his Hotel Room door and it was answered by Mr. Benny himself. (Not Rochester) :)

"He ushered me in (wearing slacks and a fancy dressing gown), and after a few pleasantries, I looked over the script, read the part for him, and that was it. I didn't get the job, and I don't even recall who did. He probably interviewed a few youngsters that morning, and he was undoubtedly looking for a specific type.

"My impressions from meeting the big star that Mr. Benny was, are as follows. A nice guy, pleasant and highly professional, (but obviously, no judge of talent. :) Sorry, folks, I'm just kidding around. I had to throw that line in for a laugh. I have a reputation to protect.

"In short, Benny seemed like a very personable guy. It was a kick for me to meet him one on one like that. I guess I was somewhere between the age of 12 and 15. I just remember being there. I can't remember dates."

The Regulars

The past few months have brought some rather interesting tidbits about various regular members of the Benny cast. Here's a tray full of newsbytes on the names after Jack and Mary (and one that wasn't, whom we all know anyway!).

Artie Auerbach
(From Shelly Lester, niece of Artie Auerbach) "I was 11 when my uncle died. He was born in New York City of Polish descent. His father was a dancer in London and won a medal from Queen Victoria (my twin brother has it). I believe he was born in 1903, but I have to check my records. His father (Wolfgang, also known as William) died young and the family was poor. He (nor did his two sisters, my mother Dorothy and Aunt Anne) never went to high school. He got a job as a photographer for the Daily Mirror. SUPPOSEDLY, he took a picture (illegally) of a person in the electric chair, but I could never substantiate that although I have seen the picture in the paper . According to my mother he got his education in the New York Public Library. They spoke Yiddish in the home, but he had no accent in real life.

"He lived in Hollywood with his wife Doris (in fact, I lost touch with her and I presume she is dead, but she was a good deal younger than he and I wonder if she is alive somewhere). They never had kids. Supposedly he was married to Lucille Ball's half sister (first wife) but I cannot substantiate that either.

"He was funny even before radio and TV - always playing practical jokes on the family. When we were toddlers he brought me those wooden beads with the shoe strings - we sat on the floor and played with them for hours. He adored us, but we did not see him that often. One thing he used to say - my mother used to quiz him about the actors he lived next to (Hopalong Cassidy) and he said, 'They all sh*t the same way.' He was the most down to earth person - I only wish I knew him better as I was so young when he died. He never made it big, but did okay!

"He died of an embolism in the aorta, not a heart attack as originally thought. He was in his fifties. I have a picture of him somewhere. My mother had very little memorabilia, which I feel bad about.

"Here is the clincher. I found out a few years ago that I was adopted and that Uncle Artie arranged for the adoption and paid for it."

(Shelly is looking for videos, DVD, photos, or other media that feature her father. If you are able to help, please let me know at the address at the end of this newsletter and I will put you in touch with her. - LL)

Dennis Day's death date coincidence
(From Brad Zinn) "June 22 marks the anniversary of the passing of Dennis Day in 1988. I find it interesting that this same day marks the passing of Fred Astaire and Judy Garland."

Dennis Day's recording career
(Not an exhaustive discussion...anyone want to write an article?)
(From Tom Wagner) "In 1946, right after he got out of the service, he recorded for Capitol Records. He recorded about 12 songs and then moved on to RCA Victor."

At Victor, he had several hit records which were (according to Joel Whitburn's Pop Memories):

Label/#	Title	Charted	Peak	Weeks
Victor 2211	Mam'selle	5/3/47	8	5
Victor 2810	Clancy Lowered the Boom	3/26/49	23	1
Victor 3102	Dear Hearts and Gentle People	1/14/50	14	4
Victor 3870	Goodnight Irene	8/26/50	17	8
Victor 3753	Mona Lisa	8/26/50	29	1
Victor 3870	All My Love	10/14/50	22	4
Victor 4140	Mister and Mississippi	6/9/51	13	7

Eddie Anderson's singing, dancing, and other performances
(Again not an exhaustive discussion...another potential article.) (From Michael) "I just got through watching my copy of "Buck Benny Rides Again", and all I have to say is WOW is Eddie Anderson a great dancer! I especially love the song he sings with Josephine (while Jack is standing outside in the rain)! Now for the question. Are there any other films where one can see Eddie Anderson in action? I've seen him in the Charlie McCarthy film "You can't cheat an honest man" but I feel he is SADLY wasted in that movie."

- Two great dance numbers in Man About Town
- (From Gerry O.) MGM's "Cabin In The Sky". Eddie has a leading role in this musical, and he does a great dance while Ethel Waters sings "Taking A Chance On Love".
- (From Gerry O.) Paramount's "Star Spangled Rhythm". This WWII musical was one of those all-star revues which featured many specialty acts and only a HINT of a plot line! Eddie is dressed in a zoot suit and performs the lively number "Sharp As A Tack".

- (From Kurt) Anderson had two good dramatic parts in pictures: With Bette Davis in "Jezebel" and as Uncle Peter in "Gone With The Wind," in which he's so heavily made up, you wonder why they cast him. He's also very funny in "Topper Returns" and "It's a Mad, Mad, Mad Mad World," although both performances are marred by racist stereotyping.

Eddie Anderson's recording of "My, My"
(From the OTR Digest) Anderson made a commercial recording of "My! My!" that was released on a Columbia 78 rpm single, catalogue number 35442. "Let's Scuffle" was on the flip side.

Eddie Anderson's racehorse
(From Kurt, excerpted from Paul Moran's story "Black Owner Seeks Date with History" in Newsday, May 5, 1988; the article discusses Jim Cottrell's horse in the Kentucky Derby)

"Black owners have been few and far between in the Derby's first 113 years. Since 1943, Cottrell is only the second black owner of a Derby starter, and he is believed to be the first black man to breed a Derby horse.

"Henry Greene, who was co-owner of a colt named Partez, the third finisher in the 1981 Derby, claimed to be the first black owner of a Derby starter, but there were at least four others before him. An exact number is unknown because black jockeys and trainers were regular participants during the Derby's early years, and it is believed that blacks occasionally owned Derby starters then.

"There is a gap of 38 years between Greene's appearance here and 1943, when actor Eddie Anderson, who played Rochester on the Jack Benny radio and television programs, sent a colt named Burnt Cork to the Derby. The colt was beaten by 38 lengths, and Anderson was criticized for using the Derby for publicity purposes, a charge he denied."

Phil Harris' bar order
(From Kurt, excerpted from a larger Los Angeles Times article on Boardner's)
"It was a 20-year golden age for Steve Boardner and his cocktail lounge, a time when former Tommy Dorsey singer Jack Leonard (Scotch and water) would regularly drop in, as would Errol Flynn (beer), and members of Xavier Cugat's band after playing at their boss' club. Another big presence was Boardner's longtime friend, the singer and bandleader Phil Harris (coffee and anisette), whose routine was to say goodbye to his wife, Alice Faye, after the two dined at Musso & Frank, then head over to Boardner's for a rendezvous with his mistress."

Don Wilson on Batman
(From Walt Pattinson) "I just saw Don Wilson as a newscaster on a Batman episode with the
Penguin, episode titled "Dizzoner the Penguin," second of a two parter where Penguin and Batman run for mayor. Don plays the role of Walter Klondike. What a surprise!"

Don Wilson on children's records
(From Charlie Willer) CLASSICS FOR CHILDREN Vol. 1 and 2, "Delightful stories introducing young people to great music"
Performed by The Continental Symphony Orchestra   Narrated by: Art Gilmore and Don Wilson

Don Wilson obituary
(From The Washington Post, April 27, 1982, Tuesday)

Teamed in 1934; Don Wilson Dies; Was Jack Benny Foil for 40 Years

PALM SPRINGS, Calif. - Don Wilson, 81, the rotund announcer who was Jack Benny's foil on radio and television for more than 40 years, died Sunday in a hospital here after a stroke.

Mr. Wilson was found unconscious Sunday afternoon by his wife, the retired actress Lois Corbet, at their home in Cathedral City, Calif. He was pronounced dead at the Eisenhower Medical Center. Mr. Wilson moved to the Palm Springs resort area after Benny's television show went out of production in 1965. During the past several years, Mr. Wilson had done commercials and hosted a local afternoon television talk show produced by his wife, often interviewing old friends from Benny's radio and television shows.

Mr. Wilson became Benny's announcer on radio in 1934. He stayed with the show when it successfully moved to television in 1950.

"I'm not really an announcer for Benny in the sense that fellows are on other shows," Mr. Wilson once said in an interview. "The reason for that is because Jack worked me into the cast over the years."

Benny, who died in 1974, often joked on the show about Mr. Wilson's weight. The 6-foot-2 announcer weighed about 240 pounds. The comedian made him sound a lot bigger.

Mr. Wilson's show-business career also included appearances in several Broadway plays, movies and other television shows.

"Jack has been very nice to me," he said. "He doesn't mind me doing other things. Some comedians wouldn't think of letting a character from their show work with other comics, but Jack doesn't even object to that."

Mr. Wilson was born in Lincoln, Neb. He began his career as a singer with a trio that made its radio debut in 1924 on Denver's radio station KFEL. The group toured the mountain states until 1927 and then signed up to sing for one year in San Francisco over KFRC.

Mr. Wilson later moved to Los Angeles where he was an NBC staff announcer. He took his first straight announcing job in 1929. He was a sports announcer for the next four years before joining the Benny show.

He married Miss Corbet in 1950, one year after receiving a divorce from his third wife, dress designer and former Polish countess Marusia Rudunska.

Jack On Stage

Bryan Olsen asked on our Web Forum about Jack's work onstage, and if there are any tapes of it. Here is my response, and I would be interested to know if anyone else has more information about recordings of Jack's work live on stage:

An excellent question, and one I've heard many times. The nightclub/Vegas routines (I assume that's what you mean by "stand up act") are one of those great, lost Benny treasures. We do have some members who were lucky enough to see him live, but I know of very few videos. I believe someone mentioned to me that there is a bootleg from Vegas where someone sneaked in a camera and shot a show (or part of it), but I have not yet seen it.

However, there are a few things that we did know about the nightclub/Vegas work. I have copies of portions of Jack's monologues from Vegas appearances in 1968-72. Jack's character and style is so firmly established that reading the scripts is, to me, almost the same as watching a tape of the performance. You can clearly hear and see (in your mind's ear/eye) Jack doing the material.
Some of these are in the UCLA and Wyoming collections of Jack's papers.

Also, he reused some routines on the air and his stage performances. A couple of them were gags that went all the way back to Harry Conn (one of Jack's first radio writers, who worked for him until 1936). The first of two skits that come to mind is the Boswell Sisters (evolved over time to a variety of names, finally becoming the Smothers Sisters). The group includes a very homely and/or tough woman (at one time played by Iris Adrian), a very heavy-set woman (originally played by Mary Kelly), and a very pretty woman. The skit goes through a conversation between Jack and the ladies, then into a rather bad musical number by them.

The other Conn skit is the Japanese wrestler bit. Jack talks about a Japanese wrestler that he'd seen, who can take on some amazing number of guys at the same time. So out onto the stage comes a tiny man, and four or five burly stagehands. Jack makes a big deal about how amazing this little wrestler is. Finally he tells the guys to go at it, and within a few seconds, the stagehands pummel the tiny guy into the floor. They walk off leaving what's left of the guy, and Jack doing a classic stare from the failed wrestler, to the audience, back to the wrestler...

Jack worked on stage with Gisele MacKenzie, and they did their "Getting to Know You" routine, among others. Jack reprised that same bit on stage and TV with Toni Marcus, a 12-year-old violinist. Jack also used the two older ladies as "President and Vice-President of the Jack Benny Fan Club....Pasadena Chapter" on both his TV and stage performances. There is a photo in one of the biographies (I think it's Irving Fein's) that shows Jack standing on stage with a group of ladies holding instruments. I have a feeling that was a stage version of the 12-13-59 show where Jack visits a meeting of the Jack Benny Fan Club and plays his violin for them. As they all gasp and swoon on the high notes of "Love in Bloom", eventually some join in on instruments and end the episode by parading around the room with Jack in the lead. (This is one of my favorite JB TV episodes...wonder why...)

I wish there was more audiovisual documentation of Jack's nightclub/Vegas work, but I hope that gives you a taste of what it was.

Jack Benny, Musical Interludes, and Minstrels
(A question was asked on the OTR Digest about why so many non-musical shows had musical interludes, such as Dennis' song. Here is the analysis provided by the ever-informative Elizabeth McLeod.)

"This actually goes back even further than vaudeville in the United States—all the way back to the traditional American minstrel show. From its beginning in the 1840s, the standard minstrel format was a mixture of music, comedy, and "specialty acts"—you'd start with the opening chorus routine featuring the byplay with the end men (the origin of the concept of the two-man comedy team, with the Interlocutor the original "straight man,") and then a tenor solo (the origin of the Dennis Day-type singer in American popular entertainment), followed by an "olio" of specialty acts—instrumental novelties, comedy monologues, singers, eccentric dancers—and then a Grand Finale which was often a broad comedy sketch satirizing some current touchstone.

"If this format sounds familiar, even to those who've never studied minstrelsy, it's because this is the basic skeleton of the radio comedy format pioneered in the 1930s by Jack Benny. It had been strained through the filters of vaudeville and the Broadway revue by this time—but it still retains recognizable roots in an entertainment form created ninety years before.

"To illustrate—the roles of Interlocutor and End Man shift around quite a bit among the cast members at the start of a typical Benny show, but whoever fills the specific role at a given moment, the dynamic is precisely the same, as is the basic feel of the opening sequence—all that's missing is a call of "Gentlemen Be Seated!" and "Jell-O again" sort of fills that role. And Phil Harris' character, especially, is a figure with deep roots in minstrelsy—the swaggering, hard-drinking, comically ignorant 'dawwwwwg'.

"To continue the analogy, the tenor vocal selection by Kenny/Dennis and the middle band number represent the Olio portion of the show, and the sketches satirizing movies and plays that conclude most 1930s Benny shows are straight out of minstrelsy by way of Broadway. (When you examine the structure of his 1930s programs closely, it becomes evident that Benny owes far more to the classical minstrel show than 'Amos 'n' Andy' ever did!) Benny's influence in the 1930s was such that his format became the standard, imitated by dozens of other performers over the years—which is why the conventions he established became so common.

"The minstrel format may be the single most enduring institution in American popular entertainment—you can find traces of it in vaudeville, the circus, radio, the stage revue, burlesque, and even modern television. (The 'end men' dynamic lives on in the exchanges between any late night comedian and his announcer/bandleader/stooge, and the broadly satirical spirit of minstrelsy lives on in the sketches of SNL, MadTV, etc.)"

Do You Know?

Was pleased to recently get a photo on Ebay of Jack Benny's first….painting. And here it is:

Typed on the back of the picture is this information: "THE HOUSE THAT JACK BUILT – Jack Benny, star of Paramount's 'Artists and Models Abroad', turns artist in all seriousness. Here's his first work of art, after lessons from Ruth Faison Shaw, the originator of 'finger-painting.' Jack apparently found his artistic mood influenced by the fact that he has just moved into his new home in Beverly Hills." (Funny…it doesn't **look** like 1002 North Roxbury…)

Anyone know any more about Jack's painting or where any of the canvases are today?

(From Jim Hilliker) "When was the first time that Jack Benny spoke over the radio? I had always heard that it took place in 1932 on a nationally broadcast program hosted by newspaper columnist Ed Sullivan from New York. But, in doing some of my radio history research of early radio in Southern California, I see that Jack took part in a radio broadcast in 1930 in Los Angeles, over Hollywood station KFWB (owned by Warner Brothers Pictures). This was 2 years before he did the Sullivan radio show.

"I'll quote from the ad printed in the Los Angeles Times on April 26, 1930:

"'Tune in Tonight! Hear Eddie Cantor, Al Jolson, Jack Benny, Benny Rubin, George Olsen, Abe Lyman, Ben Bernie, and scores of other stars of the stage and screen. One of the greatest arrays of talent ever paraded before the microphone is offered you tonight when the National Vaudeville Association Benefit Show will be broadcast from Shrine Auditorium over KFWB, starting at 8:30 p.m. Dont miss it! Program broadcast through the courtesy of Packers of MJB Coffee'

"What would Jack have done on this program? His vaudeville act? And would this have been different than the Jack Benny we became familiar with through his later radio and TV programs on his own shows?"

(From Jim Hilliker) "This doesn't have to do with the Benny program specifically, but I had a book with photos of radio performers...The short bio for Kenny Baker said he got his start singing professionally on a radio station in Long Beach, CA. They had 2 radio stations in Long Beach for many years, so my question is, was it KFOX or KGER?"

(From Mark) "Does anyone have a list of charities that Jack Benny donated to?"
(From James Darnell) "I'm not sure of every charity he gave to, but am certain he was supportive of the Heart Fund, American Cancer Society, and also contributed to the effort for the state of Israel."

(From C. Caramella) "At the Democrat Convention in Orlando, Florida, there were many gatherings of VEPs (Very Earnest People) holding VECs (Very Earnest Conversations)—heaven knows that I have attended enough political gatherings over the years to know what he was describing. These people were described as standing around and holding their arms and hands in certain positions. After describing what is acceptable, he added: 'Whatever you do, never put TWO fingers against your cheek; that's known in political circles as 'doing a Jack Benny'. It is a faux pas of the first order and you will never be taken seriously in politics again.'

"I wonder if anyone still around remembers or even knows how or when it started after all these years. It would be interesting to know the answers, because, when I was active, the term was not used (of course, Jack was alive); thus it had to have started after he left us, but when and by whom?"

(From me) I was running off the first Jell-O program (10/14/34) for an IJBFC library order, and did a quick sound check on it. Unless my ears are out of whack, it sounds like Jack goes to say a line in a southern drawl like, "That's a durn good idea" but it comes out "That's a damn...uh...durn good idea."

The word "idea" is just my filler in the line, I wasn't focusing on the rest of it. Does it sound to anyone else like Jack slips and says "damn"? And on the very first show for a new sponsor. People talk all the time about when Bing Crosby said "hell" on the show, but I've never heard anyone mention this slip.

(From me) For 39 Forever, I would like to play the full Jack Benny eulogy delivered by Bob Hope. Can anyone suggest a tribute or recording that has the *complete* eulogy (the KCRW tribute has only portions of it, but well-edited)?

(From TEADJones) "Has anybody made or acquired any Jack Benny Desktop Themes, Icons, etc.?"

(From Michael) "I've recently downloaded some Jack's Canada Dry Programs. The only problem is the opening theme (sounds weird not to hear Love In Bloom) is just distorted enough that I can't make out all of what they're singing. Can anyone out there help me out with this?"

Here's my best guess on it:
(Male trio or quartet) "Here we are again, happy as can be,
All good pals and jolly good company
[Can't get this line]
All good pals and jolly good company.

(Woman's voice) Never mind the weather, never mind the rain,

(Male trio or quartet) Now we're all together, whoops she goes again,
La dee dah dee dah, la dee dah dee dee
All good pals and jolly good company."

Can anyone confirm or fill in the blank?

You Do Know!

We have talked for a long time about whether Mary Livingstone (original name Sadie Marks) was related to the Marx Brothers. Jack's autobiography says that she was a distant cousin, and Mary's ghostwritten biography of Jack says that she was no relation. Thanks to a little help from Joan, I hope to put the matter pretty much to rest.

The Marx Brothers' parents were from Germany (their father immigrated there from France). The original name in the old country was Marrix. Mary's father's name was more likely Markowitz (or similar variation), and he came from Eastern Europe, probably Roumania. Therefore, I believe it is highly unlikely that the two families are related.

(From Martin Grams) "In 1938, a short 7 minute cartoon entitled It Happened to Caruso was
released in the theaters, and it was a direct parody of radio's JACK BENNY PROGRAM. The plot concerned Weschester, the vegetarian cannibal (a parody of Rochester), who becomes Robinson Caruso's Man Friday (Jack Benny's cloned voice). Caruso ends up killing a tiger with his violining and there's even a scene where Westchester and Caruso are riding in a broken down car (the old Maxwell). It's a funny parody from 1938, I saw it last week when I purchased it on video at the Fanex convention in Baltimore, Maryland, that sadly, is not usually aired over the networks, because it supposedly contains racist material in it. The cartoon is not one of the popular "Censored Eleven", but certainly comes close."

(From David M. Lynch) "I always had a soft spot in my heart for actor Keefe Brasselle, for two reasons. One was his starring role in The Eddie Cantor Story, which I first saw as a child, and the other was that his early 1960s summer show featured Noelle Adam, who was my first celebrity 'crush' when I was only six years old. A few years ago, however, I found out that Brasselle (evidently) didn't like Jack, to the point where he used Jack as the basis for an unflattering character in his novel The CanniBalS. [sic] Does anybody out there know why Brasselle disliked Jack?"

(From Gerry O.) "In looking through a history of CBS, I was surprised to discover that although Jack had never met Keefe Brasselle, Jack INDIRECTLY was the cause of Brasselle losing his 'executive' position at the network!

"It seems that in the 1960's, after attempting a career as a performer, Brasselle became the right-hand man to James Aubrey at CBS. Aubrey was a programming executive who was known as 'The Smiling Cobra'. Aubrey was a vicious sadist who was famous for not only canceling TV series, but for also getting a sicko charge out of giving the cancelled shows' performers and staff the bad news. During Jack's last TV season on CBS, it became painfully clear that the show's ratings were going down the tubes. Stiff competition from NBC's "Bonanza" [LL: Actually, not so…Jack was opposite Bonanza in 1961-2] plus changing tastes meant certain cancellation of the weekly Benny program.

"However, William Paley had a long and friendly history with Jack and was grateful for what Jack had done through the years to help make CBS the 'Tiffany Network'. Also, Paley did not want to lose Jack's services entirely. He had some ideas in mind for hour-long Benny specials and the like. Paley wanted to handle giving the bad news to Jack personally…and he also wanted to lead into more upbeat talks about future Benny-CBS projects. However, Aubrey (who had rapidly been losing favor with Paley to begin with) beat Paley to the punch. Aubrey gave the news to Jack in a VERY rude manner…something to the effect of 'You're through, Old Man!' Jack was so humiliated and upset that he left CBS and immediately signed with NBC for a final season of weekly programs.

"When Paley found out about this, he was FURIOUS with Aubrey…It was truly the last straw!
Because of the terrible and heartless handling of Jack Benny, Paley fired both James Aubrey and Aubrey's right-hand man, KEEFE BRASSELLE!

"It was Brasselle's firing that prompted him to the write the bitter 'novel' about a TV network (which EVERYBODY knew was supposed to be CBS) and its 'loser' performers. So in some twisted way, Brasselle could have blamed Jack Benny for his being fired from CBS!"

(From Kurt) "The press book for Casablanca has an item, for release in newspapers, that says Our Jack can be seen very briefly in one scene of the Humphrey Bogart classic. Jack was then, of course, under contract to Warner Brothers (making George Washington Slept

Here), which, as emcee of the 1944 Academy Awards, he joked about as if it were The Horn Blows at Midnight."

And where is Jack, you ask? (From David M. Lynch) "Well! (to coin a phrase) At least we're all in agreement as to when and where Jack appears, i.e. over 'Sam's' right shoulder (on our left)
during Dooley Wilson's musical bit which occurs about seven minutes into Casablanca. But to clear up any confusion as to the actual number(s) being performed, the soundtrack CD to Casablanca (which didn't exist until 1997!) lists it as a medley of 'It Had to Be You' and 'Shine'. Jack's brief appearance is during the segue from one song to another, when 'Sam' is singing that his hair (Sam's, not Jack's!) is curly. By the way, although Dooley Wilson sang all of 'Sam's' material (all of which was recorded 'live' on the set, unlike the film's other musical numbers) it was Elliot Carpenter who actually played the piano.

"Hmm. Wonder if the cigarette Jack was smoking was a Lucky? Ahh, it doesn't matter anyway, they weren't his sponsor yet!"

(From LH) "Jack can be found on the 1930 census in California, Los Angeles county, E.D.# 196, page 27A, line 23."

(From Michael) "I've been listening to a number of Lucky Strike era shows and am wondering if Mr. Boone and Mr. Riggs are actually saying anything before they say 'Sold American!' I've been to real auctions where the auctioneer has gone about as fast as these two, but I could understand them.... I think Riggs starts off by saying 'Sixty-five.'"

(From Kurt) "Lee Aubrey Riggs, who died in 1987 at 79 (Congestive heart failure. Draw your own conclusions, I guess.) was able to chant at 469 words per minute, believed to be the fastest in the world. Hence the nickname of 'Speed.' He once participated in a comedy routine with Fred Allen in which he threw some extra words into the chant. But as far as what he actually was saying, only another tobacco auctioneer probably could tell you."

(From me) Going from memory, one call (I believe it's Riggs) calls "49 American", indicating the lot was sold to American Tobacco for 49 dollars (or 49 plus some number of zeros). The other call starts at 65, and has a lot of what I've heard auctioneers call "filler" (dingle-ingle-ingle doodle-oodle-oodle...) Filler is used by some auctioneers while waiting for a higher bid to keep the action moving but letting bidders consider their next move. Some will use just nonsense words, while others will just repeat the same line over and over ("I've got twenty I've got twenty I've got twenty over here Twenty twenty twenty twenty THIRTY! Now I've got thirty I've got thirty...")

(From Mike Amowitz) "The Kids in the Hall were apparently Jack Benny fans; their name was taken from the 'kids in the hall' [LL: Probably Hal Goldman and Al Gordon, whom Jack called "the kids"] who would pitch jokes to Jack Benny as he came to his office."

(From Thomas Kessel) Fred Allen is buried in the Gate of Heaven Cemetery in Hawthorne, New York (Westchester County). His tombstone lists both his birth name (John F. Sullivan) and Fred Allen.

Jack Benny Classifieds

§§§ Unbelievable offer for Jack Benny programs and appearances on 16mm:

JACK BENNY PROGRAMS:
    DON BREAKS HIS LEG
    SMOTHERS BROTHERS SHOW
    PETER, PAUL & MARY SING JACKS SONG
    THE NEW TALENT SHOW w sponsor tags
    HARLOW GETS A DATE
    ISSAC STERN STORY
    JACK MEETS A JAPANESE TALENT AGENT (Jack Soo)
    DON'S HOUSE TO DINNER (Famous scene where he's held up)
    JACK FIRES DON

THE DANNY THOMAS SHOW:
    THAT OLE DEVIL, JACK BENNY 1958
    JACK STEALS DANNY'S JOB 1950

GE THEATER:
    THE FACE IS FAMILAR

CHECKMATE: 1 HOUR SHOW
    A FUNNY THING HAPPENED

JACK BENNY LOW FADE CARTOONS:
    MALIBU BEACH PARTY- Low Fade
    THE MOUSE THAT JACK BUILT (features Jack IN COLOR @ end) Low Fade

My price is $1600 for all plus shipping. All prints are in good used condition, no vinegar. I also have a Low Fade LUCY SHOW featuring Phil Harris singing with JACK BENNY TEXACO COMMERCIALS/ CRAZY GOOGINHEIM for MALT O MILK and a PET

COOLY DRINK COMMERCIAL for $65. I am not willing to sell shows separately, it's either ALL or nothing.. Tom Williams, tfwms1@bellsouth.net

---

§§§ Alice Faye: A Life Beyond the Silver Screen by Jane Lenz Elder.
Now for the first time, fans of the fabulous Faye can enjoy a full-scale biography of the beloved star. Four years in the making, Alice Faye: A Life Beyond the Silver Screen is published by the University of Mississippi Press as part of its Hollywood Legends series. Film historian Jane Lenz Elder conducted interviews with Alice's friends and family, consulted leading oral history collections, and dug through archives in California, New York, and Linton, Indiana (home to the Phil Harris-Alice Faye Collection), to create the most compelling, comprehensive, and accurate depiction of Faye's life yet published. 6x9 inches, 256 pages, 25 black & white illustrations, filmography, bibliography, index, ISBN 1-57806-210-1. Call 1-800-737-7788 to order toll-free.

---

§§§ (From Ben Ohmart, benohmart@yahoo.com) "I wondered if you'd be interested in contributing to a new book about Jack Benny. I don't know if you know Midnight Marquee books, but they've been doing a series of books of nonfiction essays on horror films. There haven't been any books of this sort done yet on OTR, and I think it would be a good idea to start. The first would be on Jack Benny, though all major series (like Amos n Andy, Fibber McGee, etc.) could have their own volume later. To give you an idea of topics for this book: a history of the Benny-Allen feud; the changing role of Rochester from the early years in which there was an emphasis on his fondness for chicken and for playing craps to a more positive image, perhaps best illustrated by the New Year's Eve show in 1950 when he shares a toast with Jack as a colleague and friend; the railroad shows and how they captured a sense of the adventure of traveling by train; a rundown of the bloopers; the wonderful use of sound effects on the show and how they contributed to the enjoyment of the listeners by appealing to the imagination; specific writer contributions to the series; the masochistic Jack and the anatomy of an ego. There are lots more ideas possible, and in fact, I'd like to hear ideas from you rather than just take something from this brief list of samples.

"I'd like to solicit different topics from different writers, perhaps 20, plus pictures. Submissions can be between 1000 to 4000 words, however much it takes to say what you want to say. I'll start with Benny, and if it interests enough people, move on to other shows. I haven't solicited many writers about this yet, though Clair Schulz, Laura Wagner and Martin Grams Jr. have signed up so far. Already published writers and/or incredibly smart Jack Benny fans only please! I can pay $50 plus 2 copies of the book for use of the non-fiction. If you're interested, let me know. Thanks."

§§§ <u>Jack Benny's First Farewell Special</u> is available for $5.00 from Satellite Media Production, P.O. Box 638, Walkersville, MD 21793-0638, (800) 747-0856, www.satellitemediaproduction.com.

§§§ Would very much appreciate advice on how to obtain the episode "Jack Joins the Acrobats" on video (no luck from MCA). I was advised that all episodes from 1965 were filmed so hopefully this one is available. It is Episode 250, aired February 19th 1965, Production Code 24614. mail_mi_2000@yahoo.com

§§§ I am searching for the following tapes if anyone has: "A Love Letter To Jack Benny" NBC 1981,
80 years of Frank Sinatra: My Way ABC 1995, any appearances of Don Rickles on Johnny Carson. bjglaw0326@aol.com

Please send all questions, comments, corrections, and additions to:
International Jack Benny Fan Club
P.O. Box 11288
Piedmont, CA 94611

JackBenny@aol.com
www.jackbenny.org
Laura Leff, President

Please, friends, send no bombs.

The Jack Benny Times

May - August 2003   Volume XVIII, Numbers 3-4

President's Message

39 Forever is now history, and a grand story it is! Eric Brolund has provided us with an accounting of the weekend and the events leading up to it, and I hope that everyone will be able to enjoy it all over again through his words. Thanks very much Eric!

I would like to thank everyone who offered so much kindness, patience, prayers, and support for me during the time after 39 Forever. As I consider my future career, I keep thinking that if the fan club could pay as well as a regular job, I would love to devote myself to it full-time. It is an amazing thing--the effort I put in gives back as much good feeling in people's laughter and appreciation in enjoying the work of Jack Benny. It is a privilege and a pleasure.

New Members

**** Hillel Ginton (Israel) **** Mike Leach **** John Troughton **** Dean Alan Carnegie **** Gary Goodson **** John Garofano **** Daniel T. Tarnow **** Gary Pierce **** Wally Kleinfeldt **** Matt Davidson **** Ken Teutsch **** Tracy & Ryan Allred **** Bob Pennock **** Bryan Smith **** Tom O'Brien **** Christopher Eckart **** Chuck Quinn **** Mark Demos **** Mark Demos **** Don Warner **** Traci Backstedt **** Doris Fitzpatrick **** Andrew Russell **** Andrew Johnson **** Bud Reeves **** Alfred Ogbonnaya **** Jon Teboe **** David Copeland **** Eric Feman **** James A. Bittner **** Alan Chapman **** Tad K. Murphy **** Robert Henn **** Ron Barnes **** Malcolm Stuart-Fischer (Canada) **** Jarrod DellaChiesa **** Janine Preston **** Dan Leimeter **** Matthew Wilha (England) **** Joe Gandelman **** Jerry Glen **** Michael Prince **** Norman S. Hern **** Morton Paradise **** Wayne Lawless **** Greg Rosenstein **** Peter B. MacManus **** Kevin McAuliffe **** David Cada **** Chip Roehunter **** Linda Louise Schmidthuber **** Patrick Bruneni **** Steven Reeves **** Jerry Hamood **** Robert Greene **** William Kirby **** A. Bimka Chislowsky **** Jerry J. Haumberger **** Ted Hobgood **** John Williams **** Robert Saunders **** Sheila Caetta **** Matt Hurley **** Sheldon Kenin **** David M. Snyder **** Jessie Sater (Canada) **** Rob Thweatt **** Ted Hobgood **** Mickey A. Driver **** Debbie Driver **** Gordon Simbrow (Canada) **** Douglas Brock (England) **** Marilyn Anne Dean (Canada) **** Diane Wasserman **** Lauren Webbles **** Terry Poirier (Canada) **** Paul Coleman (Canada) **** Rob Schickowski **** David Creelman (Canada) **** Arthur Gagnier **** Kurt Wyman **** Paul Spagnuolo **** Terrence Jahraus **** Todd Wagner **** Mark Stephenson **** Edward Johnson **** Walter Palmer **** Edward Imperatore **** Susan Hansen **** Edward C. Moore **** Christopher Guarino **** Tad Higginson (Canada) **** Thomas Ray **** Dennis Oppenheim **** Bruce Bealer **** Cecil Stanford **** Bob Reynolds **** Gerald Tucker **** Dave Stephens **** Wesley Smith **** Andrew C. Tartaglia **** John Crawford **** Dennis Bell **** Rev. Garry L. Hickman, M.Div. **** Howard Scouten **** Erwin Boychenko **** Debbie Callanan **** Stu Berman **** Eric Butler ****

Ellen Smith **** Jim Archer (Canada) **** Ludwig van Catt **** Paul Gordon **** Andy Ciriaco **** Billy F Gibbons **** John Di Fatta **** Dr. Steven Cottingham, PhD **** Bill Skolnick **** Beth Kontos **** Don Conrad **** Jack Rhodes **** Dennis Johnson **** John C. Griffin, Jr. **** Alison Hortan **** Angela D. Harris **** Bill Allen **** Bob C. Hendrickson **** Brett Somers **** Chad Johnson **** Charle Landry **** Charles Snyder **** Christopher Filchak **** Dan Tirman **** Daniel A. Buttolph **** David Lee Guss **** David Golumbia **** David Mackson **** Debbie Grugal **** Debra Peterson **** Diane and Alan Blank **** Dr. Robert Israel **** Edna Moledor **** Emily Holbrook **** Floyd E. Riggle, Jr. **** Frank Reuben (England) **** Fred Huebscher **** George Berger (Canada) **** Hans Agneessens **** Heidi Sackerson **** Henry McDaid (Ireland) **** Howard E. Green **** Ilene and Ralph Kupler **** Jacques de Broekert **** Jake Mabe **** Jerry Hensley **** John Roberts **** Joseph G. Uribe **** K.L. Pearson (Canada) **** Karla Jo Renee **** Marcelina Lundy **** Marie Ciriello **** Mark Rubin **** Michael C. Fortner **** Mike Larson **** Mike McCune **** Jennifer J. Sikes **** Nancy Murzyn **** Paul Hermann **** Peter Kempert **** Rob Mermelstein **** Robert Glenn Allen **** Robert Zegster **** Robyn Rivero **** Rod & Karen Walker **** Ronald Shore **** Ryan Patrick **** Sara B. Tebbs **** Scott D. Vroegindewey **** Sean Dougherty **** Stephen Blackwell (Australia) **** Stephen Maitland-Lewis **** Stephen Powers **** Susan and David Schneider **** Timothy P. Irvin (Ireland) **** Valerie Sumida **** Paul DeLucchi **** John Doherty **** Jay Meade **** William E Chapman **** Arthur Gagnier **** Jamie Leavens (Canada) **** Joe Thoms **** Michelle Ortiz **** Paul A. Casner, Jr **** James Walsh **** Toby Springer **** Anthony Tardiff **** Timothy S. Gibbons **** Leaha Magee **** Diana Twombly **** Roger A. Wasby **** William J. Buckley **** Jim Pepping

Backstage at 39 Forever
By Eric Brolund

The International Jack Benny Fan Club staged their first major convention in the twenty-three year history of the organization this February in Los Angeles. The event was crowned with the formal ceremony inducting Jack Benny into the National Comedy Hall of Fame. Many members of the fan club were on hand to enjoy the weekend's events and I'm sure several of them will take the time to write about their experiences. I thought I'd do something a little different and take you backstage to show some of the hard work and fun that went into making 39 Forever so special to us all.

But first, I think I need to relate a bit of the history of this endeavor. For the International Jack Benny Fan Club, it all began with the build up to the unveiling of the Jack Benny Statue in Waukegan….

Waukegan

The Jack Benny Statue started as a project of the Events & Attractions Committee of Waukegan Sunrise in 1997 and eventually came to be managed by The Citizens' Committee for Jack Benny Statue, with Laini Zinn as Chairperson. Fund raising began in earnest and in January 2000, sculptor Erik Blome was selected to design and install the statue. As he set to work, it was time for the committee to start planning for the main event, tentatively scheduled for September 2001.

Of course, this was a perfect opportunity for the International Jack Benny Fan Club to get more involved. Laura Leff had been in regular contact with Laini and the Mayor's office of The City of Waukegan throughout the process, working together to stage a memorable weekend of activities.

Enter Tony Belmont, Executive Director of the National Comedy Hall of Fame (NCHOF). The NCHOF had wanted to induct Jack Benny for some time. But in order to do so, according to their charter, the induction required the participation of the inductee or his closet living relatives. And it should be staged in a manner befitting the status of the inductee and the other stars who would participate. The Waukegan event seemed to be a good fit.

By February 2001, during one of the monthly web chats, Laura asked the members what suggestions they had for the weekend. The idea of a Jack Benny tour and the radio show recreation came out of this session. Several of us volunteered for the re-creation and committed to the trip shortly thereafter. As the summer approached, fan club volunteers had been rehearsing the script and plans seemed to be coming together. But barely a few months later, delays and other issues forced the postponement of the event.

It seems to be a function of human nature that once initial plans fall through and time marches by, folks tend to move on. And as it happens, the National Comedy Hall of Fame decided Waukegan wasn't the right time to stage their Induction Ceremony for Jack Benny.

The statue was unveiled in June 2002, and the International Jack Benny Fan Club played a major role in the festivities. The event marked the first public performance of the *Not Ready for Sunday At Seven Players* featuring Eddie Carroll as Jack Benny. The cast included Bill Powers as Don Wilson, Tom Trethewey as Dennis Day, Dan Leff as Rochester Van Jones, Laura Leff as Rochester's lady, Charlie Willer as Mel Blanc and sound effects, Eric Brolund as Phil Harris and the lovely and talented Miss Maria Scarvelis as Mary Livingstone!

Waukegan was a fantastic success all around and when it was all over, Laura Leff went home and slept for 36 hours straight. When she awoke, she immediately started getting calls and emails saying "Wow, that was great" and asking what she had in mind for the next time.

Laura's reaction: "What are we gonna do? Unveil the statue again? What is this next time?"

Laura continues, "After talking to some people and doing a little polling to find out who was interested, we decided we were going to do the biggest and best Jack Benny tribute, and that is 39 Forever."

The IJBFC Council
As enthusiastic and energetic as Laura may be, she still felt she could still use some help getting the convention plans off the ground. She contacted some of the *Not Ready for Sunday At Seven Players* to volunteer as members of the IJBFC Council. Laura Leff serves as Chairperson, with Council members Bill Powers, Tom Trethewey, Eric Brolund and Maria Scarvelis.

It was early July with barely eight months to go before the convention. All we needed now was a budget, a venue, and a plan for the events. It wasn't long before we had some ideas. After some inquiries by Maria, Laura selected the Sheraton Gateway Hotel as the site of the convention. Plans were drawn for a birthday celebration on February 14th, complete with a radio show re-creation featuring Eddie Carroll. Saturday the 15th had panel discussions and activities during the day followed by the induction of Jack Benny into the NCHOF at the Friar's Club. On Sunday, February 16th, Laura would lead a special memorial service for Jack and Mary at Hillside Memorial Park followed by various self-guided tours and a visit to the Museum of Television and Radio.

As a council, we agreed that funding for this convention would come from two sources – advance ticket sales and sponsorships. And in order to get this show on the road, we needed to spread the word fast. Laura set to work designing and printing the convention announcement booklets as well as the sponsorship packages. In addition, we wanted Laura to attend several upcoming OTR conventions like SPERDVAC and FOTR in the fall to raise awareness of 39 Forever in the general OTR community. Laura also appeared as a guest on such radio programs as *Yesterday USA* and *The Joe Franklin Show* to promote the event.

Maria Scarvelis volunteered to create the Attendee Badges and as well as to design and print the Self-Guided Tour Booklets. Eric Brolund designed and printed the Convention Program & Souvenir Booklets. Bill Powers helped with publicity and sponsorships.

To increase fan club participation and interest, we also decided to run a few contests in the months leading up to the convention. We got the biggest response with folks suggesting categories and questions for Jackpardy!, a takeoff on the popular television quiz show Jeopardy. We also had good participation in the script-writing contest.

Star Quality
The International Jack Benny Fan Club enjoys a good relationship with Jack Benny's family. Almost from the start, Jack's daughter Joan Benny agreed to appear as a panelist along with her son Michael Rudolph. Her younger son Bobby Blumofe would join her for the induction ceremony.

Throughout the fall and into the winter, Laura worked hard with the folks at the Friar's Club and the NCHOF to publicize the event throughout their membership as well as attracting the participation of the various stars who would make this event shine. Tony Belmont helped bring in the Ink Spots and selected the comedy acts for the Friars Club. As the days went by, more and more stars committed to attending including Kay Linaker, Beverly Washburn, Gisele MacKenzie, Jay Meyer, Budd Friedman and Emma Kennedy. We were also pleased to have Jack's manager, Irving Fein and writer Al Gordon agree to appear as panelists.

Rehearsal, Dad, Rehearsal
It may interest you to know how the *Not Ready for Sunday at Seven Players* manage to rehearse the radio re-creations in the period leading up to our performances in both Waukegan and 39 Forever. After scripts are circulated, we would get together every few weeks online using Yahoo voice chat to run through our lines and practice our cues. Laura usually subs for Eddie Carroll, as Jack Benny. We continue with online rehearsals leading up to the days before the show. The *Players* arrive a day before the performance, where we are joined by Eddie Carroll, and together at last, we run through two or three times to put the finishing touches to the show.

You know, I can't say enough about Eddie Carroll. Forget that he is absolutely the best Jack Benny impressionist working today. Forget that he can play the violin almost as well as Jack. He is an amazing actor, and a truly entertaining individual on and off the stage. Eddie and his wife Carolyn have been completely supportive of the IJBFC activities both in Waukegan and at 39 Forever and he surely deserves his title of Honorary Mayor of Waukegan.

For 39 Forever, Janine Preston as Mabel Flapsaddle also joined the regular cast members in our recreation of the Jack Benny show from February 13th, 1949.

The stage was set. Everything was in place. Airline tickets and Hotel reservations were made. Time to catch my flight….

Los Angeles
Most of us on the IJBFC Council made our way to Los Angeles on Thursday, February 13th to begin setting up for the convention. Friday morning I took the opportunity to do some sightseeing with Bill Powers, his brother John, and Gene Ruechert. We made our way down to Hollywood Boulevard to see the Walk of Fame and Graumann's Chinese Theater. We also took the time to tour the lobby of the famed Roosevelt Hotel. We then took off towards Beverly Hills in search of Jack Benny's house at 1002 North Roxbury. After taking a few pictures of the house and the work that is still ongoing there, we returned to the Sheraton Gateway to begin our rehearsal at 1:00pm.

As we walked into the banquet hall, we were greeted by fan club members Hal Bogart and Melanie Aultman who were helping Maria Scarvelis assemble the Attendee Badges. Laura and Dan were bringing in the sound effects equipment loaned to us by SPERDVAC. Tom Trethewey was also there casually talking to Kay Linaker! I left briefly to get a few boxes of the convention booklets.

I stepped outside and there was Eddie Carroll with his wife Carolyn. He greeted me warmly by name – he remembered – and we talked a bit about Waukegan before heading back in.

After a bit of fussing around, setting up the A/V equipment and the sound effects, it was time to start the first reading. First reading is all about intonation – how you phrase your line. It's followed by second reading, which focuses on timing. The last read through is a technical rehearsal with music and sound effects. Complicating matters this time, at a certain point in the show, Maria, Tom, Bill and I have to sing like the Sportsman Quartet while Eddie plays the violin. We've never done this at any point before! In the audience, Kay Linaker applauds politely while Hal Bogart and Melanie Aultman worry we might call them up for help.

After a few hours, the rehearsal ends and it's time for all of us to head back to our rooms and get dressed for the birthday party. But first, Janine and I had to set up some recording equipment so we could capture the evening on tape. I also spent some time learning how to work the Jackpardy! computer program for tomorrow morning.

Happy Birthday
The hall was already fairly full when I made it back after changing. The bar was open and the caterers were preparing the buffet. I had a chance to talk to quite a few fan club members as I mingled through the crowd. I wish I could remember everyone's name like Eddie can, but by this point, my nerves were already starting to get the best of me. I don't normally get stage fright, but this time I began to second-guess myself. There were probably a hundred die-hard Jack Benny fans in this room and each of them probably has a strong sense of how the cast should behave and how each part should be read. I'm not onstage yet, but I've somehow got to get into character and put my fears behind me.

As the buffet closed down, Laura welcomed the audience to 39 Forever:
"I get asked a lot. Why Jack Benny? Why are you working so hard to keep his memory alive? And I think everybody in the room knows the answer to this. He was funny! And his work is timeless. You can listen to a radio show and it's as funny today and you laugh as much as people were laughing at him in 1940. It's wonderful to keep something like that around. You know, when something comes along and it's just so good you say, this is a real treasure. And you just want to hang on to it. Jack Benny was truly one of America's greatest treasures. And that's why we're here tonight."

After a few more minutes discussing the convention, Laura introduced the cast to the audience. Eddie Carroll came onstage for some opening remarks, and Laura presented the proclamation from James Hahn, Mayor of Los Angeles, of February 14-16 being Jack Benny Weekend in Los Angeles. Then the show began. My fingers must have been shaking as I clicked the button for the opening music since I managed to trigger the music twice. Oh well, there's our glitch for this show.

If you're like me, you probably take your time deciding whether to see a particular play or movie. You ask your friends if they liked it. You read the newspaper reviews and watch the entertainment shows. What you do not do, is take the word of the performers themselves that the show is worthwhile. So why should you take my word it went well after my initial mistake? I think everyone enjoyed themselves and I certainly heard quite a bit of laughter.

The show ended with Laura bringing a birthday cake up to the stage as all sang Happy Birthday to Jack Benny.

Memorable Moments
I had two particularly memorable moments from the birthday party I'd like to share with you. The first was my chance to sit and talk to Kay Linaker after the radio show recreation. You may remember her from Buck Benny Rides Again. But Kay Linaker is also the author of the classic 1958 film *The Blob* and she spent quite a bit of time telling me how she developed the idea for the movie. It was a lot of fun.

As the party broke up, several of us including Jim Davison, Melanie Aultman, Rizwan Kassim, Bill Powers, and Maria Scarvelis made our way to the hotel lounge, and ultimately out to poolside, as we discussed Jack Benny under the stars and a moon that seemed to hang directly above us. It was a perfect end to a magical evening.

The Convention
The convention started Saturday morning with auditions for Mary Cooper's winning script submission. As folks filtered in, I helped Maria and Tom fold the tour brochures and set up the tables. Hal Bogart volunteered to man the vendor table. Michelle Malik, of the Eddie Cantor Appreciation Society, helped Brian Gari lay out their table of Eddie Cantor tapes and discs. After I did my bit folding, I helped Laura do a sound check on the A/V system and then prepared for Jackpardy!

Jackpardy! What a great idea! We had a great computer program created by Al Baggetta that automated the questions and scoring. We projected the video out to a screen up on stage beside the teams. This was a great start to the day and everyone had fun with the questions and answers.

After Jackpardy!, the Co-worker panel began. Jack's manager Irving Fein and writer Al Gordon shared quite a few interesting anecdotes about working with Jack but it was Kay Linaker who related a very funny story about Jack in Buck Benny Rides Again. Kay informed us that Jack was scared of horses and he really wasn't much of a rider. Jack knew how to get on a horse and how to get off. He really couldn't do much more than that. This one particular time, Jack managed to get on a fairly skittish mount and a large number of the other cast were to ride beside him. As luck would have it, a sudden noise or the backfire from a nearby car started Jack's horse galloping wildly away from the set. The wranglers had to chase Jack's horse for a mile or so before they finally managed to catch up and stop him. Jack was absolutely sick from the fear and excitement and they had to postpone shooting for a few days as he recovered. I could just imagine the panicked look on Jack as Kay told the story. Beverly Washburn closed the session by sharing some memories and pictures of her appearance as a child star on Jack's TV show.

After the Co-worker panel, I joined the rest of the audience in Stan Taffel's screening of two classic Jack Benny TV shows during the lunch break. It was wonderful to see these shows in high quality, on film, projected onto the big screen in the convention hall. The sound quality was as fresh as the day it was made. We saw Benny as the Cactus Kid with Gisele MacKenzie in one episode and as Tarzan with Carol Burnett in the second.

The Family panel began after lunch with Joan Benny and Michael Rudolph sharing stories of their life with Jack. Michael Levine moderated this panel. Joan was very charming and awfully happy to talk about her father with the assembled fan club members. Michael shared a story about his grandfather giving him charge of his precious Stradivarius backstage in Las Vegas. Michael then wanted to get a soda, and decided that the best place to hide the violin would be in the shower. Upon Jack's return, panic ensued…but the violin was recovered unharmed!

The Musical panel was next. Gisele Mackenzie (at left) spoke of her career and performances with Jack. Brian Gari (below, center) spoke about his grandfather, Eddie Cantor, and read a passage from Cantor's book where he thanked Jack Benny for all the help he gave Eddie with his career. Norma Stevens (below, right) spoke briefly of her late husband, Larry Stevens, and his last musical endeavors. Then Jay Meyer (below, right), from the

Sportsman Quartet, spoke lovingly of his association with Jack and the show, and really capped off the panel by singing one of the commercials for us.

The Comedy panel started with Eddie Carroll (left in photo) discussing Jack's impact on comedy and what it was about Jack that continues to inspire him today. There was some lively discussion from Emma Kennedy (BBC), Budd Friedman (the Improv, right in photo), and Leo Gorcey Jr (author and son of Dead End Kid Leo Gorcey) on the nature of comedy before things got heated. At one point, moderator Michael Levine asked Tim Williams from TV Guide why *Jack Benny* re-runs are comparatively rare today compared to re-runs of *I Love Lucy*. This prompted quite a few questions and comments from the floor that political correctness, i.e., Rochester as Jack's valet, perhaps is at the root of television's reluctance to support the show today.

The afternoon was capped off with the performance of Mary Cooper's script submission. All of the cast were

marvelous but Joel Rothman absolutely floored me with his impression of Frank Nelson's YESSSSS! I still catch myself laughing about it whenever I think about it.

(Cast photo at right, L to R: Joel Rothman (Frank Nelson), Steve Oualline (Jack Benny), Michelle Malik (Mary Livingstone), Jim Davison (Phil Harris), Hal Bogart (Don Wilson), Scott F. Greene (Dennis Day))

The Friar's Club
After helping to pack up everything from the convention hall, I left to change for the Friar's Club. I met up with Bill Powers for the ride back to Beverly Hills. We found the Friar's Club without much effort since we had scouted it out the day before. They had valet parking! We all felt special as we emerged from the car in our tuxedos and walked up the historic steps to comedy's citadel. What can I say about the room itself? The room is covered with paintings of famous members including Ronald Reagan, Dean Martin, George Burns, and, of course, Jack Benny. The walls are painted a deep red. There is a leather-padded bar off to the far left and to the right is the banquet hall and the stage. I tried to absorb it all as I mingled with the guests and waited for the start of the ceremony

I was a little hot in my tuxedo so I took the opportunity to head outside for some fresh air. I met the guys from comedy duo Full Contact (Tim Kaminsky and Bob Jay, at left) standing out front, and talked to them a bit about Jack Benny and the induction ceremony. I apologized for not including a picture of them in the souvenir guide, but they didn't mind. As they left to head back upstairs to get ready, one of them grabbed me and kissed me hard on the cheek. So this is what it's like to live in Hollywood, huh? I decided to stay outside for a bit longer. There was another fellow hanging around outside during this time and we struck up a conversation. It turns out he's the bass player for THE INK SPOTS! We talked about the group and what he does when he's not performing. I went back inside with him, BACKSTAGE, and he introduced me to the rest of the group. What a thrill!

When I came back out front, I met up with Leonard Penner, the banquet manager of the Friar's club. Leonard said he had some folks he'd like me to meet. Who me? He introduced me to TV's Hank Garrett (Car 54 Where Are You?) and I spent a bit of time chatting with him before it was time to take our seats for dinner.

I joined the rest of the IJBFC Council members at one of the tables up near the front of the room. Tom Trethewey is really enjoying the evening so far and he points out that TV's

Rose Marie is dining right next to him. Gosh, how can this get any better? Oh yeah, the Manny Harmon Trio is starting to play some dinner music. Cool.

Dinner is served pretty much the same as any other catered affair, with Caesar salad and rolls first and the main course to follow. It's a big room and I expect it might take a while for them to get to everyone so once I've finished my salad, I decide to head to the bar to refresh my drink. I talk briefly with a few fan club members before returning to my seat.

I had the prime rib. Others had the salmon. I thought dinner was pretty good and I was anxious for the show to get started. But wait, we've got coffee and cheesecake to come next. I decide to refresh my drink in the meantime. When I get to the bar, who do I meet but Budd Friedman. He buys me a drink and I promise to return the favor after dessert. Am I the only one who feels things are getting just a little surreal?

The crowd featured many wonderful and gracious stars. Rose Marie (at right) and her daughter and son-in-law dined with IJBFC members Tom Trethewey and the Rothman family, telling stories of her work from vaudeville to Dick Van Dyke. KNX Entertainment Editor Tom Hatten escorted big band vocalist Bea Wain. Sitcom star Bill Kirchenbauer traded stories with Eddie and Carolyn Carroll. Kay Linaker sparkled in a beautiful white dress, and Beverly Washburn and her husband enjoyed the festivities. Michael Levine escorted one of the ladies of Baywatch, and it was rumored that Jason Alexander showed up incognito. Welcome to Beverly Hills!

The show started with Stan Ross, founder of Hollywood's Gold Star Recording Studios, recalling the fun of recording the Jack Benny radio shows—years before Ross' work with stars such as Herb Alpert, John Lennon, Jimi Hendrix, and the Righteous Brothers. The Ink Spots are up on stage as I start dessert. I skip the coffee and return to the bar to buy Budd his next drink. He's just standing back there because he wants to see the up-and-coming comics who will be there tonight. The guy from Full Contact who kissed me comes by and

shows me the list of planned acts and tributes. I move closer to Budd Friedman and he decides to skip the kiss this time.

The Ink Spots sang all their great hits, and the audience clapped and sang along with many of them. One member even entertained us with some fancy footwork both on and off the stage! The lead singer introduced Laura Leff, who welcomed the crowd and read a congratulatory letter from California Governor Gray Davis. Stan Irwin, former <u>Tonight Show</u> producer, reminisced about featuring Jack and George Burns in Las Vegas. Laura then introduced emcee Hank Garrett, who kicked off the evening's comedy. Hank then brought on Full Contact. This versatile duo did their own tribute to vaudeville, even bringing up IJBFC member Robert Allen from the audience to help. Hank then announced a surprise guest, and Jack Benny appeared from the wings, courtesy of Eddie Carroll. As Eddie played "Love in Bloom" on his violin, one can't help wondering whether we were also hearing the echoes of Jack himself playing the same number in this very room.

The lights then came down and two large television screens showed a montage of Benny clips selected by the National Comedy Hall of Fame. We watched and laughed as Jack reprised "Getting to Know You" (originated with Gisele MacKenzie) with twelve-year-old violinist Toni Marcus. Then Tony Belmont took the stage to announce the induction ceremony. The presentation was short and sweet, and Rose Marie spoke lovingly of Jack and his work. Joan thanked the audience and expressed her great pleasure at seeing so many people, including young ones, gathering to honor her father.

Joan is getting ready to leave and I make sure I have my camera ready. I positioned myself to take a picture of Joan Benny and Bobby holding the award downstairs next to a picture of Jack Benny. It's my favorite picture from the convention.

It's time to head back to the hotel….

Sunday Morning
Sunday morning comes a little too soon for me but I'm not about to miss the memorial service. And I've got to catch my plane shortly thereafter so I'd better start packing up and getting ready to go. I catch up with Maria in the lobby and she agrees to drive me to the service and the airport afterwards. But first, she has also promised to take Mike Amowitz and Anne Noznisky over to the car rental place so they can take pick up their own car for the self-guided tour. No problem.

Have you ever wondered how many IJBFC members can fit into a 2002 Neon? The answer is six! Along with Mike and Anne, we also brought Melanie Aultman and Rizwan Kassim

Memorial Service

I almost wanted to talk about the memorial service first. It's a bit hard to describe in words what this moment meant to me. Jack is almost, but not quite, as close and important to me as anyone else in my life. But it's a one-sided relationship where Jack did all the giving and I never had a chance to thank him while he was alive. And yet, I can still listen to his radio shows and watch his television shows. So at this moment, I'm about to confront this paradox in which Jack is still alive to me, yet gone.

As I enter Hillside Memorial Park, I see the row upon row of gravestones lined up along the hill. We travel on, up to the main mausoleum and I hesitate before walking the last few steps inside. It is a very quiet place and I'm starting to wonder if perhaps my visit is an intrusion. I catch a glimpse of Laura setting up for the service and I follow Maria inside.

Laura has positioned some seating and a podium in front of Jack and Mary's sarcophagus. A large picture of Jack, Mary and Rochester sits on a stand just behind her. An attendant hands me the memorial service card and I take a seat next to Dan.

Laura began the service, and read the eulogy delivered by Bob Hope upon Jack's passing. It was quite stirring and it reminded me of just how much we've lost in Jack's passing. Laura recited part of the service in Hebrew but I was able to read an English translation in the card I was given. And then Laura began to sing. It was as though Laura reached deep inside of me to find the pain and loss I was now feeling, pulled it out and proceeded to lift it up and away from me. I can't describe it any better than that.

I was numbed and silent as I joined the others in marking his grave with a small stone handed to me by the attendant. After placing the stone, I walked back outside and considered what this moment meant to me. Jack is surely gone. He has touched the lives of millions like me and left a wonderful legacy of dignity, gentleness, and the humility of sharing and enjoying life through friendship and laughter. I said a small prayer and shed some tears in private. I then returned to join the others back inside.

And then…

Eric had to catch his plane, and after seeing the crowd at Canter's Deli, figured that he should make that a priority. Dan helped by hitting the nearby newsstand to pick up copies of the Los Angeles Times, The Jewish Journal, and Variety, all of which had articles about 39 Forever. As we relaxed in a booth in Canter's Kibitz Room, we paged over the papers. More fan club members and their companions came in and took booths and tables around us. For those who have never been there, Canter's is a close as you can get to an East Coast deli and still be in California; rye bread stacked with inches of pastrami, corned beef, chicken liver, etc., and a bowl of half- and full-sour pickles on your table. They have sandwiches named after various stars (their Eddie Cantor looks delightful), including a Buck Benny, which is a knackwurst with onions.

A quick story about Canter's and Jack: once Jack and Irving Fein had walked up from CBS to get a bite to eat. As they enjoyed their sandwiches, they noticed that the restaurant suddenly seemed much busier than usual. When they left, they noticed a hastily hand-lettered sign in the window saying "Jack Benny is eating inside".

After eating more than our fill, we went to the Museum of Television and Radio in Beverly Hills. The front desk attendant informed me that people had been coming in since their noon opening, asking to see the Jack Benny exhibit. The museum had given us one of their theatres for big-screen viewing of rare Benny shows from their collection. I came in at the end of the Harry Truman show, followed by Jack dedicating the Jack Benny Junior High School in Waukegan. The room was reasonably full, and it is wonderful to be able to watch Jack's work with so many other devoted fans, everyone getting all the "in jokes." I sat at the back, and the seat next to me rotated with various members, occasionally leaning over to ask a question or for the year of the show. Hope we didn't bother any of you too much with our running commentary. The museum obliged us by running Jack and Audrey Meadows doing their version of "The Honeymooners" again for the finale.

As I made my way out of the theatre, someone stopped me and said, "This is a weekend that we will all treasure for the rest of our lives."

Answers and Thank Yous

Here are answers to the question, "What happened to Robert Clary, Harry Shearer, and Sid Caesar?" Robert Clary had a cold that weekend and couldn't be with us. Harry Shearer's recording schedule changed at the last minute and he was recording all that Saturday. As for Sid Caesar, a member of the Friars Club staff determined on Friday night that Sid would not be able to stay for the whole show. So we were very happy that Rose Marie graciously stepped forward to present the National Comedy Hall of Fame award in his stead. We wish them all well, and are sorry that they could not be with us that weekend.

I've also had many people ask me who was the striking woman who looked like a movie star and sat at Joan Benny's table. Well, of course, that was Joan herself! OK, besides her...her name is Dottie Goddard.

Many thank yous are in order, and hopefully I don't forget anyone. First off, a big thank you to the Council: Eric Brolund, Bill Powers, Maria Scarvelis, and Tom Trethewey. All of them had a part to play in this (not just the recreation), and everyone worked together admirably, took initiative, and pitched in whenever they were needed. Others that worked hard behind the scenes at the event were Hal Bogart, Melanie Aultman, and Rizwan Kassim. As Eric said, Eddie Carroll continues to be one of our greatest blessings in many ways. SPERDVAC was generous and accommodating in loaning us the sound effects equipment for Friday's recreation. Of course, thanks to everyone on the panels who gave generously of their time and memories. A hand for Stan Taffel, who came up with the idea of Jackpardy!

and brought his own equipment and 16mm shows for exhibition on Saturday. Kudos as well to Al Baggetta, who took it upon himself to create and enhance the program for Jackpardy!. Tony Belmont of the National Comedy Hall of Fame spent many months working on the preparation for the event, finding and contracting the talent for the Friars Club show, and organizing the myriad of things that go into such a production. Jill Glasband of Hillside Cemetery was also wonderful, coming up with a variety of ideas to make the service memorable and creating the beautiful service brochure. Perry Gee of the Museum of Television and Radio also worked with me to recommend various services they could provide, and help arrange for the theatre screening and private viewing of 30 Benny shows and specials.

Of course, we must recognize our sponsors, without whose support 39 Forever would not have been possible:

Corporate Sponsors	Individual Sponsors
Platinum	**39ers**
Levine Communications Office (also provided advance publicity)	Laura Leff Joel Rothman
Gold	**Benny Boosters**
Entertainment Today	Eric Brolund Bill Powers
Silver	Maria Scarvelis
Jell-O KNX 1070 Newsradio	**Friends of the IJBFC**
	Jay Hickerson
Dealer	K and K Creations
Ben Ohmart	MSBL Colonels
McCoy's Recording	Southern Sports

39 Forever T-Shirts and Memorabilia

There are still some remaining T-shirts commemorating 39 Forever. These sharp-looking shirts are 100% preshrunk cotton Hanes Beefy Tees, black with the photo of Jack in a tuxedo playing the violin. The shirts also feature the fan club name, 39 Forever Celebration, and the date below the photograph. Available in adult S (1), L (1), XL(5), XXL(2); (numbers indicate quantity still on hand). The cost is $16 per shirt plus $4 postage for the first shirt, and $2 postage for each additional shirt.

Two of the sample Jack Benny Middle School shirts are still available. The first is an Adult Large 50/50 cotton-poly t-shirt in green with white lettering ($16), and the second is an Adult Medium 100% cotton long-sleeve crew collar shirt in white with the school name and emblem embroidered on the left breast ($30). Add $4 for shipping. More shirts are available directly from the school; E-mail jackbenny@aol.com to request more information.

Also available are the commemorative books. These include: the 28-page book containing a complete outline of the weekend, including photos and biographies of panelists and guests; the color "Remembering Jack Benny" booklet from the Hillside memorial service; and the 39 Forever self-guided tour of Los Angeles Jack Benny sites. All three of these can be yours for $5.00.

Please send checks (payable to IJBFC) to: P.O. Box 11288, Piedmont, CA 94611, or use Paypal.com and send payment to jackbenny@aol.com.

Backstage
With Eddie Carroll

In 1983, I had the distinction of presenting my first one-man show of JACK BENNY that opened in Los Angeles. I had spent a year in preparation, developing Jack's speech, his timing and delivery and his mannerisms so that my presentation would be an accurate and honest portrayal and not just another "impression." I also had to learn to play the violin, but that's another story!!

It was a heady experience, performing for enthusiastic audiences who were delighted to once again spend an evening enjoying the company of America's most beloved comedian. An even bigger thrill was the pleasure of having so many illustrious people in attendance. There were Jack's writers: George Balzer, Sam Perrin, Milt Josefsberg, Al Gordon, and Hal Goldman…co-workers: Dennis Day and Mel Blanc…Jack's manager, Irving Fein…his daughter Joan and granddaughter Joanna…and celebrities too numerous to mention.

Amid the glow of that first engagement, there were also several "well intentioned" people who said, "Enjoy doing your show while you can, because it won't last. A few years from now, no one will remember who Jack Benny was."

WELLL….! It's now twenty years later and to my eternal delight and personal satisfaction those people have all been proven wrong! Jack's image is alive and well and enthusiastic audiences continue to fill theatres and venues wherever I appear all over the country.

More important, what has become even bigger proof of his unending popularity is the success of the IJBFC and the continual growth of its membership. The enthusiasm of the members is heartwarming, as was confirmed by those members who came from all over the U.S., Canada, and the U.K. to attend the IJBFC gathering in Los Angeles in February.

There were many convention highlights, but for me personally, it was a privilege on opening night to take part in recreating Jack's classic radio show wherein he discovers that he still is only 39! (Especially since we performed it on his birthday.) The show was a wonderful success due to the devotion and enthusiasm of talented fan club members: Maria Scarvelis, Tom Trethewey, Bill Powers, Eric Brolund, Janine Preston, and our "Prez" and her husband Dan who all did a grand job in portraying the colorful cast members of the Jack Benny Show. Many thanks to them all for a great job…great fun and a great memory!

I think everyone who had the pleasure of attending will agree that the success of the convention was far beyond anyone's expectations, and it was all due to the hard work and devotion of our President, Laura Leff. Very few members will ever really know what an enormous undertaking it was for one person, with months of preparation and planning, trips to L.A., countless phone calls, attention to details and sacrificing personal time and expense. Not to mention that Laura and Dan went without sleep during the convention itself seeing to all the details for the following day's events.

There are not enough bouquets available to show our gratitude. So here's to you Madame President.

I think I speak for all the attending members and join them all in applauding you with a standing ovation and our heartfelt thanks for providing us with three magical days that we will long remember and know that we were part of something rare and special.

Our love and best wishes and may you truly stay 39 forever!

And more thank yous…

Dear Laura & Dan,

To me, the 39 Forever Celebration was a very joyous weekend. I had the opportunity to invite my former film professor and his girlfriend to the celebration and they said they loved every minute of it!! My fiancée (who is a IJBFC member) also enjoyed every second of the celebration that she attended - (especially the Friars Club Celebrity Banquet).

Of course, celebrating the life, career and comedy of Jack Benny for an entire weekend was heaven for me. I enjoyed everything - from the Opening Program at the Gateway Sheraton to the Radio & Television Museum. Actor Eddie Carroll was so good as Jack Benny, I almost felt that Jack was still with us - and in a lot of ways, he really is. I was so amused by writer Al Gordon, who had us in tears from laughter with his comments during one of the panel discussions. I also had the privilege of meeting Jack's grandson Bob, Irving Fein, Rose Marie, Leo Gorcey, Jr., and the many wonderful people who were in attendance as Jack's fans. I am also very grateful and thankful that I was able to have the privilege of playing "Dennis Day" during a re-creation of the winning script of the Jack Benny Script Contest. It was so much fun, and I'm glad that I was a part of a talented group who entertained those in attendance. I often think that I would have thrived during the Golden Days of Radio.

I was also deeply moved by the Memorial Service at Hillside in Culver City on 2/16/03. It was a loving tribute to Jack and Mary, as they will always be in our hearts and minds. Jack Benny gave us so much in his long career, and I am grateful that a tribute like "39 Forever" was held - as it is a once-in-a-lifetime event.

Much respect and admiration go to both of you for all the hard work that it took to put this event together. I can't even conceive what it was like to plan such an event. But I will be eternally grateful that it was successfully accomplished. I wish to say to you both - "THANK YOU, THANK YOU, THANK YOU!!!"

Sincerely,
Scott Ferguson Greene

Dear Laura,

Just wanted to thank you for having The Ink Spots participate in your wonderful event for the induction of Jack Benny into the National Comedy Hall of Fame. It was a real privilege to honor a man who gave The Ink Spots so much recognition in their early days.

Jim Nabbie, who was our lead singer for many years before his death in 1992, did a great imitation of Jack Benny's introducing The Ink Spots on his show. He did this during our shows for many years. So Jack Benny has been a part of our lives for a long time.

Again, please accept our deep appreciation for allowing us to be included in your gala. Harold, Sonny, Morris, and Herman join me in sending you our warmest regards.

Sincerely,
Mili Della Lilley
THE INK SPOTS' Manager

The Tale Piece

(From Kurt Jensen) So I'm talking to Ward Grant today, and we're talking about other comedians who worked with Bob Hope, because I'm trying to help assemble the 100th birthday package for USAT. (Tomorrow I interview Frances Langford.)

And I bring up the subject of Jack and Bob, since they worked so well together. And he told me the story of what he thought was the 1970 departure for the annual Christmas USO trip.

For that, Jack dressed up like Santa to see them off. There's a tiny film clip of that on Hope's special that ran the following January, because Hope tossed a quarter at Jack, and Jack dove for it. Very funny.

And Ward Grant said that it was his job to pick up Jack, get him to the airport, and get him into the Santa suit. And nothing was scripted, so Grant suggested some things. He said, "You know, I have the rental receipt for the suit here," and Jack's reply was, "Great, I can use that." So Jack improvised a bit with Bob.

And then Grant said that after the plane took off, Jack asked him to drive to the end of the runway, just the two of them. And Grant did, and asked why, and Jack's reply was: "I want to wave goodbye."

(From Frank Reuben) I saw and enjoyed Jack Benny every time he played at the London Palladium. On my first visit to the States in the early 70's, I went with my wife and daughter to The Brown Derby in Beverly Hills for an early meal before visiting our first drive-in movie. When we went into the restaurant it was practically empty, except for a large table of about eight or ten people, you can probably guess - it was Jack Benny and his family and grandchildren. I told him that we had seen him a few months earlier in London; he was very friendly and introduced us to his family. It was a certainly one of the highlights of our visit.

(From Charles Kaufman) I was a production assistant (read: gofer) for one season of Bob Hope's shows and met Mr. Benny when I was only delivering food from a deli. He was a gracious as could be. Where the rest of the big stars that were guesting on the Hope special barely acknowledged me, Mr. Benny thanked me, asked me where I was from, etc. In a world of phonies, he struck me as a sincerely nice guy who took the time. That's it: for a 21-year-old guy beginning in the biz, Mr. Benny "took the time."

As long ago as it was and as many varied life experiences as I've had, I've thought about the brief encounter many times. In two ways: First: what a tiny little event in Mr. Benny's life, I was. I wonder how many, many lives he effected and that remained unknown to him. Second: I've achieved a fair amount of success in my life, and his behavior toward me -small as it was - has served as an outstanding model of humility and grace.

Do You Know?

(From Michael Clahr, doctorson3@webtv.net) I hope that you can help me. My late mother, Irene Etkin, was one of Jack's New York agents. She worked as Affiliated Artists, Lyons & Lyons, etc. from the 1930s-50s, and also handled the likes of Jackie Gleason, Lee Marvin, Jayne Mansfield, Patsy Kelly, and others. I'm always looking for information about her.

Have you ever come across any? On my birthday, Jack and Mary would always send flowers, and I still have all the enclosure cards from them.

(From Donald Solem, at right) I served aboard the aircraft carrier USS SARATOGA during WWII. Jack Benny broadcast his then regular Sunday show aboard this ship on April 21, 1946. I made a small violin for him from teak wood of the flight deck, just wondering if it is still around. The USS SARATOGA association hopes to acquire this violin for a permanent museum soon, and we are looking for display memorabilia. You may check our web site at www.saratogamuseum.org to review progress of this endeavor. I can assure you this artifact would be displayed with pride and honor to him for devoted cause of entertaining the service men & women of our country. (LL: Please contact me at jackbenny@aol.com if you have any information.)

(From David Golumbia, dgolumbi@panix.com) I am writing an article for an academic conference on Radio studies about some episodes of the Jack Benny program. Specifically, I want to talk about the episodes where Butterfly McQueen appears as Mary's maid Butterfly (she speaks in a high voice and talks a lot about her boyfriend Jerome) in 1943-44. In a book about Gone with the Wind, in which Butterfly McQueen appeared as Prissy, the author Roland Flamini writes that Butterfly McQueen "walked out of a Jack Benny program rather than resurrect Prissy." I can find no other references to this event in any of the literature. Do you have any idea where I might track down some more information about it?

I should mention that I am a huge fan of Jack Benny and old-time radio generally, and I admire these performances and also Thelma McQueen; I'm not interested in anything but writing a thorough and accurate historical account, especially of the role the Jack Benny program played in promoting strong views about racial equality. (My view is that the program was among the very most important cultural forces that helped to create this monumental change in American society).

(From Bill Henry, wstonehenry@adelphia.net) I am a collector of Cleveland Indians memorabilia and recently acquired an interesting baseball. On the baseball is printed the following: "Opening of 1936 Season at Cleveland between Cleveland & Tigers. 1st Ball Pitched by Joe Louis; caught by Jack Benny; batted at by Mary Livingstone, lost bat & fell." I wanted to see if you have any information about this event or whether you may even have any pictures from that day (April 14, 1936). I would appreciate any help you can provide and would be happy to email pictures of this ball to you if you would like them for your website. Thank you very much.

(From John Hawksley of England) I would dearly like to buy a few TV cassettes in PAL format of the half hour shows made Jack Benny...I have tried many avenues before the BBC, but all efforts proved in vain...hoping you can help.

(From Tony Olson, aolson@calpoly.edu) My grandfather was a guest on the Jack Benny TV show. He and Jack did a skit. If you come across the skit please let me know. By the way, my grandfather was the violinist on the old CBS radio shows. His name was Anthon Fredrick Olson. He was known as Fred. However, I think he told me Jack Benny insisted on calling him Anthon.

You Do Know!

(From Nate Gordon) As a Jack Benny historian, I thought you might be interested in this: You may recall that I asked you if you knew where Jack and the gang might have done the radio show before NBC opened its Sunset & Vine studios in 1938. At http://www.angelfire.com/ca7/loyaltubist/OTR.HTML (I hope I copied it correctly), it states, "NBC's first home in Hollywood was the RKO Movie Studios located off Melrose Avenue, near Vine Street (behind the present Musician's Union complex). This is further corroborated by, of all people, Bob Hope, in an introduction that he wrote for a book that I just purchased through EBAY, a book authorized by NBC to celebrate its then 50-year history (it was published in 1976). Also see http://www.seeing-stars.com; check out the KCAL studios link and you will even see a picture of NBC radio in 1935. The building seems to still be up.

(From Mary Lou Wallace) According to the April 26 - May 2 TV Guide article about TV shows on DVD, the DVD of the 1st season of "The Mary Tyler Moore Show" has bonus footage of Jack Benny and Lucille Ball presenting Emmy Awards to Ed Asner and Valerie Harper in 1971.

(From Art Chimes, of the Voice of America) I was reading on your FAQ page about whether Benny was an accomplished violinist. Are you familiar with his appearance at the 1970 "Honor America" event at the Lincoln Memorial in Washington? It was sort of flag-waving, bash-the-counterculture event that I would have sneered at the time. But a few years later I got a copy of the 2-disc album of the rally that includes at least two outstanding cuts: Kate Smith's smashing "God Bless America" and a red-hot Jack Benny (on his Strad, if I remember correctly) playing "Sweet Georgia Brown." Maybe no Mischa Elman, but not too shabby, and the crowd certainly loved it.

(From Russell Myers) A while back I told you that I had discovered the location of Rochester's house in Los Angeles. After some more detective work, here is what I found. The [postcard at left] shows the house in its glory days, some time in the 1930s or 1940s. I don't know when it was built. It is on a cul-de-sac with eight to ten other houses and the street is named Rochester Circle. It's located about a mile south of the Santa Monica freeway (10) and about a mile west of the USC campus. The most unusual thing is that it is in an area of much smaller two or three bedroom homes on small lots. It's completely out of proportion to the other houses in the area. It is also surprisingly similar in size and style to Jack's most famous residence on Roxbury in Beverly Hills.

I drove by and snapped this photo. It's not very good but you can't find an angle where you can frame the entire house. The house is not in very good condition. The shutters are gone and I couldn't tell if it was being prepared to be painted or had just fallen on hard times and been left that way.

Jack Benny Classifieds

§§§ The First Generation Radio Archives has uncovered a 15 ips unedited reel tape master recording of "The Lucky Strike Program with Jack Benny," as recorded on April 15, 1954. It contains exactly what the audience for that program heard, from the last minute orchestra and vocal warm-ups before the show to the final applause at the end - and the fidelity is astounding. As you might imagine, this is a very rare item: the master tape the engineers used to edit together the final show as broadcast, cutting in pre-recorded commercials and removing slight delays in cues or flubbed lines. Most of these tapes were erased for re-use once the final version was made - this one survived.

You'll get another Jack Benny program - this one from February 25th of the same year - from the final edit CBS network master tape recording. Even if you have heard these shows before, you've never really heard them until you hear these CDs: high fidelity sound, far better than any radio was capable of receiving at the time. Hearing these shows is just like being there - only better, because once you have them, you can hear and enjoy them time and time again.

The Archives is offering the members of the IJBFC the chance to obtain a CD copy of both of these great shows FREE, just for joining the First Generation Radio Archives. Yep, in addition to the ten free CD library loans and the free Membership CD all of our new members are sent, people who join the Archives and state "I'm a member of the IJBFC" when they fill out the on-line membership form will get this free CD as well (http://www.radioarchives.org/membership.HTML). A decent deal, I'd say, and believe me, it's worth the $15.00 one-year membership in the Archives just to get to hear these shows (not to mention all the other great shows that Archives members have access to, of course).

§§§ Shokus Video is offering a discount to all IJBFC members when ordering from their extensive and impressive list of Jack Benny rarities. Order any or all of the six Benny volumes, and mention "IJBFC 10% DISCOUNT" in the SPECIAL INSTRUCTIONS box. For more information, see their Web site at http://www.shokus.com/benny.html or write for a catalog: P.O. Box 3125, Chatsworth, CA 91313.

§§§ From the National Lum and Abner Society: It's about time for all of us to start making that annual trip through the beautiful Ouachita Mts. to Mena for the annual NLAS Convention! It is hard to believe that next year will be the 20th of these blowouts that we have blown up... but first we have our #19 event this year, where we are celebrating the 60th anniversary of the two L&A movies released during 1943, Two Weeks to Live and So This is Washington.

Unfortunately, there are no living cast members from the Washington film. However, we are very thankful that one of the main performers from Two Weeks is not only very much alive and well, but loves visiting Mena. Those of you who were around for our 1998 convention will remember that KAY LINAKER (a.k.a. KATE PHILLIPS) visited with us, even though her L&A movie was not celebrating its anniversary. At that time she promised that she would return in 2003, and sure enough, she already has her bags packed and is ready to go!

Heavens to cameo guest stars, that isn't all! In our February 2003 issue you saw the tribute to Two Weeks to Live's ROSEMARY LaPLANCHE, written by her daughter, CAROL KOPLAN, which told all about Rosemary's varied career as Miss America 1941, and later as an actress and artist. Carol plans to be with us for a portion of the weekend to speak about her late mother, and display rare photos and memorabilia from Rosemary's collection. And, keep your whiskers crossed... One of last years guests, cartoon voice legend DAL McKENNON, had such a good time in Mena that wild Gumbys couldn't keep him away this year, and he too plans to be on hand. Those of you who met him last year will agree that there are few people who make one feel so good just to be around them. We should all be that jolly!

By now you should be picking up the phone and calling the Lime Tree Inn in Mena to make your room reservation. Don't depend on your speed dial or your little black address book, because since last year the area code for Mena has been changed. The correct number is (479) 394-6350. Don't delay, do it today, and all that other rhyming stuff. In our June issue we plan to have a more complete schedule of events, but we usually begin around 5 p.m. on Friday and then have events at various times on Saturday. Well be lookin fer ya there!

---

§§§ Leo Gorcey Jr.'s book, <u>Me and the Dead End Kid,</u> will be available soon. Leo Gorcey's life had it all: The rebellious youth, the big break, domestic spats, divorces, the battle with the bottle, and the decline and fall. The celebrity's life had something else in it: Leo Gorcey, Jr.

Witnessing his famous father being loved and adored by those around him, 'Little Leo' yearned to be accepted by the star. Writing with the perfect balance of courage and edgy humor, the author takes an honest look at the ups and downs of a father/son relationship - from anger and grief to compassion and forgiveness. Leo Gorcey Jr. is a gifted storyteller. He makes us feel the joys and pains, not only of his life with the Dead End Kid, but of our lives as well - the common experience of growing up in an imperfect world, overcoming obstacles, and moving on. Watch for the website also coming soon at http://www.leogorcey.com.

The Jack Benny Times

September - December 2003   Volume XVIII, Numbers 5-6

President's Message

Hello again, folks. This summer has been a good one for me. I have been enjoying the break from working (it's a little like having a summer vacation again), and spending lots of time on the IJBFC, the Web site, and associated E-mails. I would like to thank everyone for staying in touch and keeping me even busier outside the 9-to-5 world than I had a regular job! As I said in the last issue, it is a pleasure and a privilege to correspond with so many enthusiastic Benny fans.

On our back cover this issue, we have a picture of Jack standing next to some sketches from the cartoon <u>The Mouse That Jack Built</u>. As many of you know, it was this cartoon that got me started on my love for Jack Benny. Here are the full stats:

Released 4/4/59 - Prod 1520 - MPAA 18955
Director: Robert McKimson
Cast: Jack Benny; Mary Livingstone; Rochester; Don Wilson; Ed and The Maxwell: Mel Blanc.
Story: Tedd Pierce - Anim: Tom Ray, George Grandpré, Ted Bonnicksen, Warren Batchelder - Layout: Robert Gribbroek - Backgrounds: Bob Singer - Film Editor: Treg Brown - Music: Milt Franklyn

New Members

**** Mitchell Lutsky **** Steve Keiser **** Frank E. Bales **** Alan L. Stone **** Peter Riches **** Robb Hill **** John Swanson **** Harold A. Allen **** Lori Rustin **** Ross Wagman **** Lucinda Boone **** Tony Gosmer **** Efrem Krisher **** David Lowe **** John Blascak **** Lindsay Curcio **** Tony Lee **** Robert Mechner **** Brice A Baird **** Terry Bellows **** John D. Rutledge **** Joe Sell **** Scott Freeling **** Brian O'Dell **** Larry Cheney **** Nichole Marie Baxter **** Eric Cooper **** Zach Eastman **** Hilda Katz Phillips **** Janice Spiecker **** Joe Gruzleski **** Paul J. Stamas **** Martha E. Torres **** Darrell W. Brown **** Gary Smullen **** Michael Cain **** Daniel Marbell, Jr. **** George Dranchak **** Jim Inman **** Kevin Milus **** Elizabeth Reich **** William A. Bailey **** Martin Dougherty **** J. Vincent Fitzpatrick **** Robert B. Evans **** Michael McDermott **** Michael Gibbs **** Lee F. Bartoletti **** Kent Salomon **** Cody Morgan **** Bob Watson **** John Gray **** Steven Harris **** Christina Kyriacou **** Brett Danalake **** Jack Raymond **** Randy Russi **** David Massengill **** Malcolm

Fisher **** Debbie Ekhoff **** Jay Mayfield **** Martin J. Dzik **** Jon S. Harwood **** David Coursey **** Deborah Blanton **** Robert L. Westman **** Frederick Kandera **** Dennis Norfolk **** Chris Morton **** H. Hunter George **** Karen Murray **** Janice Bleibaum **** Thomas Chuey **** Tony Miller **** Dave Koker **** Ian Krieger **** Mike Duffin **** James L. Jones **** Mark Fleischer **** Alphonse Dattolo **** Theodore V Zudyk **** Dr Graham McCann **** Gene Dench **** Jon Mark Lundell **** Loran J. Skinkis **** Dennis David Smith **** Laurence Tuccori **** Pamela Sigmon **** Richard Sutton **** Mike Antonucci **** Steve Gibbs **** Lara Hoffman **** Jason Leznek **** Barry Baldwin **** Andrew Sheardown **** James J Varela **** Michael Amaro **** Lee Seiden **** Dr. Charles Beckett

The Big Benny Deal

I want to take this opportunity to thank all the people who supported 39 Forever both before and after the event. Through your generous donations, we have reduced the event's financial loss to approximately $3,800. I think most of you know my current job situation, and having this additional outlay from our personal pocket is difficult on us. However, there are several ways that you can help, and get some great stuff in the bargain.

39 Forever Videos

We have four tapes that chronicle the weekend's activities during the Friday opening gala and Saturday's marathon. VHS, NTSC format. These videos will be ordered on September 20 based on demand, and very few additional copies will be available after this offer.

- Opening gala and radio recreation, Jackpardy, and script contest winner (2 hours) - **$15.00**
- Coworker panel: Al Gordon, Irving Fein, Kay Linaker, Beverly Washburn (2 hours) - **$15.00**
- Family panel: Joan Benny and Michael Rudolph, and Music panel: Gisele MacKenzie, Brian Gari, Norma Stevens, and Jay Meyer (2 hours) - **$15.00**
- Jack Benny's impact on comedy: Tim Williams (TV Guide), Eddie Carroll, Budd Friedman (The Improv), Emma Kennedy (BBC), Leo Gorcey Jr. (Me and the Dead End Kid), and Michael Levine (1 hour) - **$10.00**

ORDER ALL FOUR VIDEOS FOR $50!

39 Forever Program Blowout

We still have a quantity of 39 Forever programs, which include the self-guided tour map and color brochure from Hillside Cemetery. Previously available for $5.00, now on sale for $2.00! PRICE REDUCED! (Shipping included if ordered with another item)

The BIG DEAL!
For anyone making a tax-deductible donation of $39.00 or more (i.e., not in the purchase of above items), we will give a CD copy of a previously unreleased rarity. It is Jack Benny's last performance at Las Vegas' Congo Room on November 28, 1972, with Mac Davis and Hilliard "Hickey" Marks (Mary's brother). It gives a very rare glimpse into Jack's live monologue work, and the sound quality is exceptional. Don't miss this opportunity!

Shipping
Orders will be sent via Priority Mail within the U.S., and Air Mail to non-U.S. addresses. Please add the appropriate shipping charges to your order:
- First item: $4.00 within the U.S., $8.00 outside the U.S.
- Each additional item: $2.00 within the U.S., $3.00 outside the U.S.

(One or two videos count as one item, three or four count as two items)

Payment
Send Paypal payment to jackbenny@aol.com, or make checks payable to IJBFC and mail to the address at the end of this newsletter. Thank you very much for your support!

In Memoriam

It is sad to say that we have lost a number of Jack Benny-related people in the past few months. I am sure that the first one that will jump to most minds is Bob Hope on July 27. For those on the Web, you have probably already seen the photo and audio tribute on jackbenny.org. The question was posed on the OTR Digest whether Jack Benny or Bob Hope was funnier and ultimately more important to the history of comedy. Paul Fornatar wrote the following excellent response to this question:

"First, it's an unfair question since they weren't the same kind of comedian. When speaking of radio, consider my experience. Is it typical? When I listen to a Jack Benny radio show, I'm there, even if I've heard the show ten times. When

I listen to an old Bob Hope radio show, I don't quite take the trip back. I find a few things that are amusing but it's not the same.

"As for ad-libbing, neither man is a master. Milton Berle wore that hat in my opinion. He was funny on radio but not very. Milton was a comedian that had to be seen in person. I once saw him at the Chicago Theater do six live shows in one day. Every show was different. A fly came into view in one show and Milton did ten minutes on the fly. I'm afraid Jack and Bob needed writers for something like that.

"I think Benny might have been a better actor, especially in dramas he did in early television. I think Bob did one fairly dramatic role in the movies. Which leads to Bob's strength: movies. Say what you like, they were always fun. Jack's few were mostly just good tries.

"As for television, here again, they weren't the same. Jack was wise in bringing the radio family to TV because he didn't do stand up. Bob was wise and stayed with the things that made him the center. Jack was always on the outside looking in, and Bob was always on the inside looking out. Someone mentioned that Jack's television shows weren't on TV land. True, but neither are Bob's. As a guest on TV talk shows, Bob had a chance to use his prepared jokes. Jack on the other hand offered a different side of himself usually.

"They were both great "givers" of their time. No one can deny the great efforts of Bob. We who were in the midst of their primes must be thankful for having had them in our lives. I met Bob once in 1950 at a big Hollywood Bowl blast. He was very nice to me, a young man at the time. He introduced me to Peggy Lee (who was godawful gorgeous). It made my life for quite a few months. Bob  was a supreme MC that night and many nights on TV and private shows. Unfortunately, I never had a chance to meet Jack. I would have loved that.

"One last thing, which is probably personal. Try it. When you think of both men, I like Bob Hope but I love Jack Benny. Does that make sense? Or, is it just preference? I don't know. I do know I've collected a lot more Benny than Hope, even though I had more opportunity to get Hope. Someone either on this list or another said something to the effect that they both left 'Big footprints, it's just that they wore different shoes.' I think that's a wonderful way to compare two great entertainers, the likes we will not see again."

On July 23, Bob Blumofe passed away at the age of 93. He is survived by his son Bobby and daughter Joanna, and is missed by many friends and relatives.

From <u>Sunday Nights at Seven</u> by Joan Benny:

After four years of playing the Gay Divorcee, flying back and forth between jobs in New York and my children in Los Angeles, pursuing my so-called career halfheartedly and jet-setting around the world, I decided it was time to settle down again. At home between trips, I had been going out with Bob Blumofe, who was then head of production at United Artists. We had been seeing each other for about a year when one morning he called me. I was in New York.

"What are you doing?" he asked.
"I'm leaving for the south of France tonight," I replied.
"That plane's going in the wrong direction," he said. "Get one heading west. Come home and marry me."

I did. Would I never learn? This time I really thought I was in love. Bob was much older than I--twenty-five years to be exact--a settled, solid, law school-trained businessman, who would be good for me, who would keep me and my capricious tendencies in line. Unlike my previous husbands he was in show business. That was a plus. He was enormously bright, well read and knowledgeable. (I used to laughingly say, "He's the only person I know who can spell all the 'twenty most misspelled words in the English language' correctly!") He played the violin, loved going to concerts and owned a record collection more extensive than mine. We had so much in common.

Mother and Daddy thought I was making another mistake. "He's too old for you," they said, but again they knew I would do exactly what I wanted. Mother arranged a small wedding--and this time it really was small--at their house, with just the immediate family and my two children [Michael and Maria]. My favorite memory of the event is of six-year-old Maria, who was standing next to me holding my hand, announcing right smack in the middle of the "I do's" that she had to go to the bathroom. The ceremony came to a dead halt, as though someone had said "Freeze," and resumed when she returned. Daddy fell on the floor laughing--and never let her forget it!

(From Gerry O.) Mention of Gregory Peck's passing (June 12) should be made, as he and his wife Veronique were part of Jack Benny's "Inner Circle" of close friends. A number of years ago Mr. Peck did one of those one-man "An Evening With..." shows here in town, and a large part of the evening consisted of questions from the audience. Someone asked Mr. Peck about his friendship with Jack Benny, and Mr. Peck spoke of their close friendship...then after a second or two of silence, he added, "I still miss him".

Additionally, Robert Stack, the last surviving member of the main cast of <u>To Be Or Not To Be</u> (Lt. Stanislav Sobinski), passed away on May 14.

Backstage With Eddie Carroll

<u>Laughter in Bloom</u>…Imitation?…Impression?…or Art?

Over the past four decades, I've had the good fortune to enjoy success in films, television, commercials and the legitimate stage. I've also had the distinct pleasure of being the voice of Jiminy Cricket for the past thirty years and still continue to work on projects for Disney.

As much fulfillment as all this has brought me, nothing has given me as much pleasure in the last decade as performing my one-man show…<u>JACK BENNY: Laughter in Bloom</u> in theatres and venues across the country. I've also had the distinction of receiving the support and approval of the IJBFC, the Benny family and Estate, Irving Fein (who was Jack's manager for thirty years), and Jack's hometown of Waukegan. To receive all these notable endorsements is extremely flattering and rewarding, both personally and professionally. However, it also carries with it a burden of responsibility to protect and retain Jack Benny's image with honesty, dignity, and respect.

This responsibility is continually challenged, especially when I'm being interviewed by members of the media and press for upcoming performances. Some of the interviewers who had not yet seen the show make an immediate assumption that since I'm emulating a legendary figure, then the show automatically belongs in the same category as many of the glitzy imitation acts that we've all seen. Others try to find a label for what I do, as "mimic", "look-alike", "Benny act", "imitator", and most often, "impressionist". As a result, I take great pains with each interview (especially articles that appear in print) to explain the reasons why Jack Benny's image does not belong in any of those categories.

So where does it belong? To explain, let me share with you my comments to the press. Over the years, we've all seen comedians and performers do imitations and impressions of well-known celebrities. By its very nature, an impression is usually an over-exaggerated "caricature" of vocal and physical traits of a famous person, and in some instances, it's deliberately over-done to satirize or make fun of the celebrity.

Now don't get me wrong. I'm not faulting impressionists. There are some very talented people in this field and I thoroughly enjoy watching them perform a variety of impressions or imitations as entertaining moments during an entire act. However, when an actor is called upon to create and sustain just <u>one</u> character for an entire evening, doing an impression of "caricature" wears thin very quickly. Also, when you go to see Rich Little for example, who is very good at what he does, during his entire show you're always aware that it's Rich Little on stage "doing" Benny or Burns or whoever.

The difference is that when you buy a ticket for <u>JACK BENNY: Laughter in Bloom</u>, they're not coming to watch Eddie Carroll being clever…they're coming to see Jack Benny again, *in person!*

In 1983 I was given an opportunity to do my first one-man show as Jack. As a theatre-trained actor, I knew that to portray Jack with proper respect, I had to get past surface imitation and try to capture and re-create the essence of his humanity, his reality and honest persona. In preparation, I spent months watching video tapes and listening to radio shows, practicing his vocal qualities…the timbre of his voice…the Midwest drawl…and most importantly, his timing and delivery. Hours were also spent working on facial expressions, posture and body language until it all became effortless and second nature.

My purpose was to lose my own identity and create a portrait so authentic that when I made my entrance on stage, the audience would have their expectations fulfilled and accept the theatrical illusion that it really <u>was</u> Jack on stage. For the next hour and forty minutes, they could suspend reality and delight in hearing the fascinating story of his life and once again enjoy the distinctive trademarks and matchless humor that made him a household word and America's most beloved comedian.

So getting back to my original point, is there a label for what I do, or a category for my show? If there is a category to which it belongs, then it's best described by a noted drama critic who said, "<u>Laughter in Bloom</u> is an evening of pure nostalgic joy and brings Benny to life with such clarity that it belongs in the same illustrious company as Hal Holbrook's <u>Mark Twain</u>…James Whitmore's <u>Will Rogers</u>…Robert Morse in <u>Tru</u> and Christopher Plummer in <u>Barrymore</u>."

I don't think anyone would label these accomplished actors as impressionists or imitators, but rather as consummate artists who use their talent and craft to pay homage to a legend and create an evening of theatrical magic. I hope Jack is proud to be included in such esteemed company and I will continue to be responsible in protecting his legacy.

ଔ ଓ

As a note to all IJBFC members, the show is booked in various theatres around the country from August through May of 2004. If you're interested in seeing it, please check the IJBFC

Web site under Goodies (Eddie Carroll) and you'll find a list of dates and locations. After every performance, I go out in the lobby to greet the audience and if you happen to attend, it will be a pleasure to meet you.

The one question I get asked most often is, "What made you decide to perform as Benny and how did it come about?" Well, dear members, that is a story in itself and I'll save that for next time. Until then, take time every day to share a laugh with someone and perform one act of kindness. You'll not only feel better, you'll truly stay 39 forever!

The Jack Bloom Pasadena Chapter

The Jack Bloom Pasadena Chapter was started in 1990 as an honorary society for IJBFC members who have been active for four or more consecutive years. Jack Bloom was a dedicated member of the IJBFC, doing extensive research on him for the <u>Times</u> and the original edition of <u>39 Forever</u>, plus donating hundreds of shows to kick off the IJBFC tape library. Additionally, Jack and I kept a running correspondence for years, discussing Jack Benny and other shared passions, ranging from George Gershwin to bird watching to bad puns. His passing in June of 1990 was a tremendous loss for all the IJBFC members. I still miss him, and am grateful for the warmth and humor that he shared with me.

(Members added this year are indicated by an asterisk.)

Michael Avedissian	Bryan Haigood	Howard Mandelbaum	John Sauciunas
Louis Bianco	Franklin Heynemann	Hooman Mehran	Clair Schulz
James G. Burke	Jimmie Hicks	Steve Metzger	Mel Simons
C.A. Caramella	The Hornbergers	Walt Mitchell	Gary Smith
Jim Davison*	David Howell	Richard Nathan*	Scott J. Smith
Warren Debenham	Will Jordan	Jack Palmer	W. Robert Smith
Anthony DiFlorio	Thomas Kessel	Chris Reale*	Helen Songer
Matthew M. Drew	Raymond L. Krysl*	Richard Rieve	Gus Storm
Robert L. Garland	Stephen Lake	The Robertses	Barbara Thunell
Joe Goff	James A. Link	A. Joseph Ross	Harvey Walker
Frank Gregory	Stephen H. Loeb	Joel S. Rothman	Mary Lou Wallace
Joseph F. Gross	Bobb Lynes	Richard Rubenstein	

Emeritus Members (15+ years)

Hal Bogart	Alan Grossman	Tom Mastel	The Tintorris
Rob Cohen	Tim Hollis	Robert Olsen	Barbara Watkins
Robert Duncan	George Lillie	Donnie Pitchford	Doug Wood
J. Ed Galloway			

Tape Trading List

- Rob Cohen, robcohen@ameritech.net (Rob would also like to trade Jack Benny MP3 for other radio comedy shows--e.g., Fibber McGee, etc.)
- Steven Cottingham, steven@stevencottinghamchess.com

- George Grube, Ontime6402@aol.com
- Janet Maday, maydaymayday@aol.com
- John Matthews, glowingdial@yahoo.com
- Jay Meade, jmeade@starfishnet.com
- Jack Palmer, vdalhart@prodigy.net
- Brendan Scherer, goldenstar4@juno.com
- Jeff Tanner, P. O. Box 65787, Vancouver, WA 98686, USA; TannerJeff@aol.com
- John Tisinger, jdtisinger@peachnet.campuscwix.net
- Lynn Wagar, philcolynn@yahoo.com (cassette only)
- Bob Westman, leniro@aol.com
- Drew Wiest, 6109 NE 197th St, Kenmore, WA 98028, USA; dwiest12@hotmail.com
- Bob Wombacher, Jr., bashfulbobmotel@webtv.net
- Ken Yesson; yesandno@telusplanet.net

The Tale Piece

(From Dick Osgood's <u>WYXIE Wonderland</u>) There was excitement at the studio. Jack Benny was going to do one of his broadcasts from Detroit. He was on NBC's Blue Network then which meant the Detroit broadcast would originate from WXYZ. No sound men were coming with him, so a script from the Detroit show was sent in advance and Ted Robertson and Fred Flowerday went over it listing sound requirements. One was to be the sound of a wheezy old automobile.

Flowerday remembered it vividly. "Ted and I got this big wash tub and an old electric fan. We removed two of the blades of the fan and rewired the thing into the tub and that was a live prop on Jack Benny's show. I'm not saying that the sound was not improved upon later but this was the first time he had used the Maxwell.

"We didn't have the advantage of a tape recorder. We did not have the advantage of a wire recorder. They had not been invented. Some of our sounds were on records done by the Gennett Company or Major Standard Sound Effects. But most of our sounds were live sounds which we had to invent ourselves."

One standard prop was an empty cigar box with one end partly removed. Each actor had his own with his name on it. To give the effect of talking from the far side of a closed door, the actor would speak his lines into the cigar box.

The Benny broadcast was on Sunday night. Sunday morning, Robertson and Flowerday showed up for rehearsals with their paraphernalia at Masonic Auditorium, a huge concert hall where the broadcast would originate before a live audience. Don Wilson, Benny's announcer, was already there.

"Can either of you do any acting?" he asked.
"I can't," Flowerday admitted.
"I've done a little," said Robertson.
"Let me hear you read this bit."
Robertson read it for him.
"Well, we'll see."

Detroit actors appeared throughout the day hoping to pick up a little work. By afternoon, one of them had been given Robertson's bit. But Ted had the last laugh. The actor's bit was not funny. But the sound of the old car invented by Ted and Fred Flowerday was a sensation. It won the biggest howl of the show. It was even applauded. It broke up Jack Benny.

The WXYZ sound department, now made up of six men--Robertson, Flowerday, Ernie Winstanley, Dewey Cole, Jimmy Fletcher and a newcomer named Fred Fry--was often considered the best in the country. The National Broadcasting Company tried to lure it to New York in toto, but for varying reasons the six men decided to stay in Detroit. [EN: Strangely, Don's announcement at the end of the show states that the broadcast originated from the Venetian Room of the Book-Cadillac Hotel!]

(From Bill Murtough) During the spring of 1946 I was laid off at CBS. I was immediately hired to go to Palm Springs and build a new station (KCMJ) for announcer Dick Joy and his partner, Don McBain, a former Don Lee engineer turned United Airlines captain. To celebrate the opening of the new CBS affiliate, the network originated their Frank Sinatra show from there, using the local movie theater, to be followed by a local dedication program, with a welcoming bit by the Palm Springs mayor. During the afternoon Benny passed by and seeing a KNX studio manager sunning himself outside the theater, inquired as why he was there. After George explained what was going on, Jack said he would stop by that evening and give us a hand. Due to the fact that the Frank Sinatra was no novelty to them (they were used to sharing the soda fountain at the local drug store with him) the audience response was poor. Fifteen minutes later we went back on the air locally, and Jack, as he promised showed up and took over the mike, ad libbing and had the audience "rolling in the aisles". The only one not laughing was the irate Sinatra director who swore he would never take his show out of town again. Our local announcer finally had to take over in order to get the mayor on. This proved that Jack was a natural comedian and could do a great performance without the help of scriptwriters!

We liked Jack. Always friendly. Also he was very loyal to his people. When he switched from NBC to CBS, CBS paid a million dollars to him, as we understood. However another stipulation was that he would bring his NBC engineer, George Foster, with him. This locked up our seniority list. In other words, if CBS wanted to cut back, as broadcasters did from time to time, they could not lay off any engineers beyond George. George was a fine chap who I was pleased to know. Also Jack took his people, including George, in on his investment deals. Consequently they were financially well off, including George. Last I knew he owned a ski resort up in the mountains. I would usually be in the Master Control room at the time of his show, which was behind glass at the end of the lobby. After the show, the entire cast would pass single file with Jack in the lead. Jack would always give with a big, hearty wave, and the entire group would do the same.

One Sunday afternoon I was in small studio six on the third floor (where Amos and Andy and Steve Allen first started) to feed Jack doing a live insert to a "special" program for B'nai B'rith originating from New York. Two guys from the organization were in the studio and were plotting how they could perhaps get Jack to attend their dinner that night which would inflate their ego. Jack must have had "ESP", as when he entered the studio he turned toward me and gave me a warm greeting, acted like he didn't see these two "cats", went on to the table where he would be seated, recorded his bit, then a farewell to me and left, the two bewildered guys still sitting there with a look of amazement on their faces. I am sure he was aware of their little plot. He was a pretty sharp "cookie". I said that I recorded the bit, but the more I think about it, it was a live insert into a "special" originating in New York.

(From Ruth Filstead) My grandmother, Lillian Streed Goding, did talk about playing in the same school orchestra or band as "Jack" Benny did, but as they were different ages, they were not that close. I do recall her saying that "Jack" always acted like the comedian. My sister, Mimi, recalls hearing from Aunt Lil that Jack Benny was always a "cut-up" in the Waukegan schoolrooms.

(From Randy Russi) According to Billboard Magazine (March 25, 1963), a brief bio of the Rocky Fellers, 4 Filipino brothers who recorded the hit song "Killer Joe", they were on the following TV shows: Dinah Shore, Jack Benny, Jackie Gleason and Ed Sullivan. [EN: They appeared on the November 27, 1962 show with guests Jack Soo and Romi Yamada.] I spoke with the original lead singer of the group, Albert Maligmat, and he confirms this. He says they were working in nightclubs all over Asia when they were approached by producers from Dinah Shore to come to the U.S. They ranged in ages from 8 to 18 and their father was also a part of their act. According to the oldest brother of the Rocky Fellers, Jun (Junior) Maligmat, "All I remember of Jack was that he was funny (besides making jokes) in person, a real gentleman and cared for the people who worked for him."

Is Nothing Sacred? (Apparently Not!)
By David M. Lynch

One often hears that the earlier years of this century were more "sexually innocent." And generally speaking, that's certainly true. Anyone who came of age during the last two or three decades (as well as those older folks whose sensibilities have progressed with the times) has to laugh at the thought that people were once shocked by Elvis Presley's swivel-hipped stage gyrations and the illicit implications of the Everly Brothers' "Wake Up, Little Susie." Years earlier, Mae West was banned from NBC radio for ten years after her 1937 appearance on *The Chase and Sanborn Hour* with Edgar Bergen and Charlie McCarthy. Her suggestive dialogue with Charlie, as well as her "Adam and Eve" sketch with Don Ameche, caused quite a furor. And plenty of the members of the IJBFC know how much agonizing the censor did over exactly how many fraternity pins would be needed to cover Veola Vonn's ample bust!

Well, regardless of what MTV, *Maxim* magazine, TV commercials, and their ilk would suggest, sex has been around a lot longer than Bill Clinton, longer than Elvis, longer than Hugh Hefner... It's been around since, well, the *real* Adam and Eve (Sorry, Mae)! It's only during the last 30-40 years that sex has hit the so-called mainstream. It was always "there;" we just didn't talk about it in what was called "mixed company," or "polite company." *"Keep it clean, guys, there are girls around!"*

And anytime something is suppressed, its "black marketability" (to coin a phrase, perhaps?) is heightened considerably. And so, dearly beloved, we are gathered here today to focus on just one of those underground outlets for the curious, the peculiar publications best-known as "Tijuana Bibles." Let's see how deeply we can delve into the subject without losing sight of the fact that the IJBFC's membership includes pre-teens and other minors...

Tijuana Bibles (known by a few other names as well, "eight-pagers" being the most descriptive, albeit most simplistic) presumably originated sometime in the 1920s, and remained popular (well, clandestinely "popular," if that's possible) until the late 1940s, although I personally am aware of some produced as recently as the early 1970s.

The subject matter was out-and-out sex, but the subjects themselves ranged from movie stars (Bob Hope, Clark Gable, Jean Harlow, and of course, Mae West) to gangsters (Al Capone, John Dillinger) to political and /or newsworthy figures (the Duke of Windsor, Alger Hiss) to comic strip & comic book characters (Popeye, Blondie & Dagwood, Superman, Maggie & Jiggs)! In fact, comic strip characters seem to be the most-used type, probably because the TJBs were themselves comic books, and their artists were cartoonists. Also, it was easier to imitate Elzie Segar's Popeye and Olive Oyl, or Chester Gould's Dick Tracy, than it was to do a true likeness of Jean Harlow or "Pretty Boy" Floyd.

The term "Tijuana" is a tip of the hat to the fact that "foreign" publications seemed more exotic to Americans, so many domestically produced items were given added spice by the claim that they'd originated in Mexico or France. But these books were "bibles" (using that term to mean "authoritative" or "reliable," rather than in any religious context) only in the strictest sense.

The "TJBs," as I like to call them, were traditionally eight pages in length. Quite often, the best likeness of the book's star was on the cover; inside, the artistic standards were generally looser. The usual size was 3" by 4½". Each page had one illustration. They were usually unsigned, and when they were credited to someone, it was an obvious alias. Juvenile "names" like "Juan Goof-Ball," "I.P. Freely," and much cruder *noms de plume* abounded. (Would you sign *your* name to something which was blatantly illegal?) They showcased explicit, straightforward "action" which was doubtlessly instructional only to the most uninformed readers of the era. Plots were minimal. The sex was what was most important, and nothing was allowed to postpone that (Again, keep in mind that we're discussing underground publications designed for a specific, taboo purpose.), although some of them were admittedly clever. Most were produced hastily, with all misspellings and other grammatical errors intact.

Once in a while, an artist more talented than the norm would come along, and one of the larger (approximately 4" by 51/2 ") TJBs would result. Some of these were relatively well-drawn and well-written. "Eddie Cantor in *The Torso Teaser*" was drawn by someone who did a fair likeness of Eddie, and I've seen a 16-page Gracie Allen TJB with a mediocre Gracie but an excellent likeness of George Burns (from the neck up, anyway, as I can't vouch for the rest, nor would I want to).

As for any Jack Benny connections (which could hopefully justify this article's inclusion in the IJBFC newsletter!), I have yet to find one featuring Jack himself. Frankly, that surprises me, since so many big names from the entertainment world were used as subject matter by the TJBs, and, as IJBFC members are well aware, Jack was a star in both radio and motion pictures.

However, I have located one which features Jack's wife ("*Mary Livingstone Hocks Her Benny*"), wherein Mary is shown how to make a little extra money by none other than Bing Crosby! Bing also appears in the Bob Hope TJB I've seen, but neither artist captured Bing's likeness particularly well.

Other Benny-related titles would include another TJB featuring Gracie, "Gracie Allen in *Dumb Like a Fox,*" which features a tryst between Gracie and Phil Baker, which is interrupted by George Burns! There's also one featuring Phil Harris' wife, Alice Faye, in which Alice appears with all three of the Ritz Brothers. The less said about that one, the better, except to say that there's no Phil Harris in sight, probably because it would have made things far too crowded!

I'm not easily offended, so if I ever do find a "Benny Bible," I doubt I'll have a bad reaction to the inevitable treatment Jack would receive (my primary guess would be a story line involving his legendary stinginess). The Tijuana Bibles need to be placed in their proper historical context to be appreciated for what they were. These books fulfilled a need for illicit material (specifically that featuring celebrities, whether fictional -- like cartoon characters -- or real) which existed in the days long before nude scenes became commonplace in Hollywood offerings, long before celebrities posed for *Playboy*, and lonnnng before Pam Anderson and Tommy Lee made their infamous home video. As blatantly sexual as they are, the passage of time has defused their shock value. As such, they're not only inoffensive, but actually rather quaint!

But... really now... *Alger Hiss*?!?

Do You Know?

It has long been an accepted story that Mary recorded her lines from home (in her room or the library) and had an actress, Joan, or Jeanette Eyemann (the script secretary) standing in for her at the live radio performance. However, there seems to be an increasing amount of evidence that Mary did continue to come to the studio for some broadcasts. Part of this evidence is the show recordings, as it would have been almost impossible to have the audience reactions (or other performers) overlapping with Mary's lines. There are some shows where it is fairly noticeable that her lines are edited in at a later date, and have no overlap with any other sound. Additionally, member Barbara Thunell worked at CBS during the early 50s and recalls seeing Mary in the studio performing some shows. I consulted Joan about it, and she recalled that there was at least half a season when Mary recorded her part at home, and Joan read her part for the studio audience. This was probably the winter of 1951, as she left for Stanford the September afterwards. If anyone has additional information on this puzzle, it would be appreciated!

(From D.A. Berryhill) I have heard that there was a child prodigy pianist in the LA area who once had the opportunity to appear on the Jack Benny TV Show. His name was Keith

Green. This pianist grew up to become a very influential singer-songwriter in the area of contemporary Christian music, until his death in an airplane crash several years ago. Since he would have been a minor guest on the TV Show, his name never appears in episode logs or descriptions that I have seen. I am very interested in learning the date of his TV appearance and, assuming that the show is still in existence, if and how I could obtain a copy of the show.

Here's another little mystery for you. I was recently contacted about a boat called "La Jota" which supposedly belonged to Jack. I asked Joan about it, and the only boat she ever recalled was the rowboat in their backyard pool. So I have serious doubts that the boat belonged to Jack, but may have belonged to one of his associates (Eddie Anderson?) or another of his contemporaries. Here's the information I have:

"Today I learned more about La Jota - It was designed by a Frenchman named Mercer as a one-off and built in San Pedro in 1921. It was named La Jota after Jack Benny's writer as it translates in Spanish as 'The Joker'. Jack's writer was also of Basque descent and La Jota is a happy traditional Basque dance.

"In WWII the boat was commissioned by the Navy as an officers booze cruise between Tijuana and San Diego and was painted all gray and carried torpedoes. The 65' boat is now berthed on E dock of the Sausalito Yacht Harbor.

"From the looks of her she needs a lot of work. I understand that she is listed with the Classic Yacht Association."

Any thoughts on who the comedian with the Basque writer might be? While the Basque region was known for being a heavily Jewish area before the Inquisition, I think most (if not all) of Jack's Jewish writers were from Eastern European backgrounds. And I don't think that George or John or Bill were of Basque origin. Thoughts, anyone?

Your help is appreciated in locating Christine Cox. She is related in some way to TV's "Mr. Peepers" Wally Cox, but the link is uncertain. She and three others attended the 39 Forever Celebrity Banquet at the Friars Club, and told the National Comedy Hall of Fame that they would pay that night. Unfortunately she did not, and we would like to collect our $400 from her. If anyone knows her or sat with her and can provide any leads of how we can contact her, please let me know at jackbenny@aol.com. Thank you for your help.

I have seen a number of 39-cent checks signed by Jack floating around in collectors' circles and Ebay. It seems that these checks were a prize awarded to State Farm Agents when they sponsored Jack's television show during the late 50s. Does anyone know more about this award, what agents needed to do to get it, and if the signature is original?

Eric Brolund provided me with a few quotes that have been attributed to Jack. I'm dubious that all of them are really Jack, and am curious if anyone can either confirm or deny their origin:

- A cannibal is a guy who goes into a restaurant and orders the waiter.
- I don't want to tell you how much insurance I carry with the Prudential, but all I can say is: when I go, they go too.
- Give me golf clubs, fresh air and a beautiful partner, and you can keep the clubs and the fresh air.
- I don't deserve this award, but I have arthritis and I don't deserve that either. [EN: This is Jack, because I've heard the recording of it.]
- A scout troop consists of twelve little kids dressed like schmucks following a big schmuck dressed like a kid.
- Age is strictly a case of mind over matter. If you don't mind, it doesn't matter. [EN: I think this was Jack on a special quoting Mark Twain.]

You Do Know!

(From Philip Harwood) I just finished viewing George Washington Slept Here with Jack Benny and Ann Sheridan, from a wonderful Kaufman and Hart play, and directed by William Keighley for Warner Brothers in 1942. Did you know that the main title from George Washington Slept Here had lyrics? Originally, a chorus was supposed to be included in the prelude, but because the main title was edited down before the release, the chorus was booted. However, lyrics were originally written for the Main Title. Here they are:

George Washington Slept Here-
Original Main Title Lyrics

The books all say-a Gen'ral came this way,
He took off his shoes-to have a snooze,
Ding! Dong!
It is ver-y clear, George Wash-ing-ton slept here.

The proof we found, right on this ver-y ground,
He didn't count sheep, far and

near,
George Wash-ing-ton slept here.

If he had de-ci-ded to stay up.
The price of this an-tique would not be way up.
To bed, to bed, a very sleep-y head!
Turned in for the night, blew out the light
On eight hours sleep,
How he could fight,
Ding! Dong!
Give him a rous-ing cheer
George Wash-ing-ton slept here.
(Music by Adolph Deutsch; Lyricist Unknown)

(From Kurt Jensen) At the end of the 34-35 season, an item in the radio column of the LA Times had Jack explaining why the program dropped the romance between Mary Livingstone and Frank Parker. Jack said listeners didn't like it, "but I'm only her husband, so what do I know?"

There were also ads and a review for his stage show at the Paramount Theater, billing him as "the master of ad-lib comedy." Mary Livingstone was the only other billed performer. A later mention of the show describes the bit at the end in which Jack attempted to play "Love in Bloom" as the pictured opened. I think in Irving Fein's version, Jack would attempt to play the violin as the newsreel opened, preferably with as loud an opening as possible. But here was the bit back in 1935. Which means that that, too, originated with Harry Conn, as did the funny bit with the girls' trio.

(From Gerry O.) : Mary Livingstone's maid Pauline was played by different actresses during the 1940's and 50's, but probably the best-known "Pauline" was Doris Singleton, who also played "Carolyn Appleby" on "I Love Lucy".

(From Bob Macandrew) The Rich Little Christmas tape is "Rich Little's A Christmas Carol",
produced for CBC television (English) around 1978. Rich Little played all the adult lead parts as famous people would have. The "cast" included W.C. Fields as Scrooge, and Jack Benny as one of the men talking about Scrooge after he "died" and as the little boy who talks to Scrooge on Christmas morning.

Etcetera

(From Bryan H., courtesy of the OTR Digest) For the entire run of the Jack Benny Jell-O program the Pacific Coast airtime was 8:30 PM . (7:30 PM in communities that did not observe daylight savings time when such applied). The cast did two live shows (one for the east and one for the west).

Towards the end of the General Foods sponsorship that second live West Coast performance was discontinued. This happened around the fall of 1942 or so or most likely when General Foods switched the product advertised from Jell-O to Grape Nuts Flakes.

Jack Benny was then heard live out west at 4pm on connected red network stations but a RECORDED playback of the earlier program was heard at 8:30 PM on Blue network stations. The Blue network had been allowing some recorded programming on their western stations to accommodate time zone differences already .

Not too much later the 8:30 playback was heard on Don Lee Mutual stations instead of Blue network stations. (around 1943-44) . By this time the Blue network was not part of NBC. I have no information as to what the arrangements were in regard to removing the program from western blue network stations and placing the recorded playback on Don Lee stations.

In 1944 the Lucky Strike sponsorship began and until 1955 when it ended (whether on NBC or CBS) Jack Benny was heard live at 4pm Pacific Time with the recorded playback at 9:30pm on the same station it was heard on at 4pm.

(From Mike) Time magazine 8-18-03 page 65 tells of "the people's encyclopedia": www.wikipedia.org According to the article and the site, anyone can write anything about anything (and no annoying login required). There is currently a nice, moderate length entry about Jack Benny. Maybe some of you have already contributed to it. There is an open link for a contribution for Mary Livingstone.

I recently viewed a two-part episode of Batman entitled "Dizzoner the Penguin". Don Wilson plays a substantial, although uncredited, role as reporter Walter Klondike in part 2. In addition, I spotted two other Benny semi-regulars in part 1. Benny Rubin (yes, I'm sure it's him here) appears as a father who wants his baby kissed by Batman, and Madge Blake appears as Aunt Harriet Cooper. Blake's role was a regular one on the Batman series, but it took seeing her for me to make the connection. She also played the Vice-President of the Jack Benny Fan Club, Pasadena Chapter.

(From Anthony Tollin) Sheldon Leonard often portrayed the racetrack tout on The Jack Benny Program, but the role was portrayed by Benny Rubin (with Jack in photo at right in mid-1920s) when the tout was first introduced in the January 7, 1945 episode of The Jack Benny Program. That's the incredible episode that introduced three of Jack's most famous comedy devices. Jack made his first trip down to his underground vault during the broadcast, encountered the racetrack tout (played by Rubin in the broadcast) ... and we also heard Mel Blanc utter "Anaheim ... Azusa and Cuc-amonga for the very first time. (And Jack got rebuffed by Frank Nelson at the railroad ticket counter too.) [EN: Can anyone confirm this? I've listened to it and am not completely convinced that it's Benny Rubin.]

(From Greg Van Beek) I was watching the Tonight Show this evening and Lisa Marie Presley was one of the guests. Before introducing her, Jay Leno said "the two people I always wanted to meet but never did are Elvis Presley and Jack Benny".

(From Raymond Langewen, the Netherlands) This weekend I went to a stage play, the world famous stage play by Arthur Miller: "Death of a Salesman". Of course it was all in the Dutch language, as you'll understand. But in the Second Act, I was flabbergasted by a dialogue between the leading part (Willy Loman) and the role of the manager (Howard Wagner). Did you know that the name "JACK BENNY" was in this play? If a world famous playwright like Arthur Miller mentions the name of Jack Benny, it means HOW FAMOUS JB must have been in those days!!!

Here is the excerpt:

(Willy Loman tries to speak to Howard to ask for a better job, a better position and a better salary. But Howard is completely fascinated and absorbed by his latest purchase: a wire-recorder.)

HOWARD: I tell you, Willy, I'm gonna take my camera, and my bandsaw, and all my hobbies, and out they go. This is the most fascinating relaxation I ever found.

WILLY: I think I'll get one myself.
HOWARD: Sure, they're only a hundred and a half. You can't do without it. Supposing you wanna hear Jack Benny, see? But you can't be at home at that hour. So you tell the maid to turn the radio on when Jack Benny comes on, and this automatically goes on with the radio...

WILLY:	And when you come home you...
HOWARD:	You can come home twelve o'clock, one o'clock, any time you like, and you get yourself a Coke and sit yourself down, throw the switch, and there's Jack Benny's program in the middle of the night!
WILLY:	I'm definitely going to get one. Because lots of time I'm on the road, and I think to myself, what I must be missing on the radio!
HOWARD:	Don't you have a radio in the car?
WILLY:	Well, yeah, but who ever thinks of turning it on?

(From David Lynch) Fred also reminds me that Jack Webb made his final appearance in the role of Sgt. Joe Friday on Jack Benny's final TV special. It was called Jack Benny's Second Farewell Special and it ran in early '74. (Benny's previous special was his First Farewell Special; the premise was that he was going to do Farewell Specials, ad infinitum. Unfortunately, he passed away during the preparations for what would have been #3.)

(From John Burns) From New Yorker, "Talk of the Town"; 15 April 1996:
Ben and Benny - Damned if the Treasury Department hasn't revised the portrait of Benjamin Franklin on its new hundred dollar bill in the spitting image of Jack Benny. The comedian's head is cocked at an almost imperceptibly coy angle. His lips are pure Benny-- pursed. He looks as though he's just told a good joke and is turning deadpan to look at us for the laugh........he seems to be far more bemuscd.....than the more noticeably baldish, not quite smiling portrait on the old hundred. Benny might have liked the figure "100" in the new, bigger size......"

(From Melanie Aultman) I just got Wheeler and Woolsey: Vaudeville Comic Duo Films. There are two short references to Jack Benny. One mentions that JB and some other comedians grouped together to back a play or film that didn't do well. The other is that either Wheeler or Woolsey (don't remember which now) said he'd done things for JB but JB hadn't done anything for him (but he still liked JB anyway).

Jack Benny Classifieds

§§§ A fully remastered CD of the Waukegan Statue Celebration and Not Ready for Sunday at Seven Players recreation is now available! It can be had for $16 plus $4 S&H from Charlie Willer. Contact him at ChasWiller@aol.com with "Jack Benny CD" in the subject to get the address for payment.

By purchasing this CD, you support two causes. Charlie is selling these CDs to raise money for his fight with cancer, as he has no insurance. Additionally, Charlie has volunteered that for every CD sold, he will donate $5 to the IJBFC. It's never too early to buy holiday gifts!

---

§§§ From Rick Du Bose, dubosem@dchealth.com, (202) 535-2288 - I would like to purchase all seventeen of the Jack Benny Program shows that featured Frank Nelson (the comedian who portrayed floor walkers, detectives, etc., with his trademark "Yeessss?" when Benny approached him. The programs are as follows:

JACK TAKES IN A BOARDER	SLOGAN CONTEST
CRAZY AIRPORT	JACK IS ARRESTED
JACK GETS A PASSPORT	BACHELOR TV LIVES
CHRISTMAS PARTY	RAILROAD STATION SHOW
DEATH ROW SKETCH	CHRISTMAS SHOPPING SHOW
JACK AT THE SUPERMARKET	THE AIRPORT
LUNCH COUNTER MURDER	FOUR O'CLOCK IN THE MORNING
NIGHBEAT TAKEOFF	JACK DOES CHRISTMAS SHOPPING
	HONOLULU TRIP

---

§§§ Kevin Byrne found that the skit "The Slowest Gun in the West" is now available from www.encorevideo.com. He notes, "I received my copy of it today and it's excellent. Jack Benny only features in it for about the last 20 minutes, but he plays a great part. It's mainly a Phil Silvers film, but Jack has an integral part. The quality of the copy was excellent. The film lasts 54 minutes.

---

§§§ Does ANYONE out there have a copy of the special Jack Benny's Bag? It was originally broadcast on NBC on Saturday, November 16, 1968 (my twelfth birthday). Jack's guests included Phyllis Diller, Lou Rawls, and Eddie Fisher. My main birthday present that year was a CASSETTE tape recorder (the first I'd ever seen!), with which I recorded an audio tape (long since gone) of Jack Benny's Bag that very evening. The nostalgic appeal of this show, and thus, its necessity to my collection, should be obvious. David M. Lynch, dml@expose-epistle.com

Jack with sketches from The Mouse That Jack Built

The Jack Benny Times

January – April 2004   Volume XIX, Numbers 1-2

Jack and Gisele MacKenzie
During rehearsal for Las Vegas show – 1957

President's Message

Jell-O again, folks…as probably all of you know by now, we lost one of our dearest honorary members, Gisele MacKenzie, on September 5. I had the privilege of visiting her at her home in North Hollywood last year in July, and one of the first things she pointed out was that she kept The Jack Benny Times on her coffee table. Now we dedicate this issue to her.

Many of the 39 Forever attendees fondly remembered this beautiful woman and her stories. My personal recollection was of being concerned when the music panel was to start at 2, and she had not arrived by the end of the previous panel. I didn't know if she might have gotten lost, or had become unable to attend at the last moment. So I was shuffling stuff at the registration desk, trying to decide how long to hold the panel to wait for her. I looked up, and there was Gisele smiling at me! Only a few times in my life was I that happy to see someone. We whisked the panel members to the stage, right on schedule. As you'll see below, Jack taught Gisele to never miss her cue.

Many, many thanks to Jim Stewart, Gisele's official number one fan, for providing the photos of Jack and Gisele used in this issue.

New Members

**** James Turck **** Robert F. Greene **** Bob Scott **** Kenneth Snellgrove **** Mike Morell **** Sue Sieger **** Scott Bell **** Nick Wyche **** Pete Casey **** David Ballarotto **** Michael Hardesty **** Michael Ertel **** Stephanie Hinkle **** Ben Kelly **** David Walker **** Katie Dreisbach **** Jack H. Haase **** Lt. Col. Arthur Emerson **** Gary Zichittella **** Alice R. Coleman **** Anthony Akins **** Andrew Trethewey **** Ashley Trethewey **** Gracie Trethewey (Gracie's our youngest member ever…joined when she was less than 1 day old!)**** Becky Jean Borsody **** Carson Schreiber **** David Muise **** Eddy Lauterback **** Erik Bates **** Gary Leonard **** Gregory R. Jackson, Jr. **** Henry Rice **** Holly Jones **** Jaime Meadows **** Jason Logan **** Jerry Van Vactor **** Jessica Paige Brown **** John L. Cesaletti **** John Futch **** John Jay Lindsey **** John Pidliswyj **** Katrina M. Wilkins **** Kevin Segura **** Larry Waldman **** Lee Eric Shackleford **** Louis Fineberg **** Matthew Dietz **** Mike Sheets **** Paula Keiser **** Phil Ratzsch **** Rob Constantine **** Robin Peel **** Roger Helvey **** Ron Bleile **** Scott D. Vroegindewey **** Stephen Mullen **** Steve Verity **** Susan Graham **** Ted L. Riggs **** Terry Thompson **** Trista Brant **** William D. (Dale) Clark **** William Rogers

Remembering Gisele
By Mike Stratton

Early meeting with Bob Crosby and pianist

Gisele MacKenzie came to me late in life. A few years ago I was driving along Wilshire Boulevard late on a drizzly night in Los Angeles, while listening with one ear to a pop standards radio station. All of a sudden, the most beautiful sound I had ever heard jumped out at me from the radio and took hold of me. It was the voice of an angel, a muse, a madonna, the Virgin Mary.

I didn't know who it was at first. "Who's THAT?" I thought to myself. I listened intently for the announcer to identify the vocalist. It may have been "Answer Me My Love" that was played. The voice belonged to Gisele MacKenzie.

I had a very vague recollection of Gisele MacKenzie when I was very young. I had remembered seeing her at some time or other, possibly on Ed Sullivan or another similar show. I could only remember a dark haired woman wearing a long dress while singing. I had heard her hit song "Hard To Get" a few times on the radio over the years and was familiar with that melody. There may even have been very faint memories of her playing the violin buried within the deep recesses of my memory. But I had never REALLY heard her sing until that night.

That night my life changed. That night I started a journey to learn of the music, the songs, the woman, and the personality behind what I believe to be the most beautiful voice in the world.

I immediately began scouring used record stores and the Internet for Gisele's recordings. Most of her albums were reasonably easy to come by. There were about a dozen or so albums in all. Her first, entitled "Gisele MacKenzie," is my favorite. I would take it to a desert island. She is pictured on the cover of that one in a pink dress on a blue background with her two dogs. (Note: There are two versions of that album, one with "Tiptoe Through The Tulips," and the other without).

The singles, however, were a different matter. Most of them were very '"hard to get." I could only find a relatively few of them. I was very fortunate to make the acquaintance of another collector who very generously shared his collection of Gisele's 45's, of which there are about three dozen in all, making a total of approximately 70 + something songs.

I think Gisele excelled at singing slow ballads, such as the aforementioned "Answer Me My Love," and "Too Young." In these, every note of her rich, resonant voice can be heard and savored at its best. Someone once commented that her voice could be compared to the "finely tuned strings of a violin." I think both descriptions are apropos.

I think my favorite of Gisele's songs is "This I Know," which is on the Collector's Choice "Best Of Gisele MacKenzie" CD. The timbre and conviction in her voice on that song is

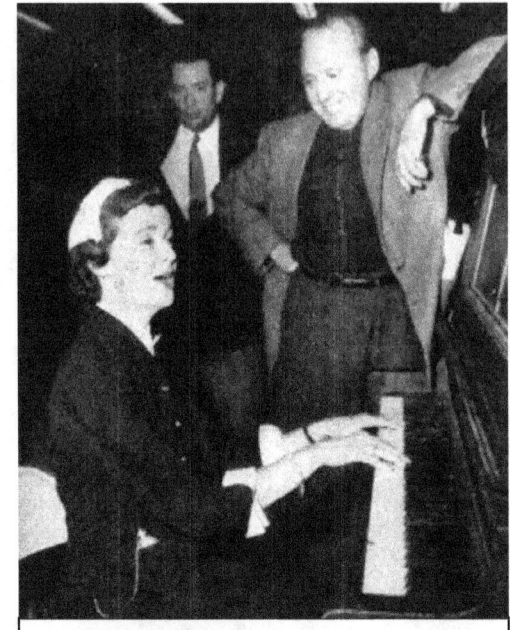

Gisele serenades Jack (Bob Shuttleworth, her future husband, in background)

guaranteed to leave the listener breathless. A close second is the Camden version of "Unchained Melody" (conducted by Alvey West - a different version than that on one of her LP albums.) This Camden version Of "Unchained Melody" has an ethereal, haunting quality that is *unforgettable*.

Some of Gisele's overlooked singles include: "Dance If You Want To Dance", "Mr. Telephone", "The Waltz That Broke My Heart",

"In Milano", "Embrasse", and the LUSCIOUS "A Letter And A Ring", among many others.

You probably know Gisele's story. Trained from a young age on the piano and violin, she began her career as a singer in her native Canada. She came to the USA to sing with Bob Crosby, and began a recording career. She then came to the attention of Jack Benny, who became sort of a mentor to Gisele, and was instrumental in furthering her career. While touring together, their famous comedic violin act was developed in which Gisele upstaged a flustered Jack, who tried in vain to keep up with Gisele's virtuostic violin skills. All in great fun, of course. Their "violin skit" was hugely popular.

One variation of this act was immortalized in the "Hong Kong Suit" episode of Jack's TV show. This episode undoubtedly ranks as one of THE funniest in all of television history, (along with that of Lucy's famous "chocolate factory").

Gisele was a frequent musical guest on many early television shows, including "The Ed Sullivan Show," "The Colgate Comedy Hour," and of course, "The Jack Benny Program." She hosted her own television show, "The Gisele MacKenzie Show" in 1957-58.

Gisele recorded on various record labels throughout her career, most notably on Capitol and RCA. She sang in both English and French. Her biggest selling hit single, "Hard To Get," was originally telecast in 1955 as part of a dramatic program, and quickly became a top 10 seller.

Dining with Bob Shuttleworth, Rosemary Portaro, and Bob Hope

Of course, Gisele was best known as a cast member of the very popular TV show "Your Hit Parade" during the mid-1950s. A few (about three dozen +) of those live telecasts have survived and are available from various sources. The March 6, 1954 show features an especially ebullient Gisele singing "That's Amore," ~ one not to be missed.

Sometime during the process of collecting Gisele's recordings, I began to wonder if it might be possible to write a letter to Gisele and perhaps receive a reply. I began to search for an address to which to write. Gisele had been out of the public spotlight for a very long time by then, and it was very difficult to find an address through which I could reach her. (This was prior to the creation of her Pierce and Shelly Internet "home page"). Finally through perseverance and a stroke of good luck, I was able to get a letter delivered to her. To my great delight about two weeks later I received a handwritten reply from her. I was overjoyed that such a magnificent talent would actually reply to me, my letter having come out of the blue like that. I followed up with some more correspondence, and a few small tokens of my appreciation.

Sometime later, I learned that Gisele volunteered at a thrift shop in Los Angeles. I decided that I just had to meet this woman, someone who had left an indelible impression on my life. I decided one day that I would take the plunge and go to the shop and try my luck. On that day I approached the shop very nervously, and took a deep breath as I entered. I was afraid I would be brushed aside with a comment like, "I'm sorry, but I'm busy right now." or something like that. But my fears melted away as Gisele received me very graciously and without reservation. She was just as nice in person as she was on TV. I had many things to ask her: (her favorite song? "Stardust." Her favorite singer? It was Matt Monroe and/or Roger Whittaker. And so on). She graciously answered the many questions that I posed. I probably lingered a little too long that day, but Gisele showed no impatience towards me. I was a Nobody, but she treated me like a Somebody.

With Bob Montgomery and Dinah Shore

As I left I felt I was in a sort of daze, having just spoken face to face with the woman who I consider to be the greatest female vocalist of all time.

I continued writing to Gisele, and after a while she consented to let me take her to lunch. We had a nice long talk that day. I held her hand and kissed it. That was one of the most wonderful moments of my life. I'll remember it forever. I wished there could have been many more of those talks, but I knew Gisele was a very busy woman, and as I learned later, she was receiving treatments as well.

Some have criticized Gisele's lack of sexuality in her persona, but that is one of the things that makes her so appealing to me. There was nothing tawdry or cheap about her. She didn't wear skimpy clothes or racy costumes. She didn't need to. Her talent surpassed all that. She was as one's mother, sister, or wife, perhaps. She was a LADY. As Dean Martin commented on one of his variety shows on which Gisele guested in 1966, she needed "no gimmicks," she was just "pure talent." It's no wonder that Jack Benny was so impressed with her!

I was somewhat surprised at Gisele's innate comic ability, which I witnessed during the one live performance of hers that I attended in Orange County, California in 2001. Having mostly heard her only on recordings, I was previously unaware that she was such an accomplished comedienne. While doing her "act", she held her own with jokes and one liners as well as any current stand up comic.

During the course of correspondence with Gisele, my own sister had passed away from breast cancer. Being a music hobbyist, she had left behind a song written out on sheet music that was never sung by anyone else. Feeling very low one day, I included it as a memento in a letter to Gisele. To my astonishment a while later I received a cassette tape in the mail on which Gisele had sung my sister's song while accompanying herself on her piano at home! I was astounded that the best singer in the world had recorded it as an unasked favor for me. That was something I'll NEVER forget, as you can imagine.

Gisele's appearance at the "39 Forever" gathering in Los Angeles was a joyous occasion, although it turned out to be a very bittersweet one as well. Watching her on the videotape of the musical guest panel one can appreciate her great wit, talent, humor and charm, and her love of Jack Benny. Her passing came as a great shock to me, because she had never seemed ill to me.

The last letter I received from Gisele was sort of a cryptic "Dear John" type one, in which she seemed to be bidding adieu while at the same time not wanting to make me ill at ease. The meaning of it didn't become clear to me until after her passing. Gisele had been known to be a very private type of person, and I respected her privacy.

Thanks Laura, for creating the opportunity to get a final glimpse of one of the greatest talents the world has ever known. As Newsweek magazine said in 1956, Gisele was the girl who could "do anything", sing, dance, act, and also play the piano and violin, as well as make people laugh.

I wish I could have been there for you near the end, Gisele. There will never be another talent that will equal yours. I love you, and I hope that your music and talent will be rediscovered by many more generations to come. -- Mike Stratton

Those interested may contact me: 2016 Daly St. #102, Los Angeles, CA 90031 - 323-227-0600
mikestraton@webtv.net (single "T").

Gisele…in her own words
(Recorded July 5, 2002)

L: …So talking about the inflated egos of so many of the performers, it seems like Jack Benny was absolutely the antithesis of that.

G: Yeah, he wasn't like that. He was…he was an amazing man because he knew that popularity came and went. He was wise enough to know that. First of all, I thought that he was a very wise person, and people just didn't bother to "look up" his other side, you know, the man's side…what a nice, generous person he was, and how sweet he was…a very sweet person. And people just kept talking about his incredible timing, and his this and that. They talked about his personality as a performer…but they forgot that he was a wonderful guy, and generous and easy to get along with, and sweet. That's how I knew him, and the rest was all working with him, especially with the violin and all.

L: …What was it that kept him humble, where other stars go off on an ego tangent?

G: I think he was just plain wise. I don't know who wised him up, maybe somebody early in his career in vaudeville or something, but somebody must have wised him up and said, "Always surround yourself with the best." Then all he'd have to do was look around. He'd look around at Milton Berle, who would watch the rehearsals and if somebody got a bigger laugh than he did, he was out or the line was cut and that actor wasn't used again. And that's what I call cutting off your nose to spite your face. You are not helping yourself. And I asked Jack about that, I said, "How do you feel about those?" Especially Milton Berle who stole material from everybody and didn't make any bones about it. [Berle] said, "If I hear something great, I want it for myself." And some other performer or comedian paid money for that material, and [Berle] couldn't care less. So I said to Jack, "Why do you surround yourself with the very best?" Like it took a lot to have Mel Blanc…Mel Blanc was pretty strong stuff…and at first, I guess, Mel Blanc would say, "How far do you want me to go?" and [Jack would] say "All the way." And everybody, they'd say, "Do you want me to play it down, so it doesn't…" [Jack would] say, "Look, you're on my show, I want you to get the best people, do your best." And he said finally, it got to the point where he just couldn't stand it if an actor wouldn't go all the way and wasn't the best, if he held back, because they worked with other comedians. And he said, "When you come down and think about it"…he'd say, "Dollface"—he always called me Dollface—he'd say, "Well, Dollface, you see I figure that if somebody said so-n-so the other night was just *so great* on the *Jack Benny Show*, that's your answer. They were great *on the Benny show.* Not on…" whatever. He got the last accolade…And he said, "I suggest that to everybody I work with, especially you." He said, "Always work with the best." The best musicians, the best arrangers, the best whatever if you have a show of your own, which I did, he said, "Surround yourself with the best people." You don't want to be with someone who's half-baked because they won't take away from you, he said, "What is that?" And you can see that because even Bob Hope the other night on that little interview thing, there was an actress on, an Italian actress I think, but she pulled a funny out of a hat. You know, a natural funny. And he appreciated it, but he was a little bit…it wouldn't be like Jack. Jack would laugh and hit the floor and say, "Oh my God, isn't that wonderful?"…Whereas Bob was a little bit resentful like, "How dare she top me?" And that's happened with so many people. Now when I think of all these wonderful people that are gone, and now the new generation doesn't know anybody but rock stars. That's all they do, and they don't even know them for very long….There's a new star every night. Either on the Jay Leno show, on Conan O'Brien, on Letterman…there's a new star always. Oh she is the newest ta-da, and then you don't hear about them again, or maybe twice, and then that's the end of that. And then there's a new star. And in our day, they'd *build* a star. You didn't have that many shows, so you were seen more often and it builds your name.

L: When I was giving a speech in Waukegan, one of the things I pointed out was that Jack was on radio alone for 23 years. And shows like Ally McBeal or Jerry Seinfeld are on for maybe seven years at the most.

G: And that's considered a long time. Especially Jerry Seinfeld, who I think is probably the freshest funnyman since Bob Hope and Jack Benny, because his humor was so different. And I actually knew a man who had that exact humor. You know, you suddenly say, "Who does Jerry Seinfeld remind me of in my own life?", and I zeroed in on this friend of mine, and I predicted to this friend, I said, "You may be alive or not, but…somebody's going to come out and be a star with your sense of humor." And he considered that quite a thrill. So when Jerry Seinfeld came out, I said, "Morey, I've finally found a comedian who's got you down pat and doesn't even know it! He's got your sense of humor, your delivery, and your little whine." He said, 'I don't WHINE!" I said, "Watch Jerry Seinfeld, and that little whiney tone."…

May 17, 1953 show

L: There have been a number of people who have said to me that Seinfeld sold itself as the show about nothing, but Jack Benny was the original show about nothing…Jack would talk with Don, and Mary would come in…and they weren't necessarily going anywhere with it.

G: It established a situation, so that it made you feel like it was part of their life. But it was just an excuse to use the jokes, and that's why he had such great writers.

L: Another thing you mentioned was that people would talk about Jack's personality as a performer, like his cheapness…

G: But then they would talk about his cleverness and his timing and his artistry. They would use those two things. They forgot about the man altogether. That always upset me, because I knew him as a wonderful man…He was passed over as far as a *man* was concerned, he's a wonderful *man*.

L: When you look at so many of the characters on the show, Phil Harris had commented to me that they were amplifications of the personalities of the actors. So Phil might like a drink, but on the show he was a swaggering drunk. But Jack was the one where it was just the opposite, he was not his character.

G: He had found the formula. He was putting himself down by being the personality that an awful lot of people are, you know. A lot of people have those personalities. When you have that,

Rehearsing in Vegas, 1957

237

he just dared to say there are a lot of personalities around who are stingy, and who are vain. Well the vain part, nearly every man is vain…but a lot of men think they're better looking than they are…But he just picked the little weaknesses on an awful lot of people and put them all together. And see, the others have tried to copy that, like Bob Hope tried to copy his cheapness…and they both had the same walk. I'll never forget a thing once, I had some lines with Jack, Jack said, "You know, Ji-ZELLE"—cause that's the way he said it—"You know, Gi-SELE…we're very much alike. We both play the violin, and we both love to laugh," and he went through all the ways in which we are similar. And he said, "You know, we kind of move alike, we even talk alike, I think we kind of even *look* alike, and you know, we even *walk* alike!" And I said, "Jack, I'm *supposed* to walk like that!" So you know…he always gave you the best. But it was still the Jack Benny show.

So anyway, he put all those things together just to appeal to most people's weaknesses…and he made the people laugh at his personal faults. Like when he said, "I'm thinking, I'm thinking"…that kind of thing. And I notice since then that Kelsey Grammar has taken a lot of his gestures, and he does the same thing about being vain. He's also…the money part, no, because he's always spending too much because he's such a snob. The over-exaggeration of his importance as a personality, like nobody's as great as he is…His brother is the only one who can come up to his kind of snobbishness, because they went to the same schools and they took the same courses, and they work in the same profession. And Kelsey has actually admitted it, that he's taken a few things from Jack Benny, because he knew the formula.

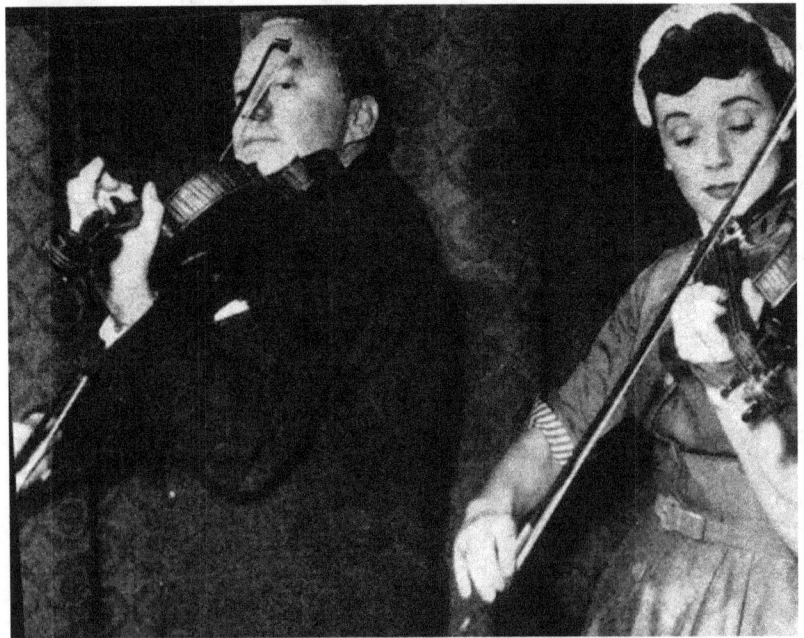

L: But nobody's completely duplicated it.

G: Because he had other things like his gestures, and his…well, not so much his walk, but his pauses. I said to him once, "You have to take the longest pauses I have ever seen in my life." He said, "You know, I'm the bravest comedian I know…I stare at them until they feel they *have* to laugh, or they'll never leave the room."…I said, "Well, with that face of yours and with those eyes, and the way you look, like you can't believe they're not laughing…that's enough to start people laughing right there." See, he had all the tricks. So he said, "I'm the bravest comedian I know."

L: There was a story of Jack playing a theatre in England and entering and staring at the audience, then after the laughter went on for a while, a cockney accent from the balcony said, "For Gawd's sake, SAY SOMETHING!"

G: Well, that probably was a plant, but maybe it wasn't. Well, that is pretty funny.

L: The story is that it wasn't, and they discussed the possibility of making it a plant, but Jack said no, because it was spontaneous.

G: It just happened and the timing was so perfect. You know, it's so funny because he and I got along so well, I just loved him very dearly and he loved me very dearly. The thing is…we were appearing in the Jack Benny show, the road show, the stage show in Dallas…He never got mad at me, I didn't see him mad…He came to my dressing room, knocked on the door, he said, "Gi-SELE!" I thought, "Oh my God, he's mad!" I said, "Yes, Jack," opened the door smiling. He said, "I have something to tell you, and I'm so mad!" And I said, "What? What happened?" like what'd I do? He said, "You know in that sketch that we do that had nothing to do with the violin. There's a moment where…" it's just one of those little things where he's, I forget what it was, but it was something not to do with the violin, it was just the two of us, and I'm supposed to react at a certain point. He said, "Do you know that you were a TENTH of a second late?!?!" I said, "What's a tenth of a second?" He said, "I don't know, but you did it!" He was mad! A tenth of a second! He said, "Don't EVER do that AGAIN!" Mad! And he  walked out of my dressing room. I couldn't believe it. A tenth of a second! You can't even measure that. He could measure it, though. It's just that it's time for his nose to work. I used to say, "You're like a rabbit smelling lettuce when you smell the audience." You know he'd go…I don't know, he did something funny with his nose that people didn't notice, but I noticed it because I was working with him right there…since I was so close to him, I could see the nose like a rabbit smelling lettuce. Nobody had that talent.

L: …I had been looking through the books, and there's always the story about him calling you for an "A" and hanging up.

G: Well, because I have perfect pitch, so that used to just amaze him. He used to say, "I can't even *understand* that." I said, "Well, even *I* don't." So anyway, he called up and the operator from London said, "Miss MacKenzie, you have a phone call from a Mister Benny from New York. Would you like to receive his phone call?" I said, "Of course, of course." He came on and said, "Gi-SELE…I'm here at the Sherry Netherlands Hotel and I've got my violin" and he's scraping away on the violin. He said, "I was just *thinking*…since you have perfect pitch and I'm here…and I want to play my violin…I was wondering, across the ocean, would you sing me an 'A'?" So with this, I didn't even laugh at the moment because to me, he was serious. So I sang him an "A", and he's in the back tuning up. He's laughing but I'm not because I took it seriously. But then he started to laugh, and then…we both started to laugh, and he said, "Thanks a lot, honey. It's cheaper than renting a piano!" Then he waited and called back in about three minutes. He said, "I *had* to hang up after that, the line was too good!" I said, "Always a comedian!"

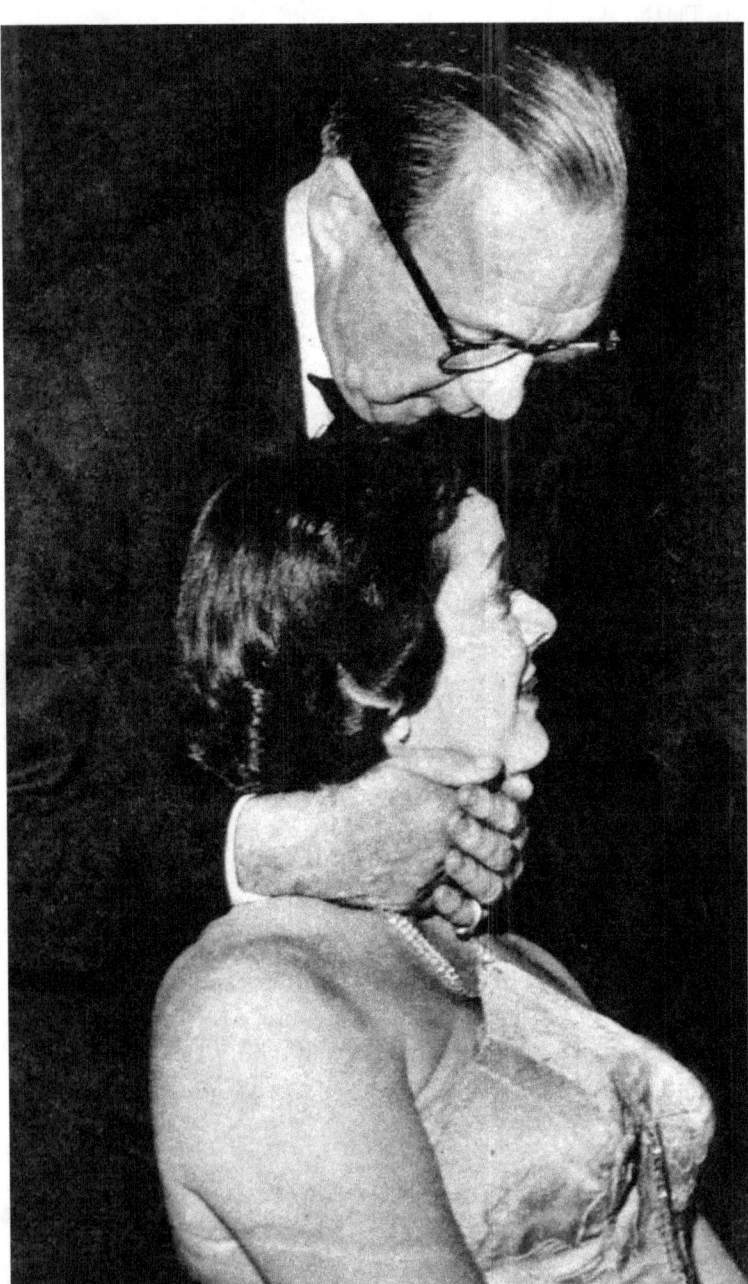

L: As I was reading all these stories, they're all facts and good stories, but they don't say as much about your relationship to him as a person.

G: He was a wonderful man. And he was so sweet, and never a demanding person, you know, just sweet as can be. When he said once, "Oh you know, because we're together so much and we travel alone, a lot of people think we're having an affair. I want you to promise me one thing: that you never say we did, and you never say we didn't. *Promise* me that." So I did…He said, "That's one promise I ask of you. That's all I ask of you…It will be good for me, and it won't hurt you." So he was funny, even about life. Oh, this is so dear…Whenever we played the duets together, which is locked up at the Museum of Television and Radio…it's in their *comedy*, so it made me think, "Isn't it marvelous that all those years of study [paid off]?" I *hated* the violin, but I always won the scholarships and I had the education at the Royal Conservatory in Toronto.

L: Why did you take it up in the first place?

G: Because my mother wanted me to. She was a stage mother, and she insisted.

L: Ironically, similar to Jack's mother.

G: Yeah, and then after I graduated and everything, I started working on radio as a singer and playing the piano for myself. And my mother was furious! And then, of course, she took the credit later, as a lot of mothers do, but especially a stage mother…But I hated the violin until I met Jack. I knew that when I played with him. Then all of a sudden, a light went on. I went through all that misery, all those years of study, intense study and hours of practice, not being able to play with the kids outside, you had to be inside…You had a lot of your teenage pleasure cut off, because you had to constantly be working and your mother says you have to constantly be practicing, and you

**MY FAVORITE PHOTO
★ By Jack Benny ★**

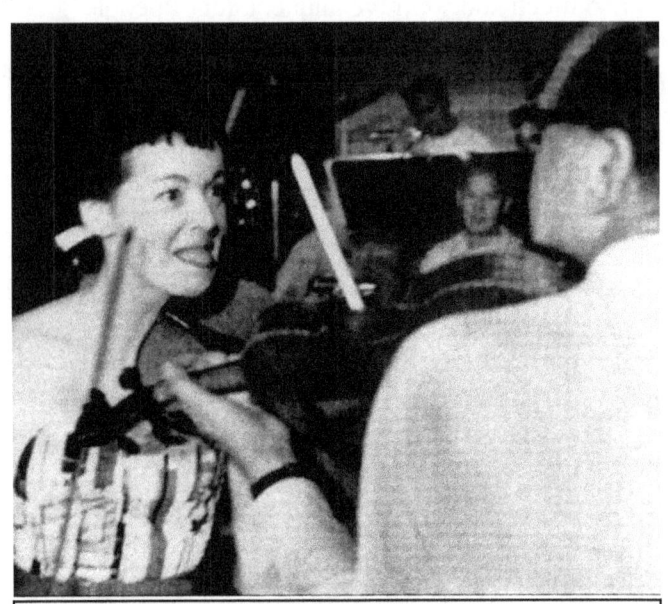

Gisele critiques Jack's playing during a 1957 Vegas rehearsal

said, "Why? I hate it." I never told my mother that because she'd throw me across a room. But in any case, I thought, "Why is this all happening?" But you see, life has a way of making you do things for a purpose. It might just drag you at the time, but it's leading to something. And you're learning, you're learning discipline, you're learning to put yourself aside, you're learning to accept the fact that you can't play with your friends. It's hard on your character, but it's character building. Then the fact that I still could play at that time, I had stopped playing because I was a singer by then when I came here. And so when Jack said, "What do you mean?"…My manager told me this, [he'd] said [to Jack], "Gisele plays the violin, she's a graduate of the Royal Conservatory in the scholarship school," which meant that you had to *win* a scholarship before you could enter the school, and each year you had to win it again. The Canadians, in those days, did not *give* anything away. It was like the Olympics, you had to win it. I don't know if they do today, but that's the way it was then. Well, anyway…I said, "I don't play any more, Jack." Today, I don't play because it's been years, and the violin is a tough, tough master. Either you play it all the time or else it leaves you. Goodbye. But I could still play enough then that I could recapture it very quickly. And so I said to Jack, "I don't play any more." He said, "Come up here, you little devil, I want you to play for me." So I went up on the stage, and we were getting ready to appear in San Francisco. So with this, he gave me the violin. And I started to play a little something, which was kind of a little boring. And he said, "My God, you play better than I do!" I said, "I haven't played in months." He said, "Well, you still play better than I do!" [EN: This would have been at the Curran Theatre in mid-1953, and Jack's serious interest in the violin had been rekindled in 1948.] So we laughed a lot, and he said, "Tonight, I just want you to show off. Do a cadenza or something. Anything you can figure out, then give me the violin back and just say, 'Great fiddle you got there, Jack.' And meanwhile, we're going to plan a number together with certain pauses for comedy, and you're going to like it." I said, "Oh thanks a lot! Since when am I a comedy writer for the violin?" And I really worked on that thing, it was hard, because I had to put the spaces in the right places. He said, "And leave us a second chorus." I said, "Jack, you're being very demanding. I'm not being paid for this, you know!" He said, "It will pay off." So we did a lot of laughing, and by the time I got it together and wrote it down, and wrote his part and wrote my part, but it was worth it. It really was…Then I knew, this was why I worked so hard. To play a duet with this great man.

L: Why, of all pieces, "Getting To Know You"?

G: That's what I said to him! I said, "What number will we use?" He said, "Getting To Know You." I said, "'Getting To Know You'? I sang that in <u>The King and I</u>!" He said, "Don't you think I know what I'm doing? This is a comedy number. I'm a comedian. I know how to pick songs." I said, "*Jack…*" And he laughed at me, he said, "You don't know comedy. *I* know comedy!...Because it's got the right spacing…'Getting to know you, getting to know all about you', then you show up. And I stand there and can't believe you, and then I finally start to get mad at you, and I finally tell you to shut up. It builds and builds and I finally tell you to shut up." Then he tries a couple of times and he loves himself and he thinks he's great, and he turns around and says, "Don't fool around with me, sister!"…And then he laughed with the others, he said to the writers, "Do you believe she *QUESTIONED* my choice?" They said, "Can't believe it, Jack! You know comedy if anybody does!" He said, "*She* didn't believe  me! So I made her write it."   Well, nobody could have written it but me. See, I'm the one who had to figure out the spaces, how much I'm going to do here, how little to do there, and here we're together and showing off together and a little flirting. I had to figure out exactly where…it took me a long time. But now that I think of it…my God, what courage I had! But he told me, he said, "You know, you have guts." I said, "Thank you, Jack!"

L: Were there variations in the lines that you used in the routine?

G: Oh sure. There were lots of different ones, and one that I use while giving my talk…I do a big cadenza at one point, and he's really boiling mad at this point, and the next thing that's going up, he turns around and he plays ya-ta-ta-too, all scratchy, ya-ta-ta-eee ya-ta-taaieee, and he says, "Don't fool around with me, sister!" The audience was on the floor because it's so bad!...And then I look at him like, "Well, there you are." And the looks between us are priceless. That's most of the comedy. I mean, with the playing, that's part of it. But the looks that we give each other, the little flirty looks and the little fun looks, and when we play something pretty together, at one point there's the little melody that we play and I'm doing the harmony, and it's very cute and he kind of [gives a little smile]. Those are the things, you couldn't buy that. You couldn't plan it. It had to be from the tune we did.

L: My mother once pointed out to me that for the passage towards the end ("All the beautiful and new things I'm learning about you"), Jack looks like he absolutely adores that part of the song.

G: Yep, that's right. All the emotions came out in that duet. The actual fact that we liked each other a lot and it shows, and then the little flirting parts, and then the part where he resents my showing him up, and then he thinks he's showing me up and he's not, and all of that kind of thing, and then we'd sometimes finish together and it was kind of pretty. And the people love it.

L: Did you ever do that with any other musical pieces?

Jack makes a surprise appearance at Gisele's Coconut Grove debut

G: Oh yes, we did "Chardice" [sp?] on my show...and then I did the harmony, you see, and he tries to play [a slower passage] and he doesn't sound too bad, actually. And then...we start to play [a faster passage], then he tries to outdo me, so he says, "Faster!...Faster!...Faster!... YOU'RE TOO FAST!" It's hysterical...We did several different things. Once we did ["Sweet Georgia Brown"], then we did all kinds of little things with that. So anyway, we played that, "Chardice", and what else did we play...mostly it was "Getting To Know You" because that became...

L: Your mutual theme song.

G: Yeah, it was. But it was so special, he said, "You have no idea how it's given *my* career a boost. It's certainly not bad for you, but for me, it was a little different side." A little thing that he could bring out every now and then, and say, "Well, now we're going to play a duet." And the amazing part was that one of the writers, one of the younger ones, I think it was the youngest one, he came up to me one time...I think it was Hal Goldman...and he came up to me, I was just going to go up and work with Jack, but he was doing something else before and I was sitting there with Hal Goldman. He says, "You know what you do up there with Jack, it is so, so fantastic because it's so different and it's just two people. We have nothing to do with it. And we've been writing for him for 25 years. It makes us feel very humble, because we realize at that moment he doesn't need us." So I said, "I never thought of it that way." And he said, "It's just two people making all that fun." And the fact that we react to each other, it's something nobody else could do. He tried it with a little girl [Toni Marcus], but it didn't work the same. It wasn't the same premise.

L: If I'm correct, you first worked with Jack in San Francisco in 1953. Before that, you had been working in Canada?

G: No, I was on the Hit Parade. [EN: Gisele was a vocalist on Your Hit Parade from 1953-57, but she was she was on Club Fifteen with Bob Crosby which ran from 8/29/49 to 1/16/53, and a frequent guest on Mario Lanza which ran from 6/10/51 to 9/26/52.]

L: Really? I thought Jack got you on Hit Parade.

G: You're right. So it wasn't that…No, I had been on the Hit Parade, but he got me the job by giving me the greatest audition I'd ever had. When we went on the road just before I had joined the Hit Parade…no, you're right!

L: The story I read was that after he had worked with you on stage, he called up the American Tobacco Company since they were also the sponsor of Your Hit Parade.

G: Yes, he said, "I'm going to give you the most expensive audition anybody's ever had. I'm going to give you my whole show." I mean, that's a very generous offer! Very generous. And I played the piano, I played the violin, I sang, I did all the funny lines, he gave me all the funny lines, and the next day they said, "Yes, that was a great audition and we want her." That's it.

L: He also was the producer of your television show.

G: Yes, he was.

L: And it was only on for one season [1957-58] because it was opposite Have Gun, Will Travel?

G: No, it was up against…it was a series of singers in a row. And I was the last one on the row [EN: Perry Como 8:00-9:00, Polly Bergen 9:00-9:30, Gisele 9:30-10:00]…Then there was a list of singers on Saturday night, doing one show after another, and I was the last one. The guy put me on as the last one. It was pretty late, I was the last singer, and they took all the tunes. And I had, you know, I had four little boys who danced with me and stuff, but I mean, they just took everything that was current and I was left with nothing. So all the shows got cancelled. It was too much to have five singers in a row. Rose Marie and Perry Como and Dean Martin and Polly Bergen, there were like five singers in a row and I was the last one. But it was a good season and I learned a lot. A television show's a big responsibility, and your name is at the helm.

L: Jack guested with you on the second of those; was he on any others?

G: He was on just once. We did "Chardice" then.

L: Do you remember a skit you did on the Benny show called "The Cactus Kid"?

G: Oh yeah! He loved to play that part.

L: I wondered if it was a partial throwback to the Buck Benny series on radio.

G: Yes, yes! That's what he said, Buck Benny drives again. And then the accent and everything, the swagger, the pushing up the hat. Oh yeah…And of course, Rochester broke me up. Whenever I worked on Jack's show and Rochester was on, I said, "Eddie…I just think that nobody can touch what you do. It's just so special with that voice of yours." He said, "Well, it's paid for my house, what you've done." And Jack said, "He's richer than I am!" In other words, he knew how to invest, and whatever he did, he took care of his money. Mary spent all of his money!

L: …How is it that Jack first learned of your work?

G: Well, this was…I came here to do the Bob Crosby show, and I was up against 500 singers, all with names. I was from Canada, and I did my own show coast-to-coast on Canadian radio, and I was known as <u>Meet Gisele</u>. And so…I had my own show, I played the piano and sang and it was a one-person show. And one day, the Campbell's Soup people, they sell a lot of soups in Canada, they called my manager and said, "Bob Crosby is interested in changing the Andrews Sisters into one singer opposite Jo Stafford. It's a five-a-week thing. And we'd like to have a tape of Gisele, of <u>Meet Gisele</u>, to play for the Campbell's Soup Company, because they've got 500 singers with names already that they've gone through. But they still haven't picked the one." So anyway, that happened to me twice. See the other thing was with Jack Benny. So anyway, we gave them the tape and I forgot about it, because I was very busy, I had my show twice a week and it was coast-to-coast and I was known as "Gisele of Canada". And all of a sudden, the phone rang and they said, "The Campbell's Soup Company wants Gisele over all the other singers." Bob Crosby was furious. He didn't talk to me for a year. I sang duets this close to Bob's face, and he wouldn't even acknowledge me. And we sang duets, that's hard! When you're singing duets like "I love you…" and he won't even talk to you. So anyway, I said, "I'd love to do that. I'd love to go to Hollywood and get into the business there. But I have to give up everything I have: my apartment, my car, my big show, and it was a two-a-week. We had three and then two. So my manager and my dog, I had a longhaired Dachshund at the time, we came on the Amtrak or whatever it was called—on the Super Chief. So we came on the Super Chief, and I took over right away. Like I came one day and I found a place to stay in a hotel, and the next day I was on the air with Bob. And he was…imagine working with a man for a year who won't talk to you. And you're costarring with him. And on the opposite days, he was fine with Jo Stafford, he liked Jo a lot…He was fine with my manager, he went out drinking with my manager.

L: It's hard not to take that personally.

G: Well, I did take it personally because I was very hurt. And I thought, "If he's mad at this choice of over 500 singers, I can't blame him because he wanted to sing with a name in the United States, and all he had was a girl from Canada, with a big name in Canada, but that's it." But he didn't have to take it out on me, he could have taken it out on the Campbell's Soup Company, which he didn't. So anyway, it was rough. But I had guts, like Jack Benny said, "You've got guts!" I thought, "Why you bum, if you think that you're going to destroy me after I've had a show of my own, I am a complete musician, I don't need an accompanist even." They tried to foist an accompanist on me and I said, "I can accompany myself! I did on my own show for years and you're going to hand me an accompanist?" You know and they had the finest musicians. But anyway, what happened was this…by happenstance. Serendipity. All of a sudden…Dixie, Bing's wife, died [EN: November 1, 1952]. And of course, everybody would call to the house, to the whole family, my God, and it was a day when Bob was performing with me, as opposed to Jo Stafford. So I said, "What's going to happen? Are we going to cancel the show or what?" I didn't say that to him because he wouldn't talk to me. [I said it] to the director. And the director said, "Well, you're going to get a big thrill. You're going to have a chance to work with Jack Benny. Jack Benny, since Bob is on his show replacing Phil Harris, is going to be coming in and we're going to quickly write a script, and you and Jack are going to work together. It'll be quite a thrill for you." I said, "Well, you're not kidding!" So I worked with Jack, but he didn't know me. I was just a singer on the show and we did some funny things, and it was cute and it was fine. Now, after that, I had worked once with Jack and knew him. Okay. But just that one time. Then, as Bob Crosby, by then he was talking to me and the year was over. One day he opened his mouth and talked to me, I thought I was going to die. Really, I thought I was going to die of shock. And after that, he was my biggest fan. Everybody came to him and said "You jerk!" They called him that! The director, the producer, they said, "We all like her, we all have fun with her, the musicians adore her because she's such a musician, and she has perfect pitch. So why don't you like her? You like her manager." He said, "I'm mad as hell that they did this to me." They said, "Well be mad at *them*, don't shoot the messenger." So anyway, that's the one time he talked to me. After that, he was my biggest fan. Then I looked into his eyes when I sang, and I almost didn't know what I was saying! You know, he had these big blue eyes.

Then we were cancelled. It was two and a half years I was on the show, the show was cancelled. So we went to Vegas, as the show, and the Modernaires were on with Johnny Green and his orchestra. So the whole show went to Las Vegas, and I did some numbers with [Bob] and I did some numbers by myself. Jack came to see Bob out of courtesy, because he was on his own show, and heard me and saw me do some comedy with Bob. So I got a wire about two weeks after that, and it said, "How would you like to join me doing An Evening with Jack Benny on the road, going to this place, that place, I'd love for you to be part of my show." The rest is history. And that's why we were in San Francisco [EN: in April-May 1953], and I didn't want to play the violin.

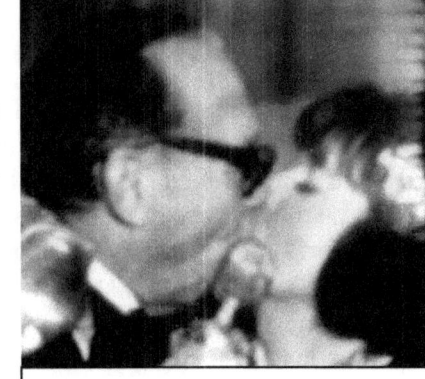

At the premiere of "Goodbye Mr. Chips"

L: I believe you were at the Curran Theatre.

G: Yes, the Curran Theatre…It has a lot of memories now.

L: Do you ever get up there any more?

G: Not often. I love San Francisco, I think it's a beautiful place. It's got such history. It's so interesting. I like everything about San Francisco. However, the work was here. I used to go as often as I could, sometimes somebody's show is up there, I'd go do that, stay a day or so. It's lovely.

L: …You had mentioned Eddie Anderson and Bob Crosby…

G: And Mel Blanc! I said to Mel Blanc, "I'm such a fan of yours, I'm embarrassed!" He said, "Well, I happen to be a fan of yours." Now he played the violin…He scratched enough to play a little number…He did that on the television show one night. He came and played just a little something, it wasn't long, enough to show that he played well. He didn't play well, he just kind of scratched away on the thing, but it got a big laugh. He came from the audience and said, "I can't stand the way you're playing, give me that," and he took the thing and he played.

L: What about some of the other cast members? Don Wilson?

G: Yeah, Don Wilson. Well, we always had laughs. Whenever I went in, the whole group was just lovely. The only one who retired was Mary.

L: Right, Mary wasn't on the show by that time. Or she was on the show, but…

G: No, she had retired. She didn't want to be on the show. Very rarely…But then she retired, she just didn't want to do the show any more.

L: She had terrible stage nerves.

G: Oh yeah. You know, nothing was right, in clothes and hair, and she seemed just a nervous wreck. So they went another way.

L: I'm intrigued that you say Jack called you Dollface, and I know that the pet names between him and Mary were Doll and Dollface…

G: Well, "Dollface" was kind of a Hollywood expression. A lot of people called each other Dollface. Men would call a woman Dollface. Well, I didn't question it. He called me Dollface, and that was fine by me! So it didn't faze me one way or the other, because it's like saying "Darlin" or "Sweetheart". You might call somebody "Sweetheart", but you'd call someone else "Sweetheart" in a different way.

L: …What other series work did you do after your own show?

G: …I became Sid Caesar's fourth television partner…I was on his show for a whole season [EN: The Sid Caesar Show, 1963-64]. His show was on ABC instead of CBS, and I was on that with Joey Forman, but I played his wife. I did some numbers. It was fun working with him because, being the last wife, and we got along, we really had fun together. So I did that, and right after the Hit Parade, I went to my own show. Then I did some freelancing, guest spots here and there, then I was Sid Caesar's fourth television wife. And after that, I just continued with…I did some serious shows like Studio One, Kraft Theatre, stuff like that as an actress, and I really enjoyed that. So I was pretty busy.

L: Are you officially retired now?

G: Well, that's what they call me. I just do some commercials once in a while…I've done some television commercials for the seniors, too. They shot it like a commercial, so everyone says, "I saw you in a commercial" when you're walking down the street, and stuff like that…And a lot of concerts, on the road, at senior citizen places and colleges. Especially senior citizen places. I've been busy off and on.

L: …You had mentioned talking about Jack as a person, and I believe there was a story about when he found out he had diabetes and he was very happy?

G: He was happy they found something. He said, "Dollface, you know what? They make me go to the hospital once a year because they have to have that, and I have to pass muster or something…and they never find anything. I'm in there for two days. It's boring as hell, but they make me do it…I'm going in to get my usual yearly checkup, and then I'll see you for lunch on Thursday." So I met him on Thursday, and he came running up to me and he said, [singsongy] "I've got diabetes! They found something!" I said, "You're quite thrilled with that? I wouldn't be thrilled with that." And I talked to him just about a week before he died. I called the hospital, I kept saying, "This is Gisele MacKenzie and I hope that I can get through." So finally, I guess they called him and said, "Do you want to speak to Gisele MacKenzie?" He said, "Yes." And he said, "Dollface, we haven't seen each other in a long time. That's no good. I tell you what—I can't keep anything down, but as soon as I can keep something down, I'll take you out to lunch." And that was the last time.

L: (Long pause)…I was recently reading some letters that Jack had written to Frankie Remley. What can you tell me about him?

G: Oh, I loved Frankie Remley. He was the funniest, silliest man. All he did was laugh. He'd laugh constantly. He was Jack's personal laugher. He said, "I could tell him the saddest story, and he'd laugh." He said, "When I told him I had diabetes, he laughed! *You* didn't laugh, but *he* laughed!" But Remley, they used to love to go and have a drink together. And he took Remley with him on trips. He'd say, "Let's go someplace," and Remley would say, "OK, Boss, where?" He'd say, "I don't know, just start the car and let's go." And he said that half the time, they didn't know where they were going, but that was the fun of it, as opposed to his life being regimented all the time. Rehearsals and meetings with the writers and material and his life. This was a relief…He said, "We didn't leave any messages behind, only when we got there. Well, we're in Timbuktu!" Or wherever. And of course, Frankie laughed the entire time. He was never serious. I can't remember talking to Remley when he was serious. I mean, when I talked to Remley as a person at rehearsals, once I caught him with a serious face and I said, "What's the matter with you? Are you sick or something?" And he started to laugh.

L: (Talks a bit about the Benny-Remley correspondence)

G: [Jack] used to write me dirty lyrics to my songs! He used to slip them under my door, and it was the song I was singing. I used to say, "Don't do that!" and he would laugh like a little kid! Just laugh and laugh and laugh…And then when I was away, let's say playing <u>The King and I</u> over the summer or playing <u>Annie Get Your Gun</u> or <u>Hello Dolly</u> or <u>Auntie Mame</u>, he would write me a dirty version of whatever song was very popular. "The Shadow of Your Smile"…well, imagine that. I had my little Jack Benny file, and it was all dirty lyrics! And some people say, "I can't imagine him saying dirty words, not Jack Benny!" I'd say, "I'm the only one who's got 'em!"

Jack surprises Gisele at <u>This Is Your Life</u>

L: I had seen his rewrite of "Young at Heart", and he did a darn good job of it, too!

G: And how! He wrote very good lyrics.

L: It's funny because you always think of him as being very clean…

G: Well, he was a gentleman…You should have seen him the night he was supposed to get me in a limo to go and do <u>This Is Your Life</u>. They picked him to get me there, and I wasn't supposed to know. And I didn't know it, no clue. And my parents had been here for almost a week, but of course they hadn't contacted me or anything because it was a secret. But he was *so* nervous. I had never seen Jack like that. I said, "You are a nervous wreck! You're like a silly schoolgirl!…What's the matter?" He said, "Well, I…uh…it's a question of timing, and I'm supposed to hear from…someone about a thing that I'm supposed to do…" And he finally said, "Well, I might as well tell ya!" And I thought, because he was so nervous, and I said, "What do you mean?" He said, "Well, I'm supposed to get a message from somebody saying 'Now is the time we're supposed to get out of here.'" It was the place across the street, a bar. We were having a drink. So he said, "I'm supposed to get in the car, the limo, you're with me, and we'll go out and eat."…So he said, "I'll sit there, and then they'll come there, and it's a thing where Bob Hope is having an opening, a special opening for us." And he kept fumbling and mumbling, and I said, "Jack, what are you saying? Bob has a new opening to a show and he wants you in it? Is that what you're trying to say?" "Well," he said, "Something like that, you see. So that I am going to just…uh…I'll just be *brief*, I'll just go out there, they'll open the door, and I'll just be *brief* and say 'Hello, hello Bob,' and then they'll close the door and then we're off…Is that okay with you?" I said, "That's fine." But he kept mumbling and stumbling, and it got worse and worse. I thought

This Is Your Life with Ralph Edwards

what is such a big deal about your doing an opening for Bob Hope? He said, "Well, I'm not used to that…uh…I'm a little bit nervous." I said, "Jack, you've done a thousand shows…" So I just sort of dismissed it. Then some guy came over, a guy dressed up from NBC, and said [whispering], "OK, Mr. Benny, NOW." And I began to get a little nervous! NOW! What's going to happen? And he said, "Oh, they're ready and Bob is going to do his opening, and they don't want me to be late because they want the thing to arrive just on time and the door will…you understand."…By then, I was a complete wreck. I didn't care what happened. So we got into the car, and then we went across the street, and I said, "Well, you better sit here, Jack. He's going to open the door and he wants to see you." He said, "No no no, it will be better if I sit over here, and you sit over there." So I'd be the first one out the door. So with this, we turned and went around and did a turn around, and I saw all these lights. So I wasn't suspicious because I saw all these lights, and Jack said, "Oh, they've got the lights on and everything. Good!" And so I said, "Okay." So with this…then I thought, "Oh yeah, we got all the lights and everything, but where's Bob?" He said, "Oh, I'll… he'll be…I'll do the opening and then he's over there…" But he was such a wreck! So the door opens, and I see two Mounties. Mounties? Two of them? Why would they need Mounties? And I said, "What is this?" And they said, "Are you Gisele MacKenzie? Gisele LaFleche MacKenzie?" I said, "Why, yes I am."

They said, "Gisele, this is your life!" And I thought I would die! Because it was so…to see two Mounties, I didn't even digest that! I thought, "What are two Mounties doing *here?*" And you know with Jack, and Jack is supposed to be sitting here, but I hadn't put everything together. I'm not that quick. It takes me a little while to put things together. So anyway, it was funny.

Jack and Gisele…together again.

The Jack Benny Times

May - August 2004 　　　　　　　　　　　　　　　　　　　　Volume XIX, Numbers 3-4

President's Message

Jell-O again, folks…Leo Gorcey, Jr. once said to me, "My most productive times have been those when I was between jobs." That is certainly the case for me, as I elected to take some time at the start of this year to work on writing two books: one Benny-related, and one business-related. The research for the Benny book and other Benny-related work has taken me all over the country, and I have met some truly wonderful and fascinating people in the process. It is amazing that Jack left such an enormous impact and body of work that I can easily fill up eight or more hours a day researching and writing about its various aspects, from the shows themselves to genealogy to interviewing all the people who knew and worked with him.

I am pleased to say that I have met my goal. I will be marketing my business book to publishers shortly, and the Jack Benny book has been released (see <u>39 Forever</u> below). The first edition of my media log (also entitled <u>39 Forever</u>) was released in 1989, coinciding with the opening of our audio library. Now the second edition is being released along with the opening of our video library. I enjoy such symmetry, and hope that you'll enjoy both of these new resources.

New Members

Terry H. Ostermeier **** Dr. Zeyd Merenkov **** Wm Powers **** Nick Thomas **** Mark Guarino **** Wayne D. Wong **** Bob Pedersen **** Joseph Crockett **** Ernest Tomlinson **** Jay Ranellucci **** Cy Gilson **** Randy Farr **** E.J. Kienzler II **** Walter C Bornemeier **** Brian D. Mount **** Steve Hanson **** Jeff Jones **** Marc Ricketts **** Wayne Yates **** Todd Gordon **** Randy Linton **** Jeffrey H. Mulvey **** Howard M. Kramer **** Jim Day **** Brad Strickland **** David M. Lowell **** Robert P. Jones **** Martin Alderoty **** Wayne Tomczak **** Ronald McDonnell **** Don Husing **** Karl Blakney **** Jeffrey Randolph Conners **** Jack Bagley **** Matthew B. Tepper **** Terence Fraser **** Phil Curry **** Laura Smith **** Bill Allendoerfer **** Michael Bedford **** Bill Schell **** Jennifer Pigoni **** Randee Mazurek **** Mark Neyrinck **** Bryan Silveira **** Richard Bell **** Greg Kilpatrick **** Julie Whitley **** Jay Stone **** Jessica Johnston **** Craig Miller **** Don and Beth Brigham **** Richard McConn **** Fran DeWysockie **** Dawn A. Eckert **** Dominick Cancilla **** Thomas L. Laham **** Paulette Farmer **** John Kehrli **** Brian Szyszko **** Colin Sutton **** Eric Caron **** Darrel Lantz **** Geoffrey H. Arnold **** John T. Rockstroh **** Troy Picklyk **** Ned Bartelt **** Randolph J. Johnston **** Larry Shank **** Jack R. Schmitt **** Ashlea Singleton **** Derek Gould **** George H. Dummer **** Alex Marsh **** Mike Stratton **** Rex Kinkade **** Scott Kent **** Andrew Steinberg **** Jerry Boehm **** Joe Riesselman **** Gary Bartole **** Jim Norcross **** Tim Smith **** Wendy Welch **** John Whitfield **** Tara Bodie **** Ric Vice **** Jaynie Behr Kane **** Marty Nerl **** Robert Sperber **** Adam Haggstrom **** Charles Kramer **** George Aust **** David Wright **** William Belaney **** Teresa Gammon **** Will Bevins **** Peter Moore **** Dan Poorman **** Anthony F. Smith **** Ken Kallick **** John Sheridan **** Mark Schlesinger **** Gary Taylor **** Peter Stark **** John Ruklick **** Greg Burton **** Stanton F. Fink **** Todd Pulliam **** Douglas Gonnelly **** Steven Wilhelmsson **** Tim Schroeder **** Alfred Balk **** Shirley M. Jones **** Joe Pinney **** Katie Larsen **** Stephen Dietz **** Bob Day **** Will Harris **** Jeffery S. Weiner, Sr. **** Charles Reiser **** Donald L Skirvin **** Amy R. Tarr **** David Gilley **** David Morgan **** Jeff Humble **** Mary Frances **** Buddy Mullaly **** Mark Zimmerman **** Stephen Turck **** Robert Fencik **** Jerry Govert **** Frank Jenks **** Benjamin Mcalister **** James M

Culver **** Ron Collins **** Sarah Nelson **** Alex Kidwell **** James M. Wester **** Kay Elliott **** David Kindred **** Julia Hann

39 Forever, Second Edition
Volume 1: Radio May 1932-May 1942 Available!

After hundreds of hours of work, I am very excited to announce that the first volume of my revised Jack Benny media log is now available!

39 Forever was originally released in 1989, and included Jack's radio and television shows, appearances, and specials, movies, books, magazine articles, and discography. Due to the level of detail involved in this revision, it will be released in multiple volumes over the coming years.

- Who were the first guest stars on the Benny program?
- When was the very first mention of a feud between Jack and Fred Allen?
- When did Jack first play Love in Bloom on the air?
- What character names did Eddie Anderson play besides Rochester?
- When did Phil Harris first call Jack "Jackson" and why?

The answers to all these questions and much, much more lie in the pages of 39 Forever, Second Edition.

Volume 1 covers Jack's regular radio programs from his debut for Canada Dry in May of 1932 through the end of the Jell-O series in May of 1942, almost exactly half of Jack's total regular radio broadcasts. Please see below for a sample of the write-up for each show. Full indexes of cast members, citics, musical artists, skits, and songs are also included.

This volume contains 536 pages of detailed information, and is truly a priceless resource for any Benny fan, and anyone looking to understand more about how the program went from its debut to the top of the ratings.

39 Forever, Second Edition - Volume 1 is available for $40.00, and will be sent to you via Media Mail. Paypal members can send payment to jackbenny@aol.com. Please make checks payable to **IJBFC**, and mail to: P.O. Box 11288, Piedmont, CA 94611.

IJBFC Starts Video Library

After decades of requests, the IJBFC is ready to start its video library. Jack Benny's work in television and movies has often been extremely elusive, and we hope to be able to make this material more readily available for our members to discover and enjoy. We plan on offering a variety of Jack Benny titles, and continuously expanding our listing through the help of the IJBFC membership.

These titles will be available on DVD only. Apologies to people who only have tape capabilities, but the cost of high-speed video duplicating equipment is beyond the finances of the IJBFC. But you can get a DVD player for about $50 now, and enjoy Benny titles and lots more.

How do I order?
- Select the titles you want from the video library.
- Send the list of your wants plus one blank DVD±RW per title to: IJBFC, P.O. Box 11288, Piedmont, CA 94611. A donation to the IJBFC of $10 per DVD is recommended, please include return postage at a minimum.
- I will copy your request onto the DVDs and return it to you.

What can I order?
- Chasing Rainbows (1929 movie) - 88 minutes
- George Washington Slept Here (1942 movie) - 94 minutes

We will be providing additional titles in the coming months, so please recheck www.jackbenny.org for updates.

NOTE: These videos are being made available for the private use of IJBFC members only. They may not be used for public exhibition, duplicated, or resold.

Hitchhiking with Rochester

Eddie Anderson, Edmond Anderson?, Eva Anderson

Member Brad Zinn helped put me in touch with his friend, Stephen Gerst, who had the unique opportunity of spending some time with Eddie Anderson and his family in Mexico. Gerst recalled:

In August of 1965 I went to Mazatlan where I was supposed to meet a friend. My friend did not show up and I was feeling ill.

The following day I was feeling better. I went down to the beach where the big hotels were. It was there I met a beautiful woman [Eva Anderson] and her children. They were playing on the beach. I learned they were going to Puerta Vallarta and since I was going there also we had something in common. I also was a bit lonely because my friend had not shown up yet. I was grateful for any companionship. I was introduced to Eddie Anderson and immediately recognized him from his voice and manner as Rochester.

I had dinner with them at the Guilded Cage that night. It is attached to one of the hotels there on the beach. I remember Eddie handing out dollar bills, smoking cigars, and enjoying being recognized. I don't know that I would have recognized him as Rochester except for his gravely voice and manner of speech.

I rode with the children in the back seat of their car to Tepic. I learned that she was a dancer and/or model. She was very beautiful and very nice. Eddie drove the car. He told me that Jack Benny built him a house near his and that it was a smaller replica of the house Jack Benny lived in. I don't recall other specific information. In Tepic I paid to have a small Cessna plane fly me to Puerta Vallarta because there was at the time a river that cut off the ability to drive there. I don't know how Eddie and the family got there but I saw them in Puerta Vallarta when I got there. I joined up with friends and, of course, shared my story with them. It, of course, became one of many stories of that summer. The attached photos were taken at the airport at Tepic.

Eva Anderson, ?, ?, Eddie Anderson

Eddie Anderson, ?, ?, Eva Anderson, , Evangela Anderson?

What's Up in Waukegan?

On February 14, a group of Waukegan citizens gathered at the Jack Benny statue in downtown Waukegan to place a wreath in honor of Jack's birthday. They were organized by Susan Tenzi, who was inspired by Stan Hickory's gesture of putting a bouquet of birthday flowers in the arms of Jack's statue two years ago.

L to R: Jack Benny Fan & Secret Admirer Stan Hickory, Susan Tenzi - Community Activist & Jack Benny fan, Mrs. Janice Hyde, Mayor Richard H. Hyde, and fellow Benny fan

Susan recalled that she watched the Jack Benny program on television when she was young, and that it "always left you lighthearted." Tapes of the Benny shows were played at the statue during the gathering, and she was impressed that younger folks would stop by and ask about Jack Benny and his work. She sees this event as part of Waukegan recreating its identity, and looks forward to making it an annual event.

The Genesee Theatre renovation project is moving along well. As many will recall, Jack debuted his film <u>Man About Town</u> at the Genesee, and broadcast his June 25, 1939 show from its stage. Steve Kolber, Executive Director of the renovation, provided us with an update on the work. It is a $24 million job, with 40 people working onsite daily to restore terra cotta to its original 1927 appearance, rebuild and expand the stage, install a new marquee, and much more. The previous incarnation held 1,800 seats and is expanding to 2,500. The storefronts that formerly surrounded the theatre have been incorporated into it, serving as patron lounges and other theatre facilities.

The Genesee Theatre is the only one of its kind between Chicago and Milwaukee, and is anticipated to bring 500,000 people to downtown Waukegan. The theatre season will feature over 250 performances, and offer patrons the opportunity to see major theatrical productions for a fraction of the ticket price in surrounding cities. There are plans for retooling of the surrounding area to serve theatregoers, including a proposal for a new parking garage and the conversion of the former Fiesta Palace (directly across the street) into a restaurant.

The main focus of the work is to meet the anticipated opening date of September. There will be various events celebrating the reopening of the Genesee, which will be announced closer to the actual date. You can see all the latest information on the renovation at www.geneseetheatre.org, or watch www.jackbenny.org for the latest Benny-related event plans.

Backstage
With Eddie Carroll
Benny And Me

At the end of every performance of my show "JACK BENNY- Laughter In Bloom" I exit the stage and walk directly to the lobby of the theater so I can have the opportunity to meet and talk to members of the audience. I enjoy this almost as much as performing the show and no matter what part of the country I'm in, the enthusiasm people still hold for Jack Benny is heartwarming and gratifying.

Quite naturally, I'm besieged with questions and the one that is most asked by the public, as well as the media, is..."What made you decide to perform as Jack Benny?" Since many of you have asked me the same question, I'd like to take a few moments and share my story with you.

There is a famous quote that says " Life is what happens to you while you are making other plans". With that thought in mind, please believe me when I say that I never chose to portray Jack Benny. It chose me.

To begin with, I was always a big Jack Benny fan, so when my agent landed me a job to act in a sketch with Jack on his Farewell TV special, you can understand how excited I became. It was a wonderful experience that resulted in a friendship with Freddie DeCordova (who produced and directed Jack's specials) and working with Jack was a joy, who was as charming and delightful a person as he was the master of timing and delivery.

Even though I had the greatest admiration for him, in all my years of working as an actor in Hollywood, no one ever said that I resembled or looked like him nor was it ever a part of my repertoire to imitate or emulate him in any way.

Anyway, to continue my story, in 1983 I was given a role in a TV movie of the week, which had a very tight shooting schedule. On the last day of filming, we were shooting a very complicated scene that was not going well. Actors were either forgetting their lines or not moving to their proper marks, or the camera was not in sync with the action and after more than twenty takes, the director was losing his patience.

On the next take everything seemed to be working perfectly and just as the scene was coming to an end, someone backstage dropped a piece of equipment that landed with a sharp clunk and bounced twice. Naturally, it ruined the take.

Expecting that the director would explode in anger and create even more tension, on sheer impulse I yelled out (in my best "Benny" voice)..." Oh for heaven's sake, ROCHESTER...if that's my Stradivarius you dropped...you better look for another job!!"   Well...it got a big laugh and released the tension on the set and on the very next take we finished the scene.

Afterwards, I was talking to the Director and he said "what I found interesting is that you not only sounded like Benny, you even started to look like him. Have you ever thought of performing as Benny on the stage?" I said, no. Why do you ask?" He said " It just so happens that a New York producer friend of mine has a script for a one-man show of Jack Benny but can't find anyone in NY who has both the vocal quality and the physical resemblance. You should get in touch with him". I replied that I was thrilled that someone was going to keep Benny's legacy alive, but with a family here and so many commitments in Hollywood, there was no way I could go to New York at this time. I thanked him and promptly forgot about it, but a week later I got a call from the NY producer's assistant. The producer was coming to Los Angeles in two weeks to audition a number of actors for the one-man show and if he found the right actor, he would open the show in LA and then take it to New York. I agreed to audition for him and asked to be the last actor on the list.

As I hung up the phone I wondered where I could find any copies of the Jack Benny television show to use a reference. Would you believe, that very week a cable channel began running the Jack Benny show every night!

I taped the segments and used them to work on voice and body language and then discovered another interesting coincidence. My receding hairline, which had caused me great concern for years, now had become a blessing in disguise.

By simply combing my hair back, I had Benny's exact hairline. I also had blue eyes, same cheek bones and facial structure which meant that I did not require any make-up or prosthetics. To complete the image, all I had to do was put on horned rimmed glasses and use facial muscles to create those famous pursed lips.

By now, so many coincidences had fallen into place that I had no doubt that fate or destiny had preordained a path that I was meant to follow.

After two weeks of intense preparation, the day came for my audition for the producer. I arrived a few minutes before my appointment, found his office and then walked passed it to the end of the darkened hallway and waited until the last actor to audition came out. As the producer stood in the open doorway with the light from his office spilling out into the darkened hallway, I began walking toward him in the dark and as Benny, I said " Oh Ted... I understand you're going to stage my life, so I got a leave of absence to come back, because nobody is going to do me...but ME!" and I walked into his light and past him into his office. He stood there just staring as his assistant, with his mouth open, handed me a copy of the script. As I started to open the pages to prepare to audition, the producer walked up, took the script out of my hand and said " you don't need to audition, you've already done it. When can you start rehearsals?"

The show opened in Los Angeles to great reviews and it was a thrill to perform for so many people who knew Jack and had worked with him. Writers, like George Balzer and Sam Perrin, Hal Goldman, Al Gordon and Milt Josefsberg. Irving Fein came, (who would also become a friend), as well as Mel Blanc and Dennis Day. Dennis, incidentally, gave me the most unique review. After the seeing the show he said " I closed my eyes and heard Jack...I opened my eyes and saw him!"

The show completed it's LA run and was slated to go to New York. However, it would be at least a year before an appropriate Broadway theater was available. In the meantime, the producer was involved in other productions and he put our show on hold. For the next few years I was busy with other projects, but I kept getting calls from people asking when I was going to perform as Benny again.

I finally realized that after four decades as a professional actor, with the hundreds of different roles I had portrayed, nothing had given me as much pleasure, fulfillment and satisfaction as performing as Jack Benny. I had literally been given the gift of carrying on his legacy and it was time to start again. Only this time, I wanted to have control of the material and do the kind of show that Jack would be proud of. Once the new show was written, I contacted booking agents and the engagements began to come in. As of this writing, the show is already booked into April of 2005.

As we all know, Jack Benny enjoyed more audience identification than any other entertainer in show business. Even today, his image is alive and well. When a man leaves as much of himself as Jack left us, then he can never truly be gone. He simply becomes…Immortal.

(For continued updates on future engagements that may be coming to your area, you check Eddie's Web site at JackBenny@eddiecarroll.com)

L.A. "Speed" Riggs

(Reprinted with the permission of the North Carolina Department of Agriculture)

The sound of the words "Sold American!" was the way many people came to know L. A. "Speed" Riggs. A son of tobacco country, he gained his nickname for the lightening-speed chant he mastered to become one of the nation's premier tobacco auctioneers as well as a radio and early television personality.

Born in the small Onslow County community of Silverdale in 1907, his family moved to Goldsboro in the mid-1920s. The son of a tobacco and produce farmer, Speed frequently went to tobacco auctions and heard the auctioneers at work. He decided to teach himself the cadences of the auctioneer, and reportedly spent time walking among the rows of tobacco on his father's farm practicing this unique chant. He once described his personal style as a steady yet rapid hypnotic monotone, different from the more usual staccato, choppy chant.

At age 18, with only a sixth-grade education, he reportedly became the world's youngest tobacco auctioneer. Several years later, he began working at the Liberty Tobacco Warehouse in Durham, where he earned the nickname "Speed," as his quick, rhythmic chant helped him sell piles of tobacco quicker than his colleagues.

In 1937, news of his distinctive voice reached New York City and the offices of George Washington Hill, president of the American Tobacco Company. Mr. Hill traveled by train to Durham to hear Speed selling tobacco at the Liberty Warehouse. After listening to the young auctioneer for a short time, Mr. Hill offered Speed a job to become "The Voice of Lucky Strike" for the American Tobacco Company. Speed asked for $550 a week, and for Liberty Warehouse to auction for charity. He was signed to a twenty-year renewable contract.

In January 1938, Speed Riggs became the radio voice of the American Tobacco Company, auctioneering on the national radio show "Your Lucky Strike Hit Parade." For many people in America, this was their introduction to the tobacco trade, a way of life not well known west of the Mississippi.

L. A. "Speed" Riggs' face became famous on Lucky Strike advertising, and he was known as the "Voice of Lucky Strike." He appeared on radio shows with Jack Benny, Fred Allen,

North Carolina's own Kay Kyser, and Jack Parr, when the shows were sponsored by American Tobacco. He would end his tobacco auctioneer's chant with his trademark "Sold American!" His radio and early television career ended with the ban of electronic advertising for the tobacco industry.

"Speed" Riggs was an ambassador for North Carolina's tobacco industry. Even when he lived in New York and California, he always insisted he be introduced as "L. A. 'Speed' Riggs from Goldsboro, North Carolina," and took great pride in North Carolina's place as a leading tobacco-producing state.

During World War II, Speed raised more than $17 million in war bonds for the United States. And he used his voice and talents to raise almost $220 million for many charitable organizations.

He moved to California after leaving American Tobacco Company, and founded a non-profit organization to teach underprivileged and physically or mentally challenged people a trade or vocation.

His beloved native state honored him in 1982 with "Speed Riggs Day," when he once again visited the old warehouse areas in Durham. He said he was saddened by the loss of prestige suffered by the tobacco industry, "because tobacco has been good to me. Tobacco helped me climb out of poverty. All my success I owe to tobacco."

Speed Riggs moved back home to Goldsboro in 1986. He died February 1, 1987, just 17 days before his 80th birthday.

Inducted to the North Carolina Agricultural Hall of Fame: February 27, 2003

The REAL Story of the Smuggling Case
By Kurt Jensen

A moment of poor judgment with a suave con man, an angry Hitler-loving maid and a rash decision to protest innocence. Sounds like the plot of a Warner Brothers potboiler, doesn't it?

But it all really happened to Jack Benny, and it nearly landed the comedian in prison in 1939.

The jewelry-smuggling caper of Benny and George Burns was recounted in Sunday Nights at Seven, the joint memoir of Jack and daughter Joan Benny published in 1990, as an embarrassment, certainly. But details of the case, as found in George Burns' FBI file and in news accounts of the investigation and trial, show that Benny came much closer to landing behind bars than he wished to later recall.

In 1939, freshly minted U.S. Attorney John T. Cahill and a federal judge were determined to make an example of a public figure in order to discourage amateur smuggling of luxury goods and the flouting of customs laws. And Jack Benny -- at the time, the number-one star of radio -- ended up being that example.

A phony diplomat
Albert Nathaniel Chaperau claimed to be a commercial attaché of the Nicaraguan consul general in New York. In fact, he was a professional confidence man, born in Poland, whose real last name was said to be Szapiro. The Nicaraguan Consulate in New York didn't even have a commercial attaché, and a judge later found that the person who supposedly appointed Chaperau lacked the authority to do so.

Chaperau, as Joan Benny recalled in Sunday Nights at Seven, "was on intimate terms with some of the finest people in the movie colony" -- he's credited as the producer of a 1937 French picture, Courier of Lyons, and as a buyer for foreign films, he brought Mayerling to the United States. But his real activity was "buying jewelry in Europe from desperate families," then smuggling the items into the United States, "where he sold them under the table, untaxed and undeclared."

"Chaperau's charm and lifestyle enabled him to cultivate relatively unsophisticated celebrities like Daddy as a cover for his criminal activities," Joan wrote. She said her father described Chaperau as looking a little like George Sanders. Photographs, however, show that he looked more like character actor George Tobias.

Jack and wife Mary Livingstone, who had met Chaperau earlier, ran into him in the summer of 1938 in Cannes, France. Chaperau "knew of a splendid bijouterie (in Paris) where the proprietor was an old friend and would give them a 'break,' " Joan wrote. "Daddy ended up buying Mother two gold clips studded with small diamonds and a gold bracelet, also set with diamonds." He paid $1,462 for them, although they later were appraised at more than $2,100.

A week or so later, Joan wrote -- and here she agrees with the prosecutors -- Chaperau arranged to deliver the jewelry into the U.S. himself, to save the Bennys about $700 in import duty. Benny gave the jewelry to Chaperau at a railroad station, and in October, Chaperau delivered the jewelry to George Burns, who gave it to Benny.

The government's case never contended that Benny and Burns had done any smuggling themselves, only that they were complicit with bringing jewelry into the United States. It was unusual for a non-commercial smuggling case to receive criminal prosecution, but Chaperau had posed as a diplomat and had induced others to smuggle, which enlarged the case.

An angry housemaid
So who blew the lid on the celebrity smugglers? It was Rosa Weber, a German housemaid at the home of New York Supreme Court Justice Edgar J. Lauer. At a dinner party at Lauer's 570 Park Avenue apartment on Oct. 21, 1938, she overheard some anti-Hitler remarks from his French and Russian guests.

Her response, according to an affidavit: "Ladies and gentlemen, I am a true German. I love Adolf Hitler. If you don't stop talking against Hitler, I will stop serving the dinner right now. It is up to you."

She was fired on the spot.

Shortly after that, Weber was talking to Treasury agents with what she knew about her employer's smuggling activities. And there was a lot to tell them. Judge Lauer's wife, Elma, had been smuggling jewelry and clothing since 1933. In her previous marriage, she had lived in Paris for 10 years and had been accustomed to bringing in her possessions duty-free.

She had been caught smuggling in 1937 and fined more than $10,000 in a civil case, but through Chaperau, she was at it again. The Lauers' apartment underwent a six-hour raid by Treasury agents on Oct. 27, the same day they arrested Chaperau. Agents left with four suitcases of clothing that had been purchased in France that summer and had been delivered by Chaperau on Oct. 6, after the Lauers returned in September.

The maid, Judge Lauer told reporters, "apparently wishes revenge for her discharge."

The search of Chaperau's apartment found correspondence with his Hollywood "friends."

A federal grand jury in New York began an investigation in December. Burns, who had purchased a bracelet and a ring through Chaperau in 1936 and in May 1938, quickly entered a guilty plea on two counts of smuggling.

But Assistant U.S. Attorney Joseph L. Delaney also grilled Benny's tenor, Kenny Baker, Jack Pearl (radio's Baron Munchausen), Sophie Tucker, Katherine Hepburn and others, although none of them were under suspicion. One wire report said Benny also was questioned at that time.

Why was Baker the only member of Benny's cast to be drawn into the probe? He was in London making The Mikado in the summer of 1938, so perhaps the Bennys met up with him during their vacation.

The indictment

Benny, although he had not been subpoenaed, flew from California to New York in early January of 1939, telling reporters, "I'm going to find what it's all about," although clearly he knew what he was in for.

On Jan. 9, Chaperau was convicted of smuggling clothing for Mrs. Lauer. His claim of diplomatic immunity through his appointment by a former Nicaraguan consul general was quickly dismissed.

On Jan. 10, Benny appeared before the grand jury, and told them that he had been persuaded by Chaperau, over cocktails, that the arrangement to bring the jewelry into the country was legal.

He was indicted on three counts of smuggling jewelry in conspiracy with Chaperau, who had arrived with the jewelry the same day he brought the clothing for Mrs. Lauer.

Although Benny and Burns had the same lawyers and undoubtedly received identical advice, on that day, Benny made up his own mind.

"Mr. Benny, how do you plead?" the court clerk asked.

"NOT guilty," was the loud reply in the voice familiar to millions of listeners.

Benny put up $1,000 bail and was fingerprinted at the U.S. Marshal's office. Each count carried a maximum of two years in prison and a $5,000 fine.

One of his attorneys, Walter N. Thayer III, issued a statement from Benny that said, in part:

"I am utterly amazed ... I have never smuggled jewelry or anything else into this country and no one can truthfully say that I intentionally committed the acts with which I am charged."

Defense collapses

Benny's trial was set for Jan. 24. But he quickly was without any legal legs on which to construct a defense.

On Jan. 11, Chaperau pleaded guilty to the jewelry smuggling charges, although he pleaded not guilty to the charges involving Burns and Mrs. Lauer.

On Jan. 14, syndicated columnist Leonard Lyons reported, "One of Jack Benny's closest friends "put the finger" on him."

On Jan. 16, Burns, wife Gracie Allen, Pearl and Baker were subpoenaed to testify in the Benny case.

On Jan. 31, Burns was the first to be convicted. He was fined $8,000, given a suspended sentence of a year and a day, and place on one year's probation. He was given 10 days to pay the fine. Cooperation with investigators had gotten him leniency.

With two guilty pleas in advance of his court appearance and Chaperau, Burns and Baker as prosecution witnesses, Benny had no chance of anything other than a conviction should his case have gone to trial.

"The executives at NBC, General Foods and the advertising agency were in a state of hysteria as the scandal erupted on the front pages of every newspaper," Benny recalled in Sunday Nights at Seven. "The fact that my life might be wrecked was beside the point. They kept talking about "public relations" and "strategy" for handling the press and what kind of statements I should make. To these people I was a pawn in a gigantic chess game of competition for ratings and the sales of boxes of powdered gelatin. ...

"I didn't want to plead guilty. I had been having meetings and conferences with network brass and sponsor representatives and they kept me in a state of nervous tension so I couldn't think straight. ... They finally decided to take a chance to continue sponsoring me -- or "risk their necks," as they put it -- and let me go on the air every Sunday."

Benny got two postponements so he could finish Man About Town. Lawyers for Paramount contended that the studio could lose $750,000 if the film was not completed.

On Feb. 26, Lyons reported, "Jack Benny has been advised that if he should be convicted, he'll receive a jail sentence."

Benny's February and March programs included the introduction of Carmichael, the polar bear sent by an admirer. Carmichael's roars came from a newcomer to the Jell-O program, Mel Blanc.

Syndicated columnist Dale Harrison visited a Benny broadcast and wrote in early March, "I was curious to observe how Benny had reacted to his trouble with the federal government. I had read somewhere in New York that his hair had turned completely white, and I had heard he had displayed signs of worry.

"Report: Benny's hair is about as gray as it was before. It isn't white. He is nervous -- jittery -- but I never saw a comedian who wasn't nervous just before his show went on."

A stiff lecture

Judgment day arrived on Tuesday, April 4. Benny was accompanied to New York by his agent, Arthur Lyons.

Benny said he was surprised when one of his lawyers, William J. "Wild Bill" Donovan, advised him, before his court appearance, to plead guilty. Donovan, a Medal of Honor winner in World War I, had been a federal prosecutor before going into private practice in New York.

"There are times, Mr. Benny, when an honest man gets into trouble without meaning to and then the bravest thing is to take your punishment even if the world -- even if the whole world -- thinks you're admitting you're bad by doing this. As long as you know in your soul that you are right -- that is all that matters. And I'll make a guess -- in the long run, you'll find that the American people will not only forgive -- they will forget."

He arrived at the courthouse with Donovan and attorneys Thayer, Carl Newton and Lloyd Wright.

The New York Times said there were 200 "admirers" in the courtroom. The Associated Press reporter, possibly including the crowds in the hallways, estimated 400 and noted that many were standing at the back of the courtroom.

When the case was called, Newton began to whisper to a court clerk.

"Well, suppose you let me in on this," said Judge Vincent Leibell.

Newton approached the bench as an attendant gestured for Benny, wearing a brown suit and twisting a gold ring on his left little finger, to stand.

"The defendant asks permission to change his plea," he said as Benny gripped the back of a chair.

"Is this the defendant?" Leibell asked after a glance at Benny.

"Yes sir," replied Newton.

"How do you plead?" the judge asked.

"Guilty," said Benny.

"To all three counts of the indictment?"

"Yes, sir."

Cahill, assisted by Delaney, outlined the charges. Before Newton could respond, the judge asked whether it had been Benny's or Chaperau's idea to smuggle the jewelry. He was told it was Chaperau.

Leibell delivered a withering lecture.

"Mr. Benny should have been bigger than to have subscribed to a plan that would have deprived his government of $700 duty. That was certainly small of Mr. Benny, letting down his own country. We have jewelers and artisans here who make their own jewelry and they should be protected.

"You must feel very much ashamed of yourself, Mr. Benny, standing here as you do today."

Benny's response was a nearly inaudible, "I do."

"I think it was a very poor return from you to the government and the citizens of this country, who have made so much of you and so much for you, to so something like this, whose object was only a pecuniary profit -- you, who make so much."

Benny got a stiffer sentence than Burns: a $10,000 fine ($5,000 on one count, $2,500 on each of the other two counts), a suspended jail sentence of a year and a day, and one year of probation. Unlike Burns, who had 10 days to pay the fine, Benny had until 4 p.m. that day. A certified check was delivered by 3.

He issued a statement saying that he thought he had dealt with Chaperau in the belief there would be "a perfectly legitimate saving" in the duty and that he had never intended to defraud the government. One wire service estimated his total bill, including trial expenses, as more than $42,000.

Chaperau, despite his cooperation with prosecutors, was sentenced to five years, fined $5,000 and received five years' probation. His sentence was later reduced to two years. Mrs. Lauer, whom the judge compared to a kleptomaniac, was sentenced to three months -- which she served in a women's detention center in Greenwich Village -- one year's probation, and fined $2,500. The total amount of the fines and penalties came to $34,344. Weber's share as an informer was to be $8,586 (one-fourth of the total).

Aftermath
The effect on Benny's popularity and career: Absolutely nothing. Milt Josefsberg (who had not yet joined the Benny writing staff in 1938), in his memoir, said he had been told there had been a slight increase in the amount of anti-Semitic mail.

"The day before I was indicted," Benny recalled in Sunday Nights at Seven, "my Crossley rating was 37.4. Three months after I pleaded guilty and had been fined and humiliated, my next Crossley rating (this would have been his season-end program, broadcast from his hometown of Waukegan, Illinois) showed a leap to 40.1.

"I am very proud of such a vote of confidence from the American people."

Benny's next program was Easter Sunday, April 9. "We bring you the man who was the highlight of the Easter Parade in his frock coat, white spats and beanie..." was Don Wilson's introduction. The sketch was a parody of Four Girls In White. Baker played a nurse called "Peaches." At one point, Benny's doctor character shouted, "Peaches, I'm going to can you if you don't behave!"

On April 16, Wilson's introduction mentioned that Benny had just returned from a one-week vacation in Palm Springs.

Cahill wrote New York Gov. Herbert Lehman to cite Judge Lauer's participation in the smuggling scheme, which in turn launched an investigation by a legislative subcommittee. Lauer, while protesting his innocence, resigned from the bench, to which he had been elected in 1933, as of June 18. Walter Winchell reported that Mrs. Lauer celebrated her release at the El Morocco.

Did getting pulled into the case hurt Baker's career? It's difficult to say.

In July, Benny started holding auditions in New York and California for another tenor, in a process that famously ended up with Dennis Day. Columnists reported that he was seeking an unknown. Baker, meanwhile, had been signed exclusively for "Star Theater" -- on which he already was a regular performer -- for the 1939-40 radio season, and the following season, he joined Fred Allen's program in New York.

Did the prosecution have the desired effect of making an example of a celebrity? Perhaps. After Benny's indictment, the assistant collector of the Port of New York told The New York Times that publicity had already resulted in an increase in duties collected by the government, and that travelers seemed "more meticulous" about declaring items they had brought in.

In 1948, when NBC was trying to keep Benny from accepting an offer from CBS, it hired Cahill, who was now in private practice, as part of its negotiating team. Benny returned from his initial meeting with them and bitterly told Josefsberg and writer John Tackaberry, "They had the colossal gall, the nerve, the chutzpah, to send three lawyers to talk me into staying with them, and one of these lawyers was the man who once caused me more mental anguish than anyone else."

Josefsberg wrote that Cahill "was the final reason" Benny left NBC. He said Benny concluded that Cahill had neglected to inform NBC of his role in the prosecution, not that the network was insensitive.

- Judge Lauer and his wife moved to Paris in 1945. He died there in 1948.
- Donovan became director of the Office of Strategic Services, the forerunner of the CIA, during World War II. He died in 1959.
- Thayer, active in Republican politics and newspaper publishing (he was the last president of the New York Herald-Tribune), died in 1989.
- Carl Newton died in 1989.
- Lloyd Wright was Charlie Chaplin's lawyer for many years.
- John T. Cahill died in 1966.
- Judge Leibell died in 1968.
- Baker made occasional guest appearances on Benny's radio program after his departure, had a starring role in One Touch of Venus on Broadway, and had his own short-lived radio series, Glamour Manor, on which Benny made one guest appearance. He was active in Christian Science for many years. He died in August 1985 in Santa Barbara, California, a month before his 73rd birthday, but his family did not make his death public for three months.
- Chaperau sued Benny and Burns in March 1945 to recover the fines he had paid, but the suit was quickly dismissed. Later that year, he tried his hand as a Broadway producer with a farce called "Make Yourself at Home," which closed after just four performances.

Accurate information concerning the outcomes of Chaperau and Rosa Weber has so far eluded inquiry.

Jack Benny
By Julius Sinykin

[EN: Julius Sinykin was one of Jack's longest friendships, lasting from Jack's teenage years to his death in 1974. Julius was born in 1883, so was Jack's senior by 11 years. This article is being printed with the permission of Jaynie Behr, who is one of the wonderful and fascinating people whom I have been privileged to meet in these past few months.]

My first recollection of meeting Jack Benny was at the Parish House at the Charity Ball in Waukegan. Benny played a violin solo and it seemed that he was the attraction of the evening. He was in his early youth at that time. Every local music critic predicted a great musical career for him.

My second recollection of him is an incident which occurred while he was a student in high School. Miss Alice Payne was the librarian in the school, and she had ordered Benny to leave the room for wisecracking. There was a dance that night at the Parish House. When Benny rose to leave the room he got as far as the door, but wanting to have the last word, he turned and said, "Alice, save me a dance tonight." Miss Payne laughed about it when she later related it to me that evening at the dance. Believe it or not, Jack had his dance with Alice that evening.

During Benny's last year in high school, he was sent home quite often for misbehavior. It was then that we became close friends. He would come to my store after being sent from school and spend much time there. At that time I had a position in the Columbia Clothing store on Washington Street, and Danny Jemison was working in the book store across the street. Between the two stores, Benny amused himself until it was time for school to close and for him to return home.

Amateur shows were popular in Waukegan during Benny's youth and I was in many of them. Benny usually played in the orchestra which accompanied the show, and while he wasn't playing, he was back stage with me. One of the plays we staged was "The Bells" and Benny was the orchestra leader in this. One of our friends named Clarence Evans was the property man. This play was a very dramatic one, making the cues for the bells and the music very important. However, Benny and Evans forgot the importance of it all as Evans started talking to a stage hand and missed his cue. The most tragic of all was Benny falling asleep in the orchestra pit. One can easily imagine what it did to our show.

A period of several days elapsed before Benny made any attempt to see me again. However, that was the longest time we were ever separated. This play was shown in the Schwartz Theatre on Water Street.

Shortly after this, Joe Howard and Mabel Barrison rented an old stable on Genesee Street and made it into a vaudeville theatre which was known as the Barrison Theatre. Arthur Frudenfeld was the manager, and I had become acquainted with him the first day he come to Waukegan. Benny and I spent a great deal of time at the Barrison Theatre and finally Frudenfeld gave Benny a job as ticket collector. However, he didn't remain on this job very long, and soon he was playing in the Barrison Theatre orchestra. Cora Salisbury was the pianist and a very remarkable one, having been in vaudeville. It took very little effort on her part to convince Benny to start on a stage career. However, his father and most of his friends tried to persuade him to practice violin, as they could see a great career in store for him. He often discussed this with me, and his version of it was that he knew too many musicians who were starving to death. Being fond of the stage, I couldn't help but agree with him.

Salisbury and Benny teamed up and went on the road. They gained considerable fame and notoriety until Salisbury's mother became ill, making it necessary for her to return to Waukegan.

While Benny was on the road, he never forgot me. He wrote me letters regularly, and all of his personal press notices came to me. I have all of his early publicity as well as the longer stories about his shows in my special "Jack Benny scrap book." During the time he was traveling with Salisbury, he never spoke a line, but he managed to get laughs from his audience from the way he would handle his violin and the motion of his little finger on his right hand.

After the Benny-Salisbury partnership severed, Benny found another pianist. This time it was a man from Chicago named Woods. One of their acts was known as the "Benny and Woods" act. This pair embarked upon a vaudeville career which was successful until the outbreak of the World War. When Benny gave up vaudeville to enter the service, he came to Waukegan and as usual visited me. We talked things over and Benny decided to join the Navy. Together we went down to Great Lakes and Benny enlisted. He stated his profession as being a musician. When his superior officer discovered that Benny couldn't play anything but a violin, he was disappointed. The Band master had no use for a violin.

Benny then went into training. I shall never forget the first time I saw him at the station. It was on a Wednesday afternoon and the temperature was exceedingly hot. Benny went marching by holding the flute—just <u>holding</u> it. He couldn't play the darn thing. After the parade I was able to see him and found him to be a very much disgusted boy. The first thing he said was, "If you don't get me out of this Navy, I'll die." At that time, I had several friends at Great Lakes, among them being Captain and Mrs. Moffett. I had promised Benny I would talk to the Captain to see if there was anything that could be done. Mrs. Moffett was at the head of the Navy Relief at that time, and they were booking entertainers for a big Navy relief show. I knew that was where Benny belonged, and where he would do the most good. I succeeded in having Benny transferred, which made him very happy. He joined the Great Lakes Review and traveled from city to city on a tour, for the duration of the war. It was in this show that he first began to speak lines.

During the time he spent at Great Lakes, he met a boy named Zez Confrey who was a talented pianist. He and Benny decided to team up after leaving the Navy, following the end of the war. However, after the war Benny was discharged but Zez seemed to be there indefinitely. Benny waited for some time, but finally after talking it over with me, he decided to get out and try to do a single.

Benny made up an act for himself and got booking on his past reputation. The skit, a monologue with bits of violin playing really gained recognition with the people. He was booked as "Ben Benny", which attracted attention. As he went along he got better write-ups with each show, and he was doing very well for himself.

No doubt very few people know why and how Ben Benny became Jack Benny. At that time, Ben Bernie was a headliner. This, of course, created considerable confusion on account of the names being so similar. Bernie had been in the show business longer, therefore it was up to Benny to change his name. That is how Ben selected the name of Jack.

Shortly after changing his name, Jack had his first big break in a Schubert show. Following that, he was offered a contract by Metro-Goldwyn-Mayer. He then went to Hollywood and everything was fine. He was offered a good salary and nothing to do all day but play golf. And life went on in this fashion for Benny in Hollywood. However, this didn't really meet with his approval, and one bright day he wired me to meet him in Chicago. While he was traveling, he always wired me when he was coming through and I always went to meet him. That morning when I met him at the train, I recall his first words, "Maybe I have made a mistake, but I was fed up with playing golf all day and doing nothing. So I went to the Manager and asked to be released from my contract." Metro-Goldwyn-Mayer released him, stating they were sorry to lose him, but if that was the way he felt, it was all right. Thus Jack Benny walked out on a good salary, California sunshine, and a daily golf game.

Perhaps another good reason why Benny left California was because he didn't like to stay away from New York too long. He didn't care to play golf and take sun baths all the time. He thought that people would forget him. Benny was an entertainer and wanted to work at his job. It was a funny thing about him—he always seemed to know what was right for him to do. He spoke of having "hunches" and usually they were always the right kind. Benny was like this also when he was a kid. Many people didn't agree with him as to his career, etc., but he usually came out on top with everything he did.

Before Benny left Chicago, he told me that he thought Earl Carroll would make him an offer for a spot in the "Vanities". He told me he expected a telegram from Carroll, and I advised him to wire me [about the result]. When I returned home, there was a wire stating that Jack was going into a show with Carroll. Thus Benny went on with his career and into a new show.

After a successful season in New York, his show—"The Vanities"—came to Chicago. Previous to this, while en route to New York, Jack told me about a girl in Hollywood whom he had met while in California. Her name was Mary [Sadye] Marks and Jack did a lot of talking about how wonderful she was. Mary had a married sister in vaudeville. Mary's sister [Babe] and her husband [Al Bernovici] were playing in Chicago at the same time Jack was there with the show—Vanities. Miss Marks came out from Hollywood to visit her sister and brother-in-law. One Sunday, Jack called me and told me he wanted to bring Mary to Waukegan. They came to visit me at my apartment in the Clayton Hotel. The following Friday, Jack called me and said that he had asked Mary to be his wife and they wished to be married in my apartment. He told me he had asked his Dad's consent to be married there, and he consented to it. [EN: This is a little unusual, as Jack's father was Orthodox Jewish and this would not be a traditional Jewish wedding in a synagogue.] At that time, his Dad was living in Lake Forest [a nearby Chicago suburb]. So Jack and Mary were married January 14, 1927. I shall never forget that day; it seemed that it snowed every day that week, in fact there was so much snow we could hardly get to the court house. It was really terrific. Dr. Farber performed the ceremony. All present besides myself were his father, his sister [Florence] and her husband [Leonard Fenchel], Mary's sister [Babe] and her husband [Al Bernovici], and Sidney Block, a mutual friend. After the ceremony, we all went to Chicago for dinner. After dinner, I took Mary to the show. Jack couldn't—he was in it. So became the partnership of Jack and Mary.

After the Carroll show closed, Jack went back into vaudeville. He used a [female] stooge, however something happened and the girl who worked for him didn't show up [EN: she became ill], so he decided to try Mary in the part. She has worked with him successfully ever since. Before appearing with Jack, she had no previous experience on the stage. Following a brief return to vaudeville, Jack went on the air. He started with Canada Dry, then Chevrolet, following with General Tires, and later turned to General Foods.

In my recollection of Jack's boyhood, I remember he was like all boys, having a lot of girls. He liked one especially whose name was Margaret. I remember the first time he took Margaret to Chicago to the show. When he came back, he came up to my apartment and kept me up the rest of the night talking about Margaret. Whenever Jack stayed out late, he never went home. He always came up and stayed with me. He was a great audience; anything that would strike him funny, he would laugh until he rolled out of bed. Another incident I recall was one time when his father left him in charge of the store. Jack had played at a dance the night before, and he was pretty tired. The easy chair was too much of a temptation and soon Jack was fast asleep. Meanwhile, someone tiptoed into the store and walked off with an entire table full of trousers. You can imagine what happened when his father came in and discovered the loss.

Jack really got started along the entertaining line in school. It was there that his talent really came to light. He was the life of every gathering with his natural flair for entertaining, which made him the target for many requests.

As I stated before, every time Jack came through Chicago, he wired me to meet him. On one of the occasions he was coming from the Coast en route to New York, and I planned to meet him in Chicago. Mayor Talcott told me he would like to join me. We drove to Chicago and on the way, I suggested it would be nice if we could have a homecoming in honor of Jack for the Waukegan people to show their appreciation for all the publicity given to the city during the years Jack had been on the air. Mayor Talcott agreed that if Benny assured me he would give us his time on a certain day, we would arrange a homecoming.

It so happened that Jack was able to stop off on the way back to the Coast. The date was set for Tuesday, March 23, 1937. It was the nicest and one of the most successful affairs ever held in the City of Waukegan. It was really a great day for Waukegan and Jack Benny. If was the day when "the local boy who made good in a big way" came to receive the honors of the citizens who used to know him way back when his Dad ran a clothing store.

Several days before the celebration, Jack wired me, "Will arrive Tuesday morning with Mary and Don. Stop. Make any plans you and Mayor Talcott and committee thing best. Stop. No parade. Stop. Remember I am nervous. Stop. Go easy on an old home boy who still likes Waukegan and his school day pals, Jack." We met Jack in Chicago, and on the way back we stopped off and met Admiral Ellis. Jack entertained the boys at the Veteran's Hospital, and our next stop was at the high school where he was greeted in the Auditorium by a packed house. The high school cadets in their uniforms lined up in the assembly. When Jack saw the splendid reception, he turned to me and said he did not deserve such honor.

Despite the fact that Jack wanted a quiet reception, Waukegan people thought differently. Jack was escorted in a gigantic parade through town. After the mass meeting was held in the school gymnasium, a dinner and dance topped off the evening. Jack was excited and pleased. More than 700 of his Waukegan friends and admirers were proud of him and his entertainment. Everyone had a genuine good time at the homecoming banquet. It was held at the Miami Ballroom. Jack admitted that he was nervous. This is what he said, "If I were to tell you I was more nervous tonight than I ever was in my life, you would think I was nuts." Jack told his banquet guests that during the 25 years of his show business career, he didn't think he ever experienced this much excitement. He went on to way, "While you all may believe I am just saying this, I am really on the level. This has indeed been the most thrilling and happy day of my life. Believe me, I am terribly nervous, but I will try to be good." And Jack Benny was good!

Preceding the dinner and dance, during the afternoon, a Jack Benny Elm tree was planted at the Court House officiated by Mayor Talcott and the Council. In thanking the Mayor for the honor, he remarked, "It was a great tribute to me and all the dogs in the county."

Jack stayed until the very last dance that evening, and after he got home, he told me it was one of the nicest things that could have happened to him. He really got a big kick out of the reception and everything that was done for him. Before saying good night to me, Jack, with tears in his eyes said, "If only my mother was alive, I would have everything." Jack never failed to mention his mother to me whenever some honor was accorded him. Naturally his father and sister were always present. His mother died shortly after he started his career in vaudeville [1917].

Jack told me right then and there that in appreciation he would like to do something for Waukegan, although at that time it looked impossible. He didn't know just how he was going to do it, but he promised me he would do one of his broadcasts from Waukegan. When Jack had his choice about the premiere of his picture "Man About Town", naturally Chicago and New York wanted it. But Jack said that a premiere was going to be held in Waukegan. He arranged to have it on Sunday so he could do a broadcast from Waukegan. Those were Waukegan Days and the celebration lasted from June 21st to June 25th, 1939.

The <u>Waukegan News Sun</u> gave daily reports, headlined as follows:

> "Days citizens of Waukegan will long remember"
> "Benny premier packed city"
> "60 to 75,000 come to Waukegan for Jack Benny days"
> "Waukegan slowly recovering today from 5-day celebration for our Number one local boy—Jack Benny and his troupe of stage and screen celebrities, climaxed last night with the wonderful premiere of his picture 'Man About Town'"
> "Nation-wide broadcast from the stage of the Genesee Theatre most colorful theatrical event the city has ever known, bringing thousands of visitors into town and spreading the name Waukegan to millions of radio listeners and newspaper readers throughout the world"
> "Waukegan was magnet for a count of 75,000 for the city parade"
> "Entertainment at the Genesee Theatre attracted an estimated 30,000"

The Hollywood celebrities who came to Waukegan included Jack Benny, Mary Livingstone, Dorothy Lamour, Mr. And Mrs. Andy Devine, Phil Harris, Don Wilson, and Rochester. Hedda Hopper was in this audience along with a score or more of nationally famous newspaper men and women.

At the time the world premiere was held in Waukegan, two of Jack's old friends, Danny Jemison and Gertrude Wilbur [EN: probably mother or wife of Stubbs Wilbur] were both paralyzed and confined to bed. They had both been in this condition for several years. Danny was in the County Hospital and Mrs. Wilbur was at her home. One afternoon, Jack managed to escape from the photographers and reporters and he and I went to the hospital to visit Danny. Although Danny could not talk, Jack managed to entertain him for a half hour. Poor Danny laughed until he cried. When we left the hospital, Jack cried.

Before leaving the hospital, Jack inquired what Danny needed. The head nurse told him that Danny could use a serving table as he spent most of his time in bed. Danny received a fine combination table which served for eating and reading. It was equipped with electric lights and everything for his convenience.

From the hospital, we went to visit Mrs. Wilbur and the same entertainment was performed by Jack. He talked about old times and at the same time threw in some new gags. Before we left Mrs. Wilbur, Jack noticed that she was sitting in an old chair which did not look very comfortable. We went directly to a furniture store and Jack purchased the best chair he could find for his old friend. On the way home, Jack got an idea that it would be nice to have these friends attend the broadcast Sunday night. With the aid of wheelchairs and an ambulance, Mrs. Wilbur and Danny were brought to the theatre. These two had the opportunity to see a show and for the first time, a broadcast of their old friend as a radio star performer. About six months later Danny died, and Mrs. Wilbur passed away six months hence.

I am always being asked this question about Jack—is he really cheap as his is pictured on radio? Jack is the most liberal man. To this day, Jack contributes to every charitable organization in Waukegan; whether it is the church, Y.M.C.A., or Community Chest. Not long ago when he met me in Chicago, he told me about an appeal he received from an organization here in Waukegan. He asked me how much I thought he should contribute. Of course, I knew about the appeal, as they generally come to me first. Therefore, I was prepared with actual figures as to the amount donated by some of the wealthiest citizens in Waukegan. I thought that if Jack matched any one of the donors, it would be very generous because Waukegan is not the only place from which he gets requests for donations. When I gave Jack the amount of the largest single donation, he made out his check for $100 more than the amount donated by any Waukegan citizen.

Jack helped many of his old friends. Not long ago, a friend of his came in and showed me a check he received from Jack for $150.00. He told me he wrote to Jack about a misfortune he had had, and asked for $150.00. He received this check by return mail.

During the depression, I was forced to sell my business. In 1932, I had the opportunity to begin again, but I had no money and so was going to take a partner. When everything was set up and about to open, my partner backed out at the last minute. I was left holding the bag. I had my new location and the merchandise bought but no money. I shall never forget the day when my "would be" partner told me his wife wouldn't let him put his money in the business. I didn't know what to do. My first thought was to walk to Lake Michigan and keep walking, but to do so I had to pass my hotel on the way. So I stopped in the lobby and the clerk handed me a wire from Jack, who was in New York at that time. The exact words of his wire were, "Will arrive Century tomorrow morning. Love, Jack". That was a message from Heaven. The way I felt, there was no one I would have rather seen. Right then I forgot about my trouble. I just wanted to see Jack and talk to him. However, I made up my mind that I was not going to tell him of my predicament.

I was in Chicago the next day to meet the train at 9 A.M. When Jack greeted me, the first thing he said was, "Florence wrote me that you were going in business, and I know you haven't any money. I also know that you will not ask me for it. That is the reason I came and I brought cash with me."

I was speechless! We got into a cab and went to Henrici's for breakfast as was always our custom when Jack arrived early in the morning. After ordering our breakfast, Jack took out his wallet and handed it to me. He said, "Here, take whatever you need and forget about it. I know if you make it, you will pay me back and if not, to hell with it."

Jack never cared for money. When he was on the road, he never used to save. However at one time he did get an idea to save, and he would send me $25.00 and $50.00 at a time to save. Then when he got home he would ask me, "How much have we got to spend?" Then we would go into Chicago and get a suite at the Edgewater Beach Hotel and spend money in great style. While doing this, Jack would manage to play one of the theatres in Chicago to make sure we had enough spending money.

The first life insurance policy Jack took out was one I had to sell him. The amount of the policy was $1,000.00. The annual premium was $29.51, and the semi-annual $15.35, or quarterly $7.82. These premiums were due the 6th day of January, April, July, and October. In this way, it was easy for Jack to keep up the payments. However, he didn't as he had too many friends to help out.

An item from the Cleveland Press dated March 25, 1938, ran as follows: "Jack Benny greets boyhood friend—Waukegan Clothier. Goes East with radio comedian. Julius

Sinykin in clothing business in Waukegan. Jack arrived in Chicago at 1:20 P.M. as was his usual custom. Sinykin went into the city to greet him between trains from California to New York. Sinykin was still greeting Benny when the radio star arrived at Grand Central Station in New York yesterday morning. Benny was so thrilled at seeing him in Chicago that he insisted Sinykin join the party, despite the fact that the bewildered clothier did not have any baggage or money with him for the trip."

I was impressed and delighted by the reception Jack got when we arrived in New York. At Grand Central Station, he was met by a delegation of twenty-five National Broadcasting Company page boys. I was told that he is the only one who received such an honor.

The week we spent in New York was a busy one. I was with Jack all of the time going from one benefit performance to another. In between times, he had to get his show ready for the Sunday night broadcast. Not until my trip to New York with Jack did I realize how much of a personal sacrifice my friend was making. Oh what price—glory! I could write about this for days, but this gives you a good idea of Jack's personality.

This is the truest story of the cheapest man in radio, and the most generous and greatest small town boy who made good in a big way and never forgot his home town or his old friends.

Meyer Kubelsky

Naomi "Emma" Kubelsky

The Jack Benny Times

September - December 2004 — Volume XIX, Numbers 5-6

President's Message

Jell-O again folks…this period of time has seen my return to work and readjustment to getting up at 6AM and packing the fan club work back into evenings and weekends. I appreciate everyone's support and patience during the time that I let E-mail take second priority to work on other things (like eating and sleeping) or just taking some time for myself. I have also had the pleasure of doing many interviews with some wonderful folks who have known and worked with Jack, and you will be seeing the results of those in many, many upcoming Jack Benny Times issues.

I am very pleased to announce that with the help of the IJBFC, the Boston Public Library has acquired the Julius Sinykin collection of Jack Benny material. As you will recall from the last Times, Julius and Jack were close friends since Jack's boyhood, spending afternoons at Julius' clothing store when Jack was sent home from school. The Sinykin collection includes hundreds of photos, clippings, personal letters, and other material dating back to 1919 and Jack's success in the Great Lakes Naval Revue. It is a fabulous collection and I am truly delighted that it will be preserved for the future of Benny fans and researchers.

Due to the amount of information included in this year's Times issues, we have not printed obituaries for Ellen Drew (Buck Benny Rides Again) or Penny Singleton (Great Temptations). If any subscribers need copies of this information and do not have Web access, please send a SASE and indication of the item you want to the address at the end of this newsletter.

New Members

**** Jan Willis **** Rita Grabel **** Eric Frazier **** Edmund Weingart **** Tim Callahan **** Rebecca K. Watson **** Kristy Fogle **** Jack R. Rininger **** Jody Bennett **** Arthur Wright **** James Brictson **** Linda Reynolds **** Ted Olech **** Perry Greer **** Jeffery S. Weiner, Sr. **** James M Culver **** D.L. Draper **** Mathew Weaver **** James Robison **** Anthony P. Bryce **** Brett M. Seamans **** David Orloff **** Julie Wilkes **** John Cavalaris **** Ryan Gatenby **** Sharon Briscoe **** Brad Yost **** James C. Gajniak **** Steven Kalka **** David Cannady **** Cathey Daniels **** Peter Farris **** Rick Roberson **** Wanda Dossey **** David Capps **** Jeffrey Chase **** Randall W. Hise **** Robert W. Newman **** Katharine Lhota **** Ray Rodriguez **** Tom Brown **** Jack Arnold **** Fred Chernoff **** Giacomo Ianieri **** James Rana **** J.C. Wells **** Charles B. Slutzky **** Carol J Mills **** Steve Archer **** Mark B. Miller **** Paul Midlick **** Liz Amos **** Craig Ferguson **** Ted D. Nichols, Jr. **** Wendy King **** Robert Barman **** Doug Iverson **** Brian Ridder **** Robert W. Coll **** Arthur Lieberman **** Joseph Planta **** Josh Alexander **** Breonna Jackson **** Richard Klee **** Michael Thompson **** Joseph Mittleman **** Mark Addison **** George Healy **** Mrs. Michelle Clipner **** Bruce E Smith **** Edward Carrington **** Jason Brimingham **** John Mathis **** Terry Cunningham **** Gloria Alfaro **** Ron Jorgenson **** Kirk Gardner **** Robert Braunstein **** Paul Williams **** Neil McCaffrey **** John Steiner **** John Fultz **** Eddie Miller **** Jack Feldman **** Sheila R. Riddle

Jack Bloom Pasadena Chapter

The Jack Bloom Pasadena Chapter was started in 1990 as an honorary society for IJBFC members who have been active for four or more consecutive years. Jack Bloom was a dedicated member of the IJBFC, doing extensive research on him for the Times and the original edition of 39 Forever, plus donating hundreds of shows to kick off the IJBFC tape library. Additionally, Jack and I kept a running correspondence for years, discussing Jack Benny and other shared passions, ranging from George Gershwin to bird watching to bad puns. His passing in June of 1990 was a tremendous loss for all the IJBFC members. I still miss him, and am grateful for the warmth and humor that he shared with me.

(Members added or promoted this year are indicated by an asterisk.)

Michael Avedissian	Frank Gregory	James A. Link	A. Joseph Ross
Albert Baggetta*	Joseph F. Gross	Mark R. Linke*	Joel S. Rothman
Louis Bianco	Bryan Haigood	Stephen H. Loeb	Richard Rubenstein
James G. Burke	Tom Heathwood*	Howard Mandelbaum	Bob Rutishauser*
C.A. Caramella	Jon Heinz*	Hooman Mehran	John Sauciunas
Patrick Carey*	Franklin Heynemann	Don Meno*	Clair Schulz
Cindy Chesser*	Jimmie Hicks	Steve Metzger	Mel Simons
Dayton Crandall*	Ellis Hogue*	Walt Mitchell	Gary Smith
Jim Davison	David Howell*	Russell Myers*	Scott J. Smith
Warren Debenham	Charles Huck	Richard Nathan	W. Robert Smith
Anthony DiFlorio	Will Jordan	Jack Palmer	Helen Songer
Matthew M. Drew	Thomas Kessel	Teresa Perry*	James Stewart*
Ray Druian*	Nik Kierniesky*	Alvin Post*	Gus Storm
The Eljases*	Kenneth Koftan*	Chris Reale	Barbara Thunell
J.E. Farst*	Raymond L. Krysl	Richard Rieve	Harvey Walker
Robert L. Garland	Stephen Lake	The Robertses	Susie Walker*
Joe Goff	Sam Levene*	Richard Ross*	Mary Lou Wallace

Emeritus Members (15+ years)

Hal Bogart	Alan Grossman	Bobb Lynes*	The Tintorris
Rob Cohen	Tim Hollis	Tom Mastel	Larry Valley*
Robert Duncan	David Howell*	Robert Olsen	Barbara Watkins
J. Ed Galloway	George Lillie	Donnie Pitchford	Doug Wood

Let's Get Together

Hey folks...we haven't gotten together since the 39 Forever convention last year. And now here's an opportunity to see each other, contribute to charity, help out the IJBFC, and enjoy some great entertainment all at the same time.

Eddie Carroll is doing his one-man tribute to Jack Benny on September 26 in Fullerton, California at the Plummer Auditorium. If you mention the IJBFC when you're purchasing your tickets, the Costa Mesa Lions Club will donate $5 to the IJBFC for each $35 and $25 ticket you buy, and $10 for each $45 ticket you buy. Everyone wins!

You can purchase your tickets by contacting Walden Hughes at (714) 545-0318, or E-mailing him at hughes1@flash.net. Visa, MasterCard, and checks are accepted.

I will be there with copies of <u>39 Forever, Second Edition</u> available for purchase, and I'd love to be able to meet or re-connect with IJBFC members. Hope to see you there!

Backstage with Eddie Carroll
<u>Benny's Timeless Appeal</u>

When I began performing my first Jack Benny one-man show in 1983, a number of well-meaning people made comments such as, "Enjoy doing the show now, because in 15 years no one will even remember who Jack Benny was."

WELLL!!! They certainly have been proven wrong because 21 years later, the show is more popular than ever. Many of my engagements are booked a year in advance and enthusiastic audiences are filling theaters wherever it plays.

Jack has been gone since 1974 and yet why does a show about his life continue to sustain, why does his name continue to draw crowds and why does the IJBFC continue to grow and draw new members?

First of all, there are millions of older people who grew up with Jack Benny on radio and later on, television. Of all the popular entertainers of his time, there is a valid reason why Jack Benny resonated so strongly with the public for more than four decades. As Americans, no matter what our background or ethnicity, we all share similar traits that give us a common bond. If you've ever traveled to a foreign country, you can instantly recognize another countryman and know that they are one of "us".

In Jack Benny, we recognized that same familiarity because he was a reflection of our commonality. His persona was woven into the very fabric of our national character and we felt a kinship with him. Unlike the glamour stars of the day, there was no way the general public could relate to their rarefied and seemingly perfect world. Those stars were looked upon as one of "them", the beautiful people who were idolized and admired from a distance.

Benny was the opposite. He wasn't one of "them", but rather one of "us" who lived in our world, with all its imperfections, faults, and frailties. The character he created was real to us, in it we saw a reflection of ourselves, and we loved him for it.

Now all of this may be a reasonable explanation for his continuing popularity with the older crowd, but what about the current generations that didn't grow up with him? Are they familiar with him and if so, do they connect with his him and his style of comedy in the same way older generations did?

I recently had a conversation with our esteemed President, Laura Leff, on this very subject and she told me how encouraged and heartened she was to see young new members joining the IJBFC, who were also eager to share the fact that they were only in their 30s, 20s, and even younger and are avid Benny fans. I've also made the same discovery in my travels around the country. After every performance, if my time and schedule allows, I go out into the lobby to talk to audience members and am always delighted to see young people in the crowd. They are eager to talk about "discovering Jack Benny" through friends or family members and becoming fans and collectors of his radio and TV shows. In every instance, I hear the same comments about how funny the shows are and how well the humor still holds up today.

And therein lies Benny's brilliance. There were no "jokes" per se, in his show. The comedy and laughter came from character and behavior. To quote an old adage, "The more things change, the more they stay the same." No matter what changes or advances we make as a society, the one thing that never changes is human behavior.

It's the reason we all loved Charlie Brown and the colorful gang of kids in the Peanuts cartoon, because we laughed at our own human foibles as seen through the eyes of children. In that same sense, Jack Benny was our grown-up Charlie Brown. Foiled at every turn, bluffing and blustering his way through life and yet somehow getting through it, not because of his strengths, but in spite of his flaws. We recognize it and respond with the spontaneous laughter of identification. It was this universal appeal that made Jack Benny a household word for more than four decades, not only here but throughout the entire English-speaking world.

So whether you're from a generation that grew up with him, or the current generation and just discovered him, Jack Benny's humor touches a common chord in us all and will always be funny and always timeless.

In this instance, the closing line from my last article is most appropriate and bears repeating:

WHEN A MAN LEAVES BEHIND AS MUCH OF HIMSELF AS JACK BENNY LEFT US, THEN HE CAN NEVER TRULY BE GONE. HE SIMPLY BECOMES....IMMORTAL.

Special note:
I have been invited to take part in the 30th Anniversary of the SPERDVAC old time radio convention on Saturday, Nov.13, 2004 in El Segundo,CA, where I will recreate one of Jack Benny's rare radio dramas. For more information and updates, contact Bobb Lynes at: www.IAIROTR@HOTMAIL.COM or www.sperdvac.org.

For additional information on my show and future engagements in your area, contact me at www.eddiecarroll.com.

What's Up in Waukegan?

Recent visitors to the Jack Benny statue in downtown Waukegan may have noticed a recent addition. It is the plaque (at right), which has been installed on a new base. The plaque was commissioned in 1976 for Jack's boyhood home on 225 South Genesee by Mayor Robert Sabonjian. When the home was demolished due to structural concerns, the plaque was the first item removed and stored at the Sabonjian family home. The plaque was recently rediscovered by his son, Robert Sabonjian, Jr. It was then passed along to local Waukegan activist, Hank Bogdala, who was also active in the creation of the Benny statue. Through Hank's efforts with the City of Waukegan, the plaque got its new home in Benny Plaza.

The Genesee Theatre's new proscenium

Which brings us just across the street from the Genesee Theatre. The construction on the Genesee is almost finished, and it is truly going to be the world-class theatre that the city had envisioned. This fall will represent a "soft launch" of the theatre, with SMG Management Group taking over responsibility for overseeing the theatre operation. Discussions are ongoing regarding an official "grand opening" celebration. We are in the talking stages of scheduling some upcoming Benny events in Waukegan, and we will keep you updated of any major developments at www.jackbenny.org.

After visiting the statue and theatre, you're probably going to be ready for something to eat. The Uptown Café is only a block away at 300 Grand Avenue, and features the Jack Benny Sandwich. This sandwich was created through the devoted gastronomical research of one of our members in the United Kingdom, Dr. Kenneth Miller, and Jaime Meadows of the Uptown Café. Waukegan News-Sun columnist Dan Moran gave the sandwich a rave review. So stop by and tell them the International Jack Benny Fan Club sent you.

Alderman John Balen views the newly-guilded Genesee Theatre auditorium ceiling

Jack Benny and George Burns
By Bev Bergeron

(Thanks to member Brad Zinn for helping make this article possible!)

When Mark Wilson and I arrived in Los Angeles in 1960 at CBS-Television City for the video taping of <u>The Magic Land of Allakazam</u>, we were steps ahead of other struggling actors and performers. We had a sponsor, Kellogg's, who was paying the bill. All we had to do was deliver the tape.

Because we were the producers and not just some lowly out of work actor, we were assigned a parking place for the VIPs of CBS. My car at the time was a relatively new car, but had the marks of hard travel, and it still supported a Texas license plate.

One morning as I was driving from Santa Monica, where I had parked my trailer, to Television city on Beverly Boulevard (No, they did not name the street after me.), I looked over to see a two-seater Mercedes stopped at the light next to me. In the Mercedes was Jack Benny. I smiled and waved. He waved back.

Traffic was very light that early Sunday morning on Beverly as we drove the next two miles to the studio. Each time we stopped at a stoplight, I would smile and wave. Benny would wave back.

When we got to Fairfax Street that the studio was on, I quickly maneuvered over to the right lane and made the turn onto the street. I looked in the mirror and saw that Benny had done the same thing. Less than half a block I made a left turn into the CBS parking lot. The guard, whom I had met a few weeks before, was from Texas also and greeted by dirty car with a very large sweep of his hands and arms pointing to my private parking place. As I drove through the gate, I looked into my rearview mirror to see that the guard was not so friendly with Mr. Benny, as his car was stopped for inspection. I pulled into my parking place and started to unload a pile of magic junk and costumes.

Benny pulled beside me; his parking place was on one side and the other side was reserved for Red Skelton. I was in good company. He stared a long look at me as we walked without talking to the guard's desk leading to the studio's dressing rooms. As I happily passed by the guard I could hear Benny saying, ever so softly, "Who is that man?"

I was even more surprised one day by having Jack Benny's number one comic on the show, Rochester, help me unload my car of magic, clowning, and wardrobe and carry a lot of it up to my dressing room. All the time I had not recognized the man until he spoke. That rasped voice of his jumped out at me as I was removing a dollar tip from my pocket. His unforgettable voice saved me a lot of embarrassment. I just thanked him for his help and praised his acting work on the Benny Show.

Jack Benny videotaped his show next door to us. When he was not taping, the studio was occupied with the Red Skelton Show. We all shared the one and only bathroom that joined the two studios. One day to our crew's and cast's surprise, in walked George Burns and Tony Curtis to watch our rehearsal. The two of them were appearing on the Jack Benny show.

I walked over and made a very courteous greeting to the pair, and that was my limit of conversation. Tony was mouthing off how he had appeared in the Houdini movie and knew about the magic and illusions we were performing. George's reputation performing card magic was far better than Tony's knowledge of magic, but he just smiled and puffed on his cigar.

While taking a break in the rehearsal, our director, Andy Sidaris, spoke over the intercom: "Mr. Burns and Mr. Curtis, you are wanted over at Mr. Benny's studio for taping." Neither one of them moved.

We continued the rehearsal for another five minutes when our director once again mentioned that Mr. Benny is waiting on them. With that George spoke: "Tell the son-of-a-bitch to get over here and see a real show." We continued again as the crew roared with laughter.

It was a good five minutes before the door to the bathroom opened and Jack Benny walked over to Burns and Curtis and said, "Come on guys, we have a show to do." Once again George cut loose using words that my mother had never heard as he put Jack's show down and praised the Saturday morning children show that we were doing. He told Jack to take a seat and shut up.

The jokes flowed from George with the crew screaming. He knew what he was doing. Benny just stood there knowing well that George was going to have his fun before giving in to leaving. Tony Curtis never opened his mouth once while the two top comedians sparred. He was outclassed.

A few minutes passed, a few more puffs on his cigar, and George turned to Tony and said, "Let's go help the old man out." The three walked out of our studio with thunderous applause from the cast and crew. A tribute to two great legends in show business.

The Great Temptations
By Kurt Jensen

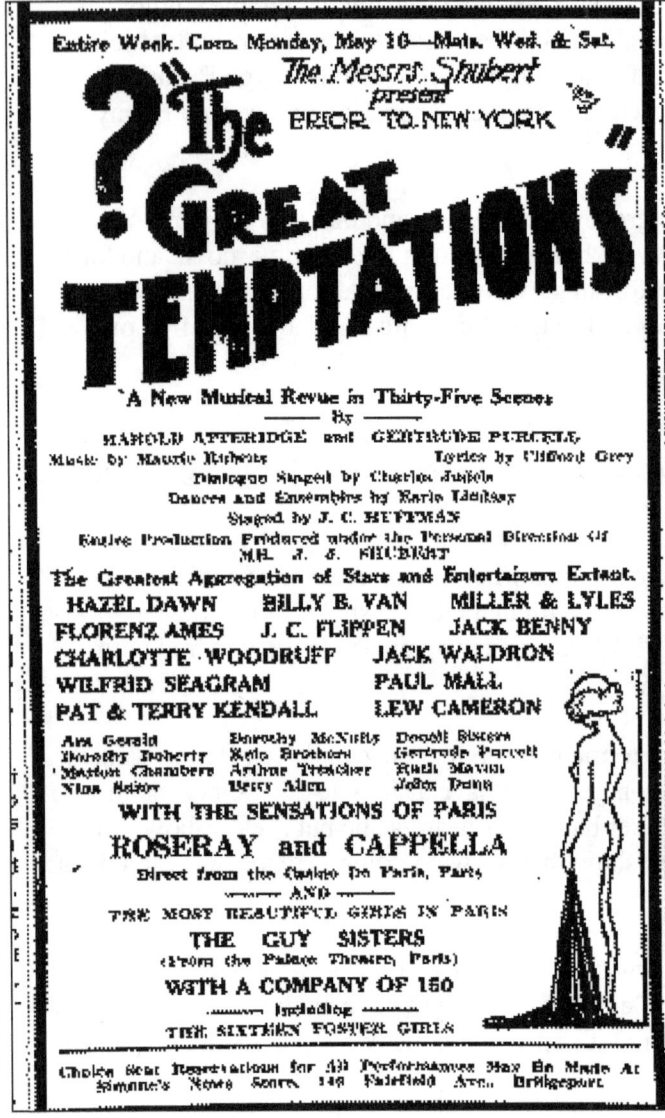

How about that ad? Not too subtle, is it?

It's for the New Haven preview run of the 1926 Shubert revue, *The Great Temptations,* which marked Jack Benny's important step up from vaudeville comic to "legit" stage actor. The show opened at the Winter Garden Theater that May, and following its Broadway run, toured throughout 1927, which is why Mary Livingstone, who married Benny that January in Chicago, spent most of their honeymoon backstage.

The bare behind and breast are a little outré for a newspaper ad even by modern standards; few, if any, papers would run that today. But it accurately reflects the provocative nature of the show. No one was actually fully nude, though; the showgirls were topless, but most of the sketches were just downright dirty. Critics of the time discreetly sniffed at the show's "smoking-room humor." Writer Milt Josefsberg recalled Benny telling him that it "was the *Oh, Calcutta* or *Hair* of its day. It was filthy, in Jack's opinion."

Benny didn't mention much about it in *Sunday Nights at Seven* other than, "My aim was to prove to [producer] Jake Shubert that I was a comedian and not a fiddler."

And that was a very big deal. Even though Benny was by then a top vaudeville master of ceremonies in the biggest venues, being a Broadway actor at the time held more prestige than introducing animal acts and jugglers in two-a-day (often three- and four-a-day, too) vaudeville shows, even at the Palace.

And producer J. J Shubert (this was his show, not in partnership with brother Lee) had a surefire formula of nudity and bawdy sketches, with a few "clean" performers thrown in. Nudity in "sophisticated" revues, and in Shubert shows particularly, was old stuff on Broadway by 1926. Up to then, it always had been presented as still-life tableaux with topless, or barely clad, showgirls in "artistic" poses during a musical number.

But J.J. Shubert was nothing if not innovative. Probably inspired by one of his visits to Parisian clubs to scout new acts, he found a way to take nudity to another level by having topless girls stroll or dance across the stage in the opening number, in which the gods of Olympus decided that nudity was really art. Zowie!

The expression "a show for the tired business man" was a cliché by the 1930s, occasionally tossed about by critics to reflect their jaded disdain for a girlie show that tried to portray itself as something else. But in 1926, Shubert's publicity wielded it proudly, touting *The Great Temptations* as "well calculated to keep the tired business man stirred up to the highest possible pitch of excitement." One can only imagine (although one doesn't really want to), an auditorium full of randy Babbitts leering at the girls.

Josefsberg wrote that the show "became a smash hit because, as Jack readily admits, the public had read how dirty the show was and they came to see a lewd nude performance." Even the headlined Parisian dance team of Roseray and Cappella were nearly nude, she in what *Variety* called "a rhinestone thingamagig judiciously spotted" and he in a rhinestone loincloth as he danced around her whitened body as if worshipping a statue.

It was a massive production, with 35 scenes in previews, 33 on Broadway and 35 in the road tour. Benny was not the comedy star. That was the now-forgotten Billy B. Van, who had been a top stage performer since the turn of the century. Although most newspaper reviews (and Robert Benchley, in *Life*) praised Benny's performance, *Variety* didn't even mention him, which must have been galling.

Brooks Atkinson, in *The New York Times*, found the show "Consistently parsimonious in humor (and occasionally foul) and none too melodious in its music," but found room to praise Benny: "After one or two flat attempts, Jack Benny manages to become successfully droll in a number with Dorothy McNulty." McNulty, no relation to Eugene McNulty/Dennis Day, was then a 18-year-old acrobatic singer, and later gained fame when she changed her name to Penny Singleton and starred in the *Blondie* films.

So what else did customers get for their money in addition to 16 minutes of Benny, who did part of his "A Few Minutes with Jack Benny" act and the skit with McNulty? For this, we can thank *Variety*, which called it "primarily ... a dancing and sight show," and helpfully detailed all the components.

Highlights included:

- Van and Jay C. Flippen (later a character actor, then a comic just breaking out of a blackface act) in a double-entendre sketch, "On My Veranda."
- Singer Hazel Dawn introduced "Valencia."
- The Guy Sisters, also from Paris, danced in expensive-looking plumed costumes.
- The blackface team of Miller and Lyles performed the sketch in which seven times 13 is "proven" to be 28 — and even then, it was considered an old chestnut! Critics pointed out that the sketch also could be seen elsewhere around New York.
- "A Harlem Incident," a blackface sketch so vile and offensive it was later ordered pulled from the show by a "play jury" organized by the Manhattan district attorney's office. *Variety* mentioned that a corked-up Flippen played "a colored woman pulling the nasty one about her shooting a colored gentleman because he said 'April Fool' at an inopportune time."
- For additional comedy relief, there was a chorus of fat girls (in tights), which critics also pointed out was a stolen bit of business from a burlesque show. Seven years later, Benny, in a routine written by Harry Conn for his stage shows, would perform a similar act with the overweight "Cherry Sisters," a spoof on tight-harmony groups like the Boswell Sisters
- For the grand finale, "March of the Lanterns," a full chorus marched up and down steps with red and yellow electric torches.

But let Jack have the final word on *The Great Temptations*, from a 1947 syndicated newspaper column:

> This was what I had always wanted — to get on Broadway and be an actor. Jack Benny ... actor. ACTOR! Boy, that was music!
>
> I wanted people on the street to point at me and exclaim, "There goes an actor!" And with the flashy Broadway outfit I bought, I'll bet I turned heads two blocks away. I must have looked like a sunset with buttons.
>
> Then one night, as I was leaving the theater, I overheard a stagehand mumble, "There goes that guy Benny. He always looks like an actor."
>
> For a moment, I floated along, engulfed in the cloud of my own conceit.
>
> "Yep, Benny always looks like an actor," came another voice. "— except when he's on the stage."

Do You Know?

Be Happy, Go Lucky music
Mike Amowitz writes: "I played another CD from the set I was telling you about (the Frank Fontaine one tonight, which is followed by the Mean Old Man show). The instrumental music that's closed each of these shows is the same melody as "Be happy, go Lucky, be happy, go Lucky Strike, be happy, go Lucky, go Lucky Strike today"...the melody repeats over and over for 2½ minutes at the close of each show."

This peppy and repetitive four-bar number seems like it would drive most people nuts if played for 2½ minutes straight. Does anyone have an idea why this music would be played over and over instead of using some other filler?

Jack Benny's mystery violins
In the past several months, we have discovered two "violins" which appear to have been created around the time of the 1937 Jack Benny-Fred Allen feud concerning Jack's ability to perform "The Bee". One is called "Jack Benny's Bee-O-Lin", pictured at left. The box features a photograph of Jack playing what looks to be an undersized violin, and a drawing of Fred Allen sticking his fingers in his ears on the right-hand side of the Box. The box claims "Anyone can play it. Even Fred Allen." A sticker on the violin itself appears to be a partial replica of the box top.

Another of these toys is called, aptly, "Jack Benny's Mystery Violin". The construction of this violin is considerably less refined than the Bee-O-Lin. The body of the violin is made of pressboard, and the fingerboard is a simple painted dowel. The "music" was made on this instrument by attaching a metal and hard rubber piece to the end of the violin as a sort of kazoo. Per the inside of the top of the box: "There's no use talking about my violin and not doing anything about it. So here it is. You can play on it as many songs as you know.

Just sing or hum in the specially toned violin-a-phone, and at the same time go through all the fingering and the fiddling motions of a real violinist like myself. I make Fred Allen jealous. You can do the same. Here's wishing you a lot of fun, and may you become the leader of your band. Musically yours, Jack Benny" The maker is listed as James McGowan Associates, New York City. The yellow lettering on the body of the violin restates the claim, "Anyone can play it – even Fred Allen".

Does anyone have additional information on these feud-related violins? When were they manufactured and for how long? The Bee-focused feud ran for only three months, so I can't imagine that this was a long-lived product. However, there was apparently enough enthusiasm for the concept to inspire two different makers to try their hand at it.

The origins of Mr. Kitzel
Kermyt Anderson asks: "I have in my notes that Mr. Kitzel's first appearance on The Jack Benny Program was on 1/6/46. (He was, I recall, selling hot dogs at the Rose Bowl.) I've recently been listening to Abbott and Costello, and was surprised to hear Mr. Kitzel as a frequent guest in 1943/44. I guess it hadn't occurred to me that the character wasn't a creation of Jack's writers; Kitzel already existed, and they simply scooped him up. (Though I believe Benny's writers added the "pickle in the middle with the mustard on top" line.) [LL: Sure did…John Tackaberry wrote that.] Does anybody know anything about this, and what prompted Kitzel's switch of programs? Were there any other characters on the Benny show that originated on other programs? Is the character of Mr. Kitzel something that Artie Auerbach developed elsewhere (say, on the stage or maybe even on vaudeville) before appearing on radio?

You Do Know

AFRS transcription editing
In listening to some of the shows from the Armed Forces Radio Service in the early and mid 1940s, I began wondering how AFRS managed to edit the commercial references out of shows that they received on disc. The answer came from Marty Halperin.

AFRS would get two copies of each show. These would then be timed by a producer, who would listen to the show with a stopwatch and note the outcue (last line) and time before the middle commercial, and the time that the time the commercial ended where the recording should start again. This was then given to an engineer, who would dub the shows into a single copy with AFRS openings and closings. When the commercial was coming, the second copy of the show would be cued to the point after the commercial. At the outcue, the first copy would be potted down (turning the volume down on it) and the second copy would be potted up, thus editing the commercial without stopping the recording disc. If a disc needed to be flipped, a disc of sound effects (applause, laughter, boos, etc.) was used to fill time at the end of a disc until it could be flipped and restarted.

Frank Remley's laugh
Doug Berryhill wrote in the Old Time Radio Digest:

This week's threads concerning Frankie Remley and audience members whose laughter is distinctive and recognizable actually merge together quite nicely in the person of guitar player Frankie Remley. For those of you who said you were listening to Benny programs in chronological order, you should have no trouble hearing Remley's distinctive laugh coming from
the orchestra pit.

Here's what to listen for: A male's voice, who laughs before the rest of the audience (perhaps because he's anticipating the joke he's already heard in rehearsal). The texture of the voice suggests a lifetime of smoking and the rhythm of the laughter suggests the machine-gun opening heard at the beginning of "Gangbusters". You'll hear this especially when the joke involves an insult (zinger) of Phil Harris, Phil's orchestra, or Frankie himself. Once you've picked out the sound of Frankie's laugh, you'll hear it over and over again in both The Jack Benny Show AND The Phil Harris/Alice Faye Show.

And no, this was not done as an audience plant or laugh generating gimmick. The real Frankie Remley laughed quite freely and loudly. I observed this first hand on a rerun episode of "This is Your Life" honoring Phil Harris. Remley was the type of person who even laughed at the straight lines!

Mike Mackey added:

The real Frank Remley made at least one appearance on Jack Benny's TV program. However, I know of no appearance by Elliot Lewis playing the part of Remley on TV.

Elliot Lewis fans know well the story about how the real Remley recommended that Lewis play him in the Harris/Faye radio show after rehearsals proved that he (Remley) simply wasn't funny. Lewis wasn't just playing a fictional character. There really was a Frank Remley, guitar-playing member of the band that played on the Jack Benny program.

According to Lewis, the whole "Frankie as a drunken, lousy guitar player" got started because Benny found the name "Frankie Remley" funny, just the way it rolled off his tongue. (He was right, I think. It is a funny name.) This running gag went on for some time culminating in the Frankie part on the spin-off series "Phil Harris/Alice Faye show." But Frankie himself didn't think he could carry the part of playing himself and recommended actor Elliot Lewis.

Later, over legal and/or financial issues [LL: some stories say it was due to a personal falling out between Phil and Frankie], it was decided to change the Frankie character's name. What did they change it to? Well, "Elliot Lewis", of course. So, instead of Remley playing Remley, it was Lewis playing Remley and, finally, Lewis playing Lewis.

The episode with Frankie Remley I am thinking of is often referred to as "The Hillbilly" episode. It is available on DVD from Diamond Entertainment on their DVD #93009A.

Because Lewis' face is not well known, I think people are easily confused when the real Frank Remley occasionally played himself. Here's a clue: Elliot Lewis was a non-musician. The real Remley was a professional guitar player. When you see the Remley character playing the guitar (as he does in the above mentioned Benny episode) then you know that it is the real Frank Remley. [LL: You can also tell it's Remley because he was a left-handed guitar player, and holds the guitar neck to his right, rather than the traditional left.]

Jack Benny's vault

In the world of Jack Benny, you just never know what "new" piece of memorabilia is going to turn up.

I received an E-mail from Roosevelt's Little White House in Warm Springs, Georgia, saying that they had found Jack Benny's vault. Evidently, the vault was used in fundraising campaigns for the March of Dimes. The vault is still intact with its lock and chain, and inside are moneybags and a newspaper dated February of 1948. The can in Jack's left hand is a March of Dimes coin can.

The vault was given to the Little White House on March 4, 1949, along with a Conestoga wagon, by Charles H. Smith of the Atlanta Junior Chamber of Commerce. The donation was accepted by Lee S. Trimble, Secretary of the Franklin D. Roosevelt Warm Springs Commision.

However by that time, the history and use of the vault had dwindled to simply the fact that it had been used in March of Dimes fund drives. It was put into storage for 50 years, as some thought it might simply be a worthless prop. David Burke, a Ranger from the Little White House, was doing research on the IJBFC Web site and found the above photo of Jack posing with their vault, which David referred to as "the holy grail of finds…This image really drives the story home…in making relevant the vault and Jack Benny and his contributions." The vault is now on display at the Little White House, and visitors are referred to the IJBFC Web site to learn more about Jack Benny.

Jack Benny calendar
Member Walt Pattinson has assembled an impressive Jack Benny calendar, featuring a full year of important dates related to Jack Benny and the Jack Benny Program. This includes milestones (e.g., first CBS broadcast = January 1), birthdays of the cast and guest, and similar information. It's a very impressive piece of work, and I recommend it to anyone interested in Jack Benny. You can see the calendar at: http://wjp-otr.com/jb/jbcal.shtml, and if you have any additions or corrections, you can contact Walt at walt@wjp-otr.com.

The Tale Piece

Larry Stevens' honorable discharge
I asked Norma Stevens, Larry Steven's widow about his honorable discharge from the military, which made it possible for him to be the singer on The Jack Benny Program during Dennis Day's tour of duty.

"Larry was honorably discharged from the service during World War 11, 1944 or early 1945, just prior to Dennis Day leaving the show. Larry had an honorable dependency discharge after 6 or 7 months of Air Force service as result of his father's illness that resulted in death at age 49, (colon cancer), his brothers' childhood diagnosis of hemophilia (a blood disease) which he later died from, resulting in Larry being the only care-giver and source of income for the family, which consisted of his mother and ill grandmother. This is the best I can tell you for now, however, after the Jack Benny show was over for Larry, he was able to get help with his family and he traveled to Europe to visit different Army camps as part of entertainers for the troops. I have many pictures of him with different officers and men in the service, along with entertainers such as Jeanette McDonald, Rita Hayworth, etc."

Mary Livingstone's radio debut
It will probably surprise you to know that Mary made her radio debut years before Jack did. It shocked the heck out of me. Here's the scoop from Benny Rubin, in his book Come Backstage With Me.

"It was some time in 1929 when Jack Benny and I were under contract to MGM. I got an offer to do a radio show for 'Orange Julius'—that is, if the *first* show was any good. I fortified myself with Mary Livingston [sic] as a singer and comedienne. Our pianist was Dave Dryer. He wrote Ain't You Coming Out Tonight Cecilia? And a lot of other song hits. It was about ten minutes to air time. Jack was there and he was more nervous than we were. I wish he hadn't been, or he wouldn't have given me this lousy joke. He said, 'In that Irish routine you do with Mary, have her ask you where you're from and you say, *Ireland*, Coney, Ireland.

"Okay, the show started and I told a couple of the best jokes I knew. Mary sang two songs. We did the Irish routine with the Coney Ireland joke. Dave Dryer played a short medley of hits, and I hate to tell you the truth, I don't remember what we did for a finish. This much I *can* tell you, we were pretty happy with ourselves. Ah ha, here comes the producer and the sponsor!

"He spoke first to Dave, 'Mister, maybe you wrote those songs, but you sure played them lousy.' To Mary he said, 'And you lady, you ain't no Sophie Tucker.' [And to me] 'And you! Boy, do you stink, especially with that Coney Ireland joke.'

"Now the way I was brought up was to very politely hit the guy a belt in the mouth. I looked around, no Mary, no Dave, no Jack. When I caught up with them in the parking lot, those three goons were laughing their heads off. And you know how Jack laughs! He was on the ground.

"Okay, fade out. A few years later, there was a gang of us at the old Trocadero Café. Mary and I got up to dance. No sooner than we hit the floor, Mary said to me, 'There's a man waving at us and he's dancing our way.' I looked and said, 'Mary, would you like to have a glass of Orange Julius?' She mumbled something like, 'Oh, no.'

"When the man and his lady sidled up to us, he said, 'Remember me, Mr. Rubin?' I said, 'Yes, one Orange Julius small.' He gave me one of those prop laughs. I introduced Mary as Mrs. Jack Benny, but he didn't recognize her. Then he went into a rave about how great she was with Jack—and get this—he loved her singing. Mary charmingly said, 'Thank you, Sir, you are very kind, but you know something I ain't no Sophie Tucker!'

"What the reaction from the guy was I'll never know. Mary and I were just learning to do the rhumba and we had enough trouble trying not to bump into everybody; when we told what happened to Jack, boom—there he was on the floor again."

Jack and Bob Hope on the links
From The World Golf Hall of Fame (www.wgv.com):

"If the Bob Hope Chrysler Classic lacked the celestial field of the Crosby Clambake, it more than made up for it with perfect weather and the enveloping presence of Hope, a peerless master of ceremonies. Along with his sometimes caddie, Phyllis Diller, who usually toted Band-Aids and a hip flask to mitigate any potential disaster, Hope oversaw a pro-am that was at least as much about the ams as the pros. Played on four courses over five days to accommodate the biggest possible field, the Classic remains a tribute to all golfers, from the sublime to the ridiculous. Until his health began to fail him, Hope still swatted the ceremonial first ball. The ardor brings to mind a story Jack Benny used to love to tell. He encountered Hope one afternoon limping off a course in Palm Springs, California moaning about how badly he was playing. Benny went through a whole litany of excuses on Hope's behalf, concluding that with his busy schedule he couldn't possibly play enough golf to keep his game in good shape.

"'You damn fool,' Hope snarled, 'I play every day.'"

Etcetera

Many of you are probably already aware that the DVD release of The Sunshine Boys includes the long-sought footage of Jack's screen tests for the part. The footage is silent, and shows both Jack and Walter Matthau in makeup in an apartment setting. For part of the time, Matthau and Jack seem to be having a conversation, and Matthau is occasionally joking around with Jack. Jack laughs at some of his pranks, but generally appears quite tired and fragile. Finding any audio or video of Jack this late in his life is rare, and it is an interesting window into the last few months of Jack's life. This DVD is still available through commercial outlets, including [CENSORED].

McFarland will be releasing a book entitled Children of Hollywood by Michelle Vogel, which includes an interview with Joan Benny and features Joan and Jack on the cover (pictured at left).

For more information, check out the McFarland Web page:
http://www.mcfarlandpub.com/book-2.php?isbn=0-7864-2046-4

Tape Trading List

- Rob Cohen, rob@conrads.com (Rob would also like to trade Jack Benny MP3 for other radio comedy shows--e.g., Fibber McGee, etc.)
- Steven Cottingham, steven@stevencottinghamchess.com
- George Grube, Ontime6402@aol.com
- Ellis Hogue, rtdj@att.net

- E.J. Kienzler II, afanofoldradio@aol.com or iluvotr@sbcglobal.net; P.O. Box 5775 Springfield, Illinois 62705-5775; 1441 N. 5th Street, Springfield, Illinois 62702-2611; www.reeloldtimegreatradioshows.tictacwebsites.com
- Janet Maday, maydaymayday@aol.com
- John Matthews, glowingdial@yahoo.com
- Jay Meade, jmeade@starfishnet.com
- Jack Palmer, vdalhart@prodigy.net
- Brendan Scherer, goldenstar4@juno.com
- Jeff Tanner, P. O. Box 65787, Vancouver, WA 98686, USA; TannerJeff@aol.com
- John Tisinger, jdtisinger@peachnet.campuscwix.net
- Lynn Wagar, philcolynn@yahoo.com (cassette only)
- Bob Westman, leniro@aol.com
- Drew Wiest, 6109 NE 197th St, Kenmore, WA 98028, USA; dwiest12@hotmail.com
- Bob Wombacher, Jr., bashfulbobmotel@webtv.net
- Ken Yesson; yesandno@telusplanet.net

Video Library – Updated Holdings

Movies
- Chasing Rainbows (1929) - 88 minutes
- Taxi Tangles (1931 short) – 10 minutes
- This Way Please (1937) - 73 minutes (note: Mary Livingstone, no Jack - poor sound)
- Buck Benny Rides Again (1940) – 84 minutes (occasional distortion at top of screen)
- Charley's Aunt (1941) - 80 minutes - NEW 6/26
- To Be Or Not To Be (1942) - 99 minutes - NEW 6/26
- George Washington Slept Here (1942) - 94 minutes
- The Horn Blows at Midnight (1945) – 78 minutes

Television programs
- The Jack Benny Program – 11/30/58 – Oscar Levant – 30 minutes
- The Jack Benny Program - 3/4/62 - Julie London, Toni Marcus - 30 minutes
- The Jack Benny Program – 3/11/62 – Jack dreams he is Alexander Hamilton – 30 minutes
- The Jack Benny Program – 10/30/62 – Darla Hood (Our Gang) – 30 minutes (poor quality)
- The Jack Benny Program - 11/13/62 - Carol Burnett (Tarzan) - 30 minutes

- The Jack Benny Program – 11/27/62 – Jack Soo, Romi Yamada – 30 minutes
- The Jack Benny Program - 1/22/63 - Peter Lorre, Joanie Sommers - 30 minutes
- The Jack Benny Program - 2/19/63 – Connie Francis (Stephen Foster) – 30 minutes
- The Jack Benny Program - 2/12/65 - Stuart Canin - 30 minutes

Other items
- The Mouse That Jack Built (cartoon) - 1958 - 7 minutes
- CBS Tribute to Jack Benny - 12/29/74 - (poor video) - 60 minutes

The Jack Benny Times

January – April 2005　　　　　　　　　　　　　　　　　　　Volume XX, Numbers 1-2

Jack's writers 1943+: (L to R) Sam Perrin (seated), Milt Josefsberg, John Tackaberry, George Balzer

President's Message

Jell-O again folks…it's been a good few months since the last newsletter, ranging from my usual October break to three events that enabled various IJBFC members to come together to share each other's company and our love of Jack Benny. The first of these was Eddie Carroll's one-man show in Fullerton, CA in late September. It was a pleasure to be able to talk with many of the members and hear your stories of discovering Jack Benny, and even one member who recalled attending a taping of a Benny television show (or almost…he was judged to be too young to be in the audience…I hope to bring you more of his story in a future issue). The second was the SPERDVAC convention, about which Melanie Aultman will tell you in a separate article.

The third was an enjoyable evening in San Francisco on December 18, with members convening for dinner at David's Deli (directly across the street from the Curran Theatre where Jack performed in 1953) and then attending a performance of Fred Raker's It Could Have Been a Wonderful Life (www.wonderfullife.org). Fred (that's him on the right) is a big Benny fan who has been doing this show for several years. It traces the story of comedian Phil Resnick, who struggles to come to terms with his Jewish identity while being guided by his guardian angel, Jack Benny. The show has gotten excellent reviews in the local papers, and Fred deftly handles playing 25 characters in his one-man show. A good time was had by all.

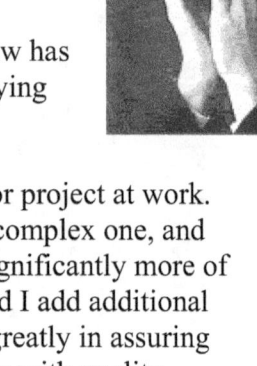

The end of this year has also brought me a leadership position on a major project at work. The balancing act between work, the club, and my own life is always a complex one, and this new development means that the first of those will be demanding significantly more of my attention. You always show patience for my usual balancing act, and I add additional thanks in advance over the coming months. Your understanding helps greatly in assuring that I am able to keep everything in balance, and continue to provide you with quality service and products. Many, many good wishes to everyone for a prosperous new year filled with laughter!

New Members

**** Marty Halperin **** George T Mathias **** David Dressler **** Roy C. Pollitt **** Peggie Coll **** Stephen Vanden Heuvel **** John Hawksley **** Abram S. Feuerstein **** Frank Miller **** M. David Lopez **** John Senechal **** Rachel Solorzano **** Sammy Jones **** Scott Southard **** Dana Eddy **** Keith Anstine **** Chris Frear **** Susan Bednar **** Steven Vink **** Gabriel Gentile **** Becky Fairclough **** E. Gerry Hoard **** Ted Davenport **** Allen Singer **** Rick Apt **** Kristopher Plank **** Alan Cook **** Chris Duvall **** Kevin Deevey **** Rick Ellis **** Eric Obermeyer **** Peter D. Kinder **** Anthony Azcona **** Gregg Hammond **** Dave Amaral **** Dave Griem **** Bud Bresnahan **** Margaret Thompson **** Maria Williams **** Herbert Altman **** Charles Francis **** David Maria **** Ross Levine **** Marc Thorner **** Paul Kornman **** John Thomason **** Rick

Payne **** Sherry Moore **** Michael J. Green **** Nicholas Moreau **** Vernon Balbert **** Scott Levine **** John Bickham **** William D. Hardie **** Michael Cunningham **** Wayne Craddock **** Steve Newvine **** Kelly Jack **** Ben Okuly **** Chad Hay **** Robert I. Hughes **** David M. Stover **** Rick Parrish **** Val Gordon **** Dean Barrett **** William Mackinnon **** John P. Morton **** Stella Meltzer **** Dick Harrold **** Russ Youmans **** Gentry Little **** Kevin Wondrash **** Thomas E. Brown **** Jude V. Domanski **** John Honeycutt **** Beverly Oldham **** Gbemisola Adekunle **** John Owen **** James M. Pelfrey **** Jane Stevenett **** Eric Hoyer **** Debbie Lascuola **** John Hahn **** Dennis Campa, II **** Gary Behnke **** Ken Candela **** Graham Ferguson **** Christopher Caruso **** Keith Wilcox **** Guenter Grossmann **** David Rubin **** Judee Clare **** Everett Seamans **** Don Pettee **** Chase Clark **** Walter Thomas **** Jay Katz **** Alan Crowder **** Gareth Hedges **** Randy Rayeburn **** Robert Seoane **** Jeremy Meyers **** Jonathan M Budd **** Tom Nee **** Dan Lamott **** Clarence Anthony **** Justin Palmer **** Bonnie L Hockin **** Thea Hockin **** Bryan Nicely **** Adele Y Lohman **** William T. Leonard **** Megan Anne Magistrelli **** Charles Berman **** Helen Grimes **** Michael Modes **** Kevin O'Brien **** Comrad Nelson **** Tim Gammon **** Michael Moslow **** Ryan Kaiserman **** Cindy Kloosterman **** Kathy Fuller-Seeley **** Chuck Schaden **** Danilo Castro

Jack Benny, Joke Books and the Public Library: How a Newbie found OTR
By Melanie Aultman

Melanie and Eddie Carroll

What do Jack Benny, joke books and the public library have in common? They helped me find OTR. I attended my first SPERDVAC (Society to Preserve and Encourage Radio Drama, Variety and Comedy) (http://sperdvac.org/) convention, their 30th by the way, held at the Hacienda Hotel in El Segundo, CA, November 12-14, 2004. The most oft-asked getting-to-know-you question was, "How did you become interested in OTR?"

Hmm-how DID that happen? I don't remember listening to any radio shows as a child. Mother says I begged to stay home from church to watch Gildersleeve on TV and although I don't remember the actual shows, I must have watched Jack Benny too because I do remember wishing that man would actually PLAY the violin…

Fast forward to 1990, the first year it can be admitted that a conscious decision to collect joke books and humorous materials was made. Many years, book sales and eBay later, the quest for older and older items led me to Vaudeville and thus to some by and for radio stars. It became obvious that some acts had transitioned to radio and television.

About that time, Laura posted an FYI about the IJBFC in a Usenet group. I checked it out and joined immediately. When notice of the 39 Forever gathering was posted, it was impossible to resist its lure.

Enter the public library. I thankfully live in a community with a tax based system and an unbelievably supportive "Friends" group. Funding allows for things beyond the "basics", including many tapes from Radio Spirits. Benny items were ordered and listened to in anticipation of attending 39 Forever (Shamefully I've never taken advantage of Laura's great offers—soon to be rectified.)

Next came the purchase of Chase and Sandborn-sponsored Eddie Cantor shows 1931-33 on CD from Brian Gari. Laura provided links to the Friends of Old Time Radio and SPERDVAC sites. I'd review them from time to time and hope to attend a meeting one day.

You may POSSIBLY have heard that Florida had a few hurricanes this year. During the last one, I vowed that if I came through it without any damage, I would "get out of Dodge", and the SPERDVAC convention seemed a logical choice. After registering, every OTR item in the library catalog was reserved and I was lucky enough to find a Green Hornet tape at the Goodwill. In an effort to hear every show possible, I listened in the car, kitchen, bedroom and even in the shower!

Laura and Jack French - OTR Club panel

Friday afternoon's convention schedule included a panel open to representatives of any OTR club. Our own Laura Leff headed up the panel, and, as always, did us proud. Though one of the Saturday panels was Al Jolson and Eddie Cantor remembered, Laura was included and more Benny insights were shared with attendees. A Saturday night highlight of SPERDVAC 2004 was Eddie Carroll as Jack Benny in a special version of "The Horn Blows at Midnight". Gracious as always, he and the Mrs. (Carolyn) patiently posed for pictures afterward.

The dealer's room was no place for a card-carrying bibliophile. Mr. Benny was well represented with back issues of The Jack Benny Times and assorted extra copies of programs, etc. from previous club activities. The second edition of 39 Forever sold out the first afternoon! Various Benny books, tapes and CDs were available from several vendors as well.

I settled on four books, secure in the knowledge that I could order more later through the internet or by attending other conventions. I actually have a bit more compassion for addicts of any stripe than I used to—there's a certain feeling that comes over me when I simple MUST have a book—never mind that I couldn't possibly even read the ones currently owned. Sunday morning, after packing and realizing there was room for at least ONE more book, I mentally went through my list of usual rationalizations—don't need to buy groceries next week, can use what's already on hand. No, used that one yesterday. How about...an hour with a therapist has to be at least $90. Isn't a good book better therapy? That's it—at least for now. With that "logic", I raced down to the dealer's room where everyone was packing up and made that last purchase. After all, the reasoning went, it IS a reference book on OTR.

The convention concluded with a brunch featuring the one and only Art Linkletter. He still has "it" and through a presentation punctuated with laughter, several Benny mentions were made.

Though I found my way to OTR through a love of comedy, joke books, Jack Benny (thanks to the tireless efforts of Laura with the IJBFC), and the availability of tapes through the public library to get me started, one would have to look long and hard and still not find any group more welcoming and dedicated than OTR fans. They have encouraged me and made gracious offers of information and program exchanges.

The folks at SPERDVAC run a class act and are to be commended for having organized a great event. Their hard work is appreciated. Get thee to a convention!

Melanie and Art Linkletter

What's Up in Waukegan?

The old marquee

The new marquee

Another of my adventures over the past few months was to attend the grand opening of the Genesee Theatre in Waukegan, Illinois. This occurred on December 3rd, and featured legendary comedian Bill Cosby. Both the 6:30 and 9:30 shows sold out within 3 hours of being offered for sale. Through a little derring-do, I was able to secure a seat in the 5th row for the 6:30PM show.

Looking up at stage right box seats

The theatre had been closed for many years. Jack broadcast his June 25, 1939 program from the theatre, as well as debuting <u>Man About Town</u> there the same evening. The photos from that event show the intersection of Genesee and Clayton teeming with people, probably the largest crowd to ever hit Waukegan to that date. I had the good fortune of a private tour of the theatre in 1987 during my first trip to Waukegan for a Jack Benny birthday celebration. While it was a thrill to be able to "trod the boards" of the old theatre, the 1950s renovation had removed the impressive crystal chandelier in the lobby (although there are conflicting stories of how and when it happened) and added an odd and badly faded color scheme. It was like seeing a withered old person and knowing that they were once very beautiful. When Dan and I visited in 1994, the theatre was boarded and seemed destined for demolition.

The three-year restoration has brought back the grandeur of the theatre, the original magnificent colors, and luxurious interior. Crystal chandeliers and aluminum gilt recall the movie palaces of 1927 (when the Genesee first opened), the place that people went to escape the realities of the Depression. The previous lobby fronting Clayton Street has been removed (you can see it and the now-gone snack bar featured in the original opening of Siskel and Ebert's <u>At the Movies</u> television program) in favor of expanded seating, going from 1,799 seats to 2,461. The waiting line was long but convivial, stretching around the block and down Clayton. Music from the Deep Chicago Rhythm Owls (pictured at right) emanated from the Jack Benny Plaza.

Bill Cosby performed for about 90 minutes, including newer material, his classic "Dentists" routine, and a good deal of improv work with front row audience members. (For those who are wondering, no mention was ever made of Jack.) Cosby summed the experience this way, "I am not — I am not — in Chicago. I'm in your own city. You did not have to drive someplace else to go see somebody. Nobody is saying, 'Wauk What?' Yeah, this is very nice, and I'm feeling good to be the first."

Jack Benny Today

There's been a lot of discussion on the www.jackbenny.org Forum Bulletin Board about where to find new (to you) Jack Benny material. Here are some highlights of the latest Benny-spottings:

- 13-year-old member Zach Eastman announced that Warner Brothers will be releasing To Be or Not To Be on DVD on March 1, 2005. Check it out on [CENSORED BY PRINTER.]

- Dave Howell sent an installment of the quirky daily comic strip Superosity which included their own tribute to Jack:

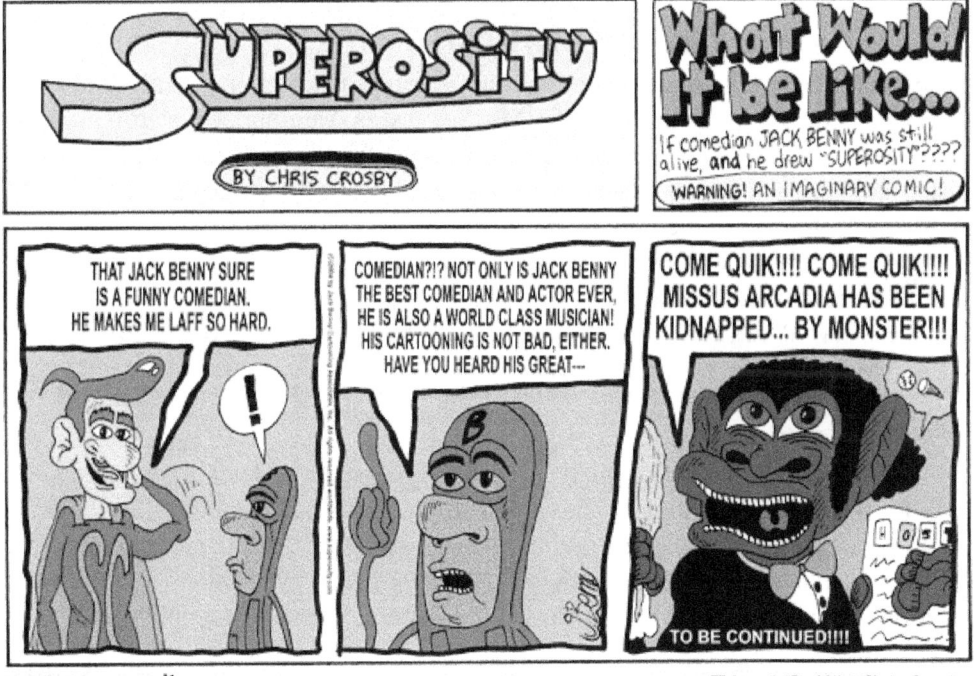

- Mike Stratton found a Jack Benny program on XM Satellite Radio, on channel 164.

- Sean Dougherty noted, "I was a proud member of the winning team for Jackpardy at Laura Leff's '39 Forever' Jack Benny convention a couple of years back. Apparently, Jack Benny figured in a critical question in the television version of Jeopardy." This was a program where the long-running Jeopardy champion Ken Jennings was almost upset by a rival, and the Benny question about "Your money or your life" tipped the score against Jennings.

- A. Joseph Ross reported, "In an interview in <u>TV Guide</u>, John Kerry was asked 'What shows or TV moments had an impact on you growing up?' His answer: 'I go back to Hopalong Cassidy, Howdy Doody, Jack Benny. I love TV. I love the Laugh-In Days.'"

- In working on <u>39 Forever, Second Edition</u> Volume 2, I became curious about the comments on a Jack Benny statue in St. Joe ("They love me in St. Joe!"). In talking with the St. Joseph Mayor's office, I offered a copy of the program that Jack broadcast from their city. The Mayor happily accepted, and the show has now become a part of the city's archives. You see, they *still* love Jack in St. Joe.

- Mike Stratton also found Gisele Mackenzie in an Abbott and Costello program recently released on DVD. "The Colgate Comedy Hour/s hosted by Abbott and Costello: she sings 'Don't Let The Stars Get In Your Eyes'. I think it was one of her best TV gigs ever. Good choreography too. I understand the DVD is for sale at some Target stores for one dollar."

Jack Benny in Print

Three books with Jack Benny connections have come across my path in recent months. The first is <u>Memoirs in Toe Shoes</u> by Erna Segal. Ms. Segal was Chiquita of the athletic dance team Chiquita and Johnson, who performed on a <u>Shower of Stars</u> episode hosted by Jack and soon after in his Miami Beach stage show. It is a colorful story of Segal's upbringing in Czechoslovakia, her young escape onto the international stage, and her experiences with a long list of immortal celebrities. The book is $28, hardcover, 360 pages with 48 pages of photographs. To get your copy, mail a check or money order to FictionSpin, P.O. Box 885, Pacific Palisades, CA 90272, call (310) 456-5251, or send E-mail to FictionSpin@aol.com.

The second book is <u>Confessions of a Small Time Name Dropper</u> by Dick Dodderidge. Dick was working for the advertising agency that serviced the American Republic Life Insurance Company during the time that Jack was their spokesman for the "Americare 39" plan, featuring "Life insurance at Jack Benny prices." With this, Dick was able to spend some memorable moments with Jack that are included in his book. Here's a sample:

"Several months after the very successful introduction of 'Americare 39', we developed a second phase of the campaign. This featured Jack talking with people who had bought the insurance. The first satisfied customer to be featured was a New York City subway guard who lived in a modest neighborhood in Queens. We hired a <u>LIFE</u> magazine photographer, loaded two stretch limos with Jack and a small entourage, and made our way into Queens. The word had spread that Jack was making a visit, and a crowd of neighbors began to gather. Jack was gracious, signed a lot of autographs, and we met and photographed the policyholder.

"By now it was lunchtime and Jack made a suggestion. 'Let's eat at a McDonald's. I've never been to one.' So the limos pulled into a McDonald's and I volunteered to get Jack some takeout so he could eat in the car. But he wanted to have the complete experience, so we joined the customers inside and again caused a real stir with the crowd. One thing about Jack, he looked like Jack Benny and he was a huge celebrity whenever he went out in public. By the way, he loved his Big Mac and probably became a regular customer after that."

The book is $15, softbound, 163 pages including 15 pages of photographs. To get your copy, mail a check or money order (payable to Dick Dodderidge) to 1660 Valley Drive, Venice, FL 34292, or E-mail dickdodd@hotmail.com. The price covers book, postage, handling, tip and Dick's personal autograph.

The third is an unusual little volume called The Glass Bed by Norman Panama and Albert E. Lewin. Unlike the other two this is not a new book, being published in 1980. Its Benny connections are peripheral but unusual, as the book's first chapter is a detailed (and slightly anachronistic) dramatization of rehearsing "Your money or your life." The rest of the book is a novel about Rob Gardner, a comedy writer on the rise, and Johnny Malone, a radio comedian whose career is threatening to be on the descent. Between them is Darleen Dawn in the perpetual love triangle, and the story unfolds around their radio politics and erotic escapades. Not a book to read to the kiddies, but how often does one find an X-rated book about old time radio comedy? Light reading for a cold winter evening, look for it at your used book store.

Of course, I can't go without mentioning my own current book, 39 Forever, Second Edition – Volume 1. As Melanie noted, I sold out the first printing almost before the SPERDVAC dealer room opened. I am very gratified and honored at the response it has gotten, and at the wonderful comments and compliments it's gotten all around. I have the second printing, so if you haven't yet gotten your copy, do it now! Softbound, 536 pages, $40 (includes shipping). You can go to www.jackbenny.org and use the Paypal buttons to pay by credit card, or send a check or money order (payable to IJBFC) to the address at the end of this newsletter.

The Tale Piece

Many thanks to Frank Rosin for sharing this unique story of his own Jack Benny encounter:

I was teaching the 6th grade and had been chosen to represent my school district at a conference being held at the Davenport Hotel in Spokane Washington. This location was chosen because the World Fair was going on at the time in Spokane.

The Davenport Hotel located in downtown Spokane was one of those elegant hotels of the past. The Hotel was built in 1914 during the boom days of Spokane. It was still resisting change in the 1970s but soon afterwards went into decline. At the time, they were known and still were polishing all the silver coins. If you got a dollar, half, or quarter in change, it was clean and polished like new. It closed in 1985. After a number of years, a Spokane business man purchased the hotel and spent several million in restoration. It opened after 17 years of being closed in July of 2002, in 105 degree heat. The wing that held the coffee shop where we ate was demolished for parking. But the hotel is again one of the elegant places it once was.

Because I was driving alone from Kirkland to Spokane and I was in charge of the Sea Scout group in Kirkland, I took 4 of the older youngsters along. They could enjoy the fair while I was at meetings and do some of the driving there and back. Spokane was an all day drive from Western Washington.

When we first arrived and checked in, we walked over to the elevator area. There was a group of people waiting for the elevator but in their midst was Jack Benny. He was chatting with them all. We joined in and at one point I mentioned that in listening to some of his old programs, the comedy held up unlike some of the others at that time. His response was that, yes, he had been told that by many people, but now needed to go up to his room. As we were going up to our room we got in the elevator with him and got off on our floor with no other conversation. He continued on up.

The room given us was too small. I went back to the lobby and asked for a different room. They had one on an upper floor that was larger and would not charge any extra. We moved up and being from cool Western Washington promptly opened the windows. It was about 110 out and much warmer in the room. Not being used to air-conditioning almost everyone else at the conference opened their windows also. This overloaded the hotel air conditioning system, and it broke down. We should have left the windows closed as the next 4 days were uncomfortable at that 110 heat.

At several of the conferences the next day, I would hear people say they had seen Jack Benny and even been in the elevator with him. He had been spending time in the lobby talking to people.

The second day at breakfast time, the kids I had with me and I left the room to go to the coffee shop for breakfast. Lo and behold, we didn't know it but the room next to us was occupied by Jack Benny. He came out the door at the same time we did, he was alone.

When we got into the elevator, he turned and stepped back, stepping on one of the young fellows toes. He was so sorry he said, if we were going to breakfast would we join him for breakfast to make up for it. He was dressed in a white suit.

The service in the coffee shop was slow, but that gave us time to chat. Benny chatted with the boys, asking them what they were doing in school and other small talk. He seemed sincere and pleasant. He only sipped on the coffee and took one or two bites of his toast.

At one point a woman walked into the coffee shop and came to the table and asked for an autograph. He said NO, can't you see I am talking to my friends, I don't give autographs in the coffee shop, and seemed a little annoyed. He had been spending time before in the lobby talking to people and I presume doing autographs. What a thrill it was to be called one of his friends!

Now this is all over 30 years ago, I do not recall now everything we talked about. He told us he was alone, but had a 'dresser' with him to see to it he had the clothes he needed and got to his scheduled appointments. He did not bring his wife to a two- or three-day event because it took too many people. She need an hairdresser, maid, other helpers, and many bundles of baggage and it was too much trouble. He talked about some of the other members of his cast and friends but the only comment I recall now was that Eddie Anderson, Rochester, was spending too much time at the races in his opinion.

I had a cassette from the Jell-O days among other programs we had listened to in the car on the way to Spokane. I did not know he was going to be there. I asked him if he would like to listen to the program. He didn't say yes or no but said, perhaps later on. That never happened as we never got together again.

I think he was doing two or possibly three performances at the Fair. There was a poster with Benny's Image and the performance times about 16 x 30 in size on the wall. One of the fellows went over and took the poster off the wall and asked him to sign it. He did. That particular young fellow is now an engineer at Boeing.

When breakfast was over, Benny paid for our meals and left a generous tip. It is unfortunate that he died only a few months later. The stomach problems were probably already plaguing him judging by the small amount he ate.

I saw him once more from afar on the other side of the lobby as I was going to an evening meeting and I presume he was going out the door to one of his performances. Because of my schedule I was not able to go to see him at one of the performances, I always regret that but did get the chance to talk and spend some time with him and will have that to remember always.

I also received the following compendium on the career of Michael Bartlett, the singer on the Jack Benny show from September 29 to October 27, 1935 (just five shows):

"He was hired on The Jack Benny Program as an interim singer until they could find 'a permanent singer.' [EN: Who ended up being Kenny Baker.] When Bartlett first appeared on Benny's show, he was already a well established star—three Broadway shows, three motion pictures (The Gem of the Ocean (1934), Love Me Forever (1935), and She Married her Boss (1935)), numerous radio appearances, and a star of the concert and operatic stage. From 1930 until he entered the Marine Corps in 1942, he was one of the most popular tenors in America. The plan was for Bartlett to be only on a handful of Benny's shows…Bartlett and I in the late 1950s listened to one of the shows where he sang "Through the Years" and "Ah! Sweet Mystery of Life." The reason we decided to listen to this particular show was because Bartlett received more fan mail for a singer for this show than Frank Parker and James Melton ever did on any single Benny show that they appeared on. After Bartlett left The Jack Benny Program, he made three more motion pictures: Follow Your Heart (1936) with Marion Talley and Nigel Bruce; The Music Goes Round (1936) with Harry Richman; and The Lilac Domino (1937) with June Knight. In 1941 and 1942, he made a number of Soundies—filmed musicals—the most popular ones being Mother Machree, The Little Grey House in the West, and Streets of New York. After World War II, he appeared in every operatic house in America, was a featured singer on Great Moments in Music and the Chicago Theater on the Air, and in 1946 he toured the country (44 cities) with the Order of Purple Heart Chorus and the Jersey City Philharmonic Orchestra. His last starring role was as a member of the original cast in Stephen Sondheim's Follies that was on Broadway in 1971 and 1972. He played the role of Roscoe, an aging tenor, and sang the opening number, "These Beautiful Girls." He died in 1978 in his 77th year.

Do You Know?

Waldonj@earthlink.net asks:

"I was wondering if you have any material or documentation on Jack Benny's stint in vaudeville. What I am looking for is information on a straight man named Jacob Rosenfield who lived in Baltimore and said he acted as straight man to Jack Benny during his vaudeville days. I would presume such appearances might have been limited to those in the Baltimore area. I am doing a family genealogy that includes descendants of this Jacob Rosenfield, and am trying to confirm that his representations to his family that he performed with Jack Benny were authentic or wishful thinking."

Karl Van Zoggel of Germany is doing research on Maria Callas (referred to as Mary) and asks:

"The competition Jackie refers to must have taken place in New York in late 1934, when Mary was eleven. It was a competition for juvenile talent in any field, not just singing, with children reciting poetry, telling stories, and so on, and it was broadcast nationwide. Jackie accompanied Mary (who wore her hair in bangs at her forehead) in La Paloma and A Heart That's Free. The studio audience applauded enthusiastically and, according to Jackie and Litsa, the judges awarded her first prize, which was a Bulova watch. But here the problems begin. On three different instances Maria herself said that the watch was a consolation prize, the competition having been won by an accordion player. And in all her accounts she added that the emcee of the competition was the well-known comedian Jack Benny, who was "furious" or "disappointed" that she had not won. It seems odd that neither Jackie nor Litsa ever mentioned such a popular celebrity as Jack Benny; so perhaps they were thinking about a different occasion. Be that as it may, the competition or competitions took place in New York. John Ardoin's assertion that one of Mary's radio performances was broadcast from Chicago probably arises from misinterpretation of an interview Maria once gave in Chicago, for we may be sure that a trip to Chicago would not have gone unremarked by either Jackie or Litsa."

David Fairweather writes:

"I am the proprietor of "The Dobie Pages!" http://home1.gte.net/res09cc9/index.html Have you ever noticed what a huge debt Dwayne Hickman owes to Jack Benny? I'm sure Dwayne would be the first to acknowledge that many of his comedic mannerisms are directly lifted from Mr. Benny's act."

[EN: Not being that familiar with Dwayne Hickman's work, I can't judge. What do you think?]

You Do Know!

I am frequently asked for a photograph of Veola Vonn, who despite her renowned beauty, seems to be very difficult to find photographically (surprisingly, even more so than her husband, Frank Nelson). But boys, you'll be happy to know that Gregg Oppenheimer, son of Jess Oppenheimer, provided the photograph of Veola at left. So there's the face of the Lady known as Lou.

On the Benny show of October 29, 1944, there is a loss of the network feed early in the show, just after Jack has sliced an orange (and sliced and sliced and sliced) for his visiting cast members. During the loss, there is a piano interlude with a song I could not identify, but has a bar or two of the same theme as

"Love in Bloom". Walden Hughes identified the number as "Until I Met You".

The running gag of "Symmmmmpathy Soothing Syrup" on the Benny show included the repeated reminder that "Symmmmpathy spelled backwards is Yhtapamys." This was a parody of another product of the day, Serutan, which reminded customers that "Serutan spelled backwards is Nature's." Thanks to Yesterday USA listener W. Hagen for jogging the memory banks for that item.

The Laughing Man
By Alan R. Josefsberg

Before I begin my story, I feel you need a little background about myself. I'll try to keep it short, but brevity is not a Josefsberg trait.

Growing up the son of a comedy writer has its own set of challenges. Throughout our dad's life neither Steven nor I believe we ever told a joke right and to our recollection, it was on only one occasion that Dad was left speechless. This is that story.

Milt Josefsberg, was one of the original four comedy writers for Jack Benny. He worked for Jack from 1943 – 1955. I am the elder of Milt Josefsberg's two sons. (However, my brother looks older.) I was born in 1943, and from my birth, Dad's objective was to teach me one thing. He would always tell me, "Your dad writes for Jack Benny. Jack Benny, funny man." I cannot emphasize how proud my dad was that his little Alan could tell everyone, "Jack Benny, funny man."

In 1948 Dad began working for Bob Hope, and thus my reprogramming began. While in Mr. Hope's employ, Dad did a special with Jack, and the family, Hilda, Alan age 5 and Steven 2 got to go to Palm Springs while he was working for Jack Benny.

During a leisurely break, Dad took me to the pool to meet Mr. Benny. We walked over to him, hand in hand, and Dad introduced me, "Jack, this is my son, Alan. Alan, this is Jack Benny. Jack Benny, funny man." I remember looking up at Mr. Benny and without hesitation I proudly stated exactly what my father had taught me ...… "NO! Bob Hope, funny man."

Jack collapsed at the pool's edge, and laid on the ground laughing harder than I had ever seen anyone laugh. Needless to say, Dad was speechless and Jack Benny became known to me as, "The Laughing Man."

That is one of many Jack Benny stories. If you didn't like it, don't tell anyone. However, if you did like it, do me a favor. Tell Laura to ask me to write more stories of "Jack Benny, funny man." [EN: Too late, kids…I already did.] And, while you're at it, help me follow in my dad's footsteps. Last year, my partner, Barry Paul Silver, and I began writing for television. We wrote three scripts for Boston Public, but, oops, it was canceled. Then we wrote a script for Law and Order, featuring Jerry Orbach's character, but, oops, Mr. Orbach left the show. We have recently written two scripts for Two and a Half Men. We have found a show that is here to stay. All we need is someone out there to get our scripts to Chuck Lorre or anyone on the show that is willing to read our work. We'd enjoy feedback. Any help or any suggestions would be greatly appreciated.

Sincerely yours,
Alan R. Josefsberg
(818) 763-4270   E-mail: farj@earthlink.net

John Tackaberry: Unemployed Used Car Salesman

On June 17, 2001, I had the pleasure of spending time on the phone with Stace Tackaberry, son of John Tackaberry. My sincerest thanks to him for sharing these memories of his father, one of Jack's most undocumented writers.

L: Your father was born…

S: He was born on the 9th of October of 1912…He was actually born in Adelaide, Australia…Stace was my father's mother's maiden name. She was a Kiwi, she was born and raised in Palmerson, North New Zealand. So when my grandfather, my paternal grandfather, left Texas under some rather…cloudy circumstances, he went…this would be back just before New Year's Eve of 1901, he went to England, is my understanding, and was there for a few years and then decided—I have no knowledge as to why—to go down to the Southern Hemisphere, and he first went to New Zealand and he met my grandmother there, supposedly at a horse race. They were married in Sydney, Australia…in 1910, I believe it was in March of 1910…my father's father was actually an M.D. He had graduated from Tulane University in New Orleans in 1896 as an M.D. And so he became the doctor for the Ghan…Railroad which goes from Adelaide up through Alice Springs…near Ayers Rock…They had to live out in a tiny, tiny—it still is—out in the middle of absolutely nowhere in the Simpson Desert, a town called Oodnadatta. And they lived in this rock house, and my father's sister was born first in 1911 in Sydney, and then apparently some time after that, he got this job with the railroad and they moved out to…Oodnadatta. My father was born in Adelaide, which is in the very southern part of Australia. They lived there until about 1920, so my father was 8 years old when they came back to Houston, because his father—my grandfather—was originally from East Texas…He continued his medical practice and my father started school there, and he never did go back to Australia in his whole life.

L: Do you know much about the atmosphere your father grew up in? Was there a lot of laughter and humor?

S: I really don't know, to tell you the truth. My grandfather was a very warm, kind man. My grandmother, on the other hand, was a very cold, severe woman. So I don't know if there was a lot of laughter. My father as an adult used to get a lot of laughter *out* of the two of them, they prompted a lot of laughter in him by the things they did. But I really don't know. I don't think my grandmother thought that in the world there was too much funny. My father, on the other hand, had a totally different attitude about comedy, which was that you could kid about anything. You could make a joke about anything. There was nothing that was sacrosanct, as far as he was concerned, as long as it was funny. If it wasn't funny, then it didn't make any difference anyway. And he would have loved to have been writing in more modern times where they could do more things, because at the time he was writing, they couldn't even use the word "God" on the radio. It was not done. The stuff that they, I'm sure, came up with in their sessions was probably some great stuff, but they could never use it on the radio.

L: Did he go to college?

S: Yes, he did…I'm not sure, to be honest with you, how long it was. He went for a year or so to the University of Texas, and then the Depression became more serious, and of course his father being an M.D., probably was the last person to get paid…So he had to drop out of college. But I think that's where he first got some inkling that he had some level of competence at writing because he was the editor of the Law School paper.

L: Was he going for a law degree?

S: Yes, he was. Of course when he dropped out, he didn't have a law degree and he never went back to college. He went to work for an oil field equipment company that was headquartered, I believe, in West Virginia and he was their salesman and representative in Texas, which, of course, was fairly big business back then. But in order to get to these places, these oil wells, they were way out in the middle of nowhere, almost all of them had a landing strip beside them because that's how people got there was to fly in. So he learned to fly, and got his pilot's license and…flew to these different places. That's how he made his sales calls.

L: So at what point did he start trying his hand at writing comedy?

S: I can tell you that the story is a little bit fuzzy…keep in mind my father died in 1969. I was, at that time, 27 years old and you just weren't as interested as I became later in what he was doing and how he did it. So a lot of these things I just kind of remember…He used to tell a story that in Houston…keep in mind, in Texas and many parts of the South, the drinking laws were quite restrictive in those years. They used to be decided by counties rather than state drinking laws. So in many of the counties at that time, Texas was controlled by the Baptists. And what they call "hard shell Baptists", they didn't believe in drinking. Well, in Houston at that time, they had what they called lounges, and basically they were beer bars. To get a mixed drink, you had to be a member of a private club…So he and my mother were married in 1939, and they were sitting in one of these lounges at that time, and they had one of these travelling variety shows known as Big Band shows. The more famous ones were Tommy Dorsey, and you know. They played mostly music, but they had singers and a comedian person on there. Well, apparently this particular show…it was Horace Heidt…there was an announcement that something had happened to a comedy writer, and there was an announcement that if there were any budding writers out there who wanted to write a script, they would be willing to pay…I think the number he mentioned was $100, which was a fair amount of money back then. A little sidebar here…I was born in February of 1942, and on my birth certificate, it states that his occupation was an unemployed used car salesman. I mean, it doesn't get much lower than that…Anyway, my mother said, "Why don't you do this? Submit the script, you're kind of a funny guy." My mother didn't have the world's greatest sense of humor, either. So I guess he did it and they loved the script, they thought it was fabulous, they paid him his $100, and he told me that the show was headquartered out of Los Angeles and they wanted to keep him on writing these scripts. So what he had to do was he had to type up two scripts and put it on two different airplanes in case one of the airplanes crashed. Well, the logistics of that became a little bit difficult, so finally they decided to move to Los Angeles. I'm not sure exactly when that was, but I know it was before July of 1943 because my sister was born in Los Angeles…I somehow think I was around a year old, so it would have been December-January-February of 1943…

L: Where did they settle?

S: …It's now called Lake Hollywood. They rented a house up there, and I know that he got into a very acrimonious battle with Horace Heidt because he left the show and in his later years talked about how he didn't like the guy at all. Ironically, when he died, his grave is about 100 or so yards from Horace Heidt's! So anyway…I don't know how long we lived there, but then we moved to an area of Beverly Hills called Benedict Canyon…and then I know in 1946, we bought a home in Beverly Hills that is on a street called Rexford Drive, on the corner of Rexford and Elevado…And our house, strangely enough when I looked on a plat map of Beverly Hills, was lot 1 of track 1. It was the first lot ever laid out in Beverly Hills…It's a pretty ugly house.

L: Is the house still there?

S: Yes, it is…700 North Rexford…it's right across from a grammar school where I went called Hawthorne School.

L: To back up a bit, how did your father and mother meet?

S: …Well, when he was a little boy, they lived near them in the same neighborhood. He met her then, and then they moved away to some other part of Houston. Some years later, they ran into each other as grown people…My mother was three years younger than him…And they were married in 1939, and my father was 27 years old.

L: I'm curious that you said she didn't have as much of a sense of humor about things.

S: I didn't think so. She'd think that some things were kind of cute, but she didn't have this amazingly…snappy sense of humor like my father…I remember I was growing up, I'm certain that a lot of times my friends came over to visit just to spend time around him! But anyway, he had that kind of personality, very sharp, very witty…He probably married someone who was more like his mother. She was the youngest of four sisters, and they were a very proper family. She was an absolutely gorgeous woman physically…At TCU she was elected most beautiful woman in the school…and was many years later, she only died in 1997…

L: So he left Horace Heidt, and do you know if he worked for anyone else in the interim before joining Jack?

S: I think that he…did some things for an old movie actor, a guy named Jack Carson. But what he did for him, I don't know…At the time the way you applied for a job was you wrote a script. And so I guess he heard there was an opening at Benny…I don't know what his thinking processes were, but he wanted to go for it, I guess. He wrote a script and they like it and hired him. And it turned out to be pretty successful…

L: Do you still have any of his writings?

S: Yes, I have things that he used to send me…(laughing) They were very, very dirty! And I remember one that he wrote, he used to love to write limericks and was very good at it. When Jackie Kennedy married Aristotle Onassis, he went crazy and was writing limericks all about that. He must have written 10 or 15 of them, and he'd send them to Jack Benny and would send copies to me….I've got that stuff around. I'm sort of the genealogist of the family, and I've traced the name all the way back to the Domesday Book in 1086…There's the name of an estate in Cornwall, England by that name….[side discussion of the dirty limericks] You know, I knew his fellow writers and they were all like that. A lot of that came out of the frustration of not being able to use the things they would have liked to put on the air. So they tended to in their personal lives and relationships be much more crude. But he used to tell me…a lot about the different cast members on the show and particularly the other three writers.

L: Well, let's talk about that. What do you remember of his stories and comments about everybody?

S: As you may or may not know, my father and George Balzer were the two Gentiles on the writing team, and Sam Perrin and Milt Josefsberg were the two Jews. But they kind of reversed roles quite a bit in the sense of what you think of as traditional Gentile-Jewish roles in approach to life. My father and George were very close with a nickel, and the other two guys would spend money on the craziest things…George Balzer…probably in the 40s some time, bought a house for his family, but it was a little house that Lockheed had built for their employees out in the San Fernando Valley. And these were little, boxy houses. And then after the War they sold them…Now I know the house that we bought on Rexford and Elevado, in 1946 we bought that house for $66,000. Today that house in that location probably sells for $3-4 million…I know this, my father had very bad taste in things. I mean, I thought the clothes he wore…I just don't think he had good taste in stuff…He was big on gimmicks. He'd buy these stupid glass knives on television, and I remember one time he bought 5,000 pairs of paper underwear. At the end of the day instead of washing it, you'd just throw it away. That's the kind of thing he would do. There was a chain of drug stores, Thrifty Drug Stores, and that's where he'd buy his shoes. Here's a man who got paid a lot of money! We had a three-car garage in that house, and we could only fit one car in it because every week, a truck would pull up with a couple cases of beer, a couple cases of Canada Dry product, and a couple of cases…of all the stuff they *give* you. That was back in the days of Payola…Dick Fashel (sp?) was a man whose livelihood…was like the agent for big corporations, like a lobbyist in Washington…He would always see to it that if someone mentioned the name of one of his company's products, that they got [something]. We never paid for refrigerators or appliances of any sort, they were always free. He'd get credits of $1000 at a big men's store in Beverly Hills, and he'd never use it! He'd give it away because he liked the stuff he got at Thrifty Drug Store. He was not a big spender…there was always a concern that it could disappear some day. But with the kind of money they were making…they were getting paid $2000-2500 a week…My father used to tell me all the time that Jack Benny was *extremely* dependent on writers, unlike a guy like Bob Hope who needed writers, but he could ad lib a lot. Benny, his whole thing was delivery, and he needed material. So he paid to get the very best…They used to have an office in Beverly Hills. At that time, Beverly Hills—the downtown part—was all little two-story Spanish buildings that had been there since the 20s and 30s. And they had an upstairs office—the writers did—in one of these buildings. Their secretary was Jeanette Eyemann…She was always very, very sweet and very nice to my sister and myself when she would come over. She used to come over once a month, and my father hired her on the side to write out all his bills and checks. Why he did that, I really don't know…That was not a nice time. My mother always tried to make sure that my sister and myself, and herself, were out of the house, out having dinner or doing something that afternoon or evening. He became an unhappy man during that period. My mother, on the other hand, was not a cheap person. She would spend a lot of money.

L: He was unhappy about going over finances?

S: Well, just looking at the bills and saying, "My God, why do we have to spend $400 or 500 a month at Saks?" The only thing he'd spend money on himself was that he always liked to have a nice, nice car…

L: So getting back to the cast, what are your memories of Jack?

S: Well, my father…loved that man a lot. He thought that he was an extremely generous, very kind, good man. He always said that all his life. He used to tell me that the only reason that Jack Benny could be funny about being cheap was because he wasn't at all, and if he were, he couldn't be as funny as he was about it. When he'd come over to the house, which was not unbelievably often but for a party or something…he would be nice to my sister and I. Not overwhelmingly wonderful, but I've often thought in later years that he probably wasn't *that* fond of children. But I don't know that to be true. He was nice to us, but just not gushing. But maybe we didn't deserve overwhelmingly gushing!…I remembered some years later that I was in Las Vegas when they opened Caesar's Palace, and he was the opening act. I believe it was 1962. So I phoned the hotel and said, "I'd like to speak to Jack Benny." [loss due to end of tape] And he got us tickets to his opening night, six tickets. That's the kind of thing he would do. He certainly had no allegiance to me, who was I? He was a very nice man, my father always loved him a lot. And I guess for that reason, I always had high regard for him because my father did…My father wrote a song you know, "Pickle in the Middle". It was actually written as a joke for one of the show's characters, Mr. Kitzel, who Benny ran into in different circumstances. He was going to run into him at a baseball game, and he thought it would be funny to have him sing this little ditty. The darn thing caught on, and it was number one in the country for two weeks! I used to get tiny bits of residuals where they would play it in Australia or something…Dr. Demento used to play it occasionally and some little check would turn up. I knew they'd made sheet music out of it, but I was in an antique mall in some little tiny town in West Virginia, and there was a big stack of sheet music…for a buck. And so I looked down and saw this piece of sheet music sticking out with this ugly color…and I must have remembered that color from my childhood. And that was it! I'd been looking for it for years trying to find it!…So who else?

L: How about Mary?

S: I knew her not at all…I knew Mary's sister fairly well, Babe Marks then she married this guy, Myrt Blum, and they were divorced and at the time I really got to know her, she was married to a postman…And the producer of the show for years was Hickey Marks, who was Mary's brother…This would have been in the late 50s or early 60s. My father had retired, and there was a little bar down at the western end of the Sunset Strip which has long since been knocked down, it was called the Rondele. A little bar and restaurant, and a lot of people in show business would hang out in that. And my father hung out in that a lot. And my father and I would go in there and have dinner, and I was somewhere around 18 or 19 years old, and we'd have dinner with her and the postman. I don't remember his name at all [EN: Clem]. She was kind of a bleached blonde person. She had a lot of money, but I assume that came from her settlement with Myrt Blum, who was Jack's business manager…She never worked. But the postman moved into the house in Beverly Hills, and continued to be a postman. He was a pretty nice guy as I remember, a really down-to-earth sort of a guy…

L: How about Eddie Anderson?

S: My main memory of him is that my father wrote something for him, something other than the Jack Benny show, and my father wrote this script for him…And as an appreciation for that, he gave my father a ring, a yellow gold ring, with four pretty good-sized diamonds across the ring. And this was not my father, he didn't wear any jewelry at all. So he didn't want this ring, but what he decided to do was have the diamonds taken out of there and made into…a cocktail ring for my mother. So they make this ring with the diamonds and freshwater pearls, and they made the gold setting into an initial ring with the initials "J.T." Everybody called my father Tack, including my sister and myself. The only people who did not were his parents and his sister…

L: Dennis Day?

S: I remember meeting him. Even as a child, he didn't seem like he was very tall. He just didn't seem as tall as everybody else, maybe about 5'6…I remember something, my father was convinced that Jack Benny was having affairs with various people…But my father enjoyed stuff like that, he enjoyed talking about it. He'd make jokes about just about anything. I remember one time…he and Phil Harris, they were pretty close. And Phil was over at the house one day, and my sister and I were having a particularly bad day, at least from my father's perspective, running around and making noise. And he looked at Phil Harris and said, "You know Phil, it's at times like this that I wish Dr. Salk hadn't found a cure for polio!" He saw that as very funny. I, in retrospect, think it's funny. And he would do stuff like that. And obviously everyone knew he didn't mean it. It was just his way of saying, "This is getting on my nerves." But my father was not a particularly good father. My mother was great as long as you were nursing her. After that, she kind of faded out of the picture as far as a motherly influence on her children. And then my father didn't care about children until they got old enough to carry on some level of dialogue. So there was this gap between the time we stopped nursing and the time we could talk with my father. We didn't have a lot in the way of parental contact…My father never ate until very late at night. If we ate with either of our parents, we'd eat with our mother because she ate earlier. He would eat maybe at 10:00, and usually he'd eat standing up at his bar…Mostly he was by himself…[The writers would] get up and meet in the aforementioned office in Beverly Hills around 9:30 to 10:00, and they would get through about 2:00 to 2:30 and he'd come home. And then they usually went out in the evening. We'd eat with both of our parents about three times a year…

L: Tell me more about Phil Harris.

S: Well, probably one of the reasons that they were very good friends was they both liked to drink a lot. Phil Harris' drinking, although they made jokes about it on the show, was real.

So would my father. My father actually died an alcoholic. That's why he died. His heart stopped, but if you look at the results of the autopsy, he had no liver left at all. So it was a time in that business where there was just a lot of that going on…I think that was one of their connections. He was pretty much in person like he was on the radio. He referred to Jack Benny as Jackson…I did not know Don Wilson. I probably met him but I don't remember him.

L: How about Milt Josefsberg, since I know he worked closely with your father?

S: The way they did the writing, Milt and my father would take half the show. They played a lot of gin, I remember the penny-a-point. Milt was a very nice man, and his wife Hilda was a lovely lady as well. And they had children around our age…I went to work as a salesman for a large paper mill in Chicago, and my territory was half of California. They were the largest manufacturer in the world for mat boards. So Milt's son owned a picture frame shop, and we chatted. I used to call on him as a salesman back in the 1960s. Milt was a very kind and good man, he was originally from New York, and one of the biggest things in his life he talked about was when his mother was going to come out to visit. She had never gone outside of the city limits of New York in her whole life…He was talking about it for months that she was going to come out and finally leave New York and stay with them for a month. You'd think that when you work with someone so closely that you'd want to get away from them, but they'd socialize in the evening. A lot of their work was done on the weekends, with rewrites and rehearsals. They'd write during the week, then have a rehearsal on Saturday and a rewrite, and then a mini-rehearsal on Sunday afternoon before the show.

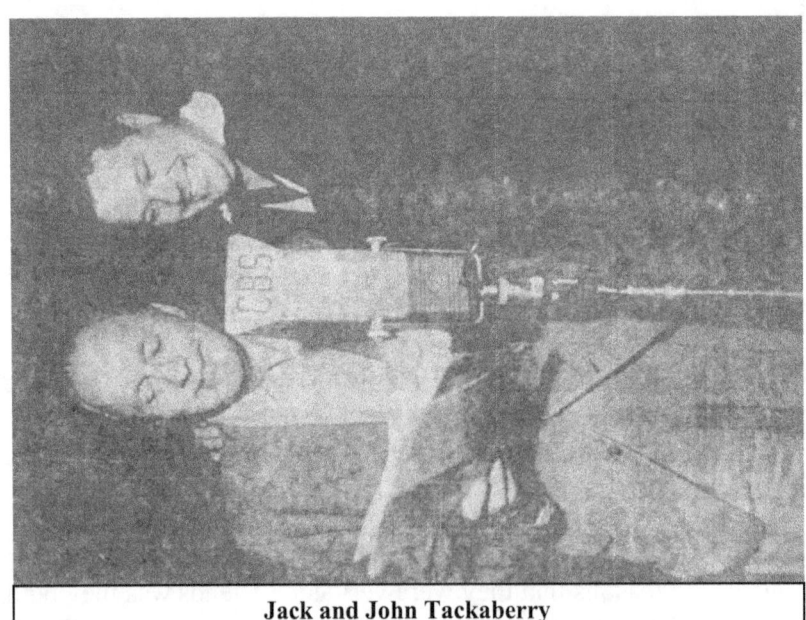

Jack and John Tackaberry

The Jack Benny Times

May - August 2005   Volume XX, Numbers 3-4

Jack Benny in Korea – Summer 1951
Photographed by Ralph Pyle

President's Message

Jell-O again folks…as usual, never a dull moment around here. In my last message, I had forewarned people about the impending heavy demands of my job. Now having put in my 60-hour weeks, I finished the contract and am looking for new opportunities. If anyone needs a good Project Manager in the San Francisco area, let me know! (www.lauraleff.com) However, it's very nice to have some time to devote to *really important* things, like Jack Benny research, before being swept back into the world of paying work. You were all very kind and patient as I had asked, and I greatly appreciate it. I've long said that Jack Benny fans are, by and large, the best bunch of people around.

39 Forever, Second Edition Volume 1 is still selling well. If you are going to be at the Cincinnati old radio convention, copies will be available at Ted Davenport/Mike Hamm's table. You'll be able to heft a copy yourself and see why it's well worth the $40 price tag. Or if you're not going to be at the convention and haven't gotten your copy yet, you can use Paypal on www.jackbenny.org or send a check payable to IJBFC to the address at the end of this newsletter. I periodically get the question on when Volume 2 will come out. It (and just about everything else) was put on the shelf during my recent heavy months on the job, but I am looking forward to getting back to it within the next few weeks.

I am also very pleased about the recent additions to our video library. Two generous donors have added quite a bit of new material, ranging from ten discs of Jack Benny programs to a rare interview of Jack by David Frost and two of Jack's color specials. You can see Jack as Ralph Kramden with guest Audrey Meadows (Alice), Jack caught in the Twilight Zone with guest Rod Serling, Jack reviving Buck Benny as the Cactus Kid with guest Gisele MacKenzie, Jack in hippie garb and a Nehru jacket in Jack Benny's New Look, and much more. For full details, go to www.jackbenny.org and click on Programs, then Video Library. If you don't have Web access, drop a letter to the address at the end of this newsletter. Please note that all offerings are in DVD format only.

New Members

**** Ray Ginn **** James Gauthier **** Mike Curran **** Susan Barba **** Don K. Tamblyn **** Dr. John Maguire **** Pamela J. Dunn **** Cobham Still **** Patrick Picciarelli **** Frank Green **** Joseph Plowman **** Kevin A. Mueller **** Rusty Baldwin **** Tom Mazur **** Sonya Carlson **** Hal Vickery **** Evan Garbe **** Bryan Walker **** Philip Satterley **** Sandy Irwin **** Joseph T. Cherry **** David Dougherty **** Daniel A. Sloan **** Skip Dunbar **** Ralph Norris **** William M Zielinski **** Mike Michell **** Wendy Braswell **** Bruce Rychlik **** Ann Linderman **** Martha Lowry **** Brian Boswell **** Mariah L. David **** Michelle Allen **** Dana Weber **** Ray Fowler **** Bret Winters **** Gayland Darnell **** Rand E. Gerald **** Catherine A. Snodgrass **** George Anderson **** Christopher Lowry **** Dave Simmons **** Penny Weichel **** Ken Kostovich **** Milton Broome **** David Bishop **** Allyson Thompson **** Gary Faligowski **** John M. Pastore **** P S Ranganathan **** Paul Daniggelis **** John Pomeroy **** Andy Klein **** Peter Greco **** William L.

Abbott **** Dick Dodderidge **** Karen Hegmann **** Nik Mohamed **** Dwayne E Landen **** Brian L. Johnson **** Brian Haas **** Jared Driskill **** Gary Stark **** Gary Bancroft **** Ed Dillio **** Alan Chengary **** Andrew L. Hurwitz **** Jim Engel **** Patricia Gulick **** Frank M. St. John **** Wayne E. Seelinger **** Mort Palin **** Jessica Dunn **** Melinda Cole **** Clinton E. Case **** Bob Grochowski **** Beverly Bennett **** Dave Anderson **** David Farber **** Samantha Darby **** Luke McKean **** Jennifer Neumann **** Christopher Annear **** Suzanne Frye Wells **** Steve Caron **** Bob Colleton **** James Johanson **** Joan Leya **** Deborah Underwood ***** Dr. David Reuben

Do You Know?

Lorene Bryant Epps, John Bryant (son of Jimmy), and Fred L. Jack are looking for the following show: Jack takes in boarders, Episode 175, April 22, 1962. "In it was a gal named Cousin Emmy, playing banjo, a guitar player named Jimmy Bryant and another guitar player named Geo Winston. The plot of the show was Don Wilson wanted Jack to hire a hillbilly band for some reason and got Jack to audition this group. I would appreciate any help you may give."

Art from the OTR Digest asks:
"While driving today on I-66 in Arlington, VA, I found myself behind a red VW Cabrio with Virginia vanity tags JCKBNY. (It was a special animal welfare plate.) One of your IJBFC members?"

You Do Know!

Questions come up from time to time about Petrillo, since he was the subject of so many jokes on Jack's program and others. Member Brad Vereen found a vintage Time cover article on Petrillo, which answers the questions in great depth. I contacted Time about being able to reprint it here, but the royalties are just too high. So if you're a Time subscriber, you can read the story online for free. Here's a taste:

Jan. 26, 1948
"James Caesar Petrillo cannot see germs, at least not very well, but they do not fool him. He knows there are armies of them all around him : hairy ones with millions of eyes, wiggly ones with transparent heads, sloppy ones shaped like tomato surprises, stiff ones which look like piccolos in aspic. He never forgets that they are coming at him, morning, noon & night. But he is not intimidated. He fights them. As grand sachem, lord paramount and international president of the American Federation of Musicians, Caesar Petrillo has an imperial disdain for convention, and, when..."

Article: http://www.time.com/time/archive/preview/0,10987,779602,00.html
Cover: http://www.time.com/time/covers/0,16641,1101480126,00.html

A while back, I was chasing a rumor that State Farm Insurance had a vintage, full-size Maxwell that they had used during the days that they sponsored Jack's television program. Dan Barringer of State Farm's Company History Unit was kind enough to answer this question and also provide a little more detail on the various offerings that State Farm had relating to the Benny program:

"Laura, got you letter inquiring about us having a Maxwell. Sorry to say we don't. I think they were referring to a 1922 Model T Ford we have in our lobby to symbolize the year we started. We did give out an award of the Maxwell to agents in 1960."

- Ed Rust (State Farm President) appeared on Jack Benny Show with Don Wilson, 1960.
- In October of 1960, a bronze replica of Benny's famous Maxwell was offered to agents as an award. Also included was an record album <u>Music to Write Apps By</u>.

LL: I am happy to say that I have both of these items. The Maxwell replica is of a 1910 model (same as the cover of the record at left), and the front crank plays the five-note State Farm Insurance jingle. The record goes into great detail about how Madison Avenue settled on that jingle, and includes a skit with Jack, Rochester, and Don.

The qualifications for the Maxwell award are also outlined inside the record jacket as follows:

Each Agent, in the applicable classification, will be recognized as a Maxwell Award Qualifier, who produces, during October, Auto Points (Career Club basis) equal to 10% of his 1959 Auto Points, subject to these respective minimums:

    1959-60 Convention Qualifiers, Minimum – 172 Total Points (Auto, Life and Fire)
    1959 Career Club Qualifiers, Minimum – 115 Total Points (Auto, Life and Fire)
    All others (including new Agents), Minimum – 60 Total Points (Auto only)

Points will be determined as follows:
- A. Auto – 2 points for each new, added or reinstated section.
- B. Life – 2 points for each $5.00 of submitted premium in cash. Bankable time checks will be considered as cash.
- C. Fire – each new and renewal Fire Policy – 1 point; Homeowners – 4 points

Business produced during the qualifying period (October 1-31) and received in the State Office, Agency Records Section or Operating Division, not later than November 4th, will qualify. NOTE: Agents in New York and Wisconsin to receive one (1) extra point for every four (4) points for Auto or Fire production.

Each Manager who has 75% of his total Agency qualified will also be recognized as a Maxwell Award Winner.

Inside the jacket, it shows how Jack was being marketed to the State Farm agents:

"It finally happened! Jack Benny pays off for State Farm Insurance agents!

"On Oct. 16, 1960, The Jack Benny Show begins its 11th season, this year on CBS-TV under the co-sponsorship of the State Farm Insurance Companies and Lever Bros. Your sales story will be reaching 23 million night-time family-viewers; nearly 10,000,000 adult male insurance prospects!

"Imagine! Television's stingiest man paying-off for you! Yes, Jack Benny will be paying you handsome dividends this fall. Not in musty old bills from his vault, but in red-hot prospects! Your State Farm message via the Jack Benny Show will be beamed to 40% of the nation's Sunday evening television audience, creating a massive awareness of your multiple line services.

"This Jack Benny pay-off gives you a tremendous edge over competition. You'll be able to reach many interested prospects still warm from the Company advertising on Benny's Show. It's your brightest opportunity for increased October production ever! Jack Benny is paying-off...for you."

- In 1961, 39 cent checks were given in celebration of State Farm's and Jack Benny's 39th birthdays. [LL: These are the 39-cent checks that show up on Ebay from time to time.]
- Jack Benny shirt. Offered in a regional agency promotion for 39 apps in 1 month, and sold at the home office. [LL: Has anyone ever seen one of these? I don't think I have. Maybe everyone wore them out.]

Natalie McLain provided the following in response to a discussion of whether there had ever been plans for a movie biography of Jack Benny:

I have been a Jack Benny fan for over 32 years when I found a tape of one of his shows in the public library when I was 16 years old. Ever since that day I was hooked. Last night, I was listening to you and Walden Hughes discuss whether there was ever a plan to film a biography of Jack Benny and you didn't think there was. However, I have access to the New York Times database and one of the things I have been doing has been reading articles about Jack of course. I seemed to remember an item about that very same subject so I went looking for it and here is what I found. I think you would be very interested.

On April 5, 1946, I found: "Dennis Day, of Jack Benny's Radio program will appear as himself in <u>Always Leave Them Laughing</u>, the Benny film at the studio." (Warner Bros. which was mentioned earlier in the column).

On July 3, 1946 I found: "Also at Warners, Jack Benny is at the studio conferring on <u>Always Leave Them Laughing</u> the projected screen story of his life. Humphrey Bogart will be costarred with Benny, and Jerry Wald will produce the comedy."

Then on January 19, 1947 from an article about Jerry Wald which indicates a slight shift in the direction of the film: "In a lighter vein he is excited about a satire on movie biographies, <u>Always Leave Them Laughing</u>. This will be a picture within a picture, being a story about the filming of the life of a great comedian (Jack Benny) who is the technical adviser on the picture and whose suggestions are brutally ignored by the movie people. "It's about time we started kidding ourselves." says Mr. Wald.

Things must have broken down though after that article because, the next time I can find mention of <u>Always Leave Them Laughing</u> was on April 5, 1949 and it is now the title for a Danny Kaye vehicle. Then on May 17, 1949, Milton Berle became the lead and Danny Kaye was scheduled for another film.

It was finally filmed with Berle and it was retooled and Berle plays a comedian named Kit Cooper and the film is loosely based on his life. I wonder about the original film with Jack. What part was Bogart playing? I guess we'll never know.

Natalie and I tossed some ideas around in E-mail, and here are my thoughts on this series of news releases. I have a feeling that there may have been varying views or a misperception in the July 1946 mention, of whether this was to be the story of *Jack's* life or a satire of movie biographies *starring* Jack as later indicated. Having Bogart costar in Jack's life story doesn't make a lot of sense to me, unless they were doing it ala <u>The Jolson Story</u> and throwing reality out the window. I read a personal letter of Jack's from September of 1946 saying that he was hoping to make another movie, but "it looks like it's been cancelled" due to script issues.

Then on December 16, 1946, Jack starred on Lux Radio Theatre in a play entitled "Killer Kates". William Keighley notes in the introduction that the piece is "based on a Warner Brothers screenplay" and adapted for radio. Jack plays actor Jeff Morley who is famous for playing a killer, but wants to be a comedian. After a nervous collapse, Morley believes that he really is his character Killer Kates, breaks into his own safe, and runs to New Jersey to lay low. With the heavy gangster element of the plot, this would make sense for a costar of Humphrey Bogart.

People sometimes ask why Jack never starred in another picture after The Horn Blows at Midnight (released April 28, 1945), often theorizing that it was such a bad movie that the studio wouldn't risk Jack in another movie vehicle. Of course, Horn wasn't nearly as bad as Jack and the gang made it out to be, and the above information seems to confirm that Warner Brothers was still trying to find the right role for Jack. Unfortunately, it seems that was not to be. If anyone has more information about Always Leave Them Laughing and its evolution, please contact me at the address at the end of this newsletter.

What's Up in Waukegan?

Waukegan continued its annual tradition of a birthday celebration at the Jack Benny statue in downtown. Per David Motley, Director of Public Relations for the City of Waukegan: "Mayor Hyde welcomed the crowd and explained the significance of Jack Benny to our community, the reason why we should celebrate his life and legacy. We next had Hank Bogdala say a few words regarding, of course, the placement of the statue and he plugged his upcoming *History of Waukegan* Class & Tour on March 24 & 25. Finally, Stan Hickory, a.k.a. the anonymous donor, talked about why he was inspired to leave flowers at the site and made some recollections about the family gathering to listen to the Jack Benny Radio Program days long ago. The wreath was placed and cake and coffee was served. It was freezing cold and very windy but everyone had a good time."

The Tale Piece

It's always fun when someone new associated with Jack Benny contacts me. Russell Kayser played George Jessel's nephew Seymour in the December 24, 1963 Jack Benny Program, which has just been added to our video library. If you've seen the show, you may remember the young man holding a giant tuba. That was Seymour/Russell:

"Well after 42 years, it seems a life time ago! As I sit here on an island off the east coast of Sweden, recalling the events of that week on the set with Jack. I remember between takes, he would sit me down, and teach me to play chess (I think he knew I was bored hanging around the set all day). And after several days, I finally got the hang of it, and would arrive early at the studio knocking at his dressing room door, wanting to play another round before they started taping (in between bugging Mel to do Daffy Duck) and Jack (being half asleep) would oblige me.

"Needless to say this was a fun week for a kid my age, mostly because of the kindness shown to me by these two men. I remember something Jack said to me as he patiently tried to teach me the rules of chess (not an easy task with a 12 year old). Quote: 'Life's a lot like this game son ,and someday you'll see why..' And after two kids and 3 grandkids, I think I see his point, while fondly recalling his face and words, he represented a time of innocence for me, and perhaps for America as well, in this age of harshness and inhumanity."

Dwight Fisher, a Scientist with the USDA, made the following recommendation for celebrating Jack's birthday:

"Well, this is not something I normally do but I think you may enjoy the story. I noticed that it was Jack Benny's birthday today since it was included in a news brief that I get via the Internet.

"I offered to get a cup of coffee for a coworker since I was going into town and passing by Starbucks. I don't like change and all that so I said she couldn't pay because it is Jack Benny's birthday today. Although he pretended to be cheap but he wasn't really cheap and you are supposed to do something generous in honor of his birthday. She was suspicious but accepted my explanation. This was over the lunch hour and when I got back she told me she had bought lunch for a friend because it was Jack Benny's birthday. Then another coworker told me that she was trying to find someone to be generous to. So, how about a new holiday? Also if someone contacts you please cover for me and tell them that, yes it is customary to be generous on Jack Benny's birthday."

Jack Benny in Korea

I was recently contacted by Ralph Pyle, who had toured with Jack as an Army photographer. Ralph generously shared both his photos and memories.

"I was an Army Combat and Aerial Photographer in Korea from Nov 1950 to Nov 1951. During my tour of duty, I received the Bronze Star for photographs made of Chinese troop concentrations and equipment from an L 19 Cessna airplane. Flying at about 1000 feet, I made over 35 flights. I also covered the combat operations of the United Nation troops. I was a veteran of WWII for 3 years in the South Pacific. As a reserve I was called back to duty in Korea Sep. 1950

"During the summer of 1951 I was assigned a very plush assignment of covering The USO Tour of Jack Benny and Co. I spent 4 days photographing his tour for the Public Relations Department of the Defense Department. The official pictures are in their archives. I have several photos taken for my personal use of Mr. Benny signing autographs and just talking to the troops.

"I have been thinking about the wonderful time I got to spend with with Jack in Korea, and how much it meant to the thousands of guys who were called back to service after serving in WWII and how little respect we got at the time. We were uprooted from our homes and families after already spending years in the war of Japan and Germany people like Jack and his whole tour left home and safety to bring a little joy to us.. It was greatly appreciated. I mailed some of these pix to him in later years and never heard from him, this was in his bad days. Benny was one of the nicest stars I ever met in Korea, a real gentleman, and Frankie Remley was sober the whole tour. Mr. Benny said that his drinking was a story just for the audience only. Benny was a wonderful Patriot and Gentleman, I'm just glad to have spent some time with him."

Frankie Remley, Jack, and ?

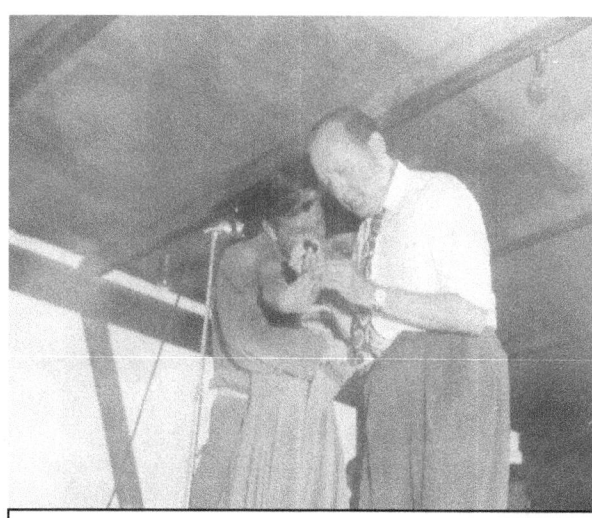

Jack inspects money paid by a GI to kiss Marjorie Reynolds

Jack signs autographs for the troops

Capt. Joe McConkey presents jack with the Korean Campaign Ribbon

L to R: Gen. Van Brunt, ?, Gen. O'Daniel, Jack, Gen. Milburn, and Deloris Gay

Jack (left jeep) and his USO troupe being escorted to a performance

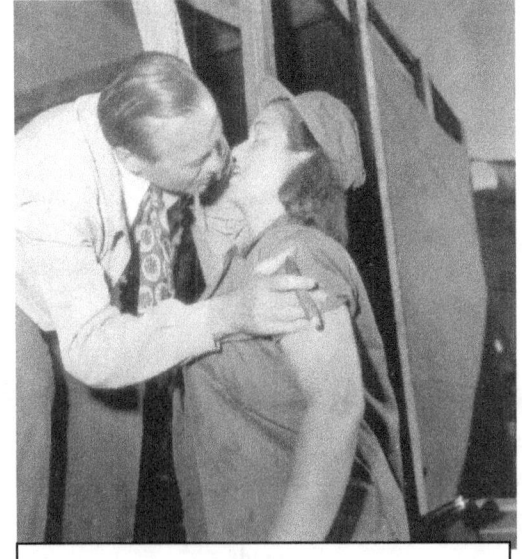
Jack kisses an Army nurse

Jack says to Ralph, "It's Coke," knowing he was a non-drinker.

Fred Allen's Side of the Feud

Lovers of old time radio are always on the lookout for "lost shows"...programs that are not currently in circulation or which are considered to no longer have any existing audio copies. As Benny fans, we are extremely fortunate to have a large number of Benny programs available to us (well over 700 of the 924 total shows done). These include pretty much every week in early 1937, when the feud between Jack Benny and Fred Allen was just starting to blossom. So we can hear Jack's cracks about Fred, but what was on the other side of this conversation?

During one of my trips to Boston, I visited the Boston Public Library to find the answer to that question. They are the owners of the Fred Allen collection, which includes (among many other things) scripts of most of his shows. In fact, it contains up to three different versions of scripts for each show with successive rewrites. What fascinated me was that the sections of the script having to do with Jack appear to have been written after the final revision and were inserted as separate sections with the title "(BENNY BIT)" at the top of the first page. This would make sense, as Fred would have had to listen to Jack's Sunday show to know what he was answering. Fred's show was on Wednesday, so the script would have had to be finalized and approved by Monday at the latest, necessitating any answer to be a last-minute insertion.

So here is a rundown of both sides of this virtual conversation between two masters of comedy, not heard since it was originally broadcast. Due to the length of the scripts, this will be published in installments; this covers to the end of January, 1937. Scripts are copied verbatim.

December 30, 1936: Town Hall Tonight, Stuart Canin appears (written as Stewart) – Fred Allen introduces Canin who plays The Bee in the unscripted "Town Hall Varieties" segment. Allen and Canin then chat briefly about the violin and Canin himself. The following exchange was transcribed from the East Coast broadcast of the program. It seems that for the West Coast broadcast, Allen revised his comment to be on the order of, "Jack Benny should be ashamed of himself."

Allen: ...Imagine if ten or fifteen years from now and you're playing the cello up on the (???)...What grade are you in at school?
Can: Public school?
Allen: Public school, do you go to public school?
Can: Yes, Five B.
Allen: Five B? Where do you live, Edgemere?
Can: Edgemere.
Allen: And you're in Five B, huh?

Can: Yes.

Allen: What do you know, Murray? A little fella in the fifth grade at school and already he plays better than Jack Benny…(4 second burst of laughter)…Well, we want to thank you very much, Stewart, and it's certainly been a pleasure to have you here, and I'm still, I'm convinced. I'm going to watch you play again, I think you've got another arm comes out of your sleeve there. I don't think you were doing that all with two arms. And thank you a lot.

Can: Thank you.

January 3, 1937: <u>The Jell-O Program</u>, very end of the closing blackout

Jack: Oh Mary…

Mary: Yes?

Jack: Take a wire to Fred Allen, will you?

Mary: Okay.

Jack: Say, "Dear Fred, I am NOT ashamed of myself. When I was ten years old, I could play <u>Flight of the Bumble Bee</u> on my violin too. NYEAH!" Do you know how to spell nyeah? Signed, Jack Benny.

January 6, 1937: <u>Town Hall Tonight</u>, no Jack Benny references in the script. Fred must have ad libbed more comments about Jack's playing, per Jack's comments the following Sunday.

January 10, 1937: <u>The Jell-O Program</u>. Almost the entire first half of the program is dedicated to the cast ribbing Jack about how great Fred Allen's program was the previous Wednesday. This is the first time any significant airtime has been dedicated to the feud. Jack continues to refer to the piece as <u>Flight of the Bumble Bee</u> instead of <u>The Bee</u>.

January 13, 1937: <u>Town Hall Tonight</u>, Benny bit inserted at the start of Town Hall Varieties. A Mister Petrie (possibly played by John Brown) interrupts Fred.

Fred: There's no trouble Mister Petrie. I just happened to say one night that Jack couldn't play a number called The Bee on his violin. That's all. Last Sunday Jack said he could play The Flight of the Bumble Bee.

John: That's another tune, ain't it?

Fred: Yes. He's off on the wrong argument. The number I meant was The Bee by Shubert. The Flight of the Bumble Bee is by two other fellows, Rimsky and Korsakoff. [sic]

John: A couple of foreigners, eh?

Fred: As a matter of fact. The talk in musical circles is that Rimsky and Korsakoff heard Jack trying to play Shubert's Bee and that's why they wrote their Bee in flight.

John: To give the bee a chance to get away, eh?

Fred: Yes. Now, Mr. Petrie, as man to man, I'm giving myself the best of it perhaps…but did you ever hear Stuff Benny play The Bee on his violin?

John: Well. I heard him play somethin in a vaudeville theatre one time.
Fred: Was it The Bee?
John: Couldn't a been. When he finished playin his violin was covered with somethin but it wasn't honey. Looked more like tomatoes to me.
Fred: I see. With all those tomatoes hanging on it, his E string must have looked like vine.
John: I ain't here to stool pigeon, Allen.
Fred: Well…
John: You fellers ought to quit this arguin. All Waukegan is agog. The Chamber of Commerce sent me down here as a committee of one to straighten this thing out.
Fred: Oh! Are you from Waukegan, Mr. Petrie?
John: Yes. I'm in the Post Office there. At the General Delivery window.
Fred: Yeah? Right across from the second spittoon as you come in the door.

January 17, 1937: The Jell-O Program. Again a good portion of the first half of the show is spent discussing Fred Allen's program. Jack shows a picture of himself at age 10 playing The Bee.

January 20, 1937: Town Hall Tonight, again at the start of Town Hall Varieties (possibly played by Charles Cantor)
Fred: Thank you. And now? Before presenting the first of our guests, ladies and gentlemen, I would like to clean up a little extraneous business that has been popping up…on the program…Helter skelter…As the saying goes every Wednesday for the past few weeks…I refer to what, in French, we would call l'affaire Benny. Last Sunday, this impetuous and self-styled virtuoso, Mr. Benny showed a picture of himself playing the "BEE" at the age of ten. A new low in composite photographic skulduggery, ladies and gentlemen. Mr. Benny could have waited for television and the entire country could have seen what the picture looked like. But…no…the picture was exhibited in a dinky, ill-lighted West Coast radio studio to a hand-picked studio audience consisting of fifteen men named Boasberg. [LL: Al Boasberg was one of Jack's writers.] We are coping with a cutie, ladies and gentlemen, but we are prepared. We'll show this pixie who is running the dell. We'll show you exactly what this picture was. Tonight, we have spared no expense to bring you the man who took this picture of Jack Benny holding the violin when he was ten years old. Mr. DeWitt Levee.
Chas: Thank you.
Fred: Now Mr. Levee. Where is your home.
Chas: Waukegan, Illinois.
Fred: What do you do in Waukegan?
Chas: I am running…strictly by appointment…the Bide a Wee combination pawn shop and delicatessen.
Fred: Pawnshop and delicatessen. What kind of a sign do you use outside the store.
Chas: Three meat balls.

Fred: I see. Do you ever listen to Jack Benny on the radio.
Chas: Who else?
Fred: Don't get personal, Mr. Levee. Just answer my questions.
Chas: Jack Benny! There's a comedian. You should live to see the day you could hold a candle to Jack Benny.
Fred: Wait a minute! I don't want to hold a candle. Don't turn this into an arson case, Mr. Levee.
Chas: Last Sunday, Jack is slaying me. He is calling you a toothpaste salesman.
Fred: That's only the half of it.
Chas: A toothpaste salesman. Hi! Yi!
Fred: Well. At least my samples don't wobble around.
Chas: What's the matter you couldn't say Jello?
Fred: Did he say Ipana last Sunday.
Chas: Jack Benny. An artist. A scholar.
Fred: But not a violin player.
Chas: Look! I'm giving Jack Benny a little plug. And he can't take it.
Fred: You know what happens if you give Jack a little plug, don't you?
Chas: So what happens?
Fred: Buck Benny rides again!
Chas: Oy! Buck Benny. What a cowboy!
Fred: Now…Look, Mr. Levee. You were brought her tonight to tell our radio audience about a certain picture.
Chas: Could I get a word in endwise…Up to now?
Fred: Quiet, please! Did you…or did you not…on the afternoon of July 7th, 1904 take a picture of Jack Benny holding his violin.
Chas: I did.
Fred: Where was this picture taken?
Chas: In the Bide-A-Wee Pawn Shop at Waukegan, Illinois with a Brownie Number Two.
Fred: Fine. What was Jack Benny doing in the Bide-A-Wee Pawnshop at the time.
Chas: He was practising on his violin.
Fred: He practised his violin in your pawnshop?
Chas: Where else? You think I am letting the violin out of mine sight.
Fred: I see.
Chas: The violin was in hock, a technical term, but I was letting Jackie come into the pawnshop to practise.
Fred: How did you come to take this picture.
Chas: Confidentially, one day a party is relinquishing for money a Brownie Number Two. Jackie, a little boy, is asking me to take his picture to see if he will coming out a Brownie.
Fred: You have one of these pictures with you.
Chas: Right here. See! It's Jasha Benny with the violin.
Fred: Yes. Uh huh! Which is Jack?

Chas: The one that goes in the middle there.
Fred: According to this picture he was standing on his head at the time.
Chas: No. It was me. I was holding the camera upside down.
Fred: Ha ha. Look at this. He didn't even know how to hold a violin.
Chas: Yi! Yi! The strings is underneath.
Fred: Not only that. The thin end he's got stuck in his neck.
Chas: It ain't right?
Fred: No. The fat end of the violin goes under a violin player's chin to keep his head company.
Chas: Hi! Yi! A schlemiel!
Fred: Now one vital question, Mr. Levee. Was Jack playing the Bee on this violin when you took this picture?
Chas: Is the right arm blurred?
Fred: No. The right arm isn't blurred.
Chas: Then he wasn't even playing.
Fred: Now, Mr. Levee, you heard Jack play around your pawnshop a good many times.
Chas: To destruction!
Fred: And what did he play?
Chas: You got a fiddle.
Fred: Yes…A violin for Mr. Levee, Peter. Thank. Here you are. (KNOCK ON WOOD)
Chas: A violin. By me, in hock for this fiddle, you are getting two dollars only after an argument.
Fred: Never mind that. Just show us what Jack Benny played around the Bide-A-Wee Pawnshop back in Waukegan.
Chas: Okay.
(VIOLIN STARTS EXERCISES…GOES INTO "MUZZALTOFF"…BACK TO EXERCISES)
Fred: Thank you Mr. Levee, you have definitely proved that the Bee was not played by Mr. Jack Benny in your Pawnshop. Thank you.
Chas: How do I get out now. It's falling flat.
Fred: I'll just lift up this applause card and you beat it.
Chas: Hokay.

January 24, 1937: The Jell-O Program.
Show starts with Jack in the other room practicing The Bee. Again, much of the early part of the show is devoted to jokes about Fred Allen. Jack is infatuated with Phil's sister, Lucy-Belle, but she thinks Fred Allen is wonderful.

January 27, 1937: Town Hall Tonight . One Benny joke in the opening dialogue between Fred and Portland, plus the inserted Benny Bit at the top of Town Hall Varieties, possibly played by John Brown and Charles Cantor.

Fred: Before presenting our first guest, ladies and gentlemen, I would like to mention a gentleman…and the word gentleman is used loosely here…I won't stoop to mention his name…But…He is a picture star…His initials are J.B…and I don't mean John Barrymore. Last Sunday, on a comedy radio program—J.B., referring to my profile, said that there was a limit to what the makeup man could do for me when I come out to Hollywood to make a picture this summer. All right. I'll admit I'm no middle Ritz Brother. I know that the stork flew backwards so he wouldn't have to confront me in case the bundle flew open…Still I had hoped we could keep this altercation on a dignified plane—but—If Mr. J.B. wants to get personal…all right. I quote from a Hollywood gossip column…Quote…what radio and movie star was seen trying to get into a grapefruit-skin so that he could go to a masquerade as a little squirt…Unquote. J.B. isn't exactly little but a big squirt would spoil the joke. All I said, originally, ladies and gentlemen, was that Mr. J.B…

Harry: The character J.B. is entirely fictional, folks, and any incident that might be construed as having reference to any living person…or Jack Benny…is entirely co-incidental…signed…the management.

Fred: I only said that when J.B. was ten years old he couldn't play the Bee on his violin. Tonight…I shall go even farther. Statistics don't lie ladies and gentlemen and tonight's statistics will prove conclusively that J.B. will <u>never</u> play the Bee on his violin. At this time…I present Mr. Myrt Plum, [LL: Jack's manager was Myrt Blum] vice-president of the Neapolitan Insurance Company. Mr. Plum

John: Yes, Mr. Allen.

Fred: As an insurance man you have a thorough knowledge of the life span in different parts of the world.

John: Yes. Our insurance charts are authentic and complete.

Fred: If I ask you the life expectancy of a person you can tell me approximately how long the person will live.

John: Oh yes! If you're a Hindu, aged ten, under normal conditions your life expectancy is 48 point 5. That means you've got less than half a chance to live to be eleven.

Fred: This party isn't a Hindu.

John: Is he white?

Fred: Yes. He's scared most of the time.

John: Does he smoke cigars?

Fred: If you put a cigar down he'll take it up from where you left off. Yes.

John: Drink?

Fred: No. But he might as well. He always looks that way.

John: I see. What month was he born in?

Fred: May.

John: Under Gemini, eh? Where was he born?

Fred: Waukegan, Illinois.

John: How old is he now?

Fred: About thirty-five.

John: What business is he in?
Fred: No business. But he plays the violin.
John: I see. No business playing the violin, eh?
Fred: And how! He's got no business.
John: Well. According to our Neapolitan Life chart this party should live sixty-nine more years…and six months.
Fred: If he's thirty-five today he'll live to be 104 and six months.
John: Unless he plays the violin in public. Yes.
Fred: Thank you, Mr. Plum. And now from the South Bend Conservatory of Classical Music I present Professor Gustave Strad. Professor Strad, you are an authority on the violin.
Chas: (DUTCH) Yes, Mr. Allen.
Fred: Are you familiar with a musical composition known as "Love in Bloom"?
Chas: I am. Yes.
Fred: Are you also familiar with Shubert's immortal masterpiece…The Bee.
Chas: Bee as in Benny?
Fred: No. That's what the whole argument is about. There is no Bee in that Party. It's Shubert's Bee.
Chas: Ach, yes! I know Shubert's Bee very well.
Fred: Good. Now, in your expert estimation, Professor, how long would it take an alleged violinst who today can barely play "Love in Bloom" to render Shubert's Bee?
Chas: Speaking as an expert I would say…Three times as long.
Fred: In other words. If a man was thirty-five today and could barely play "Love in Bloom". By the time he could play The Bee…
Chas: He would be three times as old.
Fred: He's be 105.
Chas: To the day.
Fred: Thank you, Professor. That concludes my argument, ladies and gentlemen. Mr. Myrt Plum, the insurance expert says:
John: This man will live to be 104 years and 6 months of age.
Fred: Professor Gustave Strad says:
Chas: He will never play the Bee until he is 105.
Fred: So you see, ladies and gentlemen, statistics prove that Mr. J.B. will never play the Bee. He will be gone six months before he even masters the entire number. I thank you!

January 31, 1937: The Jell-O Program. Jack wants Phil to add 30 guys to his orchestra to accompany him when playing The Bee next week. Jack falls asleep and dreams of shooting Fred Allen.

Everything You Ever Wanted to Know About Dr. David Reuben and Jack Benny But Were Afraid to Ask

On March 8th, I had the pleasure of interviewing Dr. David Reuben, author of <u>Everything You Ever Wanted to Know about Sex But Were Afraid to Ask</u>, in the IJBFC chat room. Happily, the special <u>Everything You Ever Wanted to Know About Jack Benny But Were Afraid to Ask</u> had just been added to our video library. Little did I know that Dr. Reuben's appearance on that special had sparked such a warm friendship between the two men.

(DR = David Reuben, LL = Laura Leff
This interview is copyright 2005 by Garland Resources, Inc. and published with permission.)

DR: Good evening! This is Dr. Reuben.

LL: Good evening! How are you doing this evening?

DR: Fine....and you?

LL: I'm doing very well. It's a beautiful spring day here in California...So to begin at the beginning, were you and your family Jack Benny fans before you met him?

DR: LIKE EVERYONE ELSE IN THE USA WE LISTENED TO JACK EVERY SUNDAY NIGHT AT 6 PM AND IT WAS IN WAUKEGAN...OF ALL PLACES.

LL: You're from Waukegan?

DR: I LIVED THERE WHEN I WAS GROWING UP...LIKE JACK BUT I DIDNT KNOW HIM THEN OF COURSE.

LL: Of course. The city put up a statue of Jack downtown back in 2002.

DR: AND NAMED A JUNIOR HIGH SCHOOL AFTER HIM...HE TOLD ME ALL ABOUT IT...BUT IN THOSE DAYS WAUKEGAN WAS LIKE THE TYPICAL AMERICAN TOWN IN THE MOVIES TREE LINED STREETS AND SMALL TOWN ATMOSPHERE...

LL: Were you there when Jack debuted "Man About Town" there in 1939? Or do you recall any of Jack's visits to the area?

DR: NO..I GREW UP AND MOVED AWAY AND JACK WAS ABOUT 20 YEARS OLDER THAN I WAS AT LEAST... I LIVED WITH MY AUNT AND UNCLE THERE ...BUT LET'S GO ON TO THE SPECIAL WHICH IS MORE INTERESTING I THINK

LL: OK, please do. How were you first approached about the name of the special?

DR: IRVING FEIN, JACK'S AGENT, GOT IN TOUCH WITH MY AGENT AND ASKED ABOUT DOING A SPECIAL WITH THE NAME OF MY BOOK ADAPTED. THAT GREW INTO ME APPEARING ON THE SHOW AND IT WAS AN AMAZING WEEK, BELIEVE ME...THE CAST WAS A LOT OF JACK'S OLD FRIENDS, INCLUDING PHIL HARRIS AND ALICE FAYE AND OF COURSE, GEORGE BURNS... JACK AND GEORGE WENT BACK A LONG WAY...

LL: Yes, a lot of legends there! Phil, Lucy, George Burns, John Wayne... Jack and George met back in vaudeville in the early 1920s. You even got to do a bit of schtick with Jack and Phil.

DR: WELL, I WOLDN'T CALL IT SCHTICK EXACTLY...JACK INSISTED THAT MY PART WAS STRAIGHTFORWARD AND DIGNIFIED...JACK WAS ONE OF THE MOST CONSIDERATE PEOPLE I EVER KNEW...HE WAS GENTLE AND POLITE AND A PERFECT GENTLEMEN...A LOT OF THE SHOW BIZ TYPES ARE ACTORS...THEY HAVE ONE PERSONA ONSTAGE AND ANOTHER QUITE DIFFERENT OFF...BUT JACK WAS GENUINE AND WE HIT IT OFF FROM THE FIRST MOMENT.

LL: Did he give you any coaching on delivering your lines?

DR: HE HELPED ME WITH MY LINES AND MADE EVERYTHING EASY FOR ME...REMEMBER I WAS EXPERIENCED BUT JACK MADE IT A PLEASURE. AND OF COURSE IT WAS JOHN WAYNE WHO SURPRISED ME. HE HAD THE IMAGE OF A TOUGH GUY....BUT DURING THE FIRST RUN THROUGH I DIDN'T GET MY LINES EXACTLY RIGHT AND JOHN STEPPED OUT OF THE SHADOWS AND PUT HIS HAND ON MY SHOULDER GENTLY AND SAID, "DOCTOR, IT'S EASY. JUST SAY IT LIKE THIS." AND JACK NODDED HIS APPROVAL.

LL: Were you using cue cards or memorized?

DR: I NEVER USE CUE CARDS....IF I CAN'T REMEMBER MY LINES HOW CAN I REMEMBER MY PATIENTS PROBLEMS?

LL: LOL...got it! Did you get to interact with Lucille Ball at all?

DR: YOU KNOW, THAT'S FUNNY. I DONT REMEMBER SEEING LUCILLE THEN ALTHOUGH I MET HER LATER ON...I MET ALMOST EVERYONE IN SHOW BIZ SOONER OR LATER.

LL: How was it working with Jack and Phil? Phil was first on Jack's show back in 1936, so they knew each other's styles very well. The bit they did about "That's What I Like About the South" was done almost verbatim about 30 years earlier on the radio show.

DR: PHIL WAS THE SAME AS USUAL...EASY GOING FRIENDLY AND ENJOYING BEING WITH JACK. IT'S HARD TO DESCRIBE THE WARMTH AND FRIENDLINESS OF JACK...

LL: Was he still in relatively strong health at that time? I've heard people say that offstage he could seem a bit fragile, but then turn it on in front of the audience.

DR: I DIDN'T SEE HIM THAT WAY...WE USED TO GO LUNCH TOGETHER AND HE VISITED ME IN SAN DIEGO...HE DROVE HIS OWN STATION WAGON...HE CALLED ME 3 DAYS BEFORE HE DIED AND SAID, "DAVID, I'M JUST NOT FEELING VERY WELL." AND THAT WAS THE LAST TIME I TALKED TO HIM.

LL: I didn't know Jack had a station wagon...he seemed more like the Cadillac convertible type. Except for the Maxwell, of course.

DR: REMEMBER THE FAMOUS CARICATURE OF JACK...THE ONE THEY USED AS BACKDROP FOR SOME OF HIS SHOWS?

LL: Right...the Rene Bouche drawing. They had several of them in the opening monologue.

DR: WELL, HE HAD JUST A FEW SOLID GOLD MONEY CLIPS MADE WITH THE DRAWING ENGRAVED ON IT...HE GAVE ONE TO DENNIS, TO PHIL, TO DON WILSON, AND PEOPLE LIKE THAT...AND HE GAVE ONE TO ME....OF COURSE I STILL HAVE IT.

LL: The gold money clips...were they holiday presents? I've seen a couple of those, one he gave to Bob Hope.

DR: THAT'S RIGHT...PEOPLE LIKE HOPE AND GEORGE BURNS...THE ONES THAT WERE CLOSEST TO HIM. NO IT WASN'T A HOLIDAY PRESENT...JUST JACK SAID ONE DAY, "DAVID, I'D LIKE YOU TO HAVE THIS."

LL: Wow...what a compliment. You must have felt great.

DR: IT WAS A NOBLE GESTURE AND I CERTAINLY FELT HONORED. I HAVE HAD THAT KIND OF KINSHIP WITH MAYBE 5 PEOPLE IN MY LIFE AND THAT KIND OF INSTANT BOND THAT IS SO RARE. AND THAT'S THE WAY IT WAS WITH JACK.

LL: Tell me about lunch with Jack. What did you talk about? Where did you go?

DR: IT WAS JUST A LUNCH BETWEEN FRIENDS...WE TALKED ABOUT FAMILY AND LIFE AND OLD TIMES...ALTHOUGH I MET JACK LATE, IT WAS AS IF WE HAD KNOWN EACH OTHER FOR YEARS.

LL: Did Jack talk about the symphony orchestra dates that he was doing then?

DR: NOT REALLY. WE NEVER ACTUALLY TALKED SHOP. OF ALL THE PEOPLE IN SHOW BIZ, I NEVER TALKED ABOUT PERFORMING WITH ANY OF THEM EXCEPT THE ONES WHO WERE MY PATIENTS, OF COURSE..

LL: Did Jack talk about his family much? Mary, Joan, and the grandkids?

DR: NOPE...A WORD OR TWO ABOUT MARY SOMETIMES...BUT NOTHING MUCH...MOST OF OUR CONVERSATIONS WERE JUST ABOUT SHOW BIZ IN

GENERAL AND COMMENTS ABOUT PEOPLE WE KNEW. THE KIND OF TALK YOU HAVE WITH OLD FRIENDS...JACK WAS NOT A GOSSIP AND I NEVER HEARD HIM SAY AND UNKIND WORD ABOUT ANYONE.

LL: Per your comment about Jack not being a gossip...Isaac Stern said the same thing, that it was so remarkable that Jack was in this gossip-ridden industry and yet he never talked badly of anyone. Back to that opening bit with Jack and Phil...they both play up the aspect of wanting to "talk with you about the book...you know...later...it's kind of personal..." Was that fairly characteristic of how people would approach you about the book?

DR: ARE YOU KIDDING? ALMOST NOBODY EVER WANTED TO APPROACH ME ABOUT THE BOOK...WHAT CAN YOU SAY TO THE AUTHOR OF A BOOK ON SEX?

LL: True...I guess since it was yet three years after the Summer of Love, I didn't know how comfortable people were with the topic yet.

DR: JACK WAS FIRST CLASS...AS I SAID, HE WAS REAL GENTLEMAN...NOT JUST PRETENDING TO BE ONE WHEN HE WAS ONSTAGE. NO BAD LANGUAGE, NEVER VULGAR.

LL: Even Jack in his opening monologue spells it out S-E-X.

DR: THAT'S RIGHT.

LL: Did you spend any time with Jack and George Burns? There are so many stories of Jack falling on the floor laughing with him.

DR: I SPENT A COUPLE OF DAYS WITH JACK AND GEORGE AND THEY HAD A KIND OF CHEMISTRY TOGETHER. BUT THEN THEY HAD KNOWN EACH FOR DECADES...

LL: What else happened during the week of filming? Any standout memories?

DR: IT WAS REALLY AND AMAZING EXPERIENCE...BETWEEN TAKES THE WRITES INVITED ME UP TO THE CONTROL BOOTH AND IT WAS AMAZING. THEY WERE ALL LIKE ONE BIG FAMILY WITH A TREMENDOUS AMOUNT OF RESPECT FOR JACK.

LL: I haven't looked at the end credits yet...who was working on it? Hal Goldman and Al Gordon and George Balzer, I'd imagine.

DR: I ESPECIALLY REMEMBER HAL...NICE FELLOW AND VERY SMART.

LL: Side note on Hal...I just transferred a Smothers Brothers Comedy Hour with Jack and George today, and noticed that Hal and Al were writing their show too. Were the writers continually refreshing the script, or did it stay fairly steady?

DR: IT SEEMED VERY PROFESSIONAL AND RAN SMOOTHER THAN ANY OTHER SHOW I HAD DONE...AND THE ATMOSPHERE WAS DIFFERENT...DIGNIFIED, NO TEMPERAMENT, EVERYONE RIGHT ON THE BEAM...THAT WAS BECAUSE OF JACK...THERE WAS NONE OF THE USUAL TENSION OR PRESSURE THAT YOU SEE ON SPECIALS.

LL: Pressure for performance, or tension because of personalities?

DR: MOST OF THE SHOWS I HAVE DONE...AND THERE HAVE BEEN PLENTY...HAVE AT LEAST SOME OF BOTH....BUT WITH JACK IT WAS LIKE A BUNCH OF OLD FRIENDS GETTING TOGETHER...AND I WAS HONORED TO BE AMONG THEM. YOU CAN'T IMAGINE HOW GRATIFYING IT IS TO WORK WITH ONE OF THE GREATS... AND EVERYONE WANTED TO PLEASE HIM BECAUSE HE WAS SUCH A GOOD PERSON. I HAVE NEVER HEARD ANYONE SAY ANYTHING BAD ABOUT JACK...

LL: I've been interviewing people for 20 years about Jack, and the obvious love that so many people had for him is just amazing. You can just say his name and watch people light up. One interviewee actually broke into tears because he missed Jack so much.

DR: WELL, I CAN TELL YOU THIS. AFTER KNOWING WAUKEGAN THE WAY WE LIVED THERE...REALLY A WONDERFUL TYPICAL AMERICAN SMALL TOWN TREE-LINED STREETS, WHITE CLAPBOARD HOUSES, AND ALL THE REST...TO FINALLY MEET JACK FORM THE SAME TOWN AND WORK WITH HIM WAS TRULY A WONDERFUL EXPERIENCE.

LL: Someone said that Jack always kept a little of Waukegan inside of him.

DR: THAT'S TRUE ABOUT WAUKEGAN....WARM, FRIENDLY, EASY GOING....TYPICAL OF THE BEST AMERICAN TRADITIONS...I KNOW WHAT YOU MEAN...WHEN JACK DIED, I FELT THAT I LOST MY BEST FRIEND...EVEN MORE, A MEMBER OF MY FAMILY.

LL: Were you able to attend the funeral?

DR: NO I DON'T GO TO FUNERALS BECAUSE THE PEOPLE WHO DIED ARE NEVER THERE.

LL: Very well said. Thank you so much for sharing your time and memories. I really appreciate it, and I know our members will too.

DR: IT'S MY PLEASURE...AND I FEEL I OWE IT TO JACK'S MEMORY. AND TO ALL THE FOLKS OUT THERE WHO LOVE HIM AS MUCH AS I DO....JACK LEFT US ALL SOMETHING THAT CAN NEVER BE LOST...A WONDERFUL WISTFUL LOOK AT THE WORLD WE LIVED IN...AND A DELIGHTFUL KIND OF OPTIMISM AND INSIGHT THAT BRIGHTENS EVERYONE'S LIFE....GOODBYE JACK, WE LOVE YOU AND WE MISS YOU...

LL: Yes...we ALL do.

DR: GOOD NIGHT LAURA...AND GOODNIGHT JACK...

Capt. Andrew G. Burt (Photo Officer), Benay Venuta, Jack, and S/Sgt. Ralph Pyle

The Jack Benny Times

September - December 2005 Volume XX, Numbers 5-6

1912 Publicity portrait of Salisbury and Benny – Jack's first vaudeville partner

President's Message

Jell-O again folks...as most of you know by now, it's been a rough few months for me health-wise. Between pneumonia in June and unexpected major surgery a couple weeks ago (early August), I am learning what I am made of in fighting these challenges. Thanks so much to everyone who has sent E-mails, cards, and similar well-wishes. I know that they help, and I am happy to say that I'm on the road to recovery. Having to focus my physical activities on sitting in my recliner and concentrating on healing still gives me time for doing computer-based things like this newsletter (and happily I have a strong, handsome husband to haul up the crate of results when the printers are done with it). However, I am still on pain medication...so if anything in the newsletter suddenly becomes incoherent, I apologize!

I am pleased to say that there has been a good amount of activity in the video library over the past few months, and I have gotten many positive remarks from members on our "Special Collections" of the television series. For a full listing of the video library holdings and how to get them, go to www.jackbenny.org and click on Programs, then Video Library.

39 Forever, Second Edition Volume 1 is still available for $40 and selling well. Over 500 pages of detailed information on Jack's radio shows from 1932 to 1942...you're sure to find something you never knew about the program. Make your check or money order payable to IJBFC and mail it to the address at the end of this newsletter.

New Members

**** Marc E. Juarez **** Scott Wallace Brown **** John W. Ray **** James Smeaton **** Kevin Conley **** Stan Shabaz **** Patrick F. Radke **** Steve Wilson **** Rick Bruno **** Harris Neil **** Thomas Osborne **** Martha M Babcock **** Mr. & Mrs. William G. Earle **** Robert Butler **** Josh Loranz **** P. Suffolk **** Craig Shemin **** Lorene Bryant Epps **** James Pantano **** Bernard Hohman **** Jack Helms **** Gregory j. Wilkin **** Chris Riesbeck **** James Shokoff **** Matt Miller **** Nick Goodspeed **** Holland MacFallister **** Steve Wilczynski **** Gary Wedge **** Thomas Kuzmarskis **** Apurva N. Gokal **** Alan Morgan **** Desma Droze **** Marc Sosnick **** Sarah Marie **** David Gustafson **** James Miller **** Jim Pykonen **** Clara Dugas **** Caroline Nickel **** Alan Feldman **** Mike Kurtenbach **** Jerry Juneau **** Steve Franklin **** Mark McCulloch **** Jim Ethington **** Michael Kazer **** John Franklin **** Victor Blecker **** Mark Nolen **** John H. Gillette **** Eryn Tormos **** Ilana Rugg **** Thomas Pawlak **** James Williams **** C. H. Hutchison **** Curtis E. Conklin **** Dan Higgins **** Tim Holt **** Greg Davis **** Russ Crowell **** Elizabeth Rinaca **** John Roman **** Rick Ostopowicz **** Darrell G. Carlisle **** Mark Jordan **** Donnie Nourie **** Amy Saunders **** Phil Hutchison **** Laural Levine **** Russell Graves **** Carl Rickards **** Joshua Chitty **** Cheree Rafferty **** Jim Rawls **** Scott Kriefall **** Mike Underwood **** David Martin **** Michael Clahr **** John Beloin **** Walt Staves **** Eddie White **** Robert Casteel **** Blayne Mayfield **** David Wilson **** Kenneth and Ursula Field **** Silvestre Segarra Soler **** John Tyler **** Tom Coyle **** Joseph Costanzo **** Lisa Glomb **** Bob Baumann **** Chuck Butkus **** Kara Bobo **** Howard Shaughnessy **** Steve Schier **** Noel Farmer **** Harry V. Jones **** Cecil West **** David Watson **** Elizabeth George **** Mark E. Billings ****

Bruce Klayman **** Jeffery Robert **** Marilyn R. Williams **** Marc Milzman **** Danny M. Sides **** Dennis Millard **** Dale Johnston **** Jonathan Smith **** Bill Ludwig **** Denis O'Leary **** Tom McQuade **** Steven Springer **** Andrew Mesulam **** Heidi Bishop **** Zachary Wayne McCammond **** Bill Robinson **** Amber D. Oles **** Bill and Anne Thompson

Jack Bloom Pasadena Chapter

The Jack Bloom Pasadena Chapter was started in 1990 as an honorary society for IJBFC members who have been active for four or more consecutive years. Jack Bloom was a dedicated member of the IJBFC, doing extensive research for the Times and the original edition of 39 Forever, plus donating hundreds of shows to kick off the IJBFC tape library. Additionally, Jack and I kept a running correspondence for years, discussing Jack Benny and other shared passions, ranging from George Gershwin to bird watching to bad puns. His passing in June of 1990 was a tremendous loss for all the IJBFC members. I still miss him, and am grateful for the warmth and humor that he shared with me.

(Members added or promoted this year are indicated by an asterisk.)

Melanie Aultman*
Michael Avedissian
Louis Bianco
Eric Brolund*
James G. Burke
C.A. Caramella
Joe Caramella
Cindy Chesser*
The Chinellos
Kim Cunningham*
Warren Debenham
Lois Dicker*
Anthony DiFlorio
Matthew M. Drew
Ray Druian*
Gerald Eskin*
J.E. Farst
Kenneth Flowers*
Sol Fox*

Robert L. Garland
Hillel M. Ginton*
Joe Goff
Nathan Gordon*
Scott F. Greene*
Bryan Haigood
Jon Heinz
Franklin Heynemann
Jimmie Hicks
H.K. Hinkley*
David Howell
Ed Howell*
Charles Huck
Thomas Kessel
Nik Kierniesky
Kenneth Koftan
Michael A. Langer*
James A. Link

Stephen H. Loeb
Howard Mandelbaum
Lon McCartt
Steve Metzger
Kenneth Miller
Glenn E. Mueller*
Russell Myers
Charles Niren*
Betty O'Brien*
George D. Paddock*
Teresa Perry
William Powers, Jr.*
Chris Reale
Mark Reesor*
Richard Rieve
The Robertses
William Rompala
A. Joseph Ross

Richard Ross
Joel S. Rothman
Richard Rubenstein
Bob Rutishauser
Rick Scheckman*
Clair Schulz
Gary Smith*
Scott J. Smith
W. Robert Smith
Helen Songer
Gus Storm
Barbara Thunell
Michelle Varteresian*
Lynn Wagar*
Harvey Walker
Susie Walker
David L. Williams*
Brad Zinn*

Emeritus Members (15+ years)

Hal Bogart
Bob Burns*
Dayton Crandall*
Robert Duncan
J. Ed Galloway
Alan Grossman
Tim Hollis

David Howell*
Will Jordan*
Glenn Laxton
Bobb Lynes
Tom Mastel
Walt Mitchell*

Robert Olsen
Jack Palmer*
Donnie Pitchford
Joyce Shooks*
Mel Simons*
Jeanette Thomas*

The Tintorris
Larry Valley*
Mary Lou Wallace*
Barbara Watkins
Tom Williams*
Doug Wood

What's Up in Waukegan?

In early June I had the pleasure of visiting the Waukegan area again. I arrived on Memorial Day and drove up into Wisconsin to visit the graves of a couple people who had been close to Jack. The first was Julius Sinykin (1883-1961), whom regular Times subscribers will know as a friend of Jack's since childhood and one of his early mentors. Julius is buried in Madison, WI at Forest Hill Cemetery. He is next to his brother, Sam, and sister-in-law Dora, and just behind his nephew Gordon who was an excellent writer and right-hand man for General Douglas MacArthur.

I also visited the grave of Louise Sinykin Hansen (1905-1981) nearer to Milwaukee, as she was a one-time fiancée of Jack's in the early 20s (before Mary Kelly). Louise is the daughter of Sam and Dora. I am told that when she and Jack were engaged, there was concern from multiple family members (including her Uncle Julius) that Jack would never make something of himself (he was not yet the vaudeville headliner, but was touring on the Orpheum circuit). So Louise broke off the engagement and later married Ray Hansen, a pharmacist in the Milwaukee area. She herself later worked for the State of Wisconsin. I left roses for both Julius and Louise.

In Waukegan the following morning, the cemetery tour continued with something towards which I have been working for some time. A group of folks gathered at Am Echod Cemetery to unveil a stone for Florence Fenchel, Jack's sister. Florence passed away in 1977, and with no children or immediate

family to follow up, there was never a stone placed on her grave. Florence's grave is between her (and, of course, Jack's) parents, Meyer and Naomi/Emma Kubelsky, and her husband, Leonard Fenchel. I first discovered this gap myself when visiting Waukegan in 2002. Rabbi Ze'ev Harari of Am Echod Synagogue said the service, and many synagogue elders attended and shared their memories of Florence and Jack. IJBFC members Joel Rothman and his family were also in attendance. Many thanks to the Benny family and everyone who helped put things right for Florence.

Then on to the Uptown Café where the Specialty of the House is the Jack Benny sandwich, a wonderful concoction originally recalled by IJBFC U.K. member Dr. Ken Miller based on his memory of the Benny sandwich at Lindy's Restaurant in New York. And finally to the Jack Benny Center for the Arts in Bowen Park, where an Autumn Blaze Maple stood ready to take its place as the new Jack Benny Tree in Waukegan. Waukegan Mayor Richard Hyde, Chuck Wilms of Senator Terry Link's staff, and several local notables and citizens turned out for the planting. The tree was donated by

Ken Erickson of Lionel & Aurelio Landscape, and we extend our thanks to him, as well as to the City of Waukegan and the Waukegan Parks District.

Do You Know?

I have received an inquiry from the daughter of James Melton, a radio, recording and opera star from the mid 1920s to the mid 50s. He appeared on Jack Benny's radio program from March to June of 1933. She is looking for any articles relating to his career and/or personal anecdotes of interest to help with a book about her father. She would appreciate any information that you may be able to provide. Contact her at: Margo Melton Nutt, margo.nutt@dartmouth.edu.

Bob Simmons is trying to identify the women in this picture in the front seat of the jeep. His father is the first man on the left, and says it was taken in North Africa or Egypt when the Benny troupe was on tour there. I have made guesses based on the women in the tour, but can anyone make a conclusive statement about them? Contact him at:

ashdownbob@yahoo.com.

Jim Hilliker writes:
"I was reading a story about a weather forecaster/ broadcaster on KFI radio in L.A. in the 1930s to about 1956, who gave citrus growers the nightly frost warning weather reports every winter. Apparently he read the temperature, dewpoint and cities, such as Anaheim, Azusa, and Cucamonga (yes, very true, all orange growing areas back then) in a monotone voice style. Uninteresting to most, except the farmers.

"Well, a Pomona newspaper story suggested that according to this man, Floyd D. Young of the U.S. Weather Bureau office in Pomona, the train conductor in the Jack Benny bits where the train was leaving for those three small towns, was based on this man's voice. Have you ever heard that bit of information before? Maybe the Benny writers heard this guy's voice and got Mel Blanc to deliver the line that way?"

Laurie Platt asks if anyone knows where Mary Kelly is buried. She died on June 7, 1941 in Los Angeles. I'd like to know that one myself, so please send information to jackbenny@aol.com.

Jim Cox says that he has discovered notes indicating that Andre Baruch was an announcer for Jack Benny. I am sure that he wasn't before Don joined, but there is always the possibility that he worked with him in later years on something other than the regular show. If you can provide more details, please E-mail me at jackbenny@aol.com.

You Do Know!

In our last issue, one of Ralph Pyle's Korea pictures included a woman playing the accordion. Here's another picture of her that was taken by the father-in-law of Darrell Carlisle, when he was a soldier in Korea. I'm happy to say that as the result of my recent research trip to Laramie, I have found her name to be June Brunner. The show was called the Carnival of Stars, and ran from July 2 to 20, 1951, and then went on to Japan for four additional shows at military hospitals. The full troupe included: Errol Flynn, singer Benay Venuta, guitarist Frankie Remley, Marjorie Reynolds, Happy Kahne, dancer Dolores Gay, and Ms. Brunner on piano and accordion.

Jim Hilliker provided the following factoids on Don Wilson:

"I was always interested in Don because of his connection to Los Angeles radio, after he started in Denver, then moved to KFRC in San Francisco as part of The Piggly Wiggly Trio, and a year or so later moved to KHJ-Los Angeles as part of that trio. Don W. then became a staff announcer at KHJ, circa 1928, and by 1929-1930 was the chief announcer for KFI/KECA at Earle C. Anthony's two L.A. radio stations, where he stayed until he did more sports for NBC and then went to work for Jack. Seems like he also did a lot of announcing, possibly free-lance for NBC and other shows or special broadcasts.

"I have a 1930 Radio Doings magazine with a younger-looking Don pictured in a tux as one of the KECA announcers. Generally, KFI was part of the NBC Red Network and KECA was NBC Blue, and later was bought by the Blue Network in 1944, to become ABC and KABC in 1954. I have also heard a snippet or two of Don Wilson and Ken Carpenter co-hosting a special broadcast for the 20th Anniversary of KFI radio in 1942, which was very interesting to hear. On the special 60 or 65th Anniversary DVD of Disney's 'Snow White and the Seven Dwarfs', they included the one-hour 1937 premiere of Snow White on NBC from Hollywood. Don was the MC, and he did an excellent job on that program."

The Tale Piece

From Genaro Gomez:

"I danced in [The Jack Benny Program of 2/12/63 with Rita Moreno as a guest star] where Dennis Day was a bullfighter and Rita was divided in love with Jose Wrecko (Jack Benny) who was a flamenco dancer and the bullfighter. We had a hilarious time, like the time when he said, 'Genaro, you got muscle but I'm gonna show you what muscle looks like.' Then he raised his pants sleeves and showed his legs and we all had fits. He was so funny that I can't explain all his humor, because he said everything so seriously that you thought he meant whatever he would say. I believe that they used that part in the show. A lot of the things in that show were improvised and then they would use them. The director [Fred deCordova] almost couldn't direct because he was always laughing at everything that Mr. Benny would do. You see, it was kind of difficult to direct him because he came out with more comical ideas that were not in the script. Anyway, the important thing is that it was done and that we had a splendid time."
[Note: This show is available in our video library.]

From Fred Essex (reprinted from Sperdvac Radiogram with permission from Patrick Lucanio):

"Frank Sinatra starred on The Hit Parade produced by the FCB Ad Agency for Lucky Strikes. Our Agency had the Jack Benny Show, also sponsored by Luckies, and one night the Benny script called for him to *turn on his radio* and hear Frank. Benny originated in Hollywood and Sinatra from New York, so I was assigned to direct the cut-in segment from NBC in Radio City.

"With 40 musicians in Studio 6B, Frank was to sing *All the Things You Are*. Earlier we had rehearsed the dialogue over the phone from his suite in the Waldorf Towers and all was well—up to that point.

"In the studio about an hour before air time the rehearsal was going smoothly, the balance with the orchestra was great and Frank was in fine voice. Then immediate chaos! The last musical phrase had him singing '*All the Things You Are, Are Mine*' in ascending notation. As he reached the higher notes, his voice began to buzz and sizzle. 'Can we have the last four bars once more?' I asked from the Control Room. Frank turned to the conductor, 'The man wants it again.' True professional, no temperament.

"But after the third try, with the clock ticking closer and closer to air time and with no resolution in sight, the engineer, after trying everything else, decided to change the ribbon mike. Voila, it worked and the broadcast went on without a hitch with little time to spare.

"Later we discovered the first mike has been used on *Truth or Consequences* and had been beaten up."

From Ryan Schroer:

"Just reading a book about the 1970's Oakland A's and something I read made me think of you. It seems that before Game 6 of '73 Series between the A's and Mets, Jack threw out the first ball. After he threw the ball out, he asked to have it back!"

An excerpt from a Playboy interview with Albert Brooks:

"Harry Shearer and I went to [Jack Benny's] office on a Monday and he died on Thursday. He had stomach cancer, but we didn't know he was that far gone. We had been working on my album, A Star Is Bought, on which every cut was a different genre of radio. The idea was to have airplay on every conceivable kind of station. One was an old-time radio show and we wanted Jack Benny to be in it. Between Harry and me, there were no two people our age on the planet who idolized a person more. So I said, 'Mr. Benny, we're doing this album and we're recreating this old radio—'

"I never got any further. He said, 'Radio! That's all they remember me for! I've done everything! I've done movies! I've done television!' We're thinking, 'Oh my God . . . oh no, please don't be like this.' I said, 'Mr. Benny, I only know you from television! I just knew you did radio. Believe me, I know you did everything.' I swear to God, I walked out of there thinking, What's the point? How do you win at this game? If Jack Benny feels like this four days before he checks out, how do you win? If anybody had the right to be calm and peaceful with his own career, it was Jack Benny."

[Note: Seeing Jack at the office on the Monday—December 23—immediately before his passing is highly unlikely. On December 18, Jack had a conference at his home about the upcoming special, but couldn't get through it because of his medication. He was diagnosed with pancreatic cancer on December 20, and the doctors kept Jack heavily sedated from then until the end. But it's possible that it might have been the previous week.]

A <u>Los Angeles Times</u> excerpt from Jim Hilliker:

"The relocation of Los Angeles' first radio station, KNX-AM (1070), to new studios in Wilshire Boulevard's Miracle Mile area will end an 85-year tradition of radio broadcasting in the place that bills itself as the world's center of entertainment. Over the years, Hollywood has been home to 68 radio stations and nine television stations. In the last few years, five television stations have left. And when Columbia Square is shut down next year, two more — KCBS-TV Channel 2 and KCAL-TV Channel 9 — will move to new headquarters being built in Studio City. That will leave just two television stations, KTLA-TV Channel 5 and KCET-TV Channel 28, in Tinseltown.

"After KCBS and KCAL depart, the Streamline Moderne building at 6121 Sunset Blvd. is expected to be demolished to make way for new development."

KNX was the originating studio for Jack's Hollywood CBS broadcasts. Sad to see it go.

Etcetera

A member (who will go unnamed unless he wants to be revealed) forwarded me a photo of a current top fashion model named Tatiana Fanego. Tatiana has a tattoo on…well…she has a prominent tattoo of the Lucky Strike logo. I'd suggest that any interested parties type her name into Google to find photos that show it. You'll know it when you find it…can't miss it. No, you won't have to go to any adult sites to see it. And for those in the know…I'm still trying to find out if it says "Means Fine Tobacco" on the other side.

Another member shared the amazing autographs at left. They almost certainly date from between March and June of 1933, as that was the time when Frank Black, Howard Claney, and James

Melton were all on the Benny program. It is difficult to date it more specifically that this, as I cannot place the other three names in any of the cast listings from shows of that time. Possibly they were crew or sound effects personnel. He pointed out that Mary was signing her autographs sans the ending "e" on Livingston, and this reflects the spelling in the scripts of that time as well.

Member Brad Zinn noticed that Time-Life has recently released a DVD of Benny television shows. These include some of the often-found public domain shows, but this one also includes the television program with Groucho Marx as a guest and a hilarious send-up of "You Bet Your Life", reminiscent in some ways of Jack and Fred Allen doing "King for a Day". This DVD has also been offered through the Publisher's Clearing House Sweepstakes, so let's hope that may inspire some folks to order the disc and discover Jack's humor.

From Gordon Rebelato:

"I thought you would find this photo interesting. I don't know if you have seen this photo before. My mom had it for years in her photo album. It was a photo taken in Vancouver, I was told when Jack did his radio show up here in 1944. It is of Jack and Mary taken in front of the White Spot Restaurant, Granville Street, Vancouver. The restaurant burnt down about 10-15 years ago. It was unfortunate as it was a Vancouver landmark. There is a picture of it on the White Spot web page. Not the best picture but it gives you an idea of what it looked like."
http://www.whitespot.ca/whitespot/historyexpansion.htm

TCM recently aired the cartoon Bacall to Arms (pictured left) after To Have and Have Not. At the end of the cartoon, there's a bit where Bogey Go-Cart shoots the Tex Avery-ish wolf over the sexy Laurie Becool's cigarette butt, only to have the cigarette blow up in Bogey's face. Then in a Rochester voice he says, "My, my…I can work for Mr. Benny now!" Apparently this bit had been excised at some point in the past due to perceptions of racism. Happily, the TCM version was complete and unedited.

Collector's Choice Music has released a DVD entitled "The Best of Mel Blanc: Man of 1000 Voices". It contains 25 tracks of material ranging from stuff tightly coupled with his Warner Brothers' work to "Yah Dis Ist Ein Christmas Tree" which graced our Web page during the last holiday season. It also includes "Woody Woodpecker", but I don't know if it's the same recording that was done with the Sportsmen Quartet. To see the full playlist and purchase your copy, go to http://www.ccmusic.com/item.cfm?itemid=CCM05932

Fred Allen's Side of the Feud

This is a continuation from the previous Times issue of the script transcriptions from the Fred Allen shows during the start of the Benny-Allen Feud in 1937. Many thanks to the folks at the Boston Public Library Special Collections, where Fred's scripts are housed. Punctuation and spelling is verbatim from the scripts.

February 3, 1937 – Town Hall Tonight

	(KNOCK AT DOOR)
ALLEN:	Come in.
	(DOOR OPENS)
ALLEN:	Well, what is it?
HARRY:	[likely BALDWIN] I want to take this opportunity of wishing you and your company a very very Happy New Year.
ALLEN:	Listen. This isn't Jack Benny's program.
HARRY:	So. I made a mistake. Sue me!
	(DOOR SLAMS)
ALLEN:	How do you like that? I'm here minding my own business and in flies a dead duck and says Jack Benny.
PORT:	Are you still trying to get even with Jack, Mr. Allen?
ALLEN:	I'd like to get even with him on the Crossley.
PORT:	Gosh. This is the tamest feud I've ever seen. You two have been fighting four weeks and there's been no bloodshed.
ALLEN:	How can there be bloodshed when that guy's anemic?
PORT:	Oh. Jack Benny's twice as healthy as you are.
ALLEN:	He could be three times as healthy as I am and still be half dead.
PORT:	I don't think you should go around saying Jack's anemic.
ALLEN:	Any guy who goes out to a nightclub and has to get a transfusion before he goes to bed so that his eyes will be bloodshot in the morning is anemic.
PORT:	I don't believe it.
ALLEN:	Have you ever heard him play the violin.
PORT:	Once. Yes.

ALLEN: Once. That's all anybody ever hears him play. Did he blush when he finished playing.
PORT: No. He didn't.
ALLEN: Then he's anemic.
PORT: Oh .. boy! I'm going to write and tell Mary everything you've said!
ALLEN: Good. And don't put off till tomorrow what you can do right now.

(Later in the show)

ALLEN: Now, before presenting our next guest I would like to react to some verbal mayhem shunted at me, from Hollywood on Sunday last, by an itinerant vender of desserts. I won't mention this gelatine hawker's name at the moment. Suffice it should be to say he has a sideline, called by some, a radio program. On this program, last Sunday evening, this gentleman…and the word gentleman is used with intent to libel…this spoilsport fell asleep..fell asleep on his own program, mark you, making it unanimous..while he was asleep he had a dream…..during which….this defiler of the Stradivarius…..shot at me six times. That same night I ate a Welch rarebit and what I didn't do to him in my dream is nobody's business. All I said originally, ladies and gentlemen, was that Mr. Benny couldn't play the Bee on his violin. Last Sunday, he had a cold. Colds are caused through vitamin deficiency proving that Mr. Benny hasn't even got a Bee in his vitamins. Plied with aspirin, and reeking of menthol he swore that he would play the Bee on his program next week. This dire news has seeped into every nook and cranny of the country. What effect will this solo have on contemporary life in America. Mr. Kut Priceler, the eminent violinist says:
JOHN: [likely BROWN] If Jack Benny plays the Bee next Sunday, it will set the violin back 200 years.
ALLEN: Mrs. Anne Levee..wife of a tin can tourist says:
DOUG: My husband and me live in a trailer, our radio's in the car. If my husband turns that radio on next Sunday….I'm cuttin' the trailer loose…with me in it….and hopin for the best.
ALLEN: Mr. Lemuel Randypone….Southern Planter….Says….
CHAS: [likely CANTOR] If Benny plays his violin next Sunday the cotton crop is saved. The South will be all ears. And the ears will be stuffed with cotton.
ALLEN: Max Raucous….prominent union organizer….says:
HARRY: [possibly VON ZELL] If somebody can get this Benny to put his violin down on a chair before Sunday, will I start a sitdown strike, And How!
ALLEN: When these are but a few of the opinions voiced, during the week, ladies and gentlemen, it is small wonder we look forward to Sunday next with apprehension. Tonight…in order to stunt Mr. Benny's growth we have brought back to the microphone the young man who made this whole argument possible….Master Stewart Canin.

How are you tonight Stewart? [Note: no lines are scripted for Canin.]
Mind if I ask you a few questions?
On December 30th, 1936 did you appear on this program?
What musical composition did you play.
Fine. As you perhaps know, Stewart, your rendition of the Bee has caused a modicum of trouble.
Do you know Jack Benny?
Did you ever hear him play the violin?
How did his playing sound to you?
Well….Mr. Benny is in a spot Stewart. He is supposed to play the Bee next Sunday and I thought if we wanted to be fair about the whole thing you and I could explain to Mr. Benny — how he can manage it. You know….we can tell him how to hold the violin and everything. Now..you show me how to hold it and I'll tell Mr. Benny. Oh yes! The violin is held in the left hand, Mr. Benny. The little finger resting lightly on the first string. The round end of the violin sets back into the neck….a little over to your left….with just a dash of Adam's apple peeking around the corner. The bow…or crop….as you cowboys call it, Mr. Benny, is held in the right hand. Now….to play the violin what do you do Stewart? I see….you scratch the bow across the strings. Fine. And now that Mr. Benny knows how to hold the violin little ten year old Stewart Canin will show little thirty-five year old Mr. Benny how to play the Bee. All right, Stewart.
(VIOLIN SOLO)

ALLEN: Thank you, Stewart. That was "The Bee" Mr. Benny. And on Sunday next we wish you well.

February 7, 1937 – <u>The Jell-O Program</u> – Jack's violin is stolen.

February 10, 1937 – <u>Town Hall Tonight</u>

ALLEN: And now ladies and gentlemen….The Mighty Allen Art Players. Tonight…these stormy petrels preen their beaks and take a peck at the tail-feathers of that eminent bird-lover Jack Benny. Mr. Benny must love the bird or he would have thrown his violin away 20 years ago. Last Sunday Mr. Benny was supposed to play the Bee. He didn't. He won't. He can't. Down through the musical ages ladies and gentlemen, the Bennys have been a sixteen bar rest in the development and progress of music. Tonight we present a calvacade of showing their contributions to the world of music from the dawn of creation to the present day and even tomorrow. This little opus is called the Benny Hit and Miss Parade. Overture, Peter.

(ORCHESTRA..."LOVE IN BLOOM"...FADES.)
          (CURTAIN RISES)

ALLEN: In the beginning Adam and Eve lived serene and contented in the Garden of Eden. The birds of the air and the beasts of the field had been named, and Adam and Eve were the happiest pair on earth. One noon Adam came in from the fields.
          (DOOR CLOSES)

MIN: [assuredly PIOUS] Welcome home, Adam, my mate.

JOHN: [likely BROWN] Why isn't my lunch ready, Eve?

MIN: I've had a splitting headache, Adam. I couldn't prepare your snack.
          (KNOCK AT DOOR)

JOHN: Who is it?

CHAS: [likely CANTOR] (Hisses)

JOHN: It's that snake again. What do you want, Serpent?

CHAS: (OFF MIKE) Any apples today?

JOHN: For the last time, No!

MIN: I wish that serpent would leave us alone, Adam.

(FLUTE PLAYS...SCALE SLOWLY UP...OFF MIKE)

JOHN: Hark! What is that squealing, Eve?

MIN: A strange reed player is trespassing in the Garden. His piping has given me this headache.

{FLUTE PLAYS SCALE...DOWN}

JOHN: That music is atrocious. I shall throw something at him.

MIN: There is nothing in our hut to throw, Adam, my husband.

JOHN: Then I shall get something.
          (DOOR OPENS)

JOHN: Hey, Snake!

CHAS: (HISS) Yes, Adam!

JOHN: Give me one of those apples.

CHAS: (HISS) At last! Here you are.

(FLUTE PLAYS SCALE UP)

JOHN: If my aim is good, I'll teach yonder reed pest a permanent lesson.

MIN: Throw straight, Adam.

JOHN: Take this, pest.

(FLUTE PLAYS HIGH NOTE)

JOHN: A bulls-eye. See Eve! He runs from the Garden.

CHAS: (HISS) And now you, too, will run from the Garden, Adam and Eve.

MIN: Adam and I will run, Serpent?

CHAS: Yes. When Adam took that apple it broke your lease.

JOHN: You brought this reed player to the Garden of Eden to trick us Serpent.

CHAS: Yes. Pick up your figs and leave.

MIN: Before we go, Serpent, what was that reed player's name?

CHAS: Beelzebub Benny!

(TO BE CONTINUED…)

Frank Nelson: The YEEEEESSSS Man

The beginning of this interview was published in the third 2001 issue, but I'm reprinting it here for easy reference and completeness. Frank was the first formal interview that I ever did for the IJBFC (back in 1984), and I had just never gotten around to publishing it. Frank passed away in 1986, but it's wonderful to have his memories recorded and to still be able to release previously unpublished material almost 20 years after his passing. Frank, I hope you and Veola are doing well, wherever you are.

L: How did you get your start in radio?

F: Well, I actually started at KOA in Denver, Colorado while I was still in high school, and the way that happened, somebody said, "They're having an audition out at KOA. Why don't you go out and see if you can get something?" I was doing nothing except amateur theatricals in school, and doing a few things with various clubs and little theatre organizations in Denver. So I went out and walked in, and this gentleman looked at me and said, "What are you here for?" I said, "Well, I understood you were having some kind of an audition for some kind of a series you were going to do." And he said, "Oh, good Lord…this is a man who's 35 years of age and he's married to a lady who is about 30, and it's their adventures and we're going to do it for a bank in Denver." And I said, "Oh," and I started to leave. And he said, "Wait a minute, have you ever read on a microphone before?" And I said, "No, no, I haven't." And he said, "Well you made a long trip out here," because KOA at that time was out on the edge of Denver, and he said, "Maybe you like to just stay and read just, you know, to see how your voice sounds over the radio." And I said, "Well, yeah, sure, why not?" So I read that day with about 30 other gentlemen, and the next day they called back 12 of us, the next day they called back 4 of us, and the next day they called me up and told me I was doing it. So I was, I guess, about a quick 15 at the time, and I played that series with the most gorgeous 30-year-old redhead I ever saw in my life. But I didn't know very much, so I didn't profit much by my experience. But that's the way I started, that was my beginning. That was in 1926.

L: When radio was really in its infancy.

F: Yes, it was.

L: So you were a regular on at least four shows: Jack Benny, Eddie Cantor, Blondie, and Meet Me at Parky's…

F: Yes, I did Blondie. I did the next door neighbor, Herb Woodley.

L: Which of those was the first one?

F: Actually, the first thing that I did…you see, transcontinental radio was coming out of Chicago and New York, but not out of Los Angeles. I had worked out here in Los Angeles for a gentleman by the name of John Swallow, and two radio stations in town which were sister stations called KFAC/KFED. And I had worked for him there for a couple of years, and finally, he was appointed the head of NBC. Well, NBC at that time consisted of one show that was done on the RKO Studios lot. That was the motion picture studio lot of RKO, and it was a sustaining show that advertised RKO pictures, and it was called "The RKO Theatre of the Air". And so John said, "How would you like to announce this thing?" And I said, "Well, sure, why not?" I think I got a quick $10 for announcing a transcontinental show, which was not sponsored by anybody. And then finally we did one sponsored show, which was called "Flywheel, Shyster, and Flywheel", and that was with Groucho and Chico Marx. And we did that from a soundstage on the RKO picture studio…Kind of an interesting thing happened to me on that. About four or five weeks into the series, they begin talking to each other in Jewish [Yiddish], and I knew they were talking about me, but I didn't know what they were saying. And that went on for a couple of weeks, and finally Groucho came over to me and he said, "Frank, can you sing?" And I said, "Oh boy! I couldn't carry a tune in a bucket…I'll give you an idea how bad I am. Last week, we were doing a serious drama down at KHJ, and at one point, the family sang Happy Birthday to George. And the director said, 'But Frank, you lay out.' That's how bad I was. I couldn't carry a tune." He says, "That's too bad, because we wanted to put you in our next picture." And that happens to be the picture that Allan Jones did Donkey Serenade in. That was what they wanted me for, but I couldn't sing, so I didn't do it. [EN: Allan Jones didn't sing Donkey Serenade in a Marx Brothers movie, but FSF was done in 1932-33. So the film in question must have been A Night At the Opera (1935).]

So then, I'm getting to this the long way, but I will answer the question, I'm actually going to get to it. So one day, Jack [Swallow] called me and he said, "Look, Jack Benny is coming out from New York to see about doing something in a movie [EN: based on the time this was probably Transatlantic Merry-Go-Round], and they want to keep him alive in the New York show, so we're going to do a five-minute insert from here, and I want you to work with him." So that was the first one that I worked with, that was Jack in 1934 [6/1/34]. And what we did, it was a little sketch on the train coming out from New York, and Jack is talking about how he's going out to Hollywood, and what a smash he's going to be, and how great he's going to be, and I'm non-committal but very polite to him, and he finally…says, "Well, you know, I think you're a very personable-looking young man, and possibly I might be able to do something for you. My name is Jack Benny, what is your name?" And my answer was, "Clark Gable." That was the joke. So we did that five minute insert, then we did another one about a week later, again a five-minute thing, and after that, Jack went back to New York, and I think it was about a year before he came out to

367

Hollywood. And as soon as he came out, he called me and I began working with him, but just in casual parts. So that was really the beginning of those shows that you spoke about. That was the first one that I did…

L: So how long was it before you started that familiar character?

F: Well, I guess I had worked for Jack now for several months, just doing casual things here and there, and one day, the writers said, "We're going to try that again." And I said, "Try what again?" They said, "Well, you remember last week, you stretched the 'yes' out, and it got a big laugh." And I had to think for a minute, and I said, "Oh yeah, and I don't even really know why I did it." And they said, "Well, we're going to try it and, you know, see if it goes again." So they wrote it a second time, and it played again, and so that became the beginning of the character. But it just kind of grew like Topsy. Nobody told me to do that or how to do it, I just happened to do it and it got a laugh, so it developed into that character. And of course the first time we ever did the "Oo", I absolutely destroyed Jack on the show, because I held back on it…Finally, we were in this fight about something, and Jack said, "You really hate me, don't you?" And I said, "OOOOOOO, do I!!!" And he went right on the floor! He fell right down on the floor began to laugh. So he was a great audience you know. I don't know whether you know this about Jack, but you see, Jack did something that no other comic did. He gave the jokes to what we term the "second bananas". We were…his supporting cast had the jokes. Jack didn't have jokes. Any joke that Jack had was a character joke about his cheapness, or something like that. But actual jokes he gave to the other people. And he's the only comic I know of that ever constructed a show in that manner.

L: As opposed to Bob Hope…

F: Who wants them all for himself. And Eddie Cantor…Eddie Cantor used to be, when you worked with Eddie, they would do a preview. You'd have an audience in there just to see how the material was going to go before you went on the air. Well, if you had a joke that got a big laugh, you knew when you came back you wouldn't have it any more. Eddie would have your joke. But Jack never worked that way.

L: Did you play the same character on the other shows that you did?

F: Oh no, no. Herb Woodley was a next-door neighbor who was just kind of a sarcastic guy on the <u>Blondie</u> show, a buddy of Arthur Lake's who did Dagwood of course. No, that was an entirely different thing. Matter of fact, I really started…before I started doing comedy, I was doing a lot of local shows out here and I worked as a leading man. And I did dramatic shows, did a lot of highly dramatic things—we have a show called "The Witches' Tales" which was one of those scary things, and very dramatic roles and I did that. And I did D'Artagnan in "The Three Musketeers" and I did Cardinal Mazeran [sp?] following Henry Stafford who had done Richelieu, and just things of that nature. But the point is you can make more money in comedy, so I finally stopped playing leads opposite stars for $25 and $35 when I could get considerably more money for doing comedy. We had a show out here called "Hollywood Hotel". I worked opposite the female stars. Now the female star was getting $3500 to $7500 a week, and I was getting $25! But I was considered capable of playing opposite that star, but they wouldn't give you any credit and they wouldn't pay you any money, so I finally said, "Well, heck with it. I'm gonna do comedy." And that's really how I began to switch over from doing drama and doing that type of thing. I think about the last show I did, and someone gave me a copy of it just recently, I did "The Egg and I" with Claudette Colbert. We did that on "Screen Director's Playhouse", and that was in the later years of my career in comedy, and I got called for that. It was fun to go back and do a lead again.

L: I know most people don't know much about the show "Meet Me at Parky's". Can you tell us a little about the show and the part you played in it?

F: …That was the Parkyakarkus show. He was a Greek restaurant owner, and I just had a running part on the show. I don't even remember what it was now. I had a rather tragic ending in that. He had some trouble with his back, and he went into the hospital and had an operation, and he came out from that and was in a wheelchair for the rest of his life. So that was really the end of doing that show. And I think we only did that show about 26 weeks…It was not one of the great shows of all time, but he was a very interesting Greek comic. He did a Greek dialect, he was not Greek. But he did a Greek dialect, and it was a cute, nice little show, friendly kind of show and it was fun to do, but when that happened to his back, that was the end of it.

L: What part did you play in the Eddie Cantor show?

F: With Eddie, I just did casual things. I didn't do anything regular with Eddie Cantor at all. As a matter of fact, Eddie did a very terrible thing to me one day. I went over to do his show and I'm reading the dialogue and all of a sudden I get to a spot in it, and here's the "yes". And I said, "Oh, I'm sorry, Eddie," I said, "I don't do that for anybody but Jack. It's on his show." And he said, "Frank, you don't think I would have asked you to do it if I hadn't asked Jack." I said, "Oh…you mean Jack said it was all right?" He said, "Oh well, certainly! Otherwise I wouldn't have it written in." So I did it. Two weeks later I'm on Jack's show, and Jack said, "Frank, why'd you do that?" And I said, "Why'd I do what?" He said, "On Cantor's show. Why…?" I said, "Wait a minute. Didn't he ask you for permission and didn't you give him permission for me to…" He said, "He never spoke to me at all." Isn't that a dirty trick? I ended up doing something that I wouldn't have done because I…lots of people would write it in, and I'd say, "No, no, I'm sorry, that's so well identified with the Jack Benny show that I simply don't do it anywhere else."

L: Are there any particular show experiences that stand out in your mind? [EN: Sorry folks, I was an eager 15-year-old and not the greatest interviewer. Fortunately Frank was a pro and gave me the ultimate classic Nelson-Benny story. You've heard it a million times, but here it is from the horse's mouth.]

F: Well, there's a story that I've told many times and you've probably heard it before about the Drew Pearson thing…First I've got to set it up this way. I had a joke where Jack said,

"Are you the doorman?" And I said, "Well, who do you think I am in this uniform? Nelson Eddy?" And he said, "I don't like the Nelson Eddy joke." He said, "We've got to get a new joke for Frank." Well, we ended up going on the show and they hadn't gotten a new joke for me. Now early on in the show, Don Wilson, the announcer, had a line about Drew Pearson, the columnist. And it didn't come out "Drew Pearson", it came out "Drear Pooson." And of course the audience broke up completely and Jack broke up, and the next thing I see is the writers are motioning for me to come into the booth. And so I went in and said, "What do you want?" They said, "Hey, when you get to the line, say 'Who do you think I am in this uniform, Drear Pooson?'" I said, "Oh come on, fellas. That doesn't even track. That doesn't make sense. You know, the Nelson Eddy joke made sense at least because Nelson Eddy was always in costumes." And they said, "Trust us." I said, "Now wait a minute. You don't ad lib with Jack." They said, "We will take responsibility for giving you the line." So I had my back to Jack and he said, "Oh Mister, Mister." And I whirled around and said, "Yeesssss?" And he said, "Oh, are you the doorman?" And I see this real dull look come into his eyes. Here comes that line, we didn't change it. I said, "Well who do you think I am in this uniform? DREAR POOSON?" Well, his eyes got like two saucers, he began to laugh. He grabbed hold of the microphone, he slid down the microphone all the way to the floor, he pounded on the floor. He got up and he staggered all the way across the studio to the far wall, hammered on the wall, turned into the drapes, grabbed the drapes, slid down the drapes, pounded on the floor some more, and the audience is in hysterics this whole time. Then he got up, staggered back to the microphone, and we went on with the show. And the funny thing is that for at least three or four weeks after that, every time I met a comedy writer from another show, they said, "Now, that whole thing was planned, wasn't it?" And I would tell them what I'm telling you now, not a *one* of them believed me! They all thought it was set up that way, meant to be that way, and it was not. And they never would have changed my line if I had had a line that Jack liked. It was just that Jack didn't like the line, we never changed it, and so when this happened, the writers said, "Hey! Let's have him do that." I really think…you've always heard that the biggest laugh on the Jack Benny show was "Your money or your life, I'm thinking, I'm thinking." I really think that this was probably a longer laugh, but it wasn't a planned laugh like that other laugh was. So if you ever saw a man break up, that was the day because Jack was completely gone when I did that.

L: You've been in comedy for quite some time, so what do you think about the comedy of today? Like <u>Saturday Night Live</u> or things like that?

F: Well, I don't happen to be a fan of <u>Saturday Night Live</u>. I did do the show once [12/5/81, with host Tim Curry]. I must tell you that I felt for the people that were on it. They had some great people on there, and they did material that, so help me, I wouldn't have done. I thought the material was just atrocious. I thought the writing was not good on that show. And I think an awful lot of the sketches have been very, very poor. And so I'm just not a fan of <u>Saturday Night Live</u>. If you want to talk about standup comedy, I do see some young comedians that I like. I think they're funny, but it's a different kind of comedy today. Back in the days when we were doing the Benny show, it was a gentle comedy. There were no barbs, you weren't political, you didn't take swipes at people, you didn't do the kind of things that comics do today. And I think that comedy today is more implied to be on the vitriolic side, on the maybe the dark side, let's say, black comedy side, than the days that I knew as comedy. And I wouldn't trade them for anything. I think the others were better, I think comedy in those days was gentler, and I think it was enjoyed more by people than it is today. Now there are some shows today that I think are just absolutely great. Barney Miller…it's off the air now of course, but I think the rapport between all the people in that show was just absolutely marvelous. WKRP in Cincinnati is another one I think of immediately as having a cast of people that are just great. That kind of comedy I think is excellent, and why it went off, I don't know. I think both those shows ought to still be on the air. The Mary Tyler Moore Show, that was a lovely show. But really, the thing I'm talking about more than anything else is standup comedy. I don't like the standup comics today as well as I did in the old days because I just don't think they're really the same kind of comedy that I enjoyed in those days. I do cartoon things now, I work for Hanna Barbera quite a bit, and I'm doing one that's on the air right now called "The Snorks". I am the Governor of Snorkland, and we're called Snorks because we're under the ocean. We have our little snorkels on. So you keep on doing something. There's always somebody that wants to dig up that character and have a touch of that character in something that they're doing currently. [EN: And isn't it ironic that all these years later that's still true, and the character is semi-recurrent on The Simpsons?] And so I've continued to perform, I don't go out looking for it today, but I get a lot of calls that keep me reasonably busy.

L: Would you have any advice for comedy writers and comedians today?

F: I wouldn't try to advise anybody in today's market as to what they ought to do. I think that each comedian does what he thinks he does best. It's just that there has become a sharpness in comedy that I kind of deplore, but I certainly wouldn't tell anybody "Don't do it" because that seems to be what everybody is doing today, so evidently it plays to a lot of people. But I'm not an advice-giver. It's like someone says, "Should I get into the business?" And I say, "Well, your chances of success are very, very limited because there are tons and tons of good performers for every available job. And an awful lot of fine performers are having a terrible time trying to make a living." But I wouldn't tell anybody "Don't try it" because you may just be the one who comes along and is an absolute sensation. So if you feel that you should, and feel that you want to, and feel driven to do it, take a chance! Try it! Worst thing that can happen is you fail, you go on to something else.

L: Thank you very much, Mr. Nelson…or rather…Frank…[EN: I asked him before the interview what to call him, and he'd said "Call me Frank"]…and if you will so indulge us, if you might be able to do that famous "yes" once again for us.

F: [Playful smile in his voice] Well…I suppose I could do that…

L: Shall I lead into it?

F: If you'd like to, you just go right ahead.

L: Oh Mister…Mister!

F: YEEEEESSSSSS? Well! Look who's here! It's Laura Lee!

[EN: That was one of the great thrills of my life. I still get tingles hearing it.]

Please send all questions, comments, corrections, and additions to:
International Jack Benny Fan Club
P.O. Box 11288
Piedmont, CA 94611
Please, friends, send no bombs.

JackBenny@aol.com
www.jackbenny.org
Laura Leff, President

Waukegan's Barrison Theatre circa 1911
Where Jack started as a ticket taker around 1908 and was soon promoted to violinist,
plus met Cora Salisbury and the Marx Brothers

Index

39 Forever book 257, 313, 328, 352
39 Forever convention 142-144, 153-158, 176-195, 205-206, 308
Abbott, Bud 14, 296, 312
Adam, Noelle 169-170
Adler, Larry 42-53, 79-80
Adrian, Iris 164
Alexander, Fay (stuntman) 60
Alexander, Jason 187
Allen, Fred ....
    35, 66, 82, 85, 100, 102-107, 120-121, 155, 171, 172, 173, 257, 264, 272, 295-296, 337-343, 361, 362-366
Allen, Gracie 16, 37, 60, 67-70, 82, 108, 111, 115, 216, 217, 268
Allen, Steve 214
Allen, Woody 51, 116
Allman, Elvia 70, 111
Ally McBeal 236
Alpert, Herb 187
Am Echod (Waukegan synagogue) 58, 140, 354-355
Ameche, Don 215
American Radio Archives 38
American Republic Life Insurance 312-313
American Tobacco Company 171, 245, 264-265
Amos 'n' Andy 104, 166, 173, 214
Anaheim, Azusa, and Cuc….amonga 222, 356-357
Anderson, Eddie "Rochester" ....
    13, 37, 38, 45, 59, 64, 65, 70, 88, 104, 112, 115, 159, 161-162, 169, 173, 185, 190, 199, 204, 218, 246, 248, 257, 258-259, 262, 279, 290-291, 315, 325, 330, 361
Anderson, Edmund (Eddie Anderson's son) 258-259
Anderson, Eva (Eddie Anderson's second wife) 258-259
Anderson, Sherwood 44
Andrews Sisters, The 87, 246
Archer, Corliss 66
Arlen, Harold 49
Armed Forces Radio Service 296-297
Asner, Ed 198
Astaire, Fred 161
Atkison, Brooks 293
Aubrey, James 170
Auerbach, Artie 14, 160-161, 296, 324
B'nai B'rith 214
Babylon 5 11
Baird, Jimmy (BH Beaver) 71, 82
Baker, Kenny 10, 34-35, 65, 166, 167, 267, 269, 272, 273, 316
Baker, Phil 14, 45, 118, 217
Baldwin, Harry (secretary) 13, 362
Ball, Lucille 25, 40, 41, 60, 82, 108, 160, 185, 198, 231, 345

Balzer, George 18, 19, 59, 62, 156, 193, 218, 263, 305, 323, 347
Bannon, Jim (Bea Benaderet's first husband) 108
Barrison Theatre 139, 274, 372
Barrison, Mabel (co-owner of the Barrison Theatre) 274
Barrymore, John 47, 60, 342
Bartlett, Michael 34, 316
Baruch, Andre 357
Batchelder, Warren (Mouse that Jack Built) 204
Beach Boys, The 82
Belmont, Tony (National Comedy Hall of Fame) 32-33, 178, 180, 188, 192
Beloin, Ed 13, 75, 156
Benaderet, Bea 107-109
Benchley, Robert 293
Bennett, Earl – See Sir Fredrick Gas
Bennett, Tony 24
Benny, Jack
    Award 39
    Baseball first pitch 198, 359
    Cartoons 109, 169, 204, 225, 361
    Census records 171
    Comedy style 116-125
    Estate 39
    First radio appearance 167
    Forest 39
    Genealogy 12, 140
    Houses 38, 111, 112, 181
    I Can't Stand contest 36
    Minstrel comparison 165-166
    Money clips 346
    Movie biography 331-333
    Nightclub shows 164-165
    Orchestra benefits 83-87, 92, 98, 123, 346
    Painting 166-167
    Sandwiches/meals 113, 289, 355, 361
    Show creation 22-23, 121-122, 325
    Smuggling case 40, 67-70, 265-273
    St. Joe 312
    Stamps 73, 74
    Statue 10, 32-34, 40-41, 57-59, 79, 101-102, 129-138, 177-178, 223-224, 259-260, 288, 333-334
    Tree 278, 355-356
    Violins 39, 92-93, 184, 295-296
    War tours 42-48, 79-80, 146-149, 327, 335-336, 349, 356, 357
    Young life 40, 116-117, 139, 140-141, 214, 273-277
Benny, Joan ....
    27, 38, 39, 45, 57, 66, 140, 141, 143, 154, 169, 180, 184, 191, 193, 205, 208, 217, 265-266, 302, 346
Benny, Mary – See Mary Livingstone
Bergen, Edgar 110, 215
Bergen, Polly 245-246
Bergeron, Bev (magician) 290-291
Bergman, Ingrid 43-46, 48, 52, 80
Berle, Milton 36, 51, 115, 116, 207, 235, 332

Berman, Shelly 116
Berner, Sara 107
Bernie, Ben 105, 167, 276
Bernovici, Al 276
Berns, Seymour 21, 82
Bernstein, Leonard..123
Bestor, Don..110
Billinglsey, Mr. 13, 36
Bishop, Joey 116, 124
Black, Frank 360
Blake, Madge 221-222
Blanc, Mel 23, 109, 113, 193, 204, 222, 235, 248-249, 263, 269, 334, 362
Blanc, Noel (Mel Blanc's son) 153
Bliss, Ted..34
Block, Sidney (Waukegan friend) 277
Blome, Erik (sculptor)..33, 129, 136, 178
Blondie 75, 215, 366-367, 368
Bloomingdale, Alfred 25
Blum Myrt (lawyer and manager) 324-325
Blum, Babe – See Babe Marks
Blumofe, Bob (son-in-law)..208
Blumofe, Robert (Bobby, grandson) 136, 144, 180, 188, 194, 208
Boardner, Steve (barkeeper) 162
Boasberg, Al..13, 115, 339
Bogart, Humphrey 170, 332-333
Bolger, Ray..20, 81
Bonanza 170
Bond, Tommy..57
Bondy, Judge William (smuggling case)..69
Bonnicksen, Ted (Mouse that Jack Built)..204
Boone, F.E. (auctioneer)..171
Borie, Marcia (biographer) 21, 71, 83, 105, 112, 139
Bouche, Rene (caricature artist) 102, 159, 346
Bow, Clara..38
Boyer, Charles..60
Brasselle, Keefe..169-170
Brice, Fanny 20, 81
Brooks, Albert 359-360
Brown, John..338-339, 341-343, 363, 365
Brown, Treg (Mouse that Jack Built) 204
Bruce, Nigel..316
Brunner, June..357
Bryant, Jimmy (guitarist)..328
Burgess, Carlton (architect) 112
Burnett, Carol 23, 60, 183
Burns, George..
...11-12, 15, 21, 26, 36, 37, 39, 40, 46, 60, 66, 67-70, 82, 85, 111, 115, 116, 119, 186, 188, 207, 210, 216, 217, 265-273, 290-291, 345, 346, 347
Burt, Captain Andrew G. (Korea)..349
Caesar, Sid..191, 249
Cahill, U.S. Attorney John T. (smuggling case) 69, 266, 271, 272-273

Cahn, Sammy	11
Callas, Maria	316-317
Canada Dry	13, 63, 168-169, 257, 277, 323
Canin, Stuart (violinist, "The Bee")	102-107, 337-338, 363-364
Canter's Deli	143, 155, 190-191
Cantor, Charles	339-341, 343, 363, 365
Cantor, Eddie	41, 51, 75, 167, 169, 183, 190, 216, 308, 366, 368, 369
Capone, Al	51, 215
Cardinal Quartet	35
Carleton, Bob (Great Lakes Naval Center)	147-148
Carmichael	36, 64, 71, 269
Carnegie Hall	86-87, 90, 91, 92, 94, 123, 155
Carpenter, Elliott	171
Carroll, Earl	276-277
Carroll, Eddie	
16-20, 101, 129-138, 143, 149, 153, 158-159, 178, 179, 180, 181-182, 185, 187, 188, 191, 193-194, 205, 209-211, 261-263, 286-287, 306, 307, 308	
Carson, Jack	322
Carson, Johnny	20, 81, 116, 174
Casablanca	170-171
Cassidy, Hopalong	160, 312
CBS	63, 66-67, 170, 213-214, 217, 221, 249, 290, 331, 360
Channing, Carol	60
Chapereau, Albert (smuggling case)	40, 67-70, 266-273
Charriff, Rabbi Iser	12
Chevalier, Maurice	116
Chevrolet	277
Claney, Howard	360
Clark, Dick	19
Clary, Robert	191
Clinton, Bill	215
Colbert, Claudette	369
Cole, Dewey (sound effects)	213
Cole, Nat "King"	38
Colman, Ronald and Benita	24, 63, 64, 123
Como, Perry	131, 245-246
Confrey, Zez	117, 148, 275
Conn, Harry	13, 109, 164-165, 294
Connery, Sean	82
Cooper, Gary	24, 65
Corbet, Lois (Don Wilson's fourth wife)	163
Cosby, Bill	310-311
Costello, Lou	14, 296, 312
Crosby, Bing	26, 72, 217, 247
Crosby, Bob	229, 231, 245, 246-248
Crystal, Billy	60
Cugat, Xavier	162
Cummings, Robert	60
Currry, Tim	370
Curtis, Tony	60, 291
Davis, Bette	162

Davis, Governor Gray (California) 188
Dawn, Hazel (Great Temptations) 294
Day, Dennis 25, 34, 62, 63, 64, 65, 113, 161, 165, 166, 193, 194, 263, 272, 293, 300, 325, 332, 358
Day, Doris 60
DeCordova, Frederick 20-27, 80-81, 261, 358
Deep Chicago Rhythm Owls 310
Delaney, U.S. Attorney Joseph L. (smuggling case) 267
DeMarco Sisters, The 105
Deutsch, Adolph 220
Devine, Andy 10, 142, 279
Devore, Bill 32, 132
Diller, Phyllis 116, 224, 301
Dillinger, John 215
Disney, Walt 34, 82, 209
Dodderidge, Dick (publicity man) 312-313
Dolly Sisters, The 148
Donovan, Attorney William J. (smuggling case) 270, 273
Dorsey, Tommy 162, 321
Drew, Ellen 284
Dryer, Dave (pianist) 300-301
Duchin, Eddy 35
Durante, Jimmy 20, 81, 88, 116
Durkin, Mayor William (Waukegan) 32
Eddy, Nelson 370
Edwards, Gus 49
Edwards, Ralph 252
Eisenhower, Dwight 48
Ellis, Admiral (Waukegan) 278
Elman, Mischa 199
Erlinborn, Ray (sound effects) 57
Etkin, Irene 196
Evans, Clarence (childhood friend) 274
Everly Brothers 215
Eyemann, Jeanette (secretary) 26, 323
Fanego, Tatiana 360
Farber, Dr. (officiated at Benny wedding) 277
Fashel, Dick 323
Fay, Frank 119
Faye, Alice 162, 173, 217, 297-298, 345
Fein, Irving 18, 20, 60, 62, 154, 165, 180, 183, 191, 193, 194, 205, 209, 220, 263, 345
Fenchel, Florence Kubelsky (sister) 12, 58, 140-141, 277, 279, 281, 354-355
Fenchel, Leonard (brother-in-law) 140, 277, 355
Fender, Harry (Great Lakes Naval Center) 148
Fields, W.C. 41, 220
First Generation Radio Archives 41, 200
Fisher, Eddie 224
Flamini, Roland 197
Fletcher, Jimmy (sound effects) 213
Flippen, Jay C. (Great Temptations) 294
Flowerday, Fred (sound effects) 212-213
Floyd, "Pretty Boy" 215

Flynn, Errol..162, 357
Fontaine, Frank...295
Ford, Phil..57
Ford, Wallace...70
Forman, Joey...249
Foster, George (engineer)..66, 213-214
Fox, Harry..148
Franklin, Ben...223
Franklin, Joe..179
Franklyn, Milt (Mouse that Jack Built)...204
Friar's Club.................................... 32-33, 91, 143, 144, 154-155, 179, 180, 186-189, 191, 194, 218
Friedman, Budd..180, 185, 187-188, 205
Frost, David...328
Frudenfeld, Arthur (Barrison Theatre manager)..274
Fry, Fred (sound effects)...213
Full Contact (comedy duo).. 186, 187-188
Furness, Betty..21
Gable, Clark..24, 75, 215, 367
Gardner, Ava..24
Gari, Brian (Eddie Cantor grandson)..183, 185, 205, 308
Garland, Judy...20, 24, 161
Garrett, Hank...186, 188
Gas, Sir Fredrick..14
Gay, Deloris (Korea)..336, 357
General Foods..68, 110, 221, 269, 277
General Tire...277
Genesee Theatre 10, 33, 59, 76, 79, 129-130, 137, 159, 260-261, 279, 289, 309-311
George Washington Slept Here lyrics 219-220
Gersh, Lenny..27
Gershwin, George...49-50, 80
Gershwin, Ira...44, 49-50
Gilmore, Art...163
Gleason, Jackie..123, 196, 214
Goding, Lillian Streed (schoolmate)..214
Goldberg, Albert..97
Goldman, Hal 59-60, 156, 172, 193, 244-245, 263, 347
Gomez, Genaro..358
Gorcey Jr., Leo...185, 194, 201, 205, 256
Gordon, Al...18, 59-60, 156, 172, 180, 183, 193, 194, 205, 263, 347
Gordon, Ben (cousin)..139, 140-141
Gordon, Claire Kubelsky (aunt) 140-141
Gordon, Cliff (cousin)..139, 140-141
Gordon, Marvin (cousin)..139, 140-142
Gould, Chester...215
Gould, Morton...50
Grammar, Kelsey..238
Grandpré, George (Mouse that Jack Built)..204
Granlund, N.T. (announcer)..105
Grant, Cary..24, 51-52, 12
Grant, Ward..195-196
Grape Nuts..63, 221

Great Lakes Naval Training Center 58, 101, 117, 146-149, 275, 284
Great Lakes Quartette (Great Lakes Naval Center) 147
Great Lakes Tumblers (Great Lakes Naval Center) 148
Great Temptations, The 292-294
Green, Johnny 21, 248
Green, Keith (pianist) 217-218
Gregory, Dick 116
Gribbroeck, Robert (Mouse that Jack Built) 204
Griffith, Melanie 24
Gulf Western Oil Company 65
Guy Sisters, The (Great Temptations) 294
Hackett, Buddy 114-115
Hahn, Mayor James (Los Angeles) 182
Halperin, Marty 296-297
Hammel, Joan 32
Hardy, Oliver 27
Harlow, Jean 215
Harper, Valerie 198
Harrah, Bill 11-12
Harris, Phil ....
    10, 16, 24, 25, 62, 64, 65, 72, 162, 166, 217, 237, 247, 257, 279, 297-298, 325-326, 343, 345-346, 347
Harris Jr., Phil 72
Harrison, Dale (columnist) 269
Harrison, Rex 109
Hatten, Tom 187
Hayworth, Rita 42
Hearn, Sam 14
Hefner, Hugh 215
Heidt, Horace 321
Heifetz, Jascha 87, 93, 96, 123
Hemingway, Ernest 51
Hendrix, Jimi 187
Hepburn, Katharine 267
Hickman, Dwayne 317
Hill, George Washington (American Tobacco) 264
Hillcrest Country Club 25
Hillside Memorial Park (Benny burial place) 143, 155, 179, 189-190, 192, 193, 195, 205
Hines, Mimi 57
Hiss, Alger 215, 217
Hitchcock, Alfred 60
Hitler, Adolf 70, 265, 267
Hitz, Ralph (hotelman) 70
Hoffa, Portland 341, 362-363
Holbrook, Hal 210
Honor America Day 198-199
Hope, Bob ....
    26, 42, 45, 70, 82, 107, 115, 116, 168, 190, 195-196, 198, 206-208, 215, 231, 235-236, 238, 251-252,
    301-302, 318, 323, 346, 368
Hopper, Hedda 279
Howard, Joe (co-owner of the Barrison Theatre) 274
Howdy Doody 312

Hudson, Rock	155
Hyde, Mayor Richard (Waukegan)	130, 158, 260, 333, 355
Ink Spots, The	154-155, 180, 186, 187-188, 195
Irwin, Stan (Tonight Show producer)	188
Ja Da Trio (Great Lakes Naval Center)	148
Jacobs, Jody	39
Jell-O	10, 63, 104, 110, 114, 166, 168, 192, 221, 228, 256, 257, 269, 315, 340
Jemison, Danny (childhood friend)	274, 279-280
Jeopardy	311-312
Jessel, George	21, 26, 39, 51, 116, 334
Jiggs and Maggie	215
Johnson, Van	38, 141
Jolson, Al	20, 24, 41, 50-51, 80, 119, 167, 308, 332
Jones, Allan	75, 367
Jones, Jack	142
Jones, Spike	14, 72
Josefsberg, Alan (Milt Josefsberg's son)	318-319
Josefsberg, Milt	18, 59-60, 156, 193, 263, 271, 272-273, 292-293, 305, 318-319, 323, 326
Joy, Dick	213
Kahne, Happy	357
Kaye, Danny	16, 83, 89, 141, 332
Kazan, Lainie	51
Keaton, Buster	115
Keighley, William	219, 333
Kelly, Gene	60
Kelly, Mary	70, 111, 164, 354, 356
Kelly, Patsy	196
Kennedy, Emma (BBC)	180, 185, 205
Kennedy, Jackie	322
Kern, Jerome	49
Kerry, John	312
Kids in the Hall, The	172
King, Larry	40
Kirchenbauer, Bill	187
Knight, June	316
Kubelsky, Meyer (father)	12, 58, 139, 140-141, 277, 279, 282, 355
Kubelsky, Naomi Emma – See Emma Sachs	
Kyser, Kay	264
La Jota (boat)	218
Ladd, Alan	38, 60
Lahr, Bert	20, 81
Lake, Arthur	368
Lamour, Dorothy	142, 279
Lane, Abbe	55
Langford, Frances	195
Lanza, Mario	245
LaPlanche, Rosemary	201
Lastfogel, Abe	42
LaToy, Harry	104
Lauer, Judge Edgar J. (smuggling case)	69-70, 267, 272, 273
Lauer, Elma N. (smuggling case)	69-70, 267, 268, 271, 272, 273

Laurel, Stan..27
Lee, Anna 42, 80
Lee, Don..213, 221
Lee, Peggy...207
Lehman, Governor Herbert (New York) 272
Leibell, Judge Vincent (smuggling case).. 40, 68-69, 270-271, 273
Lemmon, Jack...123
Lennon. John..187
Leno, Jay..222, 236
Leonard, Jack..162
Leonard, Sheldon..222
LeRoy, Mervyn..35
Letterman, David..236
Levant, Oscar..50
Lever Brothers..331
Levine, Michael..153-154, 184, 185, 187, 192, 205
Levy, Ralph...21, 82
Lewin, Albert E...313
Lewis, Elliott..297-298
Lewis, Jerry...116
Lilly, Bea...20, 81
Linaker, Kay...180-184, 187, 201, 205
Linkletter, Art...309
Little, Rich..210, 220
Livingstone, Mary ....
    10, 11-12, 21, 24, 26, 27, 39, 44, 45, 48-49, 63, 65, 67-70, 71, 73, 81, 93, 97, 110-111, 112, 113, 129,
    139, 141, 169, 190, 194, 196, 197, 198, 204, 208, 216-217, 220, 221, 237, 249, 266, 276-277, 278,
    279, 292, 300-301, 324, 346, 360-361
Loesser, Frank..49, 50
Lombard, Carole...73
Los Angeles Philharmonic...39
Louis, Joe.. 197-198
Love in Bloom.. 11, 122, 165, 168, 188, 220, 257, 318, 343, 365
Lucky Strike..63, 171, 200, 221, 264, 295, 358, 360
Lum and Abner... 41, 87, 200-201
Lyman, Abe...167
Lyons, Arthur (agent)..270
Lyons, Leonard (columnist)...268, 269
MacArthur, Douglas...47, 48, 354
MacKenzie, Gisele...57, 142, 165, 180, 184, 185, 188, 205, 227-253, 312, 328
Maligmat, Albert (The Rocky Fellers) 214
Maligmat, Jun (The Rocky Fellers) 214
Maltin, Leonard 35
Mansfield, Jayne...196
Marc, Ted (BH Beaver)...71, 82
March of Dimes, The.. 298-299
Marcus, Toni (violinist)..165, 188, 245
Marie, Rose..186-188, 191, 194, 246
Marks, Babe (Mary Livingstone's sister) 276, 324-325
Marks, Hilliard "Hickey" 21, 26, 206, 324
Marks, Sadie – See Mary Livingstone

381

Marshall, Herbert	112
Martin, Dean	38, 60, 186, 233, 246
Martin, Mary	35
Marvin, Lee	196
Marx, Chico	75, 110-111, 115. 169, 367
Marx, Groucho	35-36, 65, 75, 82, 110-111, 115, 155, 169, 361, 367
Marx, Harpo	35, 110-111, 115, 169
Marx, Zeppo	110-111, 169
Matthau, Walter	302
Maxwell	23, 37, 65, 112, 169, 204, 212-213, 330-331, 346
MCA	20, 174
McBain, Don	213
McCarthy, Charlie	40, 110, 161, 215
McConkey, Captain Joe (Korea)	336
McDonald, Jeanette	38, 217
McGee, Fibber	173
McKennon, Dal	201
McKimson, Robert (Mouse that Jack Built)	204
McNulty, Dorothy – See Penny Singleton	
McQueen, Butterfly	197
McQueen, Steve	60
Meadows, Audrey	191, 328
Meet Me at Parky's	75
Mehta, Zubin	123
Meiseles, Joanna (granddaughter)	133, 135, 144, 193, 208
Melton, James	316, 355, 360
Merrick, Mahlon	95
Meyer, Jay (Sportsmen Quartet)	180, 185, 205
Milburn, General (Korea)	336
Miller and Lyles (Great Temptations)	294
Miller, Ann	34
Miller, Arthur	222-223
Modernaires, The	248
Moffett, Captain (Great Lakes Naval Center)	149, 275
Monroe, Marilyn	16, 62
Monroe, Matt	233
Montgomery, Robert	232, 233
Moreno, Rita	358
Morrow, Bill	13, 75, 156, 218
Morse, Robert	210
Moskowitz, Joseph	70
Mouse That Jack Built, The (cartoon)	204, 225
Mulhare, Edward	19
Murray, Ken	73
Murtough, William	66, 213-214
Museum of Broadcast Communications, The	33, 58, 64, 136
Museum of Television and Radio, The	155, 191, 192, 194, 241
Nabors, Jim	60
National Comedy Hall of Fame	32-33, 58, 79, 143, 154, 177, 178, 188, 191, 192, 195, 218
Nazarro, Cliff	70, 111
NBC	16, 20, 63, 66, 110, 141, 170, 198, 212, 214, 221, 252, 269, 272, 282, 358, 367

Negri, Pola	110
Nelson, Frank	20, 74-76, 222, 224, 366-372
Nelson, Ralph	82
Newton, Attorney Carl (smuggling case)	270, 271, 273
Nicholson, Mavis	42
O'Brien, Conan	236
O'Daniel, General (Korea)	336
O'Hara, John	49
O'Keefe, James (Great Lakes Naval Center)	148
Olney, Clyde (Great Lakes Naval Center)	148
Olsen, George	167
Olson, Anthon Fredrick	198
Onassis, Aristotle	322
Orlando, Tony	60
Paley, William S.	170
Panama, Norman	313
Parker, Dorothy	44, 80
Parker, Frank	109, 220, 316
Parkington, Michael	42
Parkyakarkus	369
Parr, Jack	264
Pauline (Mary's maid)	220
Payne, Alice (Waukegan librarian)	274
Pearce, Al	14
Pearl, Jack	70, 267, 269
Pearson, Drew	369-370
Peck, Gregory	141, 209
Perrin, Sam	18, 59, 62, 156, 193, 263, 305, 323
Peterson, Walter (Great Lakes Naval Center)	148
Petrillo, James Caesar	329
Phillips, Kate – See Kay Linaker	
Piatagorsky, Gregor (cellist)	90
Pierce, Ted (Mouse that Jack Built)	204
Pious, Minerva	365
Plummer, Christopher	210
Polly the parrot	64, 109
Popeye	215
Portaro, Rosemary	231
Porter, Cole	49
Powell, Dick	72
Powers, Dudley (Waukegan conductor)	138
Presley, Elvis	52, 215, 222
Pyle, Ralph (Army photographer, Korea)	327, 335-336, 349, 357
Radio Recorders	66
Raker, Fred	306
Ralston, Marcia (Phil Harris' first wife)	72
Ravel, Maurice	53, 80
Rawls, Lou	224
Ray, Tom (Mouse that Jack Built)	204
Raymond, Gene	38
Reagan, Ronald	186

Redford, Robert 52
Remley, Frankie 25, 63, 66, 100, 250, 297-298, 335, 357
Reuben, Dr. David 344-348
Reynolds, Marjorie 335, 357
Richman, Harry 105, 316
Rickles, Don 174
Riggs, Lee Aubrey "L. A. Speed" (auctioneer) 171, 264-265
Righteous Brothers, The 187
Ripley, Robert 25, 100
Ritz Brothers, The 217, 342
Robertson, Ted (sound effects) 212-213
Robinson, Edward G. 65
Rocky Fellers, The 214
Rogers, Ginger 155
Roosevelt, Eleanor 47
Roosevelt, Franklin 47
Rose, Leonard (viola) 90
Rosenberg, Chester (Great Lakes Naval Center) 148
Rosenfield, Jacob (vaudeville) 316
Roseray and Cappella (Great Temptations) 293
Ross, Stan (Gold Star Recording) 187
Rosselini, Roberto 43
Rubin, Benny 167, 221, 222, 300-301
Rudolph, Maria (granddaughter) 133, 135, 208
Rudolph, Michael (grandson) 142, 154, 180, 184, 205, 208
Rudunska, Countess Marusia (Don Wilson's third wife) 163
Rupp & Linden (Great Lakes Naval Center) 147
Rust, Ed (State Farm President) 330
Sabonjian, Mayor Robert (Waukegan) 288
Sachs Gordon, Sudie (cousin) 140, 142
Sachs, Naomi Emma (mother) 12, 58, 140, 282, 355
Salisbury, Cora (vaudeville partner) 116-117, 274-275, 351, 372
Sanders, George 266
Saunders, Russell (stuntman) 59, 60
Schaden, Chuck 132, 134
Schlepperman – See Sam Hearn
Scott, Bert (secretary) 26
Segal, Erna (dancer, Chiquita and Johnson) 312
Segar, Elsie 215
Seinfeld, Jerry 24, 116, 236-237
Sellers, Peter 82
Selznick, David O. 52
Serling, Rod 328
Shapiro (aka Szapiro), Nate – See Albert Chapereau
Shaw, Marie 42, 80
Shaw, Ruth Faison (artist) 167
Shearer, Harry (BH Beaver) 71, 82, 111, 191, 359-360
Sheridan, Ann 219
Shore, Dinah 214, 232, 233
Shubert, Jake 117, 276, 292-293
Shuttleworth, Bob (Gisele MacKenzie's husband) 230, 231

Sidaris, Andy (director)	291
Siegel, Bugsy	51
Silvers, Phil	224
Simon, Neil	18
Simon, Simone	50
Sinatra, Frank	11, 39, 155, 174, 213, 358-359
Singer, Bob (Mouse that Jack Built)	204
Singleton, Doris	220
Singleton, Penny	284, 293
Sinykin Hansen, Louise	354
Sinykin, Julius (long-time friend)	139, 255, 273-282, 284, 354
Si-Sy routine	23, 113
Skelton, Red	51, 66, 123, 290, 291
Slowest Gun in the West, The	224
Smith, Kate	199
Smothers Brothers	26, 60
Snowden, Ted	17
Sommer, Elke	82
Sondheim, Stephen	316
Soo, Jack	214
Spielberg, Steven	52
Stack, Robert	209
Stafford, Henry	368
Stafford, Jo	38, 246-247
Staples, Duke (Great Lakes Naval Center)	147
State Farm Insurance	218-219, 330-331
Steinberg, William	123
Stern, Isaac	56, 77, 81, 83-98, 347
Stevens, Larry	63, 113, 185, 300
Stevens, Norma	113, 185, 205, 300
Stewart, Blanche	70
Stewart, Jimmy and Gloria	24, 65, 123
Stone, Hal	159-160
Stoopnagle and Budd	104
Sullivan, Ed	114, 167, 214, 229, 231
Sunshine Boys, The	36, 37, 302
Superman	215
Superosity	311
Swallow, John	75, 367
Sympathy Soothing Syrup	318
Szell, George	123
Tackaberry, John	18, 37, 59, 71, 156, 218, 272-273, 296, 305, 319-326
Tackaberry, Stace (John Tackaberry's son)	319-326
Talcott, Mayor Mancel "Bidey" (Waukegan)	277-278
Talley, Marion	316
That's What I Like About the South	15, 112, 345
Thayer III, Attorney Walter N. (smuggling case)	268, 273
Thomas, Danny	116
Thousand Oaks Library	38
Tijuana Bibles	215-217
Tilton, Martha	42, 43, 80

Tobias, George 266
Tracy, Dick 215
Truman, Harry 17, 155, 191
Trumbauer, Frankie 49
Tucker, Sophie 21, 267, 301
Twombley, Gene (sound effects) 108-109, 133
Tyler, Ginny 109
USS Saratoga 197
Van, Billy B. (Great Temptations) 293, 294
Van Brunt, General (Korea) 336
Van Dyke, Dick 187
Van Steeden, Peter 364
Vaughan Williams, Ralph 52-53, 80
Vault 23, 33, 58, 62, 102, 129, 136, 222, 298-299, 331
Venuta, Benay 349, 357
Vincent, Bob 11-12
VoicOgraph 10
Von Zell, Harry 342, 363
Vonn, Veola 215, 317
Wain, Bea 187
Wald, Jerry 332
Wallenstein, Alfred 91, 123
Warner, Jack 63
Washburn, Beverly 180, 183-184, 187, 205
Waters, Ethel 161
Waukegan ....
..10, 32-34, 40, 56, 57-59, 76, 79, 95, 101-102, 127-142, 158-159, 177-178, 180, 181, 191, 209, 214, 259-261, 273-282, 288-289, 309-311, 339-341, 342, 344-345, 348, 354-356
Wayne, John 155, 345
Webb, Jack 223
Weber, maid Rosa (smuggling case) 70, 267, 273
Welles, Orson 107
West, Mae 215
Wheeler and Woolsey 223
Whiteman, Paul 49
Whitmore, James 210
Whittaker, Roger 233
Wilbur, Gertrude 279-280
Wilde, Larry 116-125
Wilkerson, Tichi 71, 83
Williams, Tim 185, 205
Willis, Bruce 24, 52
Wilson, Don ....
...... 10, 16, 36, 64, 65, 70, 132, 142, 163-164, 204, 213, 221, 237, 249, 272, 278, 279, 326, 329, 330, 357-358, 370
Wilson, Dooley 171
Wilson, Flip 60
Winchell, Walter 105
Winstaley, Ernie (sound effects) 213
Winston, George (guitarist) 328
Winters, Jan 38

Wolff, David (Great Lakes Naval Center) 117, 148-149
Wood, Illinois Lieutenant Governor Corrine 57
Wood, Murray (Fred Allen amateur) 105-106
Woods, Lyman (vaudeville partner) 117, 275
Wooton, Stevie (BH Beaver) 71, 82
World's Fair 314-315
Wright, Attorney Lloyd (smuggling case) 270, 273
Wynn, Ed 116, 119
Yamada, Romi 214
Young, Floyd D. (announcer) 356
Youngman, Henny 46, 51, 119
Zanuck, Darryl 63

www.ingramcontent.com/pod-product-compliance
Lightning Source LLC
Chambersburg PA
CBHW082105230426
43671CB00015B/2613